LABOR RELATIONS IN PROFESSIONAL SPORTS

ROBERT C. BERRY
WILLIAM B. GOULD IV
PAUL D. STAUDOHAR

Auburn House Publishing Company
Dover, Massachusetts • London

Library of Congress Cataloging in Publication Data

Berry, Robert C.
  Labor relations in professional sports.

  Includes bibliographies and index.
  1. Professional sports--Economic aspects--United
States.   2. Professional sports--United States--
Contracts. 3. Professional sports--Laws and legislation
--United States.   4. Collective bargaining--Sports--
United States.   I. Gould, William B.   II. Staudohar,
Paul D. III. Title.
GV583.B46 1986   331.88'11796'0973   85-26806
ISBN 0-86569-137-1

Printed in the United States of America

CONTENTS

v

LIST OF TABLES

PREFACE

Professional sports have assumed expanded places of importance in American society. With their amateur counterparts, they dominate substantial portions of media attention and enter our homes through print, radio, television, and just plain conversation. The sociological, psychological, and political aspects of sports are significant. The business potentials are significant. The legal consequences are necessities.

We suggest in this book a need to examine the structural and legal underpinnings of professional sports in order to understand where sports are headed. The first two chapters introduce the backgrounds in general, developing the thesis that today labor relations and the labor laws have assumed pivotal roles in determining the development of professional sports. There follows an examination of each of the four major team sports—baseball, football, basketball, and hockey. Only after explication of the idiosyncrasies of the individual leagues and their experiences in labor relations can we probe the current unresolved issues and the predictable future problems yet to unfold. The final two chapters make no pretense at perfect analysis or forecast, but we are willing to suggest that many of the problems discussed will be realities on the professional sports scene for years to come.

This book's origins lie in a lengthy law review article written by two of the authors, appearing in *Case Western Reserve Law Review* 31 (1981), at pages 685–813. The third author had also written previously on themes developed in these pages. Up to this point, we had not had the opportunity to develop in depth and league-by-league the examination of the multifaceted relationships existing in professional sports; we welcome this occasion to do so.

This book could not have been written without the willingness of people involved in professional sports to share their experiences, observations, and information with us. Through interviews, phone conversations, and professional conferences, the following have given us valuable insights: Donald Fehr and Eugene Orza, Major League Baseball Players Association; Raymond Grebey and Elliott Azoff, Major League Baseball; Edward Garvey and Richard Berthelsen, National Football League Players Association; Jay Moyer, National Football League; Lawrence Fleisher, National Basketball Players Association; David Stern, National Basketball Association; Jan Volk, Boston Celtics; R. Alan Eagleson and Sam Simpson, National Hockey League Players Association; Clarence Campbell, Gilbert Stein, Roger Gotlieb, Carole Robertson, and Gary Meagher, National Hockey League; Leonard Koppett and Bart Wright, journalists; Robert Woolf, David Falk, and Arthur Kaminsky, player's attorneys. Not all these individuals still occupy positions directly connected with sports. Their views were, nevertheless, helpful when conveyed and persist as valid today.

What all these people had to say often conflicted with the observations of their counterparts who occupied different positions in professional sports. In large part, that is what made the writing of this book both perplexing and refreshing. The final analyses are, of course, ours alone.

A baseball manager, Danny Ozark, once remarked about one of his players, "His limitations are limitless." We now know what Ozark meant. Ours are too. Even so, in the writing, whenever we took a high, hard one just under the chin, we bounced back up, dusted ourselves off and dug back in for another swing.

R.C.B.
W.B.G.
P.D.S.

LABOR RELATIONS IN
PROFESSIONAL SPORTS

1 MODELS FOR UNDERSTANDING THE INDUSTRIAL ENVIRONMENT

The Elysian Fields, Canton's mud patch, the peach basket in Springfield, and ice ponds across Canada produced the beginnings of organized team sports in baseball, football, basketball, and hockey. From roots established by amateur sportsmen evolved the professional sports leagues that today are major industries. Other sports—notably soccer—await full development, while individual-performer sports, such as tennis, golf, and bowling, have organized along quasi-industrial lines. Multimillion dollar businesses have resulted from these sports; multimillion dollar problems are the inevitability.

The development of business and legal approaches to the professional sports industries has proceeded along traditional and predictable lines: hardly surprising considering the limited models available for reference and the constraints of existing laws. Even so, special problems are created by traditional approaches, which lead to doubts about their optimality.

Certain industry features create the façade of a common front. The potential for notoriety and money transforms pastimes into passions. This same potential also breeds conflict as various sectors of the industry fight over prospective riches. This process is highlighted by the increasing tensions in management/player relations and by the consequent upsurge of organized, aggressive players' associations. Once uncertain in their nature,[1] these associations are in reality labor unions and now recognized as such.

Where at one time it was commonly believed that sports professionals would not unionize, the strengths emanating from our nation's labor laws proved too strong to resist.[2] Unions are integral to professional sports and are here to stay. That is clear. Their ultimate function is more uncertain. The transformation of players' associations into unions may have been predictable, but the contributions they may make and the problems they may not be able to resolve await future developments.

This book examines professional sports league models as represented by the various major team sports and focuses especially on labor relations. The relatively recent development of sports labor relations has altered the ways that leagues do business. Leagues involved in collective bargaining have found themselves adopting significantly variant approaches to matters formerly deemed of common concern, such as a club retaining rights to a player beyond the initial contract term. Thus it is necessary to discuss how the different sports have experimented with alternative models of sports leagues and how they have used labor relations as a catalyst for much of this diversity.

This analysis evaluates the legal and business aspects of the sports industries. It centers on often fractious relationships, particularly between labor (the players) and management (the clubs and leagues). The construction of theories to clarify and strengthen the models is a central purpose of this analysis. Labor law and labor relations are a focus here, but other developments interweave the industrial fabric and must be examined. Any industry is complex; the sports industries are deceptively so, since they are a product in part of the seeming simplicity of their various components.

The mid-1970s saw the emergence of arm's-length bargaining and the resulting collective bargaining agreements in the major sports. It was then popular to declare that peace had come to the industries after a decade of litigation, abortive strikes, and constant wranglings. This view was myopic. Despite progress toward resolving some long-standing disputes, the true character of player/management splits was just being revealed. The revelations still are being made. The 1980s to date have provided intense infighting; more is promised.

Before beginning a detailed inquiry into the individual sports, Chapter 1 discusses the general background of the sports industry: the unique positions that leagues occupy, the components of the industries, the economics of professional sports, the political and cultural roles affecting and affected by sports. Then Chapter 2 considers the legal structure of the sports industry, notably as developed through cases relating to baseball, the oldest of the professional sports leagues.

UNIQUENESS OF THE SPORTS INDUSTRIES

The sports industries are not typical. Their product is ephemeral, seen in a moment, perhaps remembered, but generally not used by the hand or physically consumed. The product is entertainment, but of a special variety. A victor is declared, and a loser identified, but these are in many respects illusions, since all participants may well be winners where it counts: in the pocketbook.

Professional sports leagues differ both in the bases leading to their creation and in the problems each must face and attempt to solve. The nature of a sport, its potential appeal to a spectator audience, and the personalities who have involved themselves in the development of the businesses have sent the individual sports in various directions. Numerous factors influence the creation and operation of sports leagues. The number of teams per league, the number of players per team, the location and size of the arena to be used, the marketability of the sport to a national versus a regional following, the number of games in a season, the injury toll on athletes, the adaptability of the game to other media, particularly television: These and other factors dictate that sports leagues are individual entities that should not be regarded as having identical interests or necessarily common problems. While commonalities exist, they are not as pervasive as are the differences.[3]

Significant disparities exist among the market values of franchises in the major sports leagues. For example, in the summer of 1981 the Wrigley family sold the Chicago Cubs for a reported $20.5 million, a price similar to the earlier sale of their cross-town compatriot, the Chicago White Sox.[4] These figures can be contrasted with a $12 million price tag set for the Philadelphia 76ers of the National Basketball Association,[5] a price that also included the buyers' assuming outstanding future indebtedness, particularly deferred compensation to be paid players in future years. The actual net price realized by the seller was somewhat more than the announced $12 million, since he was relieved of outstanding obligations. In 1981 the 76ers were one of the more powerful teams in the NBA and had been for the past few years, drawing moderately well at the gate. The Cubs and the White Sox had not generated much excitement for any number of years. Even so, the weaker baseball franchises proved to be worth substantially more than a fairly strong basketball club.

There are multiple variables in any industrial equation: Current wealth, growth potential, market conditions, and economy provide initial input. Sports require the consideration of additional factors, including the following:

1. As industries go, the sports combines are embryonic. They are overgrown small businesses, traditionally run as such, now thrust into larger industrial settings. Even today, the sports industries generate dollar volumes far less than generally is perceived by the public, which tends to be overwhelmed by media reports about the high salaries paid players, the profits earned in the sale of franchises, and the large amounts of monies going to the leagues and clubs through television contracts with the networks and local stations. While salaries are high and profits can be substantial compared to capital investment in terms of sheer dollar volume, the sports industries are not comparable to the oil, automobile, and insurance industries.

Even so, the monies are substantial and are rising. While precise figures are difficult to obtain, since most clubs are either partnerships or closely held corporations and need not divulge income figures, available economic and other relevant data reveal sports leagues as a growth industry. Because of the relatively few people involved, the potentials for personal gain, again for a few, are substantial.

2. People working in the industries are feeling their way. Existent industrial models are either unclear, not fully appreciated, or arguably inapplicable. A sizable number of sports people still do not accept the progress that sports leagues have made. Stories abound about blunders made by team owners, general managers, or coaches who did not take the time to familiarize themselves with basic working agreements (the collective bargaining agreement, the standard player contract, or even the league by-laws and rules) that determine their relationships with their players. The Carlton Fisk free agency, discussed in Chapter 3, illustrates this type of error. A similar incident occurred when the New England Patriots neglected to renew a young lineman's contract (Phil Olsen) and allowed him to move elsewhere without receiving anything in return. John Y. Brown, for a short time the owner of the Boston Celtics, renegotiated a contract with the uniquely talented and hopelessly uncontainable Marvin Barnes. Neither party had counsel present. In the process, most guarantees that had existed in Barnes's contract were removed. This action, without advice of counsel, could well have precipitated lengthy litigation when Barnes was later released.[6]

3. Relatively small numbers of people are in the business of professional sports. This leads to potential domination or disruption by the few. The human factor can tilt any equation; in the sports industry, this factor is magnified. If MISL soccer and the USFL are added to major league baseball, the NFL, the NBA, and the NHL as major leagues, there are still no more than 3,500 professional U.S. athletes at any one time on the team rosters in these leagues. There are perhaps 500 additional touring professionals in the individual sports, such as golf, tennis, and bowling. Racing car drivers, boxers, jockeys, and minor league players in various sports add to the totals, as do club and teaching professionals. But at the core, in the offices and on the fields and courts where the substantial money is concentrated, the total number of people who are there to divide the revenues total perhaps 5,000 at best.

COMPONENTS OF THE INDUSTRIES

Five interests comprise the infrastructure of professional sports leagues: Two (leagues and clubs) are aligned on the management side; three (players' associations, individual players, and the agents/attorneys for the players) are on the other. By no means is there solidarity on either side.

Individual club owners identify certain actions by the league as inimical to their best interests. The fight between Al Davis and his Oakland (Los Angeles) Raiders against Commissioner Pete Rozelle and the other owners in the National

Football League attained legendary proportions over the course of several years.[7] The effects of the Raiders' efforts to relocate a franchise over the objections of the rest of the league have ramifications that go far beyond the legal and business questions involved in this one franchise shift. The ability of leagues to govern clubs is at stake, and ultimately this struggle works itself into labor relations within the league structure as well.

As owners fight among themselves, all is not peaceful within the player ranks either. On more than one occasion, for example, contracts drafted by a club and a player's agent have incurred the wrath of that sport's players' association. Such was the case in 1977 concerning contracts entered into between the Boston Red Sox and star players Fred Lynn, Carlton Fisk, and Rick Burleson. According to the players' association, the players' agent had agreed to a clause giving the Red Sox a right of first refusal at the end of the contract periods. The players' association, contending this contravened the collective bargaining agreement, filed a grievance. The matter was settled, before arbitration, when the club dropped the controversial clauses. This type of agreement is one of many potentially divisive actions that may pit player against club, union against club, union against agent.[8]

These relationships demand close scrutiny. Besides the five infrastructural interests, however, there are other forces at work. Always important are non-playing personnel who are not management (such as umpires and referees), television and the other broadcast industries, owners of stadia and arenas (including municipalities), and minor leagues, in the sports where they exist.

Leagues

The concept of an organized professional sports league begins with the formation of baseball's National League in 1876. Several of the original principles that prompted that league's formation have since guided the course of professional sports.[9] These league principles have forced individual clubs to cooperate with each other regarding the market supply of talent that is going to "manufacture" the product and regarding the consumers who are going to pay the bills and provide the profits.

Sports leagues are not merely joint ventures; they are cartels that exist to allocate and control the production and distribution markets and to eliminate within the cartel competition over producers (players) and consumers (fans).[10] Clubs compete today but largely in areas forced on them through legal and political sanctions. Change has not come voluntarily. Nevertheless, clubs acting collectively through a league still can maximize income and profits, so long as they proceed in accordance with the law.

Today, as a cartel, a sports league allocates territorial markets and attempts to eliminate within the league competition for the sport consumer's dollar. At the same time, by spreading itself across an expansive geographical complex, it becomes a natural monopoly and effectively discourages the establishment of rival leagues. As a league enters prime markets and establishes viable properties, it gains substantial advantages, while the opportunities for new leagues to form and to succeed are diminished.

Indeed, the history of professional sports is strewn with the corpses of departed leagues. Not all disappeared completely. Certain teams from some leagues survived. But in general the challenges by new, rival leagues are marked more by failure than success. Consider the cases of the four major team sports:

1. *Baseball.* League established, then disappeared: American Association (1882-91), Union Association (1884), Players' League (1890), Federal League 1914-15), Mexican League (1946); success story: American League (1900);

2. *Football.* The dearly departed: American Football League (1932), All-American Football Conference (1946-49) (with three teams surviving (Cleveland, Baltimore, San Francisco) through entry into the NFL), the World Football League (1974-75) (no survivors); a winner: the American Football League, (1960) (through merger with the NFL and its transition to the American Football Conference); still undecided: the United States Football League (1983);

3. *Basketball.* Loser: American Basketball League (1961-63); partial winner: American Basketball Association (1967-76) (with admission of four ABA clubs into the NBA and a money settlement for the departing franchises);

4. *Hockey.* Only one challenger, like the ABA a partial winner: the World Hockey Association (1971-79) (with a select few lasting long enough to be admitted to the NHL).

Sports leagues, to varying degrees, force a redistribution of revenue among the clubs. This is particularly true regarding broadcast income: Leaguewide contracts with one or more of the three major commercial networks yield millions that are divided on a strictly equal, all-for-one, one-for-all basis. While clubs contract individually for local broadcast revenue, the national contracts—at least for baseball, football, and basketball—provide a strong equal financial base from which the league and its clubs launch their operations.

Some leagues divide gate receipts. The National Football League provides that the visiting team receive 40 percent of the gate for regular season games and 50 percent for preseason; in baseball visitors receive 20 percent. Basketball and hockey do not split gate revenues. It is notable that the NFL, which until the advent of the rival USFL maintained the lowest average salary per player among the four major team sports, requires the greatest degree of revenue sharing.

Finally, there is the division of resources necessary to stage the game. The talent pool of players is distributed in approximately equal amounts to all clubs in the league, which is accomplished by a number of devices; initial allocations, drafts of known and available talent, restrictions on player movement to new clubs, and compensation to old clubs if a player is lost. All this is done in the name of competitive balance but has other effects as well: It restricts competitive bidding for players' services, either by outright prohibitions or by indirect persuasions. These restrictions have been a central concern of the players, who have maintained that such structures illegally suppress the market for their services.

Clubs

Individual clubs in a league enjoy dual status. They are independent legal entities that act freely, that are rewarded for their individual successes, and that are answerable for their shortcomings. As members of a cartel, however, they also find their actions legally circumscribed by their agreements with the league. In certain respects, they are equal partners in the cartel, each contributing to and sharing in the whole. But in other respects, the whole is greater than the sum of its parts, and the clubs are mere franchises that are subject to the rules of the whole, including the possibility of severe disciplinary action if the rules are too severely abrogated.

The by-laws and rules of the various leagues provide for disciplinary action, including expulsion, against a miscreant team. For example, section 8.13 of the constitution and by-laws of the National Football League (1980) define the powers of the commissioner. Where it is determined that the powers of the commissioner are insufficient to act on the matter, specifically in instances such as the cancellation or forfeiture of a franchise, the matter is referred to the league's executive committee for appropriate action (see section 8.13(B)(1). The powers of the executive committee are further discussed in section 6.5(b).

The commissioner or a league executive board has imposed sanctions against the clubs or the owners in numerous instances. Some infractions of league rules result from attempts by one club to lure away another club's player.[11] Other infractions are made by an owner or general manager who speaks out of turn concerning the progress of the collective bargaining negotiations. This happened in 1981 to Harry Dalton of the Milwaukee Brewers, who broke a league-imposed gag rule that attempted to quiet all owners concerning the progress that had been made in reaching a new baseball agreement.[12]

Unlike other industries where it is possible for one sector to seek its own market, the sports franchise cannot simply walk away from the league. Essential to its existence is having someone to compete with on the playing field. Without a rival league or the possibility of the formation of one, a professional sports team must stay with the league in order to survive.

It is generally assumed that a club will always strive to field the best team possible in order to win or finish high in the league standings. This is thought to both produce maximum current earnings and help ensure future earning potential. Serious doubts can be raised about these assumptions. A few examples reveal the fallacies. First, some clubs may be only marginally profitable. A club in this category may determine that while it could afford to enter the market for a couple of free agents, the agents would improve the team very little (by a jump from fifth to fourth or third place, for example). Unless this jump would improve the gate to compensate for the extra expenditures, there is little incentive to diminish current profits without a consequent return on the investment. This situation faces several basketball and hockey clubs and at least a few in baseball.

Consequently, the disparity in baseball in spending on free agents is particularly striking. As of 1980 the New York Yankees had signed free agents to contracts in amounts totaling $17.3 million, the California Angels had contracts in total amounts of $10.5 million, and the San Diego Padres' commitments stood at $9.8 million. At the opposite end were the St. Louis Cardinals at $240,000, the Detroit Tigers $90,000, Oakland A's $50,000, Toronto Blue Jays $36,000, and, last and clearly least, the Cincinnati Reds, with a grand total of zero dollars.[13] What these figures do not reveal, and what clearly affect a club's ability to field a team with a chance of success, are the abilities of players in the farm system and the efforts made by the club to retain its own players rather than to resort to the free-agent market.

Second, for clubs that currently approach peak earnings, there is a disincentive to spend additional monies in order to improve, and that disincentive increases as the peak is approached. To spend may be to improve and to gain glory through winning, but it will reduce profits. If a few thousand dollars will achieve the top rung, it may be worth it, but to advance and merely come close is unappealing. It often takes more than a few thousand, and there still will be no guarantees: Spending equals losing—or so goes the rationale. This scenario potentially applies to all sports but is particularly accurate for clubs in the National Football League.[14]

The attitude toward free agents varies markedly from league to league. In some instances, particularly in team sports other than professional football, shortsightedness may lead to a refusal to sign free agents or do other things that will improve a club. There are numerous instances in baseball, basketball, and hockey where clubs enjoy phenomenal but relatively short-lived success at the gate. For a few years, a club turns people away at the gate, and the waiting list for season tickets is long. A couple of losing seasons, though, combined with other management mistakes such as excessive ticket hikes, may change this.

These situations should be compared with other industries. A manufacturer of goods determines a certain quality and price range for its product and hopes to maximize both the quantity produced and the price charged. Other manufacturers seek the same market, and still other manufacturers produce similar goods but at different quality and price levels. The key ingredients are how much it costs to manufacture a certain quality good and the price-times-quantity that can be realized from such efforts.

There is one supposed difference between the regular industrial model and that for sports: In the regular industrial model, it is accepted that certain businesses will sacrifice quality in order to widen the difference between costs and price realized and thus increase profits; this should not occur in sports, since each club should strive to field the best team possible. Nevertheless, certain clubs in all sports, whether through ineptness or by design, market inferior products year after year. Professional sports has its cut-rate dealers just as do the appliance, tire, clothing, and aluminum siding industries. During the past few years, each division in the NFL, NBA, and baseball's American and National Leagues has been dominated by one or two clubs. In all divisions in the three sports, either a single team has finished first more than half the time, or two teams have turned the competition into a private grudge match and won more than 80 percent between them.

Not every owner strives to cut every corner and squeeze out every dollar. Many are concerned with quality, and some could spend less than they do and increase profits. These are probably few in number, however, and fewer still are the owners who are willing to win at all costs.

Players

"From Tinker, to Evers, to Chance . . ." That little rhyme got the three into the Baseball Hall of Fame. Though many would dispute the worthiness of the selection of one or even two of the three, it underscores a truth. The name of the game is show biz, and the players are the stars. Baseball's old-timers are particularly sensitive to who has not been selected to the Hall of Fame. "Wahoo" Sam Crawford, who is in the Hall of Fame, recounted the great players of his time and decried the fact that William "Dummy" Hoy and Tommy Leach had been ignored.[15] To like effect was Sam Jones's criticism of the exclusion of Tony Lazzeri, the old Yankees second baseman who anchored the right side with Lou Gehrig for several years.[16]

As to Joe Tinker, John "Crab" Evers, and Frank Chance, the "Peerless Leader," the snipings relate to their stats, not to the admitted intangibles they delivered to the game. Only Chance hit for percentage, and none of the three was overwhelming in career hits or RBI's. In terms of raw statistics the trio are at or near the bottom in many categories when compared with other Hall of Famers. For example, among shortstops in the Hall, Tinker's career .263 mark exceeds only that of Rabbit Maranville. Johnny Evers's .270 average is far and away the lowest average among the second basemen; Billy Herman is next lowest at .304. Frank Chance, at .297, is tied with George Kelly for lowest average among first basemen, and he is substantially lower in total hits (only 1,273) than any other first baseman. Even so, they are still Tinker to Evers to Chance, fittingly elected together to the Hall in 1946.

The magic that is sports is fast fleeting. Only the other entertainment industries are comparable. Players as actors are both the machinery and the product. Fans pour in to see the Lakers play the 'Sixers, but they are just as much paying to see Kareem, Magic, and Dr. J "do their thing." It is not just that athletes are part of the game: They are the game. Are these demigods, then, mere employees—or even independent contractors? The thought is blasphemous.

Despite the talents of players who make the major professional ranks today, only a few have qualities that will endure. Their professional lives are short, and heroes fade quickly: The player's state is a transitory one. Even so, as Lawrence Ritter (in his fine oral history) quotes from Ecclesiastes: "All these were honored in their generation, And were the glory of their times."[17]

Employee, independent contractor, entrepreneur, folk-hero, statistic: The player is all these things. This causes difficulties in legal and business contexts.

Agent/Attorneys

The talents of those who play the game are marketed by a host of people who over the past fifteen years have descended on the sports industries in a manner not contemplated or prepared for by the leagues and clubs. Although agents were active well before the 1960s, they tended to be promoters, in contrast to today's personal representatives. A notable example of the old style was C.C. (Cash and Carry) Pyle. Originally a theatrical promoter, he represented Red Grange when the latter turned professional in 1925. Pyle exacted $3,000 a game and an additional $300,000 for movie rights and endorsements for his client. Pyle also helped popularize professional tennis when he enticed the French woman tennis star, Suzanne Lenglen, to embark on a tour of the United States in 1926. His guarantee to Ms. Lenglen of $50,000 startled people at the time, but at the conclusion of the tour, Ms. Lenglen, the other players on the tour, and Pyle himself had benefitted handsomely.[18]

Today's sports agents include both attorneys and nonattorneys. There are no professional requirements: One seemingly obtains credentials by calling oneself a sports agent. For far too many, this is about as far as abilities or ethics carry them. This is regrettable because credible agents have effectively advanced the causes of their clients. Overall, sports agents have been a positive influence in pushing players' salaries higher and in securing other types of financial and secured benefits.

The player/agent relationship, however, is vulnerable to abuse: misappropriating clients' funds, dealing with athletes while they still have college eligibility, violating federal securities laws, overcharging clients while taking fees on the gross amount of the contract, and renegotiating player contracts without prior authority and in abuse of prior oral agreements. Richard Sorkin's 1978 conviction for grand larceny represents a low point. The charge was misappropriating client funds. Sorkin allegedly misappropriated money totaling more than $1.2 million from approximately fifty professional athletes whom he was representing. Sorkin's easy access to his clients' money caused him to squander it for his own uses, through gambling and bad personal investments.[19]

Agents often provide funds to college athletes while they are still eligible to play college sports. Some agents sign college athletes before the end of their senior-year playing season. Both actions defy NCAA rules.[20] Other agents develop legal devices that may or may not circumvent the NCAA rules. Mike Trope, a successful agent, has in the past provided the college athlete headed for the professional leagues an open-ended contract that the athlete signs before the end of his senior-year playing season. After the athlete's season has been completed, and after the NCAA waiting period has expired, Trope then signs the "offer," notarizes it, and completes the other preparations needed to conclude the contract. Trope has said he feels in this way he serves both his clients and the NCAA rules.[21] Agents have also provided college athletes with loans in order to induce their signing. A small loan can thus create for the agent a highly profitable client. But if the loan is made while the player has remaining college eligibility, it is most likely in violation of NCAA rules.[22]

Player/agent contracts have been questioned by the courts because of securities regulation violations. In *Zinn v. Parrish*,[23] the lower court held that the contract between agent and player was unenforceable because the contract provided that the agent recommend securities to the player for investment purposes. Since the agent was not registered under 15 U.S.C. section 80B-2(11), a contract with the player could be voided. Although the appellate court found the advice did not warrant invocation of the securities laws and thus reversed the trial court decision, the case sounds a warning, but one likely not heeded in many instances.

Agents have abused their clients by taking a percentage payment when the client signs the contract. Although the player may never realize the full benefits of the contract because of injuries or getting cut, the agent takes his or her percentage immediately. This type of percentage is ethically questionable.

Renegotiating a player's contract during its term causes difficulties for management. Many agents claim that renegotiating contracts is necessary because a player's value can change quickly and immediately must be reflected in the player's salary since injury may end that player's career.[24] Others in the field, notably Bob Woolf, strongly disagree. Woolf contends that the contract should be binding on both parties equally, according to the agreed terms. He finds the industry practice of condoning renegotiation contrary to the law and dangerous for sports.[25] Representing player contracts can have a multiplier effect, since once one player decides to renegotiate, others are sure to follow.[26] This has led one league, the NBA, to impose curbs on renegotiation.[27] Even a committee of the U.S. Congress has expressed concern about player/agent abuses. The findings of the House Select Committee on Professional Sports noted "the possible widespread abuses of the player agent-athlete relationships" and urged future inquiry into the matter.[28]

Despite these abuses, sports agents perform a variety of useful tasks. While best known for the negotiation of player contracts, they may well assume other responsibilities in counselling the athlete, managing finances, marketing name and image, and representing him or her in the appropriate forums if legal disputes arise. A sports agent in these contexts is valuable to the right type of player, usually the higher-paid star whose business affairs are complex. The marginal ballplayer receives a more questionable return from the services of an agent. This does not suggest that the player should match wits alone with a club at the bargaining table; a collective agent might do as well—and at a substantially lower cost—than the individual one.

For example, a lower-round draft choice or a player not drafted at all has little bargaining power and, aside from a small signing bonus, can exact little in the negotiation process. After signing contracts, such players typically do not make the team; they are cut before realizing anything on the contract. Surely the players' associations could provide legal advice to these players at minimal cost. Better still, a standard wage and signing bonus for the rookie year could be established by collective bargaining. Someone should look out for these players, and in their best interests perhaps it should not be the individual player agent.

Custom and usage in professional team sports today dictate a bifurcated process, however, with players' associations establishing through collective bargaining certain minimum standards and agents negotiating individual contracts with the clubs. The important issues of salary, length of contract, bonuses, and guarantees are primarily left for individual negotiations, underscoring the power of the sports agent.

An agent's influence is also measured by whom he or she represents and by how many professional athletes are among that agent's clientele. Each professional sport has a handful of agents that dominate. Bob Woolf is highly regarded as an agent in many sports, but his influence in basketball is particularly extensive. Woolf has represented several first-round draft choices in recent years and can thereby affect the going price for these athletes.[29] Jerry Kapstein is a well-known name in professional baseball. At one time, Kapstein represented five pitchers on the world champion Reds. Owners admit that agents such as Kapstein, who represent so many sports stars, are powerful forces in the industry.[30] Art Kaminsky reportedly represents one-third of all players in the National Hockey League. Kaminsky's concentration in this one professional sport allows him to make decisions that influence the sport itself.[31] Six to ten agents per sport have particular power and prestige in their respective sports.

The contrast between the minimum salaries established by collective bargaining and the reported average salaries in a league are instructive in illustrating the importance of the efforts of the individual agent. (See accompanying Table 1-1.) The figures for average salaries are accurate, but there are variations depending on the source. Much depends on whether the players or owners are releasing the figures and whether deferred salaries are discounted or included at full face amount.

Table 1-1. Minimum and Average Salaries per League.

	Minimum Salary	Average Salary
Baseball 1984	$40,000	$330,000
NFL 1984	40,000	150,000
NHL 1984–85	25,000	120,000
NBA 1984–85	65,000	340,000

Note: The National Football League established minimums for each year of service in the league. While the rookie minimum for 1984 was $40,000, each year of service raised a player's minimum in increments of approximately $10,000. The top minimum is $200,000 for players in their 17th year, or above.

Source: For minimum salaries, the various leagues' collective bargaining agreements; for average salaries, data released by leagues and/or players' associations (where data conflict, best estimate is used).

Whether contracts are guaranteed or not varies greatly from league to league. In the NFL, until the advent of the USFL, it was likely that no more than 3 percent of all contracts were guaranteed. That figure has increased but still does not approach baseball and basketball, where well over 50 percent of the contracts are guaranteed.

The types of bonuses used in the different sports also vary widely. Certain bonuses are prohibited. In baseball bonuses can be awarded for the quantity of play (for example, innings pitched, games played, at bats) but not for the statistical quality of play (such as wins by a pitcher, batting average, home runs). The latter are banned by the major league rules. In the NBA a bonus based on the outcome of a particular game or series of games is prohibited.[32] Most other types of bonuses, however, are allowed. The NFL probably uses bonuses more than any other league. A typical contract may have eight or ten ways a player can earn additional money by achieving certain performance or recognition standards. The many alternatives that must be weighed in deciding a particular player's contract make the agent's role a distinctive one.

Although many of the reasons for the bifurcation are historical and arguably inappropriate today, the system nevertheless prevails. As a consequence, the role and influence of the agent/attorneys are unquestionable and shape the infrastructure of professional team sports. They are a force with which the other sports interests must deal.

Players' Associations

Following leagues, clubs, players, and agents have emerged the players' collectives, called associations but in reality unions. Their role is not easily defined. They emerged late in the process, roughly concurrently with the ascendancy of the agent/attorneys. They face hurdles that may be endemic to the nature of the industries. The history of players groups reveals their progress to be uncertain, discontinuous, frustrating, but fascinating.[33] Their many failures tend to be overshadowed by the triumphs gained in the late 1960s and through the 1970s, but the failures reveal substantial obstacles to making a players' union a vital force. These problems persist as inevitable adjuncts of the industries involved and the players to be served.

A players' union is not an ordinary trade association. It deals with a special kind of management and attempts to serve the needs of a very select group of workers. Although professional ballplayers cannot be classified with doctors, lawyers, engineers, and other academically trained professionals, professional athletes are nevertheless an "elite." They are highly trained, though not in the academic sense. They are an exceptionally skilled, select group, and few in numbers. Multitudes seek to enter these professions; a relative handful succeed. The odds against succeeding as a professional athlete are overwhelming, and as monetary rewards grow, the odds become even greater as more talented individuals seek entry into the professions.

The National Football League holds seventeen rounds to draft eligible college players. In addition to those seventeen per team, the typical club may sign another twenty to thirty free agents, either those just completing college eligibility who were not drafted or those who signed with a professional club in earlier years but had not made a team on the first, second, or even third try. Of the thirty-five to forty-five new signees per club, probably no more than five on the average will make the active roster, making the odds seven to one against making a club among those considered good enough to be signed in the first place.

Basketball is perhaps more elitist. Of the 570,000 boys who play high school basketball each year, perhaps fifty will play in the NBA: That figures to be 0.009 percent (or 9/1000 of 1 percent).[34] The NBA has seven rounds in its draft. It is the exception for anyone below the second round to make the twelve-man squad. Many lower-round picks do not even sign with the clubs that draft them; they head directly for Europe, graduate school, or a nonbasketball career.

Each aspect of these challenges to a players' union threatens the cohesiveness of a union effort. Each must be addressed in the union's plans for its members. Other unions may experience some of these problems but to a lesser degree; sports unions wrestle with them on an unprecedented scale.

The membership of a players' association is diverse. Differing skill levels, star appeal, crafts, and attained salaries, produce different outlooks and interests among the players. Even so, within a union the million-dollar-a-year superstar corresponds to the $40,000-a-year rookie. The person who has started every game for the past six years is paired with the person who may stay with the squad through preseason, make the active roster, but sit on the bench for the remainder of the season. The pitcher, the quarterback, the goalie, or the dominant NBA center is aligned with the utility man, the member of the kick-off and punt-return squads, the skater on the fourth line, or the twelfth-man "garbage time" fifth guard. To suggest that all interests are equal and all solutions to their problems are the same, or even compatible, ignores reality. There may be ways to reduce the differences, such as by having the union abrogate any role in the individual negotiations of salaries beyond a league minimum, but for each temporizing solution, there is likely an onset of new problems.

The players themselves recognize the division in their ranks. In gearing for the next round of collective bargaining negotiations in the NFL in 1982, the players' head of the union, Gene Upshaw of the Oakland Raiders, stated that it was his job to communicate with all players and convince them that the union proposal was a fair and equitable one. He clearly felt that the pending problems were as much internal within the union as they were with management. His fears were well founded. Though he, the union's executive director, Ed Garvey, and other union leaders persuaded the NFL players to strike, there was always division, which at length helped undermine the strike effort (see Chapter 5).

The varying amounts of money available to the members of the union create special problems. This is particularly true at the high end. A player earning several hundred thousand per year may not be interested in striking over meal money or other travel allowances or even over such substantial issues as pensions and the volatile freedom issues. He has his; let others get theirs the same way. That many players in the salary stratospheres do identify themselves with the lower ranks is all the more remarkable. But it may not continue, and this has to be worrisome to association officials.

The relatively short life of the professional athlete is perhaps his or her greatest problem. The average career of the professional player is between four and five years, depending on the sport and the position played. This is the average for those who actually make a major team roster. It does not include the host of hopefuls who sign professional contracts but are cut before the actual season begins.

All of this means a constantly shifting union membership. By the time a protest is pursued or collective bargaining is concluded, a new majority among the union membership may have emerged. Given the shortness of the professional career, a fact acutely apparent to the average player, his concerns must inevitably be weighted toward the here-and-now.

Not only is there a short life overall, there is a floating membership composed of those who are on a major team roster one day, off the next, then reinstated or signed by another club on yet the next. Players are waived, not claimed, released, then signed by other clubs. In addition, in baseball and to a lesser extent in hockey there is the shuffle by a certain cadre of players between the minors and the major league rosters. This difficulty in ascertaining at any given point the precise union membership presents substantial problems in labor relations.

In dimensions that far exceed any other union situation, certain nonunion members have strong interests in union undertakings: (1) prospective professional athletes (college players who will be taken in the draft or signed as free agents, others who did not make the first round but are still trying, foreign league players looking for a move, and ex-league players looking for another chance) and (2) retired players, a larger group (relatively speaking) than is usual for a union. These retired players range in age from mid-twenties to normal retirement age. In time this will become a larger and ever more persistent constituency. One of the most vocal retired player groups has been in the NFL. After threatening litigation, players who retired before the union implementation plan became eligible for union benefits. For example, every former NFL player with a disability, and who played five or more seasons is now assured of an income of $10,000 a year. The NFL, under the Bert Bell pension plan, provides needed assistance to both disabled and needy former professional players. Because of the increased veteran benefits, the NFL alumni association should grow and thus become more effective in its demands.

Finally, there are the agent/attorneys. Their intimate dealings with the individual players make the union's role ever more delicate. A good union should monitor the activities of the agents, however, and at least some players' associations have undertaken monitoring functions.[35] An ambitious project was undertaken by the NFL players' association (NFLPA) when it aligned itself with a group of agents to form ARPA, the Association of Representatives of Professional Athletes. Among ARPA's early functions was drafting a code of ethics for its members and distributing a directory that listed approved agents.[36] Eventually, for reasons hotly disputed by both sides, the NFLPA and ARPA come to a parting of the ways, and any meaningful monitoring through this joint effort collapsed. The NFLPA next sought control over agents through guarantees contained in their 1982 collective bargaining agreement with the NFL clubs, an effort that is analyzed at later points in the book.

Obviously, monitoring can cause difficulties, and if agents feel threatened, they may retaliate. In what became known as the Trope Revolt, agent Mike Trope and others announced in May 1980 that they were forming a labor organization to rival the NFLPA and would move for decertification of the incumbent union.[37] The coalition of agents joining together to launch this effort were, from the beginning, a group unlikely to cooperate for long. Although, as predicted, the effort resulted in sound and fury and little else,[38] the NFLPA was sufficiently concerned about the threat to initiate legal action, claiming that certain agents conspired to violate the antitrust laws.[39] All was still not peaceful in the NFLPA, as was underscored by reports (in August 1981) that the player representatives in the union, in a motion for a vote of confidence on Ed Garvey's leadership, did so, but with seven of the 28 votes in the negative. Gene Upshaw's comments about his mission as NFLPA president suggests that the felt need to improve the cohesiveness of the union is still present.[40]

Another source of friction between the agents and the union is equally basic. The agents and the union are in natural conflict, since in many respects they are doing the same job—that of representing the athlete. It is perfectly feasible that one could totally supplant the other. The two entities are vying for the same economic unit—the player—and the more they vie, the more likely it is that struggles will ensue.

A union exists to represent all workers in its membership. In sports this is not a simple premise. Most players view themselves as special, which makes it likely that they will find other loyalties to supersede loyalty to the union: self-loyalty, loyalty to the player's perceived best interests, and loyalty to the persons or entities that best fulfill the player's interests, which may be an agent, other counsellors, even the club owners. There may be no animosity toward the union, but there may be no fidelity either.

CHALLENGES TO THE UNIONS

The economics of the sports industry are complicated, at least for some of the leagues. It is big business, but not all sports share equally in the pie. Some would say that politics have intruded; others, merely that needed regulation has taken place and perhaps more is needed. The media, particularly television and now cable, have changed in many respects the nature of the business, not only in terms of economics but how the businesses and even the games themselves are run or played. There is still a heavy emphasis on litigation, but other dispute resolution devices are coming more into use, with positive, yet controversial, results. Several questions are posed by the current state of labor relations in the industries:

1. Have unions brought about great economic benefits to their members? If they have, where have the unions been most and least successful? Also, as illustrated above with the NFL, under what circumstances may the union succeed when an external threat—such as that posed by the USFL—appears?
2. Have unions acted so as to pose legitimate threats to the economic stability of a league?
3. How successful have unions been in gaining job security for their members? Is this a proper role for a union?
4. Have unions effectively addressed safety issues for their members?
5. How successfully have unions dealt with problems of defining their membership? Could more effective demarcation lines be drawn? For example, should unions cut across sports? Or should they recognize certain specialties within a sport?
6. Have unions fully utilized their powers as the exclusive bargaining agents for their members? Or have the unions conceded too many areas concerning individual negotiations to outside representatives?
7. Have unions effectively accommodated the collective versus the individual interest?

8.   Are sports unions fully aware of the economic potentials of the leagues in which they are situated? Are they addressing these issues—especially television—via collective bargaining?

These questions cannot be examined from only the union side. The perspectives of both labor and management must be addressed, even though often, if not generally, the union has to aggressively frame the issues and make the demands.

NOTES TO CHAPTER 1

1.   In the early days of union activities in sports leagues, both players and their counsel feared declaring their organizations to be unions. Creighton Miller was for many years the counsel for the National Football League Players' Association. Throughout this period, he generally resisted labeling the NFLPA as a union. *See, e.g.*, Krasnow and Levy, Unionization and Professional Sports, 51 Geo. L.J. 749 (1963), where the authors cite their correspondence with Miller in which he was extremely reluctant to talk of the NFLPA in terms of being a union. *Id.* at 773 n. 72. *Also see* Chapter 4. Football was not alone in this reluctance. The original and persisting position by baseball players, dating from the formation of their own association in 1954, was that theirs was not really a union. *See* further discussion in Chapter 3. An early study of the growth of players' associations by Paul Gregory concluded that the baseball association was "definitely not a union." *See* P. Gregory, The Baseball Player: An Economic Study 204 (1956).

2.   Krasnow and Levy, *supra* note 1, urged in 1963 that the players aggressively have their associations seek union status. The authors expressed some doubts, however, whether the association as unions could be very affective unless they affiliated with larger, established unions. *Id.* at 774–76. This idea has not completely died. For example, the NFLPA and the Major Indoor Soccer League Players' Association have aligned themselves with the AFL-CIO. Even so, other unions in sports have found that collective bargaining can be effectively concluded without other affiliation.

3.   Some interesting discussions of the peculiarities of sports leagues have emanated from various decisions. Of particular note is North American Soccer League v. National Football League, 465 F. Supp. 665 (1979), and 505 F. Supp. 659 (1980). In the report in 465 F. Supp., there is a telling comparison between the position of the established, well-endowed NFL, as opposed to the struggling new league, NASL. Also, see Philadelphia World Hockey Club v. Philadelphia Hockey Club, 351 F. Supp. 1462 (1972), which contains several pages of discussion of the respective positions and strengths in hockey of the old league (NHL) and the new (WHA). Finally, a good example of basic factual analysis of basketball professional leagues can be found in Robertson v. National Basketball Ass'n, 389 F. Supp. 867 (1975).

As stated by Jay Moyer, counsel to the commissioner of the NFL, a good case can be made for each sports league being sui generis. Moyer, Review of the Law of Sports, 79 Columbia L. Rev. 1590, 1592 (1979).

4. Chicago Fans in a Whirl of Expectations, N.Y. Times, June 18, 1981, at B18, col. 1.

5. Rogers, Katz Says He Paid $12 Million for 76ers, N.Y. Times, July 10, 1981, at A17, col. 1.

6. D. Kowet, in The Rich Who Own Sports, (1977), relates other tales about the contrast between old-style owners such as Phil Wrigley and Art Rooney and the new breed, Lamar Hunt and Clint Murchison, the ever-volatile Charlie Finley and his battles with almost everyone, and Ray Kroc and his taking over the mike to the public address system at his ballpark and publicly castigating both his players and the visiting team for their sloppy play. *Id.* at 97, 119–36, 147. *See also* such disparate accounts as Briner, Making Sport of Us All, Sports Illustrated, Dec. 10, 1973, at 36–42; McGraw, Memo to Delettante Owners: Sports Are Not a Joke, N.Y. Times, Jan. 22, 1978, §5, at 2, col. 1; Ryan, Sparky Sees Money Root of All Evil, Boston Globe, Dec. 7, 1976, at 31, col. 1; Smith, Charlie I and His Subjects, N.Y. Times, Oct. 17, 1973, at 49, col. 1.

7. See Los Angeles Memorial Coliseum Commission v. NFL, 468 F. Supp. 154 (1979), *modified,* 484 F. Supp. 1274 (1980), *aff'd,* 726 F. 2d 1381 (1984). It was clear, though, from the earliest hearings that this case would involve a long, protracted struggle. When preliminary rulings maintained the status quo, so that the Oakland Raiders were temporarily still in Oakland, a long and vociferous trial began in the summer of 1981. After fifty-five days of trial and two weeks of deliberation, the jury was unable to reach a unanimous decision; a mistrial was declared, not without rancor and name-calling, particularly from the Oakland Raiders' side. An accusation was launched that the NFL had planted a person on the jury favorable to its cause. At a second trial, the jury found in favor of the plaintiffs, and a subsequent damages finding resulted in an award of almost $50 million against the NFL and its clubs. For contemporary accounts and highlights of this trial, see particularly, Lindsey, N.F.L. Assailed as Trial Opens, May 20, 1981, at B7, col. 2; Lindsey, Raiders Trial Could Affect N.F.L. Power, N.Y. Times, May 10, 1981, §5, at 9, col. 4; Maher, Judge Crushes Major NFL Line of Defense, L.A. Times, July 25, 1981, at II–1, col. 5; Maher, NFL Tries to Refute Raiders Profit Claim, L.A. Times, July 22, 1981, at I–3, col. 2; Maher, Some Notice Shifting in Raider Trial, L.A. Times, July 20, 1981, at II–1, col. 6; Maher, Al Davis Has a Tough Day on Stand, L.A. Times, June 18, 1981, at II–3, col. 1; Maher, Davis Scores Some Points at NFL Trial, L.A. Times, June 15, 1981, at II–1, col. 1; Davis Calls Holdout Juror a "Plant," N.Y. Times, Aug. 15, 1981, at 17, col. 1; NFL Mistrial Imminent, Lawyer Says, Boston Globe, Aug. 14, 1981, at 29, col. 1; Rozelle Questioned at Antitrust Trial, N.Y. Times, May 22, 1981, at A19, col. 1. Other notable cases included Finley v. Kuhn, 569 F.2d 527 (1978), and Atlanta National League Baseball Club and Turner v. Kuhn, 432 F. Supp. 1213 (1977).

8. Among other accounts, *see* Miller's Feud with Kapstein Backfires on Red Sox, Boston Globe, Feb. 9, 1977, at 29, col. 1.

9. The basic principles on which the early baseball leagues were founded are discussed in Chapter 3.

10. Several disparate sources refer to professional sports leagues as cartels and discuss these implications. This is done by Lance Davis in his chapter entitled Self-Regulation in Baseball 1909–71, in R. Noll, ed., Government and the Sports Business 349–86 (1974) [hereinafter cited as Noll]. In discussing the congressional maneuverings leading to the 1966 approved merger of the NFL and AFL, James Michener noted that after the bill slipped through Congress via a conference committee report, "a cartel could (once again) be established." J. Michener, Sports in America 390 (1976) [hereinafter cited as Michener]. The dictionary definition of a cartel seems to apply to most professional sports leagues, at least to many of their activities, because it describes a "combination of individual private enterprises supplying like commodities or services that agree to limit their competitive activities (as by allocating customers or markets, negotiating quantity or quality of output, pooling returns or profits, fixing prices or terms of sale . . .)." 1 Webster's Third New International Dictionary 344 (1976).

11. *See, e.g.,* Atlanta National League Baseball Club v. Kuhn, 432 F. Supp. 1213 (1977); Kroc, Citing $100,000 Fine, Gives Up Control of Padres, N.Y. Times, Aug. 25, 1979, at 11, col. 4.

12. Owners Fine Executive $50,000, N.Y. Times, May 6, 1981, at B9, col. 1.

13. *See* 2 Inside Sports 14 (June 30, 1980).

14. *See* Garvey, NFL Snubs Free Agents, N.Y. Times, Aug. 12, 1979, §5, at 2, col. 1.

15. *See* L. Ritter, The Glory of Their Times 53 (1966).

16. *Id.* at 229.

17. Ritter, *supra* note 15.

18. P. Gardner, Nice Guys Finish Last 102 (1975). *See also* F. Menke, ed., The Encyclopedia of Football 959–60 (6th ed. 1977).

19. Montgomery, The Spectacular Rise and Ignoble Fall of Richard Sorkin, Pros' Agent, N.Y. Times, Oct. 9, 1977, §5 at 1, col. 1. *See also* N.Y. Times, Feb. 2, 1978, §4, at 15, col. 3.

20. NCAA Constitution, art. 3, §1. *See also* Ruby, What Agents Do for Clients, 2 Inside Sports 106 (June 30, 1980).

21. Johnson and Reid, Some Offers They Couldn't Refuse, Sports Illustrated, May 21, 1979, at 28.

22. Florence, Jean-Clad Trope Hardly a Penny Ante Agent, The Sporting News, March 19, 1977, at 13. *See generally* Berry, The NCAA, the Agent and the Athlete, in Current Issues in Professional Sports 31–54 (M. Jones ed. 1980).

23. 644 F.2d 360 (7th Cir. 1981).

24. Weiner, Erving's Manager Says Nets Reneged, N.Y. Times, Nov. 11, 1976, at 51, col. 1.

25. Woolf, His Ex-Manager Talks of Commitment, N.Y. Times, Nov. 11, 1976, at 51, col. 1. *See also* Woolf, Contract Renegotiating Feared as Fire for Cooking the Goose, Nat'l L. J. Aug. 7, 1978, at 27, col. 1.
26. Buck, Argovitz, Herzedg Cross Swords over Fairness to Campbell, Houston Post, Feb. 6, 1981, at C-1, col. 5.
27. National Basketball Association, Collective Bargaining Agreement, art. 20, §4 (1980).
28. Final Report of the House Select Comm. on Professional Sports, H.R. Doc. No. 94-1786, 94th Cong., 2d Sess. 177 (1977).
29. Ryan, Woolf's the Key, Boston Globe, Sept. 4, 1980, at 47, col. 5.
30. Kapstein, Could This Agent Be Too Powerful?, Boston Globe, March 21, 1976, at 90, col. 5.
31. Eskenazi, How One Man Dominates Agents' Game, N.Y. Times, March 23, 1980, §5, at 2, col. 1. *See generally* Gammons, The Restraint of Trade, Boston Globe, Dec. 14, 1980, at 49, col. 2.
32. NBA Uniform Player Contract, par. 13. On bonuses in general, see Berry, Sports in the 80's: Legal and Business Challenges (ABA 1980), in particular ch. 8, Contract Negotiations.
33. Several good accounts relate the history of attempts to establish players' associations or unions. Particularly well-documented are baseball's associations, starting with the Brotherhood in 1885, several other unsuccessful attempts, and finally the Major League Baseball Players' Association. In particular, see J. Dworkin, Owners versus Players 8-21, 25-39, 231, 243-246, 261 (1981); P. Gregory, The Baseball Player: An Economic Study 182-207 (1956); L. Lowenfish and T. Lupien, The Imperfect Diamond 27-53, 56-72, 73-95, 139-53, 183-205 (1980).
34. The figure of 570,000 high school players is based on an estimate in Underwood, A Game Plan for America, Sports Illustrated, Feb. 23, 1981; at 64.
35. Baseball Players' Union Takes Aim at "Gouging" Agents; Miller Raps Kapstein, Boston Globe, Jan. 27, 1977, at 29, col. 1. Note should also be made of the NFLPA Regulations Governing Contract Advisors, first promulgated in 1983. These are discussed further in Chapters 5 and 9.
36. *See* N.Y. Times, Jan. 15, 1978, §5, at 13, col. 4.
37. *See* N.Y. Times, May 14, 1980, at 22, col. 2.
38. *See, e.g.*, McDonough, Trope's New Union "a Joke," Boston Globe, June 8, 1980, at 94, col. 1; Visser, It's Trope vs. Argovitz . . . and Both vs. Garvey, Boston Globe, June 22, 1980, at 61, col. 2.
39. National Football League Players Association v. Trope, U.S.D.C., C.D. Calif., Docket #80-03680, complaint filed Aug. 20, 1980.
40. Wallace, N.F.L. Players Set Sales Pitch, N.Y. Times, Sept. 20, 1981, §5, at 5, col. 2.

2 THE SPORTS INDUSTRY AND THE LEGAL OVERLAY

THE CONTROLLING AREAS OF THE LAW

As the various participants in the sports industry contemplate what can be done to further their interests, laws and legal procedures become important weapons. Legal skirmishes in the sports industries are almost as old as the leagues themselves.[1] This is not surprising: Whenever parties come together to make money, disputes arise. Either unintentionally or by design, people fail to honor their obligations or disagree about what those obligations mean. People seek ways to break a contract, and the matter heads to court.

Understanding the legal background of other entertainment industries helps clarify the legal principles that apply to sports as well. Many of the early sports cases looked directly to the entertainment precedent,[2] and the other entertainment fields continue to exert great influence on sports.

Contract, antitrust, and labor law have shaped the legal framework for sports.[3] Each has exerted its distinctive influence in a roughly chronological pattern: first contracts, then antitrust, and then today, labor.[4] The interrelationship of these three areas of the law has defined the legal limits of the sports industry. Labor principles today, for example, owe much to the groundwork laid by early contract and antitrust disputes. Most cases discussed in this chapter are baseball cases. Baseball was the first of the professional team sports and one that generated a high volume of early, important cases.

THE ONE-ON-ONE: CONTRACTS

Principles of contract and its remedies were the earliest battlegrounds for the sports industry. The salvos began in the related entertainment fields but soon spilled over into sports. Much of the early litigation centered around the right of a theatrical employer to prevent an entertainer from heading to a more lucrative engagement. One of the most famous of these early cases, *Lumley v. Wagner*, involved a young opera singer, Johanna Wagner, and her attempts to abandon Her Majesty's Theatre of London and join a nearby rival troupe.[5] The court held that while it could not order Wagner to perform for her first employer, it could prevent her from performing elsewhere in the immediate geographical area. This negative injunction was to become a standard for the industry.

The sports cases, as they emerged, provided a few new twists. The sports leagues operate as cartels: They internalize rules that reduce if not eliminate competition for players' services. Until the advent of free agency, there was no bidding for services of players once they had signed with their first team, and the implementation of the draft in the various sports eliminated even that form of competition. No competition existed except for rival leagues. Consequently, the history of sports cases that involved contract jumping is also a tale of the efforts, mainly failures, of new leagues to establish themselves and challenge the established order.[6]

In 1890 the National Brotherhood of Professional Baseball Players unsuccessfully attempted to start its own league.[7] Association leaders, many of them considered among the best in the National League, led the defections to the Players' League and were, not surprisingly, among the first sued. The old clubs sought restraining orders against the players' participation in the new league. These early sports cases can be distinguished from the entertainment cases because the basic enforceability of the contracts, and not just the appropriateness of the remedy, was at issue. The existence of reserve clauses in the players' contracts raised basic issues not confronted in the entertainment cases.[8]

The reserve clause, which later was adjudicated in antitrust and labor contexts, was an early focus in contract litigation. The courts raised questions about the legal enforceability of the reserve clauses in two of the five elements necessary to qualify for injunctory relief. These clauses were examined to see if they were sufficiently definite to meet normal contractual requirements and if they, taken in conjunction with other contractual provisions, evidenced a sufficient mutuality of obligation. Initial inquiries by both a federal and a state court resulted in victories for the players. Buck Ewing, an established National League star who was to become player/manager of the New York entry in the Players' League, was singled out. In *Metropolitan Exhibition Co. v. Ewing*[9] a U.S district court, however, found that the reserve clause in his contract did not adequately define what would appear in a new contract if that clause was invoked by the club. The court held that reference to trade custom and usage did not resolve the indefiniteness. It refused to grant injunctory relief and held that damages would be inappropriate as well.

In a companion case in the state courts of New York, *Metropolitan Exhibition Co. v. Ward*,[10] one of the Brotherhood organizers, John Montgomery Ward, successfully defeated his National League club's request for an injunction on the grounds that the contract clause was indefinite and, in addition, that the contract lacked mutuality in that Ward could be let go on ten days' notice but be bound, at the club's option, for an indefinite period. After its loss in *Ewing*, the club in *Ward* tried to argue that the reserve clause was the club's right to reserve the ballplayer for only the ensuing season at not less than the present season's salary. The court, however, found that the clause did not explain or define any of the terms of the subsequent contract and thus rejected the club's attempts to explain away the ambiguities. As to the mutuality issue, the court said that the concentration of power in one party to a contract — where, as here, a club could either bind a player in perpetuity or release him on ten days' notice — could lead to great inequities. The club, for example, might hold the player until the time had passed when he reasonably could gain employment with another club, then release him with no further obligations. This imbalance in the positions of the parties was sufficient, in equity at least, to constitute a lack of mutuality and be fatal to a claim for injunctive relief.[11]

For Ewing and Ward and the other Players' League defectors, these substantial victories in court were hollow ones. By the time the legal dust had cleared, the Players' League was itself ashes. The league lasted a year, undermined in large measure by the new group of owners brought in by the players to help finance the operation. This new group found that they had more in common with the National League owners than they did with their own players. The tale is somewhat more complicated than that,[12] but it underscores that there is more to winning than having the law on one's side. Ewing and Ward returned to the National League, played out their careers in brilliant fashion, and are now in the Hall of Fame as two of the early stalwarts of the national pastime. But their great dream was defeated, not by the law but by business maneuverings.[13]

The next round of litigation came ten years after *Ewing* and *Ward*. Much happened in the 1890s. After the Players' League folded, the two remaining leagues that had operated in relative harmony since 1884 under a national agreement fell into dispute. The American Association withdrew from the agreement and attempted to operate alone. This shortsighted move was compounded by a number of economic mistakes, perhaps fostered in part by National League actions, that led to the American Association's demise in 1891.[14] For a few years the National League stood alone, but professional baseball was a young and growing sport, and people wanted to get in on the action: Thus, the American League was born in 1900.[15] Following the usual formula it started luring established players away from National League teams,[16] and the Nationals retaliated by filing lawsuits against the fleeing players.

Enter Napoleon Lajoie, whose case became a legal standard in the early years of sports litigation. By 1900 Lajoie was a leading player in the National League, holding down second base for the Philadelphia Nationals.[17] At the same time, he was forced to labor under the $2,400 maximum salary imposed by National League rules. He was ripe for a move, and he moved all the way across town to the new Philadelphia club of the equally new American League. The National League club brought suit.

The first round of *Philadelphia Base-Ball Club v. Lajoie* went to Lajoie.[18] The trial court, relying heavily on English and U.S. precedent, found that Lajoie's work at second base and at the plate was not sufficiently unique to place his services in the category of impossible to replace. The court also dismissed the complaint on the grounds that the contract was unenforceable due to a lack of mutuality.[19] As in *Ewing* and *Ward* the court noted that the club could terminate the contract at any time after giving ten days' notice but that it could at the same time, if it chose, extend the agreement from time to time for a total of three years. In light of the earlier sports cases, albeit in other jurisdictions, the trial court's holdings were not particularly surprising. The case was appealed, nevertheless. In the interim Lajoie played the 1901 season and batted .422, which is still the American League single season high.[20]

This fact was not noted by the supreme court of Pennsylvania, but it did regard the case in substantially different fashion than had the trial judge. The high court's opinion of April 21, 1902, established in its analysis a memorable precedent for the professional sports industry. The court thought that the trial judge regarded Lajoie's talents too lightly and that the evidence warranted a stronger finding as to his baseball acumen. The court concluded about Lajoie's ability that "He may not be the sun in the baseball firmament, but he is certainly a bright particular star."[21] The mutuality issue presented more difficulty; however, the court noted two points: (1) It is not necessary for sides in a contract to have identical rights or remedies; and (2) Lajoie's "large salary" was in part consideration received for the ten-day termination powers given the club. Thus, the court neutralized the termination powers through the salary, leaving the length of the contract as not unreasonable.[22] Since plaintiff had exercised its right of renewal of the contract for the 1902 season, the defendant was enjoined from playing for any other club for that season.

This time there was a hollow quality to the legal victory obtained by the league. Lajoie did not meekly return to the Nationals, nor did the American League roll over. Instead, Lajoie was traded to Cleveland, safe there from the impact of the Pennsylvania injunction because the Ohio courts refused to adhere to the Pennsylvania decree.[23] Lajoie was inconvenienced only by not being able to travel with his club to Philadelphia, which lasted only until the two leagues came to a new national agreement a year later.[24]

The standards set in *Lajoie* have prevailed. In most cases, ballplayers have been held to be unique and have been held to somewhat one-sided contracts that might be unenforceable in other industries.[25]

Beyond the narrow issues decided by these cases, however, was a challenge to the way a sports league conducts its affairs as a cartel. A central part of a league's operations is a system of allocating player resources. This system was challenged in the 1890 and 1900 cases. The challenge was partially successful in *Ewing* and *Ward* but lost through other circumstances; the challenge was totally unsuccessful in *Lajoie*. Although some later cases, tried in contract, questioned the system,[26] none made serious inroads. The leagues as cartels went forward. Players and rival leagues had to look elsewhere for legal assistance.

The initial contracts cases gave limited victories to the players. The leagues were forced to rewrite the contracts, but with *Lajoie* even this became largely unnecessary. The injunctory weapon, though an extraordinary one in theory, became the usual remedy in practice and a significant roadblock for most professional ballplayers and for any new leagues that wished to tap the talent pools of the established leagues. Although some objections were voiced against the indiscriminate use of the injunction, these were only temporary. Ways were found to avoid them. For those who wished to loosen the established leagues' hold on professional sports, it was obvious that new legal strategies would have to be devised. When it came to the one-on-one contract, the players were overmatched and undersized.

THE SLAM DUNK: ANTITRUST

In 1890 Congress passed the Sherman Act,[27] which was aimed at the huge industrial monopolies that threatened to consume the nation's economy. No legislative history suggests that Congress was concerned with professional baseball and its monopolistic tendencies, and the other professional team sports did not yet exist. Although the Players' League was born and died in the year of the Sherman Act's passage and though the American League arrived amid bitter feuding with the National just ten years later, there is no record of antitrust litigation concerning those two leagues and their complaints against the established order. Not until the Clayton Act came along in 1914[28] were private individuals, and not just the U.S. government, vested with rights and remedies under the antitrust laws. It was only in 1914 with the formation of yet another baseball league, the Federal, that the possibility was raised of applying the antitrust laws to the sports industry.

The Federal Baseball Cases

The first of these cases was similar to *Ward, Ewing*, and *Lajoie*. A well-known first baseman, Hal Chase,[29] signed with Buffalo of the new Federal League while under contract to Chicago of the American League. Although the court held in *American League Basketball Club of Chicago v. Chase*[30] that Chase's services were sufficiently unique to suggest, initially, the appropriateness of injunctive relief, the court further held that the contract evidenced an "absolute lack of mutuality" and would not be enforced. As in *Ward* the court contrasted the ten-day termination clause that could end the player's contractual rights with the option clause that could extend them, both of which were exercisable only by the club. In this respect the case affirms *Ward* and disagrees with *Lajoie*. But the court went further and examined both the federal and state antitrust implications of the system under which the established baseball leagues operated. While it concluded that there had been no violations of the Sherman Act because it felt that baseball was not interstate commerce covered by the act, the court did determine that "organized baseball" was an illegal combination "in contravention of the common law." It was "as complete a monopoly . . . as any monopoly can be made,"[31] invaded the right to labor as a property right and the right to contract as a property right, and was the result of a combination illegally restraining the rights to exercise one's profession.

This wedge, provided by the application of state concepts of restraint of trade, was nevertheless an inadequate one. It required each jurisdiction to interpret the common law aspects of trade restraints, and it directed itself mainly at the contracts of individual players. The Federal League lasted little longer than the Players' League had in 1890. It folded amid allegations that the established leagues engaged in activities that went beyond holding players to allegedly improper contracts. Several Federal League owners felt they had been undermined in numerous ways, particularly by fellow owners who sold out to the established leagues. One frustrated owner, who had incorporated a ball club in Maryland, brought suit against each of the sixteen teams in the National and American Leagues, against the two league presidents and a third person who together comprised what was then called the National Commission,[32] and against three former owners or persons having powers in the Federal League. The complaint held that a conspiracy among the defendants, in violation of the Sherman Act, had severely damaged the plaintiff in its attempts to launch a viable baseball team. Plaintiff prevailed at the trial level and won a verdict for $80,000, which was trebled under the provisions of the Sherman Act.[33] On appeal, however, the court held that the activities of the defendants were not within the act.[34] The U.S. Supreme Court then considered the matter.

Justice Holmes in *Federal Baseball Club of Baltimore v. National League of Professional Baseball Clubs* spoke for a unanimous Court. He concluded that baseball, while a business, was purely a state matter and did not involve interstate commerce within the meaning of the Sherman Act. Said Justice Holmes:[35]

> The business is giving exhibitions of baseball, which are purely state affairs. ... [T]he fact that in order to give the exhibitions the Leagues must induce free persons to cross state lines and must arrange and pay for their doing so is not enough to change the character of the business. ... [T]he transport is a mere incident, not the essential thing. That to which it is incident, the exhibition, although made for money, would not be called trade or commerce as in the commonly accepted use of those words. As it is put by the defendants, personal effort, not related to production, is not a subject of commerce.

The Later Baseball Cases

Major league baseball's immunity from the federal antitrust laws continues today and does so despite nearly sixty years of landmark cases that have dramatically expanded the definition of interstate commerce.[36] To many critics the non-action toward baseball is stare decisis run amuck.[37] Shortly after World War II, in a case involving a ballplayer blacklisted from the major leagues because of his defection to the shortlived Mexican League, the Court of Appeals for the Second Circuit examined the changed nature of the game of professional baseball and ruled that baseball's activities were covered by the Sherman Act.[38] Because that case was settled before reaching the U.S. Supreme Court and because other cases arising from the same general set of circumstances were decided at the lower courts contrary to the Second Circuit opinion,[39] the matter remained unresolved. Finally, in 1953 the Court ignored the logic of the Second Circuit opinion and in *Toolson v. New York Yankees*[40] held once again that baseball was not within the scope of the federal antitrust laws. The Court said that Congress had been aware of *Federal Baseball* and yet had not taken the legislative initiative to reverse what had become accepted statutory interpretation of the Sherman Act.[41]

Again, in 1972 in *Flood v. Kuhn*[42] the Court affirmed its hand-off posture, though it candidly admitted that other sports had come under the antitrust laws in the intervening years but that baseball "[w]ith its reserve system enjoying exemption from the federal antitrust law . . . is, in a very distinct sense, an exception and an anomaly."[43] In referring to the other cases in which professional sports leagues and clubs were held subject to the antitrust laws, the Court could only assert vis-à-vis baseball that[44]

> It is an aberration that has been with us now for half a century, one heretofore deemed fully entitled to the benefit of stare decisis, and one that has survived to the Court's expanding terms of interstate commerce. It rests on a recognition and an acceptance of baseball's unique characteristics and needs.

Accordingly, Justice Blackmun said that the Court must adhere to its previous decisions and that if there was any "inconsistency or illogic in all of this, it is an inconsistency and illogic of long standing that is to be remedied by the Congress and not by this Court."[45] The final word, though, may have been that of Justice Marshall in dissent. He stated that the Court's majority was depriving the baseball players of "needed" muscle and that an accommodation between labor law and antitrust law was required in this as in other sports. In his view the players had not agreed to the reserve clause, and if the antitrust laws were applicable to baseball, the labor exemption would not be, since the reserve clause was imposed by management and was not the result of bargaining.[46]

Contract principles gave limited help to those in baseball who challenged the established order. With *Lajoie* and it progeny, however, this help soon faded. Antitrust actions were almost totally unsuccessful because an antiquated opinion dictated what could be covered under the interstate rubric and what could not. That later Supreme Court decisions adhered to a rigid concept of stare decisis exacerbated the problem. Surely, then, after *Flood* in 1972 it was clear that a third wave of legal attack was needed. That this attack was to be generated by principally one man, sitting as a labor arbitrator, makes the story all the more remarkable.[47]

Antitrust and the Other Sports

Before examining the third phase of baseball litigation, however, we scrutinize the fate of the other sports industries under antitrust litigation. Their story is much different than baseball's, and the second wave accordingly was much more sweeping in its immediate effects for these sports than for baseball.

Between the time of *Federal Baseball* and the next serious challenges to sports leagues' practices under the antitrust laws, a number of changes in both U.S. laws in general and the sports businesses in particular had occurred. The most dramatic change was that professional baseball no longer was alone. Football started with a league in 1920 that officially became the National Football league in 1922. The National Hockey League came into existence in 1917, and basketball, which had seen attempts at professionalism come and go, saw the Basketball Association of America unite its roster of eleven teams in 1946 and then merge in 1948 with the National Basketball League, changing its name to the National Basketball Association. This increase in sports leagues gave greater visibility to all professional sports. The advent of radio and early experiments in television carried the games from the major league cities to people's homes. Attendance, down in the 1930s, picked up markedly.[48]

Other entertainment industries also were expanding, notably the movies and later television. These industries were inevitably scrutinized. The great shift in Supreme Court attitudes toward the interstate commerce clause of the Constitution and the attending expanded ability of Congress to act under the clause, made it only a matter of time until questions about activities in the entertainment fields would reach the courts via antitrust litigation. Beginning in the

1930s and continuing with great momentum into the 1940s, antitrust actions were brought in rapid succession in the theatre, motion picture, and other entertainment industries. With minor exceptions, these industries were held subject to antitrust constraints.[49]

With these precedents on the one hand, and with *Federal Baseball* and *Toolson* on the other, the Court faced the question of whether to apply antitrust laws to professional boxing. This single-event sport was a mixture: some sport, some show. The Court had little difficulty holding that boxing was subject to the Sherman and Clayton Acts.[50] With misgivings by only a small minority of the Court, football, hockey, basketball, and other sports experienced the sting of antitrust scrutiny.[51] Lawyers for various leagues continued to press in court for antitrust immunity into the early 1970s but that battle was clearly lost.[52] At least at one time all of professional sports may have been able to convince Congress to grant to their leagues the same sweeping immunity as that accorded baseball. Attempts came close to realizing this aim[53] but ultimately fell short of the total package. Certain exemptions passed into law, however, particularly those relating to leaguewide television contracts[54] and to the merging of the NFL and the AFL.[55] These actions by Congress have had effects that are perhaps still not fully appreciated or resolved.

THE PICK-AND-ROLL: LABOR

Even after winning some victories in the contracts and antitrust cases, the players perceived that more had to be done. Certain restrictive practices, long embedded in professional sports, had been eliminated, but what might take their place was unresolved. By 1974, 1975, and 1976,[56] labor law and labor relations began to assume a central role in shaping the future of professional sports. This was a giant step forward from where unionism in sports had been only a few years earlier. To understand this progression, it is necessary first to review the National Labor Relations Act as it bears on sports and then to examine how the National Labor Relations Board asserted jurisdiction over most aspects of professional sports.

National Labor Relations Act

Workers involved in interstate commerce, which includes professional team sports, are covered by the National Labor Relations Act (NLRA), as amended.[57] Section 7 of this law provides for three basic rights that form the heart of U.S. labor relations policy: (1) the right to self-organization (to form, join, or assist labor organizations); (2) the right to bargain collectively through representatives of the employees' own choosing; and (3) the right to engage in "concerted activities" for employees' mutual aid or protection. In short, workers are permitted to unionize, collectively bargain, and use pressure tactics (e.g., to strike and picket) to achieve their legitimate objectives. Administration is carried out by the National Labor Relations Board (NLRB) and the federal courts.

The NLRB enforces the law by policing unfair labor practices committed by either labor or management. For example, under Section 7 the employer and union are forbidden from interfering with employees' rights, and allegations of such violations are handled by the NLRB. Also administered by the NLRB is the machinery for determining appropriate units or groups of employees qualified to vote in a union representation election and for conducting such elections by secret ballot vote. The NLRB does not currently administer unit determination and elections in the four major sports. *Units* include active players, and elections involving players have resulted in the choice of an exclusive bargaining agency. Finally, the NLRB reviews questions concerning what issues are subject to negotiation under the law. Most of the NLRB's current work in sports involves unfair labor practices and scope of bargaining.

On unfair labor practices, two common allegations in sports are (1) that the employer has disciplined or discharged players for engaging in union activities and (2) that the employer has refused to bargain in *good faith*. Good-faith bargaining requires that the parties communicate through proposals and counter-proposals and that they make every reasonable effort to reach agreement. In certain cases employers must furnish basic information about finances and budgets in order to comply with good-faith dictates. This has been a recurring problem in sports, since owners are reluctant to disclose financial data to unions.

Scope of bargaining is defined in the NLRA as including wages, hours, and working conditions. *Wages* include pay, fringe benefits, and bonus payments; *hours* are time spent on the job; and *working conditions* cover factors influencing the work environment such as work rules, safety, and seniority. These areas are considered by the NLRB to be *mandatory* subjects for bargaining that must be negotiated in good faith. So-called *permissive* subjects for bargaining are those on which management is not obligated to negotiate but may do so if it wishes. This includes management rights or prerogatives that the employer has an exclusive right to determine. *Illegal* subjects are those that the law prohibits from being negotiated. From time to time the NLRB has been asked to rule on whether a subject is negotiable, as with wage scales or use of artificial turf.

Characteristics of bargaining units are generally the same throughout the team sports. All active league players are in the unit, and nearly all players are members of their respective unions. Clubs join together to form a multiemployer bargaining arrangement so that the negotiated contract in each sport applies to all teams uniformly. The formal bargaining structure influences the diversity of individual and organizational interests that must be accommodated during the negotiation of an agreement.[58] Conflict is inherent in nearly all negotiating situations, both between the parties and within the organizational structures of the union and team owners.

NLRB Jurisdiction

Before employees can benefit from the protection of the National Labor Relations Act, as described above, they must convince the NLRB that they are a labor group entitled to coverage under the act and thus entitled to bring their labor matters before the board. Until 1969 it was not clear whether the NLRB would take jurisdiction in sports industry cases. Horse racing already had been characterized as a local activity that was beyond the board's purview.[59] In 1969, however, the umpires in baseball pressed for board recognition.[60] Baseball was not the best sport to advance the cause of sports unions because of the shadow of *Federal Baseball* and Justice Holmes's declaration that baseball was not interstate in nature. As expected, the baseball leagues pressed this contention before the board and urged that the board's jurisdiction under the federal labor laws was limited to businesses engaged in interstate commerce and that baseball, as had been held, was not of this character. The board rejected this contention.[61]

Accordingly, the NLRB concluded that professional baseball was an industry affecting commerce and, as such, was within the board's jurisdiction. The Supreme Court's later decision in *Flood* actually buttressed the board's view. While expressing fidelity to the principles of stare decisis, the Court specifically stated that baseball is an interstate commerce.[62]

The NLRB also rejected the argument that jurisdiction was inappropriate both because baseball practiced internal self-regulation and because the "effective and uniform regulation of baseball's labor relations problem is not possible through Board processes because of the Sport's international aspects."[63] The umpires argued that self-regulation was entirely controlled by the employers and that lack of board regulation would make the industry subject to many different labor laws depending on the locality in which the dispute arose. The board accepted the union's argument.[64]

Additionally, the NLRB noted that many employees other than those involved in the petition for representation filed in the case were not involved in any kind of self-regulation system at all. If the board declined jurisdiction over the industry, such employees would lose the benefits of any kind of representation or dispute settlement machinery. After examining the legislative history, the board was unable to find any intent on the part of Congress to exclude sports, including baseball, from coverage under the nation's labor laws.[65]

This NLRB decision coincided with the first collective bargaining agreements forged between the nascent players' unions[66] and the various major team leagues. The baseball players were first and obtained a collective bargaining agreement in early 1968, an event that had been preceded by the arrival of Marvin Miller as director of the Major League Players' Association.[67] The agreement was modest in comparison with those that followed, but it provided significant gains for the players: It raised the minimum annual salary to $10,000, provided for arbitration of grievances, and called for a study committee to examine the reserve clause.[68] A collective bargaining agreement for football, both the NFL and the about-to-be merged AFL, followed a few months later, with similarly significant, yet rudimentary, agreements.[69] Thereafter came basketball and hockey, and with those the union movement in professional team sports became a reality.[70] All leagues showed a similar pattern: The early agreements were modest, skirting some of the tougher issues, but each succeeding agreement chipped away at traditional management prerogatives. Powers and rights slowly shifted from the owners to the players.

NOTES TO CHAPTER 2

1. *See generally* H. Seymour, Baseball: The Early Years (1960). For an account of the very earliest litigation, involving the Union Association versus the established leagues, see Seymour 141, 154–56.

    Other early examples of litigation include: Metropolitan Exhibition Co. v. Ewing, 42 F. 198 (C.C.S.D.N.Y. 1890); Allegheny Base-Ball Club v. Bennett, 14 F. 257 (C.C.W.D. Pa. 1882); Baltimore Baseball Club & Exhibition Co. v. Pickett, 78 Md. 375, 28 A. 279 (1894); Metropolitan Exhibition Co. v. Ward, 9 N.Y.S. 779 (Sup. Ct. 1890); Columbus Base-Ball Club v. Reiley, 11 Ohio Dec. 272 (1891); Harrisburg Base-Ball Club v. Athletic Ass'n, 8 Pa. County Ct. 337 (1890); Philadelphia Ball Club v. Hallman, 8 Pa. County Ct. 57 (1890). These cases predated the wave of litigation that attended the formation of the American League.

2. *See, e.g.*, Philadelphia Ball Club v. Hallman, 8 Pa. County Ct. 57, 59 (1890), which regarded Lumley v. Wagner, 42 Eng. Rep. 687 (1852), as having established precedent in this country and in England. In Harrisburg Base-Ball Club v. Athletic Ass'n, 8 Pa. County Ct. 337, 338–41 (1890), the court cited several other precedents that criticize *Lumley* and accordingly refused to follow its rationale.

    In Metropolitan Exhibition Co. v. Ward, 9 N.Y.S. 779, 780–81 (1890), the court cited *Lumley*, then turned to U.S. cases involving entertainers such as Mapleson v. Del Puente, 13 Abb. N. Cas. 144 (N.Y. 1883), and Daly v. Smith, 38 N.Y. Sup. Ct. 158 (1874).

    See also Philadelphia Base-Ball Club v. Lajoie, 10 Pa. Dist. Rpts. 309, 310–13 (1901), *rev'd*, 202 Pa. 210, 51 A. 973 (1902). This case discusses *Lumley* and *Daly* and adds to English entertainment cases such as Montague v. Flockton, L.R. 16 Eq. 189 (1873), and Webster v. Dillon, 30 L.T.R. (n.s.) 71 (1857). *Lajoie* analogizes these cases to the 1890s sports cases.

3. In addition to contracts, antitrust, and labor, tort and property concepts, although peripheral, have also been significant in shaping the legal framework of sports law. Tax law, perhaps less on the periphery than tort and property law, has also been influential. The extent to which owners could depreciate player contracts and defer compensation ameliorated some of the devastating effects of the maximum tax rates on earned income and also shaped the economic structure of professional clubs and leagues, par-

ticularly before the 1976 code revisions. The tax laws' impact, however, is somewhat separate from the interaction of contracts, antitrust, and labor law discussed in this chapter. For that reason, tax is not considered in tandem with the other areas of law.

For a thorough discussion of the interface of tax law and professional sports, particularly in light of the 1976 revisions, *see, e. g.*, Blum, Valuing Intangibles: What Are the Choices for Valuing Professional Sports Teams?, 45 J. Tax 286 (1976); Horvitz and Hoffman, New Tax Developments in the Syndication of Sports Franchises, 54 Taxes 175 (1976); Jones, Amortization and Nonamortization of Intangibles in the Sports World, 53 Taxes 777 (1975); Lowell, Deferred Compensation for Athletes, 10 Tax Adviser 68 (1979); Raabe, Professional Sports Franchises and the Treatment of League Expansion Proceeds, 57 Taxes 427 (1979); Strandell, The Impact of the 1976 Tax Reform Act on the Owners of Professional Sports Teams, 4 J. Contemp. L. 219 (1978); Weill, Depreciation of Player Contracts— The Government Is Ahead at the Half, 53 Taxes 581 (1975); Zaritsky, Taxation of Professional Sports Teams after 1976: A Whole New Ballgame, 18 Wm. & Mary L. Rev. 679 (1977).

4. Labor principles will not preempt the sports law field completely. Problems beyond the scope of labor relations or labor law are common. Depending on the nature of the problem, certain circumstances may arise that are important to the legal framework of sports but that have a limited impact on labor law. One such occurrence is the current legal dispute over the attempted move of the Oakland Raiders to Los Angeles. The NFL's action to block this move has resulted in antitrust litigation by those with financial interests in the Los Angeles Coliseum and the Raiders. For preliminary actions in this litigation, see Los Angeles Memorial Coliseum Comm'n v. NFL, 468 F. Supp. 154 (C.D. Cal. 1979), *modified*, 484 F. Supp. 1274 (C.D. Cal. 1980). *See also* Hecht v. Pro-Football, Inc., 570 F.2d 982 (D.C. Cir. 1977) (denial of stadium lease to prospective owner in one league because club owners in a rival league exercised control over the facility); AFL v. NFL, 323 F.2d 124 (4th Cir. 1963) (assorted monopolistic practices engaged in by one league to the detriment of the other); NASL v. NFL, 505 F. Supp. 659 (S.D.N.Y. 1980), *modifying* 465 F. Supp. 665 (S.D.N.Y. 1979) (restrictions on cross-ownership among sports leagues).

5. Lumley v, Wagner, 42 Eng. Rep. 687 (1852). This case also spawned actions against the rival employer who attempted to induce Johanna Wagner to break her contract—an early example of interference with a contractual relationship. Lumley v. Gye, 118 Eng. Rep. 749 (1853). This approach, particularly when injunctive relief against the defecting employee might be unobtainable or ineffective, has served occasionally as an effective alternative in the sports industries. *See* New England Patriots Football Club v. University of Colorado, 592 F.2d 1196 (1st Cir. 1979); American League Baseball Club of New York v. Pasquel, 63 N.Y.S.2d 537 (Sup. Ct. 1946).

The early entertainment cases dealing with injunctive and other forms of relief are discussed strictly from the entertainment perspective in Tannenbaum, Enforcement of Personal Service Contracts in the Entertainment Industry, 42 Cal. L. Rev. 18 (1954).

6. Until the advent of the litigious age of the 1960s and 1970s, most reported sports cases focused on the legal problems erupting when rival leagues were formed and the owners of such leagues went to war concerning rights to players, territories, and other valuable requisites of professional sports teams. Discussions of the rival leagues, in addition to what follows in Chapter 2, appear throughout the book. These were not the only causes of litigation: Contracts were terminated because of injuries, players were suspended and blacklisted, and owners were disciplined. Until the advent of grievance arbitration and the individual player's awareness of his legal rights, however, the history of the legal problems in sports and of new leagues challenging the established order were practically synonymous.

7. A few cases were decided before 1890, but most had limited precedential value. *See, e.g.*, Allegheny Base-Ball Club v. Bennett, 14 F. 257 (C.C.W.D. Pa. 1882).

8. The reserve clause, as a baseball institution, is almost as old as the National League. It is reported to have been used as early as 1879 (see Chapter 3). The term of the contract at issue in most entertainment cases was for a definite time. The alleged breach occurred during the running of that time. In contrast, many sports cases involve the club's right to hold the player for an additional term by invoking the reserve clause in the old contract. This situation did not always arise but serves to distinguish these cases from the entertainment cases. The discussion in the text of the *Ewing* and *Ward* cases illustrates this.

9. Metropolitan Exhibition Co. v. Ewing, 42 F. 198, 204 (C.C.S.D.N.Y. 1890):

    > The law implies that the option of reservation is to be exercised within a reasonable time; but when this has been done the right to reserve the player becomes the privilege, and the exclusive privilege, as between the reserving club and the other clubs, to obtain his services for another year if the parties can agree upon the terms. As a coercive condition which places the player practically, or at least measurably, in a situation where he must contract with the club that has reserved him, or face the probability of losing any engagement for the ensuing season, it is operative and valuable to the club. But, as a basis for action for damages if the player fails to contract, or for any action to enforce specific performance, it is wholly nugatory. In a legal sense, it is merely a contract to make a contract if the parties can agree.

    It is ironic that William B. "Buck" Ewing was one of the players singled out in the litigation over the Players' League. Although he was one of the original organizers of the Brotherhood in 1885, he expressed sympathy for his National League owner, John B. Day of New York, just before the formation of the Players' League was announced. According to reports, he was almost convinced to forsake the new league and announce his support for the National League, but reneged when he found no other renegade players ready to recant. His credibility with the Players' League, therefore, was temporarily damaged. *See* H. Seymour, Baseball: The Early Years 234 (1980).

10. Metropolitan Exhibition Co. v. Ward, 9 N.Y.S. 779 (Sup. Ct. 1890). Although this analysis concentrated on *Ewing* and *Ward* from the Players' League era, numerous other lawsuits were filed against players leaving the National League and American Association to join the Players' League. Most attempts to retain players were unsuccessful. *See, e.g.*, Philadelphia Ball Club v. Hallman, 9 Pa. County Ct. 57 (1890). The club was successful in only one case. John Pickett, who had been playing for the American Association's Kansas City club, was ordered not to play for any other team. *See* American Ass'n of Base-Ball of Kansas City v. Pickett, 20 Phila. Rep. 298 (1890). Pickett, however, evidently was able to ignore the injunction because he is reported to have played second base for the Philadelphia Players' League Club.

11. In the reported *Ward* decision, the court considered only whether a preliminary injunction should issue. Evidently, there was never a full trial on the issue of whether the contract lacked mutuality. The decision does express great doubts that plaintiff ball club would have succeeded on the merits. Metropolitan Exhibition Co. v. Ward, 9 N.Y.S. 779, 784 (Sup. Ct. 1890). As is often true in these cases, the preliminary injunction stage is often indicative of the ultimate decision on the merits. This observation is particularly true when, as in *Ward*, there is no jury and the full trial may be before the same judge. Accordingly, many of the injunction cases were settled after the hearing on the preliminary injunction and before the trial on the merits.

12. The Players' League is discussed at length in Chapter 3. *See also* H. Seymour, Baseball: The Early Years 240–250 (1960).

13. The players, Ewing and Ward, who were at the heart of the 1890 litigation are themselves fascinating characters. They are mentioned again in Chapter 3. As to John Montgomery Ward, there is an excellent description of his many ventures in L. Lowenfish and T. Lupien, The Imperfect Diamond 39–53 (1980).

14. *See* H. Seymour, Baseball: The Early Years 251–262 (1960).

15. In general on the creation of the American League, see the discussion in Chapter 3. *See also* L. Allen, The American League Story (1962).

16. *See id.* at 18.

17. Team nicknames are puzzling. It was not always apparent, at least prior to 1900, when a team had an individual nickname and when it simply took the league name, as evidenced by the Philadelphia Nationals. This team already may have been referred to as the Phillies in everyday parlance. Seymour refers to the Philadelphia National League entry in 1883 as the Phillies. Seymour, *supra* note 18, at 207. To be conservative, the team is called the Nationals in this chapter, just as many of their counterparts of the day were similarly designated.

18. Philadelphia Base-Ball Club v. Lajoie, 10 Pa. Dist. Rpts. 309 (1901), *rev'd*, 202 Pa. 210, 51 A. 973 (1902).

19. *Id.* at 317.

20. Lajoie's on-field achievements rank him among the game's greatest play-
     ers. Over the course of twenty-one years in the majors, Lajoie came to
     bat 9,589 times, had 3,251 hits, and compiled an enviable career batting
     average of .339. Lajoie was elected to the Hall of Fame in 1938, the
     second year of its existence, and was the first second-baseman so honored.
     Only the big five — Ty Cobb, Babe Ruth, Walter Johnson, Christy Mathew-
     son, and Honus Wagner — preceded him into the Hall. *See* National Baseball
     Hall of Fame and Museum Yearbook 22 (1976); D. Neft, R. Johnson,
     R. Cohen, and J. Deutsch, The Sports Encyclopedia: Baseball 109 (1974).
21. Philadelphia Base-Ball Club v. Lajoie, 202 Pa. 210, 217, 51 A. 973, 974
     (1902).
22. In comparing the club's right to terminate the contract with the bargained-
     for salary that Lajoie was to receive, the court noted:

> The term mutuality or lack of mutuality does not always convey a clear and defi-
> nite meaning. . . .
>   In the contract now before us, the defendant agreed to furnish his skilled profes-
> sional services to the plaintiff for a period which might be extended over three
> years by proper notice given before the close of each current year. On the other
> hand, the plaintiff retained the right to terminate the contract upon ten days'
> notice, and the payment of salary for that time, and the expenses of defendant in
> getting to his home. But the fact of this concession to the plaintiff is distinctly
> pointed out as part of the consideration for the large salary paid to the defendant,
> and is emphasized as such. And owing to the peculiar nature of the services de-
> manded by the business, and the high degree of efficiency which must be main-
> tained, the stipulation is not unreasonable. Particularly is this true when it is re-
> membered that the plaintiff has played for years under substantially the same
> regulations.

     202 Pa. at 219, 51 A. at 974–75.
         As noted in the text, Lajoie's "large salary" was $2,400, the league-
     imposed maximum, and one of the selling points in the new American
     League used to induce players to forsake the National League. It is evi-
     dent, however, that the court also was influenced by the fact that the con-
     tract was partially executed and that the club had paid Lajoie substantial
     sums of money under what was alleged to be an unenforceable agreement.
23. *See* Philadelphia Baseball Club Co. v. Lajoie, 13 Ohio Dec. 504 (1902).
24. It was, of course, in 1903 that the first of the modern World Series was
     held, arising out of the new national agreement between the National and
     American Leagues. It was somewhat fitting that one of the participant
     clubs was the Pittsburgh Pirates, since that team earned its nickname in the
     1890s for allegedly pirating away a player that should have been returned
     to the American Association after the demise of the Players' League. Pitts-
     burgh was not as fortunate this time. In a major upset, the Boston Pil-
     grims, later the Red Sox, swept the first World Series championship, five
     games to three. Neft, Johnson, Cohen, Deutsch, *supra* note 20, at 28.
25. Well into this century, courts looked with great skepticism on contracts
     that contained one-sided cancellation clauses. These contracts often were
     found to be lacking in mutuality of obligation and were voided, as in the
     leading case of Miami Coca-Cola Bottling Co. v. Orange Crush Co., 296

F. 693 (5th Cir. 1924). For twenty-five years after *Lajoie*, therefore, courts applied the mutuality doctrine more vigorously in other industrial settings. This discrepancy has eroded slowly, so that the *Lajoie* approach for sports contracts differs minimally from other problems. This development occurred over a long period óf time. *See* Gellhorn, Limitations on Contract Termination Rights—Franchise Cancellations, 1967 Duke L. J. 465.

26. *See, e.g.*, Weegan v. Killefer, 215 F. 168 (W.D. Mich.), *aff'd*, 215 F. 289 (6th Cir. 1914); Brooklyn Baseball Club v. McGuire, 116 F. 782 (E.D. Pa. 1902); Connecticut Professional Sports Corp. v. Heyman, 276 F. Supp. 618 (S.D.N.Y. 1967); American League Baseball Club of Chicago v. Chase, 86 Misc. 441, 149 N.Y.S. 6 (Sup. Ct. 1914). *But see* Cincinnati Exhibition Co. v. Marsans, 216 F. 269 (E.D. Mo. 1914); Long Island Am. Ass'n Football Club v. Manrodt, 23 N.Y.S. 2d 858 (Sup. Ct. 1940).

27. Sherman Antitrust Act, ch. 647, 26 Stat. 209 (1890) (codified at 15 U.S.C. §§1-7 (1976)).

28. *See* discussion of the Federal League in Chapter 3. *See also* L. Lowenfish and T. Lupien, The Imperfect Diamond at 73–100 (1980).

29. Harold "Prince Hal" Chase was known for his adventures outside the ballpark. In contemporary accounts, he is described as an "incorrigible gambler." Lowenfish and Lupien, *supra* note 28, at 88. Chase was thought capable of fixing games, though he was never caught. *Id.* Chase was also a superb ballplayer and briefly managed the young and struggling New York Highlanders, today's New York Yankees. Neft, Johnson, Cohen, Deutsch, *supra* note 20, at 56, 61.

30. American League Baseball Club of Chicago v. Chase, 86 Misc. 441, 149 N.Y.S. 6 (Sup. Ct. 1914). The court's discussion focused on the contract's absolute lack of mutuality, the former national agreement for the governance of professional baseball, and the rules and regulations of the national commission. The court left no doubt about its objections to such sweeping terms favoring one side of the agreement. The court summarily denied the request for an injunction against Chase. *Id.* at 456, 149 N.Y.S. at 14. Other litigation arising from Federal League efforts to raid players from the National and American Leagues, brought differing results. *Chase* was supported in Weegham v. Killefer, 215 F. 168 (W.D. Mich.), *aff'd*, 215 F. 289 (6th Cir. 1914); Cincinnati Exhibition Co. v. Johnson, 190 Ill. App. 630 (1914). *But see* Cincinnati Exhibition Co. v. Marsans, 216 F. 169 (E.D. Mo. 1914).

31. American League Baseball Club of Chicago v. Chase, 86 Misc. 441, 461, 149 N.Y.S. 6, 17 (Sup. Ct. 1914).

32. The National Commission arose from peacemaking efforts between the National and the American leagues that resulted in the new national agreement in 1903. Its duties were described in the court of appeals' decision in National League of Professional Baseball Clubs v. Federal Baseball Club of Baltimore, 269 F. 681 (D.C. Cir. 1920):

> The National Commission . . . is an unincorporated body composed of the presidents of the two leagues and a third person, selected by them. It is an administra-

tive body, not a profit making concern. The club which wins the championship
pennant in any year in one major league competes for the championship in that
year with the winner of the other. It is one of the functions of the National Commission to regulate these contests. . . .

The National Commission exists by virtue of the national agreement. . . .

Id. at 683.

One of the National Commission's functions was to oversee the World
Series. The Black Sox World Series scandal of 1919 did not speak well for
the commission's success and was a leading cause of its demise. By all
accounts, the commission operated loosely and ineffectively. Baseball
owners thought that an authority figure was needed. The owners chose
Judge Kennesaw Mountain Landis, who had already gained their admira-
tion through his sympathetic treatment of their cause in the early stages of
the Federal League litigation. In 1920 the National Commission ceased to
exist and the commissioner of baseball became a fixture. For a particularly
good account of this era, see E. Asinof, Eight Men Out: The Black Sox and
the 1919 World Series (1963). *See also* B. Veeck and E. Linn, The Hustler's
Handbook 252–99 (1965).

This suit was not the first antitrust litigation arising out of attempts to
found the Federal League. The Federal League owners, named as defendants in the Baltimore Terrapins lawsuit, were plaintiffs in an earlier action
filed against the National and American Leagues. Lowenfish and Lupien,
supra note 28, at 91. This earlier suit was important in two respects: First,
it provided leverage for the federal owners to settle with the established
leagues, resulting in the Federal League's demise; and second, Ned Hanlon
and Baltimore, however, were excluded from the settlement benefits, thus
motivating their precedent-setting lawsuit. The settlement resulted from
the dilatory tactics of the district court judge hearing the case. This judge,
Kennesaw Mountain Landis, later became baseball's first commissioner.

33.   The lower court awarded treble damages pursuant to §7 of the original
Sherman Antitrust Act, 15 U.S.C. §§1–7 (1976). This provision eventually
was repealed by Act of July 7, 1955, ch. 283, §3, 69 Stat. 283, because
§5 of the Clayton Act, 15 U.S.C. §15 (1976), a provision almost identical
to §7 of the Sherman Act, superseded the original act. Today, an action
similar to that in *Federal Baseball* would be brought under the Clayton
Act.

34.   National League of Professional Baseball Clubs v. Federal Baseball Club of
Baltimore, 269 F. 681, 688 (D.C. Cir. 1920).

35.   Federal Baseball Club of Baltimore v. National League of Professional
Baseball Clubs, 259 U.S. 200, 208–209 (1922).

36.   Article I, §8, of the Constitution grants Congress the power to regulate
trade "among the several States." In early cases, this provision was interpreted to exempt intrastate activity from congressional regulation unless it
had a "direct effect" on interstate commerce. Schechter Poultry Corp. v.
United States, 295 U.S. 495 (1935). The Supreme Court departed from
this strict standard in NLRB v. Jones & Laughlin Steel Corp., 301 U.S. 1
(1937), where it applied a more lenient "practical effect" test in upholding the constitutionality of the National Labor Relations Act. Subsequent

cases further expanded Congress's regulatory power to include all activities that have a "substantial effect" on interstate commerce. *See* United States v. Sullivan, 332 U.S. 689 (1948); United States v. Darby, 312 U.S. 100 (1941).

37. Typical of quotes concerning the courts' reliance on stare decisis to continue baseball's antitrust exemption are the following:

> To hold that the Court must protect business interests built in reliance on prior decision could dangerously limit the adaptability and growth of the law, to say nothing of the one-sided nature of this approach when considering the interests of the other parties involved.

Note, Antitrust and Professional Sport: Does Anyone Play by the Rules of of the Game?, 22 Cath. L. Rev. 403, 424 (1973).

> [W]hen notions of a stare decisis lock judicial thinking into a 1922, or even a 1953, legal framework, the law not only appears inconsistent, but periodically the courts are again confronted with either compounding the error or reversing a long-standing precedent."

Note, Baseball's Antitrust Exemption: The Limits of Stare Decisis, 12 B.C. Indus. & Com. L. Rev. 737, 746 (1971).

See also Rogers, Judicial Reinterpretation of Statutes: The Example of Baseball and the Antitrust Laws, 14 Hous. L. Rev. 611 (1977); Note, Applicability of the Antitrust Laws to Professional Baseball, 2 Mem. St. L. Rev. 299 (1972); Note, Baseball—An Exemption to the Antitrust Laws, 18 Pitt. L. Rev. 131 (1956); Note, Baseball's Antitrust Exemption and the Reserve System: Reappraisal of an Anachronism, 12 Wm. & Mary L. Rev. 859 (1971); Note, Curt Flood at Bat against Baseball's Reserve Clause, 8 San Diego L. Rev. 92 (1971); Note, Monopsony in Manpower: Organized Baseball Meets the Antitrust Laws, 62 Yale L.J. 576 (1953).

38. Gardella v. Chandler, 172 F.2d 402 (2d Cir. 1949), *rev'g* 79 F. Supp. 260 (S.D.N.Y. 1948). A divided court held that the advent of radio and television broadcasting of baseball games was sufficient to distinguish the instant case from *Federal Baseball*, thus stating a valid claim under the Sherman and Clayton antitrust acts. In a subsequent proceeding, the court refused to issue an injunction pendente lite in favor of plaintiff. Gardella v. Chandler, 174 F.2d 919 (2d Cir. 1949).

39. In Kowalski v. Chandler, 202 F.2d 413 (6th Cir. 1953), the court sided with the dissent in *Gardella*, quoting the dissenting language with approval. *Id.* at 219.

40. 346 U.S. 356 (1953).

41. In a per curiam opinion, the Court said:

> Congress has had the ruling under consideration but has not seen fit to bring such business under these laws by legislation having prospective effect. The business has thus been left out for thirty years to develop, on the understanding that it was not subject to existing antitrust legislation. The present cases ask us to overrule the prior decision and, with retrospective effect, hold the legislation applicable. We think that if there are evils in this field which now warrant application to it of the antitrust laws it should be by legislation.

346 U.S. 357 (1953).

Although per curiam, the *Toolson* decision had two dissenters. Justice Burton, joined by Justice Reed, highlighted the changed business of baseball over the years since the *Federal Baseball* decision, as substantiated by testimony elicited in congressional hearings. Consequently, these justices would have disregarded *Federal Baseball* and applied the antitrust laws *unless* there was congressional action specifically granting baseball an exemption. *Id.* at 364–65.

42. 407 U.S. 258 (1972).

43. *Id.* at 282.

44. *Id.*

45. *Id.* at 284.

46. *Id.* at 295–96.

47. See discussion in Chapter 3 of labor arbitration, particularly Andy Messersmith and Dave McNally's attempts to be rid of baseball's reserve clause.

48. Attendance figures for sports events are best illustrated by those of baseball, the only fully established professional sport during the 1930s. In 1930 attendance was ten million, dropping to six million by 1933, a significant but not horrendous drop considering the depression. By 1937 there were definite signs of recovery, with attendance increasing to nine and a half million. By 1948 the figure more than doubled to twenty-one million. *See* P. Gardner, Nice Guys Finish Last 12, 20 (1975).

49. *See, e.g.*, United States v. Paramount Pictures, 334 U.S. 131 (1948); United States v. Griffin, 334 U.S. 100 (1948); United States v. Crescent Amusement Co., 323 U.S. 173 (1944); Interstate Circuit v. United States, 306 U.S. 208 (1939); Paramount Famous Lasky Corp. v. United States, 282 U.S. 30 (1930); and Binderup v. Pathe Exchange, 263 U.S. 291 1923). For an early article discussing some of the implications of the decisions leading up to the Griffith and Paramount cases in 1948, see Reich, The Entertainment Industry and the Federal Antitrust Laws, 20 So. Cal. L.Rev. 1 (1946).

50. United States v. International Boxing Club, 348 U.S. 236 (1955). Decided at the same time was United States v. Shubert, 348 U.S. 222 (1955), which determined that the federal antitrust laws extended to the production and operation of legitimate theatrical productions throughout the United States. Both cases considered, then rejected, arguments that they should follow the *Federal Baseball* and *Toolson* rationales.

51. For football, see Radovich v. National Football League, 352 U.S. 445 (1957). For basketball, see Robertson v. National Basketball Association, 389 F. Supp. 867 (1975). For hockey, see Nassau Sports v. Hampson, 355 F. Supp. 733 (1972); Nassau Sports v. Peters, 352 F. Supp. 870 (1972); Philadelphia World Hockey Club v. Philadelphia Hockey Club, 351 F. Supp. 462 (1972); and Boston Professional Hockey Association v. Cheevers & Sanderson, 348 F. Supp. 261 (1972).

52. See Philadelphia World Hockey Club v. Philadelphia Hockey Club, 351 F. Supp. 462, 466 (1972); Boston Professional Hockey Association v. Cheevers & Sanderson, 348 F. Supp. 261, 265 (1972); Denver Rockets v. All-Pro Management, 325 F. Supp. 1049, 1060 (1971). Within a few years

after these cases, the basis of the challenges had shifted. In Kapp v. National Football League, 390 F. Supp. 73 (1974), the applicability of the antitrust laws was conceded. What followed thereafter was more likely to be attempts to distinguish the general applicability of the laws from the facts at hand (see Robertson v. National Basketball Association, 389 F. Supp. 867 (1975)) or to argue the labor exemption under the antitrust laws. (This development is discussed at length in Chapter 5.)

53. The Court in Flood v. Kuhn, 407 U.S. 258 (1972), recognizes the various efforts made by Congress to change or modify the antitrust laws. Justice Blackmun notes that most of the serious attempts would have expanded antitrust exemption to sports leagues other than baseball, rather than stripping baseball of its immunity. *Id.* at 282–83. At various times, such exempting legislation passed one house or the other, but not both.

54. *See* 15 U.S.C. §§1291–1295.

55. The authorization for the NFL–AFL merger appears in language now contained in 15 U.S.C. §1291 (1976). Originally part of the Act of Nov. 8, 1966, Pub. L. 89–800, §6(b)(1), 80 Stat. 1515, it reads in pertinent part:

> In addition, such laws shall not apply to a joint agreement by which the member clubs of two or more professional football leagues, which are exempt from income tax under section 501(c)(6) of the Internal Revenue Code of 1954 [26 U.S.C. 501(c)(6)] combine their operations in expanded single league so exempt from income tax, if such agreement increases rather than decreases the number of professional football clubs so operating, and the provisions of which are directly relevant thereto.

15 U.S.C. §1291 (1976).

When it appeared this authorization might founder if introduced through normal legislative channels, it was appended to an Income Tax Investment Credit bill and presented to Congress through a conference committee report. Under this procedure, Congress was forced either to accept the entire bill without amendment or reject it. Despite opposition to the merger by certain influential members of Congress, the bill passed. H.R. Rep. No. 2308, 89th Cong., 2d Sess. 4, *reprinted in* [1966] U.S. Code Cong. & Ad. News 4372, 4377–78.

The circumstances under which the merger authorization cleared Congress have been criticized by many commentators. *See, e.g.,* Michener, Sports in America 390 (1976).

56. In the mid-1970s the collective bargaining agreements in all four major team sports were coming to an end. Owners and players were largely at an impasse. Though the baseball owners had prevailed in Flood v. Kuhn, the players were obviously determined to try every route possible to challenge the restraints on player movement. For a time, it appeared this would come through the efforts of Bobby Tolan of the San Diego Padres. *See* Koppett, Tolan's Grievance Case Seen More Important Than Hunter's, N.Y. Times, Jan. 3, 1975, at C21, col. 5. However, his grievance against his team was withdrawn before the arbitrators had a chance to determine his fate. *See* Tolan's Case Is Withdrawn, N.Y. Times, Jan. 14, 1975, at 39, col. 7. It would then be up to Andy Messersmith and Dave McNally. (See

discussion in Chapter 3.) Of equally crucial impact in the mid-1970s were the Kapp, Mackey, and Smith litigations in football. (See discussion in Chapter 5.) In basketball, it was concern over the future of the two rival leagues, the National Basketball Association and the American Basketball Association. This of course precipitated the Robertson litigation. (See discussion in Chapter 7.)

Hockey was likewise involved. Though much of its litigation occurred in 1972 on the heels of the formation of the World Hockey Association, the mid-1970s found the two leagues still wrestling with some of the problems spawned by that circumstance. Major litigation in hockey may have been absent by 1974, but the issues caused by rival leagues remained and had to be addressed in the difficult collective bargaining that took place in the mid-1970s.

57.   Further discussion of this and other laws on labor relations can be found in W. Gould, A Primer on American Labor Law (1982).

58.   T. Kochan, Collective Bargaining and Industrial Relations: From Theory to Policy and Practice 85 (1980).

59.   Centennial Turf Club, Inc., 192 N.L.R.B. 698 (1971); Walter A. Kelley, 139 N.L.R.B. 744 (1962); Los Angeles Turf Club, 90 N.L.R.B. 20 (1950). *But see* Celebrity Sports Center, 169 N.L.R.B. 183 (1968); Harrah's Club, 150 N.L.R.B. 1702 (1965), *enforced*, 362 F.2d 425 (9th Cir. 1966), *cert. denied*, 386 U.S. 915 (1967); Aspen Skiing Corp., 143 N.L.R.B. 707 (1963).

60.   The American League of Professional Baseball Clubs, 180 N.L.R.B. 190 (1969).

61.   *Id.* at 191.

62.   Flood v. Kuhn, 407 U.S. 258, 282 (1972).

63.   180 N.L.R.B. at 191.

64.   *Id.* at 191. Major League Rodeo, Inc., 246 N.L.R.B. 113 (1979); North American Soccer League, 236 N.L.R.B. 1317 (1978); North American Soccer League, 236 N.L.R.B. 1280 (1975); Volusia Jai Alai, Inc., 221 N.L.R.B. 1280 (1975).

65.   *Id.* at 192.

66.   There have been players groups at various times since the 1880s in baseball. To label these organizations unions, however, ignores the players' attempts to disavow that their players groups were unions. (See Chapter 3.) Consequently, it is still safe to characterize their union activities as "nascent" in the late 1960s.

67.   For an account of the enormous impact that Marvin Miller has had on labor relations in baseball, see discussion in Chapter 3. *See also* Lowenfish and Lupien, *supra* note 28, at 195–205.

68.   *Id.* at 203. The $10,000 minimum salary may seem low compared to today's baseball minimum of $32,500, but it was an increase of almost 50 percent from the $7,000 base that existed before the 1968 agreement. The committee appointed to study the reserve clause merely established the principle that restraints on player mobility were proper topics for collective bargaining.

69. Although the players associations in football obtained agreements with the owners in 1968, the association did not establish with finality that their groups were the recognized bargaining agents. After the NFL–AFL merger and the consequent merging of the two players associations, the owners initially refused to recognize the combined bargaining unit. This nonrecognition served to complicate the 1970 negotiations over a new agreement. *See* Proposed Amendments to the National Labor Relations Act: Hearings on H.R. 7152 before the Special Subcomm. on Labor of the House Comm. on Education and Labor, 92d Cong., 2d Sess. 13–15 (1972) (statement of Ed Garvey).

70. *Id.*

3 LABOR RELATIONS IN BASEBALL

DEVELOPMENT OF PROFESSIONAL SPORTS

The true origins of baseball are likely never to be known. The traditional U.S. version, once affirmed by a special commission appointed by major league baseball for the task, was that Abner Doubleday stepped out the measurements for a diamond in Cooperstown, New York, in 1839. Later, somewhat more objective baseball historians concluded that Doubleday could not have been anywhere near Cooperstown at that time. These debunkers of the myth pointed instead to a game played on the Elysian Fields in New Jersey. Still others claim that baseball is not truly American in its origins at all but derives from the English game of rounders.[1] It is safe to conclude that it was in the United States that sports became professionalized in an organized, unprecedented, and seemingly permanent fashion and that baseball was the sport that started it all.

Professional baseball began with barnstorming teams, the most notable being the Cincinnati Red Stockings. Formed in 1869 the Red Stockings toured the country and took on all comers, losing but rarely. Other clubs formed and challenged the supremacy of the Red Stockings, and soon the clubs formed loose alliances, the forerunners of sports leagues.

Formation of the Leagues

The National League formed in 1876, soon after the practical demise of the National Association of Professional Baseball Players, a loose confederation playing an even looser schedule. The Cincinnati Red Stockings were in the new National

47

League as were others, such as William Hulbert and his Chicago Cubs. They gave substance to the first league and helped it to achieve an organizational structure that asserted sufficient control over member clubs to survive the rebelliousness of individual owners. As with its predecessors, the National League had problems, but it managed to survive both internal and, later, external challenges.

Several principles behind the formation of the National League have guided the course of professional sports. Still extant are the Constitution and Playing Rules of Professional Base Ball Clubs, published in 1876 in the league's first year.[2] Some of the constitution's articles are clear models for modern sports leagues. For example, after one article names the original clubs and their cities, it is provided that in no event shall more than one club be established in any city.[3] Another stipulation buttresses the notion of territorial exclusivity by providing that each league club shall have "exclusive control of the city in which it is located. . . ."[4] As to other controls over the clubs, one provision allows for expulsion of a club, by a two-thirds vote, for reasons such as failure to abide by the league's constitution and rules. The 1876 constitution contains the antithesis of a reserve clause because it expressly allows players to enter into contracts with other clubs for the players' future services,[5] a position that was reversed when the first reserve system was instituted in 1879, barely three years after the league's founding.[6]

While many of the league rules have remained in effect, the rules of the game have undergone some marked changes. For instance, under the original rules if the pitcher did not pitch in a motion where the arm stayed below hip level, a "foul balk" would be called.[7] The batter who struck out also had to be thrown out at first base.[8] A batter could call for a high, low, or fair pitch, a fair pitch being a combination of a high or low pitch.[9] The umpire, a solitary soul in those days, was prohibited from venturing into fair territory. And going far beyond the only modern analogue—Japanese umpires who seek to explain their decisions to the crowd—the umpire in 1876 could enlist the spectators' aid in making difficult calls, relying presumably on the best testimony available.[10] George Steinbrenner would love that.

As noted, the first constitution of the National League provided for procedures leading to the expulsion of miscreant clubs, which occurred in 1879. The culprit was none other than the original professional team, the Cincinnati Red Stockings, which was expelled for playing games on Sunday and allowing liquor to be consumed in the stands. This action backfired on the National League owners: Cincinnati pressed for the formation of the American Association in 1882, the first in a long line of challenges to the National League's monopoly. The formation of the American Association ignited the first sports legal disputes dealing with player contract breaches,[11] which established a litigatory pattern followed in later attempts to establish such rival leagues as the Union Association, the Players' League, the American League, the Federal League, and the Mexican League.

The Union Association lasted less than a year in 1884, and was devoured by the National League and the American Association, which had agreed to stop raiding each other's players and to form a united front against such unwelcome interlopers as the Union Association and, a few years later, the Players' League.

The attempts to form the Players' League in 1890 had several consequences. Some of the cases emerging from the contract jumping that took place by such stars as John Montgomery Ward and Buck Ewing were noted in Chapter 2. The Players' League emerged from the efforts of a labor organization that was dissatisfied with how its demands were being met by recalcitrant owners and that was convinced that its own league was the only way successfully to reach its goals. Moreover, the league was successful: All reliable sources suggest that in the one year of its attendance it outdrew in attendance the older, established leagues.[12] Yet it failed, and for reasons that are revealing.

The Players' League sought to place the control of each club in the hands of the players themselves. The great miscalculation was in recruiting outside investors who were not to be called club owners but contributors. The contributors were to share the responsibilities of running the ballclubs. Since they had the money, they at the same time also had a good deal of control over the future of the league. At the conclusion of the first year's play, the league had done better than the established leagues, but all its clubs had lost money. At this point the Players' League contributors were convinced by the other leagues' owners, most notably Albert Spaulding, to abandon the Players' League and join in ownership combinations in the other leagues. Deprived of their financial base, the players in the Players' League were forced to disband their league and ask for readmittance to their old clubs or, in the case of some, to join new clubs in the old leagues. Indeed, one club was so rapacious in going after returning players, not previously its own, that it earned a new nickname: It became, and still is, the Pittsburgh Pirates.

Partly because of the internecine warfare over the rights to players from the Players' League, the American Association withdrew from its agreement with the National League within a year of the Players' League demise. This also led, a year after that, to the collapse of the American Association, another example of miscalculation of the economic realities of its league as compared with the rival National League.

Of course, it was not long before another rival appeared, the one and only successful challenger to the National League over one hundred plus years. Although the American League was officially born in 1900, it actually evolved from a minor league, the Western.[13] Under the leadership of Ban Johnson, it cultivated major league ambitions and retitled itself in October 1899 to evoke a more national image. In a pattern that has often been emulated, most notably in recent years by the United States Football League, the American League in 1900 at first declared that it would build its own base and refrain from any raiding of National League players. Johnson, in fact, announced that his league would abide by the National Agreement and its provisions against raiding. That promise lasted one year. In late 1900, as the American League expanded into eastern cities for the 1901 season, war over the players erupted. Of the 185 players on American League rosters in 1901, 111 were former National League players, although not all had come directly from that league to the American clubs.[14] According to one estimate, seventy-four players deserted the National League for the American League during the two-year span of the 1901 and 1902 seasons.[15] Most notably, some of these players were of the caliber of Napoleon Lajoie, whose legal exploits were discussed in Chapter 2.[16] Building carefully, the American League flourished and convinced the National League that the time for détente had arrived. A new national agreement was reached, and with it came the first World Series, in 1903, appropriately won in a big upset by the American League's Boston Pilgrims (later Red Sox), who bested the Pittsburgh Pirates five games to three.

Peace had come but lasted only a decade. The Federal League was the next challenger and took on both the National and American Leagues. The league began innocuously enough, in the fashion of the American League, styling itself a minor league and saying it would not be raiding the other leagues' players. As with its predecessor, this promise lasted only one season, and the raids began. A few players decided to defect; one of them, Hal Chase, set early standards in the antitrust field.[17] Others, such as star pitchers Walter Johnson and Mordecai "Three Fingers" Brown, were tempted, according to contemporary accounts, but these two, and others like them, remained with their original clubs. This combined with other factors to thwart the success of the Federal League as it limped through two seasons, 1914 and 1915, then expired. Despite the league's collapse, many of the Federal League owners emerged in relatively good condition. Largely because of pending litigation, the owners in the established leagues admitted many of the Federal owners into their ranks, which eventually prompted the precedent-setting litigation of the *Federal Baseball Case* (discussed in Chapter 2). In addition, the league's existence had spurred increased salaries for players in the established leagues and caused the players to try again to organize along union lines. Though both the increased salaries and the union drive faded with the demise of the competitive Federal League, inroads were made that were revived thirty years later.

The final rival league to appear on the scene was the Mexican League in 1946. With flamboyancy that could not be matched by deeds, the major backers of the league announced grandiose schemes for luring to Mexico many, if not most, of the major league stars. In at least one case their boasts landed them in court, where they were charged with interference with contractual relations and faced with injunctions against proceeding in such matters.[18] Despite these setbacks the owners found receptive players elsewhere, but the players who did leave for Mexico soon found themselves in the unenviable position of both belonging to a dying league and at the same time being banned from returning to the major leagues for five years.

The major litigation contesting this blacklist, the *Danny Gardella* case, has been previously discussed,[19] along with other cases filed at the time that reached opposite results.[20] The defecting players ultimately settled with the owners, and most reentered the leagues. One of the better players, Max Lanier, later summed up the player's perspective:

> Of course, everybody who went to Mexico was suspended from the big leagues for five years. I thought that was a little stiff. Heck, we didn't go there to hurt anybody. We just didn't think we were making enough money.[21]

Early Players' Associations

Concomitant with the formation of rival leagues were attempts to organize the players into a cohesive group that would stand united against the owners. Some attempts were successful for a short time, particularly where leverage was gained because of the existence of a rival league, when owners were amenable to player concerns. Other efforts were dreams that quickly and permanently drifted away.

Until the creation of the Major League Baseball Players' Association the most successful organizing effort was the first, the National Brotherhood of Baseball Players. Founded as a secret organization in 1885, it emerged a year later as a union dedicated to ridding its members of the $3,000 yearly maximum salary and the reserve provisions imposed by the owners on all players in the National League and American Association.[22] When its efforts were at length unavailing, the Brotherhood took the decisive step of forming its own league. As examined earlier, the Players' League failed, but not before the players had shown that such a move was feasible. They were foiled, not by the foolhardiness of their scheme, but by placing too much trust and reliance in the contributing investors. The execution, not the idea, was faulty.

An additional pattern emerged from the Brotherhood and the resulting Players' League. The top stars, particularly if they were union leaders, would likely be the most immediate targets for litigation. Such was the case of John Montgomery Ward and Buck Ewing. Both were associated with the Brotherhood movement and were also at the top of the game as players. Ward in particular was an inevitable target. A great pitcher, who after injury converted to an outstanding shortstop, Ward was legally trained and was a leader in the formation of the Brotherhood. He won his law case but the Players' League folded anyway. That was not the end of Monte Ward in professional baseball, however. He returned to the National League for more years of stardom and, after retirement, served stints as president of the National League's Boston Braves and as general manager of the Brooklyn club in the Federal League, showing at a late date that he was not afraid to buck the establishment. Monte Ward was the consummate player, on and off the field, being the only player in Major League history both to record more than 100 wins as a pitcher and 2000 hits as a batter. He is one of only ten pitchers ever to hurl a perfect game.[23]

After the Players' League folded, the Brotherhood disappeared with it. Other attempts were made in regular intervals thereafter: (1) The League of Protective Associations (1899–1902) appeared roughly at the same time as the American League rose to challenge the National;[24] (2) during Federal League times the Fraternity of Professional Baseball Players of America, existed from 1912 to 1918; although its attempts to affiliate with the American Federation of Labor were repudiated, the effort underscored its claim to be a real labor organization; (3) a hasty, ill-conceived attempt to form the American Baseball Guild was made in 1946, and it raised the possibility for future activity such as the players' pension fund it created from matching contributions from clubs and players; and finally (4) a management-financed organization of baseball players began in 1947 and was rather clearly designed to blunt future meaningful player organizational activity; this tactic worked, but only for a few short years.

The Major League Baseball Players' Association

The Major League Baseball Players' Association (MLBPA) was formed in 1954 in response to widespread dissatisfaction by players with the administration of the pension fund established in 1946. Team and league representatives were elected from among the players, and a part-time lawyer was hired. In its early days the association had no legitimate power. It confronted an owners' establishment whose tradition-encrusted paternalism had been bolstered by a 1952 Supreme Court ruling upholding organized baseball's exemption from the Sherman antitrust act. A player's contract was a unilateral instrument that read like a real estate lease. On signing a contract a player swore to abide by the rules set down by management and to conform to any changes in management's rules, without even receiving a copy of these rules. The contract entitled team owners to administer discipline and required players' grievances to be appealed to the commissioner of baseball, an employee of the owners.

The players showed a general reluctance to turn their new organization into an effective bargaining force. Like others who are relatively unique employees and are paid on a nonhourly basis, the players resisted the idea that their organization was a labor union. The MLBPA's first president, fireball pitcher Bob Feller of the Cleveland Indians, claimed that "You cannot carry collective bargaining into baseball."[25] His successor, Bob Friend, a Pittsburgh Pirates pitcher, was even more explicit: "I firmly believe a union, in the fullest sense of the word, simply would not fit the situation in baseball."[26]

These statements reflected the prevailing attitude until events made it clear that the players would not get what they felt they deserved until more assertive action was taken. In 1966 the players at last realized that they possessed no effective power for negotiating with the owners and hired a full-time executive director: a man who insisted, as a condition of his employment, that the players adopt an independent stance. Marvin Miller had served for sixteen years as chief economist and bargainer for the United States Steelworkers of America and had been a member of several presidential labor/management boards and was respected by union, management, and government leaders. As could be expected, baseball owners were opposed to dealing with an experienced union negotiator and made vigorous efforts to discourage the players from selecting Miller. Their attempts were unsuccessful.

With Miller as executive director the Major League Baseball Players' Association made gains for its members that remain unmatched by any other union in a similar timespan. In the association's first eight years (1966–74), players' pensions more than tripled, the minimum salary rose from $6,000 to $16,000, and the average salary more than doubled—to $40,956.[27] The success of the association encouraged professional athletes in other sports and stimulated the adoption of models of player organizations along traditional union lines. For baseball players the key year was 1968, when their organization closely followed on the heels of the basketball players in coming to terms with the owners in reaching the first collective bargaining agreements in professional sports.

BASEBALL AND THE "NEW LAW"

The legal experiences of players and owners in the courts produced for years waves of small victories for the players and then sweeping overrides by the owners. The players tasted initial successes in the *Ewing* and *Ward* contracts cases, only to have the tide swing against them in *Lajoie* and its successors.[28] The state court's denunciation of the baseball contract that attempted to bind Hal Chase to his old club when he wanted to move to the Federal League soon gave way to the removal from antitrust scrutiny of the maneuverings of the baseball leagues and clubs. *Federal Baseball* declared the immunity, and *Toolson* and *Flood* kept the tide running in the owners' favor.[29]

The first breach of the owners' invincibility came with the *Umpire's* case[30] and the National Labor Relations Board's assertion of jurisdiction over baseball's labor organizations. This followed closely on the players' first collective bargaining agreement (won by Marvin Miller). The stage was set for a new assault by the players, not through the lengthy and largely unsuccessful route of litigation, but through negotiation, some intimidation, and, above all, arbitration.

The *Hunter* Case

In 1973 the players' association and the owners negotiated several arbitration provisions in the new collective bargaining agreement.[31] In 1974 Oakland pitcher Jim "Catfish" Hunter and Oakland's owner, Charles O. Finley, had a confrontation. Hunter had finished the previous season with an impressive 25–13 record. The twenty-eight-year-old pitcher had been a twenty-game winner for four consecutive seasons and had compiled a total of eighty-eight wins during his four years with the Oakland A's. The A's and Hunter agreed on a two-year contract whereby $50,000 would be paid to a deferment plan of Hunter's choice. Hunter had requested a specific deferred-payment provision that would enable him to avoid immediate tax liability for the $50,000. Finley agreed to the provision but later discovered that he personally would incur resultant tax liability. Finley insisted that the contract clause did not require him to assume this burden. During the 1974 season Hunter routinely received the portion of his salary that was to be paid directly to him, but the deferred payments were not made to the designated investment company. The season ended with the deferred payments still not made, despite Hunter's repeated requests. Hunter claimed that Finley's failure to make payments constituted a breach of contract, thus enabling the pitcher to exercise his right to terminate the contract. Hunter then announced that since he had no contract, he was a free agent. Finley insisted that no free-agent question was involved, that the only dispute concerned the method of payment, and that the dispute was merely a matter of contract interpretation. Finley offered the other $50,000 to Hunter as direct payment, but Hunter rejected this offer as contrary to his contractual rights.[32]

The case was submitted under the applicable collective bargaining procedures to arbitrator Peter Seitz. Seitz ruled in Hunter's favor, finding no ambiguity in the contract language outlining the club's obligations. According to Seitz the club failed to perform, thus enabling Hunter rightfully to terminate. The arbitrator rejected Finley's contention that no breach could occur until the arbitration established whether the club was obligated to meet Hunter's demands. Seitz further ruled that Hunter no longer had a valid contract with the A's. Hunter was, therefore, a free agent and could entertain offers from any other major league club.[33]

On December 31, 1974, the Catfish[34] accepted an offer from the New York Yankees for an unprecedented salary package. Hunter received a $1 million signing bonus, a $150,000 annual salary for five years, life insurance benefits worth $1 million, and a substantial amount of deferred compensation.[35] Only later was it learned that the bidding for Hunter had exceeded the Yankee's offer. At trial in the *Joe Kapp* case evidence disclosed that Hunter rejected a $3.8 million offer from the Kansas City Royals. This testimony, by Hunter's lawyers, was admitted for the limited purpose of showing how open competition for players might affect salaries.[36] This evidence apparently did not impress the *Kapp* jury, since it awarded no damages to Kapp even though he had been forced to deal in something less than a free market.[37] Later events, however, have demonstrated the value of free agency to players. Perhaps the Hunter situation was a harbinger, but it involved special circumstances. An obstinate owner materially breached a contract, thus freeing his star player. These circumstances are rare.

This was not Charlie Finley's first altercation with a player. Ken "Hawk" Harrelson was released by Finley in August 1967 after calling Finley a "menace to baseball."[38] Harrelson was released, and his fortunes were dramatically bettered: His salary went from $12,000 to $100,000. He signed with the Boston Red Sox, who were involved in a four-team pennant race and had just lost home-run hitting Tony Conigliaro who was beaned and severely injured that same month. The Hawk became a popular figure in Boston—so much so that his trade to the Cleveland Indians in the spring of 1969 (in a multiplayer deal that brought Sonny Siebert to the Red Sox along with others) produced picketing at Fenway Park. The Hawk's popularity was such that he later returned to Boston as a Red Sox broadcaster.

One final point must be made about the Catfish Hunter dispute. Like the free-agent issues that followed in its wake, it presaged one of the most important developments in baseball: the multiyear guaranteed contract. Hunter's contract with the Yankees did not use the word *guaranteed*, but a special covenant[39] provided that salary payments "shall be the obligation of the Club, notwithstanding the inability of the Player to perform the services provided for under the contract." Salary payments, notwithstanding anything to the contrary in the contract, were to be payable "as long as the inability to so perform said services is due solely and strictly to a medical condition."

As Arbitrator Goetz noted in arbitrations subsequent to Hunter, this guarantee represents a "substantial departure" from the salary obligation assumed until then by clubs under typical players agreements. There was a presumed right on the part of clubs to renew from year to year indefinitely, and the Uniform Players' Contract also gave the club the right to terminate the player if he failed, in the opinion of the club's management, to exhibit sufficient skill and competitive ability to qualify or continue as a member of the team. If the player's contract was terminated and even if the failure to render services was caused by a disability arising out of an injury in the course of employment, the club was obligated to make only limited termination payments. Where termination was due to injury in the course of employment, the player received the balance of his salary for the year. If the player was terminated prior to spring training, he received no payment at all. If termination was for the lack of skill or ability, he received thirty days' pay if terminated during spring training or sixty days' pay if during the championship season. As Arbitrator Goetz noted:

> Thus, even though Hunter's contract was for five years, without the special covenant it could have been terminated by the Club during that period in accordance with the usual terms thereof, and he would receive at most the balance of his salary for the year, or possibly nothing. With this covenant, he was assured the full five years' salary even though he might become unable to perform due to some physical disability. With or without the covenant, Hunter could not offer his services to any club for the five year contract term—in the absence of termination thereof by the Club. . . .[40]

Soon thereafter—in substantial part because of the free-agent cases discussed below—guaranteed contracts became the norm. Andy Messersmith of the Atlanta Braves became one of the first to enter into such a contract, and Ken Holtzman of the New York Yankees entered into one for the years from 1976 through 1980. In 1976 Rick Burleson, Fred Lynn, and Carlton Fisk entered into such contracts with the Red Sox, and the California Angels negotiated similar instruments with Don Baylor, Joe Rudi, and Bobby Grich. Others soon followed.[41] The Hunter dispute and his consequent contract with the New York Yankees changed the relationship between players and clubs in a fundamental way.

The *Messersmith* and *McNally* Arbitration
Over the Reserve System

The players' attack on baseball's reserve system came through the grievances of pitchers Andy Messersmith of the Los Angeles Dodgers and Dave McNally of the Montreal Expos.[42] These players claimed to be free agents and the sacred reserve clause only a one-year option. When their request to be declared free was denied, they filed a grievance.

The leagues and clubs asserted that the contract had not expired because under the option clause the contract created a new option.[43] As long as the clubs duly "reserved their players each year, new options would be created perpetually. The owners not only contested the grievance on the merits but also contended that the matter was not properly the subject of arbitration.[44] To support this contention, the owners referred to the 1973 basic agreement, article 15, which stipulated that the agreement "does not deal with the reserve system.[45] The agreement further stated that contractual language should not prejudice the position of either side. The owners' position was that article 15 deprived the arbitrator of power to arbitrate on the core of the reserve system.[46] As the arbitrator noted: "This system of reservation of exclusive control is historic in baseball and is traceable to the early days of the organized sport in the 19th century."[47] If the arbitrator accepted management's interpretation of article 15, he was confronted with a paradox: On the one hand, the standard players' contract was incorporated into the basic agreement, and part of the core of the reserve system, as characterized by the league, was in that contract; on the other hand, the owners relied on the language of article 15 to mean that the agreement did not "deal" with the reserve system.[48] Arbitrator Seitz noted that the legality of the reserve clause was at issue in *Flood*, that the parties had "agreed to disagree" about its continuation from the 1968 agreement onward, and that the reserve system remained, therefore, "untouched" and in existence.[49] The arbitrator accordingly found that the contract provisions represented a type of cease-fire over the issue while the matter was being litigated. Since the basic agreement incorporated the players' contract,[50] and since the players contended that they were free agents once their individual contracts expired, the arbitrator found that he did, in fact, have authority to resolve the dispute.[51]

The arbitrator interpreted the Uniform Players' Contract language, which provided for renewal "for a period of one year," as a renewal clause that "does not warrant interpreting the section as providing for contract renewal beyond the contract year.... When that year comes to an end, the Player no longer has contractual duties that bind him to the Club."[52] In light of the considerable impact the award would have on the parties, the arbitrator repeatedly urged them to negotiate a new system.[53] The owners were faced with two alternatives. The first alternative was to allow McNally and Messersmith to become free agents. This decision would have allowed the owners to argue that the principle of stare decisis, not being as embedded in the arbitration system as in the judiciary,[54] would not bind another arbitrator to Arbitrator Seitz's interpretation of the collective bargaining agreement. This option would have created uncertainty, especially given the expiration of the collective bargaining agreement and the imminent expiration of numerous individual contracts. The owners' second option was to negotiate more vigorously with the association about changes in the reserve system—a process initiated in the summer of 1976.

The owners, however, chose to litigate. This choice was made despite the arbitrator's indication that he would resolve the issue adversely to the owners and despite the Supreme Court's declaration in the *Steelworkers* trilogy[55] that the courts will not reverse a labor arbitration award in the absence of "clear infidelity" to the agreement. Not surprisingly, the courts, pursuant to the *Steelworkers* standards, affirmed the award. The Court of Appeals for the Eighth Circuit in *Kansas City Royals Baseball Corp. v. Major League Baseball Players' Association*[56] concluded that the arbitrator had jurisdiction to resolve the issue. The *Steelworkers* trilogy instructed that courts should conclude that an issue cannot be arbitrated only when there is explicit language or bargaining history excluding the issue from the arbitration clause.[57] Accordingly, arbitrability— one of the more difficult issues presented—was resolved against the owners.[58] The court noted that article 15 and its predecessor, article 14, were adopted as both sides maneuvered in anticipation of the *Flood* case.[59] The association was willing to negotiate language that indicated it had not addressed the free-agent issue and was concerned that the players, unhappy with the handling of the reserve-clause issue, might initiate litigation on the duty of fair representation. The association wanted to avoid this issue while *Flood* was pending. The owners wanted to utilize the labor-exemption defense in the *Flood* litigation[60] to establish that the agreement addressed the issue.[61] The court concluded that "manifest infidelity," a prerequisite for finding that the arbitrator had erroneously interpreted the agreement, was not present.

These rulings prompted new collective bargaining. Excluding those players bound by long-term contracts, the owners faced the prospect that all players would become free agents at the end of the 1976 season, or soon thereafter, because of the *Seitz* award and its affirmation in *Kansas City Royals.* The Eighth

Circuit, following *Mackey v. NFL*,[62] urged the parties to resolve their problems through collective bargaining:

> [W]e intimate no views on the merits of the reserve system. We note, however, that club Owners and the Players Association's representatives agree that some form of a reserve system is needed if the integrity of the game is to be preserved and if public confidence in baseball is to be maintained. The disagreement lies over the degree of control necessary if these goals are to be achieved. Certainly, the parties are in a better position to negotiate their differences than to have them decided in a series of arbitrations and court decisions. We commend them to that process and suggest that the time for obfuscation has passed and the time for plain talk and clear language has arrived. Baseball fans everywhere expect nothing less.[63]

Sports was no longer merely the business of giving exhibitions;[64] it was a complex of industries, each with challenges to meet in the 1980s.

SALARY ARBITRATION

The 1973 agreement, negotiated soon after the *Flood* decision, was the first to provide a method of resolving salary disputes through arbitration. That salary clause has been expanded through bargaining agreements that instituted grievance/arbitration machinery that provides for dispute resolution by a third party who makes a final, binding decision.

The 1973 agreement mandates that "[a]ny Club, or any Player with both a total of two years of Major League service in at least three different championship seasons" could submit a salary dispute to "final and binding" arbitration.[65] In the 1976 agreement, eligibility was modified: Any player's salary dispute could proceed to arbitration if both sides consented; salary arbitration could be obtained as a contract right with the same minimum service eligibility as contained in the 1973 agreement, but the player must have had less than six years service.[66]

The procedure established by the basic agreement of 1976 is called final offer arbitration. The parties propose salary figures that need not have been submitted during prior negotiations. The arbitrator, pursuant to criteria established by the contract between the association and the clubs,[67] must select one of the parties' positions as his award.

Salary arbitration has produced major gains for players.[68] The 1980 provisions, which give players with six or more years of service free-agent status if the team does not consent to arbitration of the salary dispute,[69] also have proved to be significant.[70] These provisions, in conjunction with the important 1976 contract clauses in the collective bargaining agreement regarding the free-agent draft, have altered significantly the market value of players' services.[71]

PREVIOUS JOB ACTIONS

The earliest known case of circumstances that might have led to a baseball strike occurred in 1889. Four years earlier the Brotherhood of Ball Players had been formed to help players in trouble and improve relations with club owners. As a result of the imposition of salary limits on players by the National League, the Brotherhood considered a protest strike.[72] However, the players were reluctant to strike because nearly all had signed contracts for the coming season and feared a loss of public support. When the dispute remained unsettled, some star players formed their own league in 1890. But after a year of play to poor attendance, the Players' League folded, and the maverick players returned to the National League under complete surrender.

The First Strike

Baseball's first strike occurred during the 1912 season. It lasted only a day, involved just one team, and was instigated by a single player. Ty Cobb of the Detroit Tigers was the target of "profane and vulgar words" from a persistent heckler during a game.[73] Always quick to anger, Cobb jumped into the stands and knocked the fan unconscious with fists and feet. Under indefinite suspension from the American League as a result of the fight, Cobb got his teammates to join his protest by refusing to play. The Detroit manager was ordered by the team owner to find replacement players for a game against the Philadelphia Athletics: The sandlot strikebreakers lost 24 to 2; a ground ball knocked out two teeth of the third baseman; an outfielder had a fly ball land on his head; and the pickup team committed nine errors in the game—which was counted in the official standings. Thus sobered, Cobb urged his teammates to return to work. These players were fined $100 each, while Cobb got a $50 fine and ten-day suspension.

Skirmishes in 1969 and 1972

The near strike of 1889 and the strike of 1912 were carried out by players who were generally uneducated and inexperienced in business. Professional guidance and counsel from unions, agents, and lawyers either did not exist at all or was extremely limited. The reserve clause bound players to their teams and placed them securely in a power vacuum.

Players chafed under the reserve clause over the years, but no relief was provided. In 1969 a brief and futile challenge was made. The players, by now organized into the Major League Baseball Players' Association (MLBPA), presented demands to the owners on the issues of the reserve clause and improvements in pensions. The parties disagreed in particular over the percentage of receipts the players' pension fund should receive from the leagues' national television contract. Through its player representatives, the MLBPA urged players to refuse to sign contracts for the upcoming season until the dispute over the pension fund was settled.[74] A compromise pension agreement was reached just prior to the start of spring training. Some players were late to training camps because of a threatened boycott by the MLBPA. The reserve clause remained unaffected.

In 1972 pension issues again led to a dispute between owners and the union. A three-year agreement had been reached between the parties in 1970. At the outset of spring training in 1972 the players, by almost unanimous vote, declared their intention to strike over the amount of their future pensions and how they would be calculated.[75] Unable to gain redress for their concerns, the players went on strike. The strike caused the cancellation of eighty-six games at the start of the regular season and lasted for thirteen days.

Under the agreement that was eventually reached, the owners capitulated by agreeing to the players' demands on the pension issue. A further dispute ensued over whether players would be paid for games missed during the strike. This was resolved totally in favor of the owners, who docked the players' salaries in proportion to games not played. The lost games were not rescheduled.

Spring Training Lockout—1976

To understand the issues that led to a delay in spring training in 1976, we must examine a chain of incidents that began in 1970. These events also shed light on the 1981 strike. In the 1970 collective bargaining agreement the MLBPA negotiated a provision for using grievance arbitration to settle disputes over the interpretation of the collective bargaining agreement. Prior to this time such disputes were ruled on by the commissioner of baseball.

The first significant use of grievance arbitration was by Jim Hunter of the Oakland A's. Hunter had agreed with club owner Charles Finley that half of his 1974 salary would be set aside in an insurance trust. When a dispute arose over Finley's alleged noncompliance, the matter was submitted to arbitration. The chairman of the arbitration panel, Peter Seitz, ruled that Finley had not met the conditions of the agreement and declared Hunter a free agent.

In December 1975 another ruling by Arbitrator Seitz upset the reserve clause. As noted earlier, this case involved players Andy Messersmith and Dave McNally, who contended that since they had played for one year with their clubs without a contract, their employment status could not be further extended utilaterally by the club. Seitz agreed with the players, holding that they were free agents able to negotiate on the open market.

The demise of the reserve clause was the focus of collective bargaining talks between the owners and players in 1976. In these negotiations, the owners acknowledged that they could not return to the old system of the reserve clause, in which players were committed to a single team throughout their careers unless traded or released. However, the owners were not willing to allow for free-agency status in the manner provided by Arbitrator Seitz's decision. For their part, the players were content with the status quo: that free agency could be achieved by playing for one year without signing a contract.

Ironically, conditions precipitating the 1976 dispute were very much unlike those that had been common before the *Messersmith* arbitration decision unleashing free agency. In arbitration the players tried to get the reserve clause modified in their favor, for greater opportunities for movement among teams. But in 1976 the reverse situation prevailed: The owners tried to get back at least a part of what they had lost in arbitration—that is, more restraint on player mobility through free agency. In short, the players now bargained from strength, and the owners tried to budge the players.

When the parties were unable to reach agreement on the free-agency issue, the owners shut down spring training camps in March 1976. This action, called a lockout, is management's counterpart to the strike. The owners' tough stance was motivated by fear that unless the system of free agency was changed back in their favor, free agents would continue to sell their services to the highest bidder without restraint. This, they argued, would raise salaries dramatically and tilt the competitive balance in favor of the clubs with the most money.[76] In retrospect, the owners' concerns over skyrocketing salaries were well founded. This salary escalation was a major reason for the rigid posture of the owners in the 1980–81 collective bargaining talks that eventually broke down into a prolonged strike.

The negotiators in the 1976 dispute—Marvin Miller for the union and John Gaherin for management—reached a sticking point on the number of teams with which free agents could bargain. Miller's position was that free agents should be allowed to negotiate with all twenty-four teams in the leagues, which was the same situation that the players had won through arbitration. Gaherin insisted that there be an eight-team negotiating limit.[77] Another stumbling block concerned whether the commissioner of baseball, Bowie Kuhn, would act to open training camps. Kuhn's position was that he would do so if he felt progress was being made in negotiations. Despite the MLBPA executive board's rejection of the "final" contract proposals of management, Commissioner Kuhn ordered that spring training "get under way without further delay" on March 17.[78] Although this action did not end the stalemate, it got the sport back in gear and eased the distractions on the parties to work out a settlement through reasoned compromise.

The 1976 lockout lasted seventeen days. When it was over the ensuing negotiations produced a new contract that bound players to their teams for six years, plus a one-year option. In exchange for this concession the players won substantial increases in their pension fund, from $6.85 to $8.3 million.[79] They also received increases in minimum salaries from $17,000 to $18,000 in the first year of the contract and increases of $1,000 per year for each of the next three years of the contract. The contract, signed in July, was made retroactive to January 1, 1976.

Under the modified free-agency system, players were tied to their clubs for a limited period. For individual contracts executed before August 9, 1976, clubs were allowed to renew for one additional year after the contract expired. Then, if a player remained unsigned, he could become a free agent. For contracts executed on or after August 9, 1976, any player with six or more years of major league service at the end of the contract date could become a free agent by giving notice. A procedure for drafting free agents was established that allowed players to be chosen by a maximum of twelve clubs and placed limitations on the number of players clubs could sign in the draft.[80]

The new system's impact on player performance or morale is difficult to assess. Most of the highly paid players appear to have performed well, although injuries have hampered some of these players.[81] In contrast, the performance of some players undoubtedly has declined out of fear that an injury might diminish their marketability.[82] Nonetheless, the owners sought revisions of the 1976 agreement since early 1980, nearly resulting in a players' strike and culminating in a temporary solution.

The effect of the lockout on the season was minimal. Although players were denied some opportunity to get into physical shape for the regular season, the full schedule of games was played. The agreement resulted in significant modification of the free-agency rules through what appeared at the time to be a workable system that allowed for liberal freedom of player movement coupled with some restraint on free agency to protect owners. As it turned out, however, the restraint was not strong enough for the owners' liking. Players' salaries rose substantially as a result of free-agency pressures.

NEGOTIATIONS IN 1980

Following the 1976 lockout, focus shifted to the need for increased compensation to clubs that lost free agents to signings by other clubs. This, felt the owners, would deter free agency and help put a cap on the rising salaries. Under the 1976 agreement the only compensation due the former club was a choice of a player in the amateur draft. The free-agency compensation issue emerged into the central target of owners in the 1980–81 talks and, more than any other factor, led to the strike.

Contract Talks Begin

Although the basic agreement in baseball expired at the end of 1979, the parties did not begin serious negotiations until February 1980. A new chief negotiator,

Ray Grebey, represented management, and Marvin Miller continued as the union's chief spokesman. Grebey had previously worked as a negotiator for the General Electric Company.[83] GE's bargaining policies have been closely associated with a former company vice president of labor relations, Lemuel Boulware. "Boulwarism," as it came to be known, was a sugar-coated form of "take-it-or-leave-it" negotiations that was debunked by the NLRB and the courts in the late 1960s as a failure to bargain in good faith.[84] Employment of Grebey as chief negotiator was a clear signal that the baseball owners intended to take a hard-line position.

In the 1976 negotiations the union had found itself in the anomalous position of trying to ward off the offensive of management to take away benefits previously won (through arbitration) by the union. This situation persisted in the 1980 talks, as management again sought to chip away at union rights provided in the 1976 contract.

Management takeaways or givebacks were also gaining currency in other segments of U.S. industry in 1980, as evidenced by the land mark agreement between Chrysler Corporation and the United Automobile Workers. With the continuing slide into national economic recession, takeaways later became widespread in a number of industries, such as automobiles, trucking, rubber, airlines, farm implements, meatpacking, and textiles. But the recession had no apparent adverse effect on baseball. Attendance at games set a record with 43.5 million fans in 1979 for the fourth consecutive year, a record four-year national television contract had just been reached, and publicity over free-agent signings helped promote fan enthusiasm to unprecedented levels. Nonetheless, the owners felt the players' salaries had gotten out of hand, threatening relative parity of teams and putting some of the less wealthy clubs in financial jeopardy.

Management Proposals

In response to this situation, the owners made an innovative two-part offer to the union in February 1980: (1) establishment of a wage scale providing minimum and maximum salaries for players with fewer than six years' service in the major leagues and (2) a new free-agent compensation rule whereby a team that lost a star player to free agency would get a good, though not comparable, player in return from the major league roster of the club that signed the free agent. (The wage-scale concept, which made its modern baseball debut as a management proposal, surfaced again in the 1982 football negotiations. Although criticized by the MLBPA as foreign to the essence of baseball because it deemphasized players' performance and concomitant rewards, the concept was proposed in football by the union rather than management. The reasons for this ironic turnaround in bargaining positions in football are explored in Chapter 5.)

Baseball management's proposal on the wage scale was heavily weighted for seniority, with some recognition of performance. As shown in Table 3-1, the

Table 3-1.   Baseball Owners' Proposed Pay Scale, 1980.

Maximum Incentive Bonus	Years of Service	Minimum	Maximum
$ 0	0-1	$25,000	$ 40,600
200	1-2	25,000	53,000
2,400	2-3	25,000	69,200
6,000	3-4	25,000	90,300
11,700	4-5	30,000	117,700
20,700	5-6	30,000	153,600

Source: Boswell, Baseball's Owners Pitch a Salary Curve at the Players, L. A. Times, Feb. 27, 1980, pt. 3, at 1, 8.

base salary maximums would range from $40,600 for a rookie to $153,600 for a six-year veteran. Adding the performance bonuses would mean a maximum salary for six-year players of $174,300. Players with over six years' experience would be able to negotiate contracts without any maximum.

According to the owners' free-agency compensation proposal, the practice would change from awarding a player in the amateur draft as compensation for loss of a star free agent. Each team would be allowed to protect fifteen players on its forty-man major league roster. In signings of star free agents, the losing team could select a player from the unprotected group of twenty-five players on the signing team's roster. If the free agent were not a star player, the compensation of a choice from the amateur draft would remain as under the 1976 agreement.

Union Proposals

Besides the union's objection to the wage scale on principle, as contrary to the notion of compensating players solely on the basis of performance, Miller viewed the owners' compensation proposal as merely a ploy to limit the mobility of players.[85] He protested that player pay would be reduced by about a third under the proposed wage scale. Particular inequity would occur for young star players like Jim Rice, Fred Lynn, Keith Hernandez, and Dave Parker, who would suffer even more substantial losses of salary if tied to a wage scale.

Also rejecting the owners' proposal on free-agency compensation, the union instead proposed liberalizing the rules. Under the 1976 agreement, a free-agent player who signed with another club was required to wait five years before becoming a free agent a second time. The union's proposals would change this to allow a player to become a free agent a second time immediately after the contract with his new club expired. Moreover, the union proposed that a player be allowed to opt for free agency after four years in the major leagues rather than the six years required under the 1976 agreement.[86]

Owners Drop Wage Scale

By March 4, 1980, there had been twenty-three negotiating sessions between the union and owners. At that time the MLBPA's executive board authorized a strike if an agreement was not reached.[87] The regular season was scheduled to begin on April 9. Subject to final ratification by the players, a strike was threatened any time after April 1. The players responded by voting 967 to 1 to approve the executive board's call for a strike.[88]

The owners attempted to head off a strike by making a significant concession on March 18. This was the first real evidence from either side in the talks of willingness to compromise. The owners withdrew the wage-scale proposal. Their position on free agency remained largely intact. A formula was offered that would provide no compensation for situations in which a free agent was selected in the draft by three clubs or less. If four to seven clubs selected the free agent, the team would receive an amateur draft choice as compensation. For a free agent selected by eight to thirteen clubs, compensation would be a choice in the amateur draft plus a player not on the club's fifteen-man protected list.[89] The owners also proposed increases in minimum salaries, pensions, and life insurance.

Resort to Mediation

At the end of March, the parties agreed to accept the services of Kenneth Moffett, a mediator from the Federal Mediation and Conciliation Service. Mediation is a nonbinding attempt at stimulating negotiations, usually performed by a neutral third party. Although mediators do not have any authority to require the parties to agree, their efforts to suggest areas of compromise and to keep the talks moving along can have considerable merit.

Moffett met both separately and together with the parties toward aiding them to establish common ground for agreement. The mediator helped tone down hostilities and get the parties to focus on the key area of discord, which was the number of players that a club could protect from being selected as compensation for free-agent signings. Although the union seemed willing to accept a penalty of additional compensation for free agents, it adamantly opposed the owners' position of protecting only fifteen players. Protection of thirty players on the forty-man roster would have been more acceptable to the players. It was this kind of compromise that Moffett sought to encourage.

On-Again, Off-Again

The players boycotted the remaining eight games of spring training. These exhibition games do not benefit the players monetarily because their pay does not start until the regular season. Thus owners' revenues were diminished slightly, and the action underscored the players' intention to strike sometime during the regular season. Although it was anticipated that the strike would begin on opening day, the players voted instead to strike on May 22, the eve of the heavily attended games of the Memorial Day weekend. This would allow them to collect some pay and to buy time to iron out their differences with the owners.

On May 16 the union made a proposal to resolve the impasse by deferring the free-agency compensation issue to later talks, thus accepting the status quo conditions for the present. Its proposal was conditioned on resolution of other issues being discussed in negotiations, such as minimum wages, pensions, and health and safety. A joint labor/management study committee was suggested to consider free agency. Meanwhile, the parties would operate under the free-agency rules of the 1976 agreement. The owners would have the right to reopen negotiations in the future on free-agency compensation.

Although the owners initially rejected this proposal, and the May 22 shutdown appeared inevitable, the union allowed the deadline to pass without striking. On May 30 a four-year agreement was reached that averted a strike in the 1980 season but kept open the possibility of a strike in 1981 or 1982.

1980 Agreement

There was no clear winner of the negotiations that resulted in the 1980 agreement. Both sides conceded on economic and working condition demands.[90] The key to the settlement was the establishment of a joint committee to study free agency, composed of two players and two owner representatives. By January 1, 1981, this committee was to report its conclusions. If no agreement was reached on the basis of the report, the owners were allowed to unilaterally adopt their final compensation proposal from the 1980 negotiations.[91] At this point the players would have three options: (1) accept the owners' compensation position outright, (2) accept it only for the 1981 draft if the owners allowed the players the right to strike in 1982, or (3) strike by June 1, 1981.

MOVING TOWARD A SHUTDOWN

The joint study committee did not resolve the free-agency issue. Therefore, the owners announced in February 1981 that they intended to put their free-agency compensation plan into effect. Under this revised plan, a formula was established for compensating teams that lose players to free agency. If a player is picked by eight teams or more in the annual free-agent draft and is ranked in the top half of his position in the prior season in times at bat or pitching performance, the losing team could claim a player from the signing team's roster after eighteen players had been protected. If the free agent ranked in the top third of the two categories, the signing team could freeze only fifteen players.[92]

Union Commits to Strike

Following this announcement by the owners, the MLBPA declared its intention to strike on May 29, 1981, unless there was a compromise on the free-agency issue. To strengthen its position the union filed an unfair labor practice charge with the National Labor Relations Board. The owners had contended that they needed restrictions on free-agency movement because escalating player salaries were jeopardizing the financial solvency of some clubs. Such statements were made by several owners outside the negotiating sessions and by Commissioner Bowie Kuhn.[93]

In response to this contention the union requested that the owners open their accounting books to provide justification for their plea of financial ruin. However, the owners countered that their earlier claims were really overstated, and that free agency was not threatening their economic survival afterall. Moreover, argued the owners, the accounting data were none of the union's business. This prompted the union's charge to the NLRB that the owners were not bargaining in good faith.

NLRB and Court Actions

Three days before the MLBPA's announced strike deadline, the general counsel of the NLRB, William Lubbers, upheld the union's contention that the owners did not bargain in good faith.[94] The NLRB's five-member board authorized Lubbers to request a restraining order in federal court that would prohibit the owners' compensation plan from becoming effective unless they bargained in good faith and would grant the players the right to strike on free agency by June 1, 1982.[95] The NLRB's decision had the effect of delaying the strike for a few days, pursuant to agreement between the parties, until the request for injunction was heard in court. If granted, the injunction would put the strike off for at least a year.

On June 10, U.S. District Court Judge Henry Werker dismissed the NLRB's request for an injunction, finding that there is "no reasonable cause to believe an unfair labor practice has been committed" by the owners.[96] Ironically, Judge Werker ended his ruling with the admonition: "Play ball!" This was the final opportunity to head off a baseball strike.

THE STRIKE IS ON

The baseball strike began on June 12. The chief participants in the dispute remained the same: Miller and Grebey as head negotiators and Ken Moffett as mediator. Some other figures made appearances. Bob Boone and Doug DeCinces were the primary player representatives in the talks. Secretary of Labor Raymond Donovan spent a few days trying unsuccessfully to bring the strike to an end. Grebey imposed an order of silence on owners, with noncompliance punishable by fines of up to $500,000. Conspicuous by his general absence from direct or indirect participation in the talks was Commissioner Kuhn. The position of the parties, hardened by their statements to the media and widespread publicity, made early compromise unlikely. All signs pointed to a lengthy strike.

Owners' Strike Insurance

Cushioning the impact of the strike for the owners was a $50 million strike insurance policy and a $15 million strike fund.[97] The strike insurance or "business interruption policy" was mainly provided through Lloyds of London, although the coverage was distributed among several U.S. insurance carriers as well. It was reported to have cost each of the twenty-six clubs an annual premium of $65,000. The policy did not take effect until 150 games were missed, and provided compensation at a rate of $100,000 per game. At that rate, insurance payments were expected to run out by August 8.

The strike or "mutual assistance" fund had been accumulated over the previous two years by owners who contributed to it 2 percent of their gross receipts from ticket sales. These monies were intended for use after the strike insurance payments were depleted. In contrast to the owners, the players did not have financial protection against a strike and would forgo about $4 million a week in salaries. Numerous businesses dependent on baseball for revenues stood to lose substantial amounts that were difficult to estimate accurately in total.

Nor did baseball's fans have a fund on which to draw comparable entertainment during the summer of lost games. Many would discover other diversions for personal satisfaction and sense of accomplishment. The summer probably set a record for quantity of yard work and house painting by disgruntled males. A poem satirizing the classic "Casey at the Bat" captures the essence of the dilemma.

> The sneer is gone from Casey's lips, his teeth are clenched in hate;
> He pounds with a cruel vengeance his contract on the plate.
> "It's not a game; it's just a job; that's what it's come to be."
> This is what the slugger said " . . . and we'd be agents free."
>
> Oh, somewhere in this favored land the sun is shining bright,
> The band is playing somewhere, and somewhere hearts are light;
> And somewhere men are laughing, and the kids have what they like.
> But there is no joy for most of us—when Casey's out on strike.[98]

Suggestions for Compromise

Early in July mediator Moffett made an unsolicited proposal for ending the strike. This plan, closer to the players' position than the owners', was accepted in principle by the union.[99] However, the owners rejected the plan, indicating their displeasure with what they regarded as a one-sided position by Moffett.

About a week later the players proposed a "pool concept" in which one-third of the teams would make annual contributions to a pool from which teams losing a free agent could take compensation. The owners countered with an offer that was not significantly different from the direct compensation offer previously made.[100] Negotiations had made virtually no progress since the strike began. Apart from compromise by the parties, which began to appear increasingly unlikely, the alternatives were to cancel the entire season or to allow the impasse to be finally resolved by an arbitrator. Since both these alternatives were eschewed by the parties, the only real option was to somehow bridge the negotiation gap.

The settlement that finally resulted after fifty days of strike and assessment of the aftermath of the strike are presented later in this chapter. We turn next to analysis of the strike in terms of the power and behavioral models.

STRIKE ANALYSIS

We are interested here in the applications of the power model to the baseball strike. *Power* is defined here as getting the other side to do what you want.[101] An overall assessment of the power equation between labor and management during the strike indicates that strength was pretty evenly distributed.

Power Standoff

Power is determined by costs of disagreeing, or ability to inflict damage on the other side, and costs of agreeing, or making the other side more willing to agree with you. Costs of disagreeing are negative factors; costs of agreeing are positive.

There was an almost total absence of positive elements in the baseball negotiations before and during the strike. Instead, the talks were characterized by the adversary relationship; they were geared toward conflict over the single issue of free-agency compensation. The owners were trying to acquire something (restrictions on free agency) that the players had won through arbitration and negotiations and were seeking to preserve and protect. There is simply no evidence of sustained cooperation between the parties apart from that necessitated by strike deadlines.

Emphasis was placed on offensive power tactics calculated to force the adversary to grant concessions. The players utilized their ultimate and really only effective power weapon—the strike—to achieve their objective of holding on to as much of the freedom of movement among teams as possible. The owners' primary weapons were strike insurance and the strike fund, utilized to secure a hoped-for breakthrough in the players' solidarity and to force a tightening of restrictions on player mobility. Neither side gained a significant edge through the use of power tactics. The result was a standoff that was broken, as strikes almost always are, by each side yielding in substantial part to the other's position.

Behavioral Model

The behavioral model has four major aspects: distributive, integrative, attitudinal, and intraorganizational.[102] Distributive bargaining is the predominant approach between U.S. business and unions. It involves carving up the economic pie in a manner most favorable to each; it is win/lose negotiation characterized chiefly by the adversary process. What is gained by one side in this contest over a finite economic amount must inevitably be lost by the other side.

Distributive Bargaining. Although most of the distributive issues, such as minimum salaries, pensions, and insurance, were settled in the 1980 agreement, the remaining issue of free-agency compensation is also distributive in nature. If the players accepted greater restraint on their ability to negotiate as free agents over which increased free-agency compensation would entail, their salaries might not rise as fast in the future as they had in the past. If the owners allowed the status quo or even accepted the union's early concessions on free agency, they would virtually guarantee continued rapid escalation of player salaries.

Toward maximizing their outcomes in this distributive struggle, the parties resorted to offensive and defensive power tactics. Although these tactics were significant in their impact on both sides, the relative equality of power, noted above, made it difficult to tilt the balance in one's favor. This ability to offset offensive power thrusts in the distributive setting is a major explanation for the lengthy duration of the baseball strike.

Integrative Bargaining. The elements of true cooperation, where the parties seek to put their heads together to come up with joint solutions to common problems, were not found in the baseball negotiations. Some effort at integration for mutual benefit was made by mediator Moffett, but the basis for enhancing the welfare of both sides in a win/win outcome simply did not exist.

The parties made a half-hearted attempt at integrative bargaining when the joint study committee was agreed on in 1980 to study free-agency compensation. However, this committee split on partisan lines rather than create a unified solution, so any fruits that might have sprung up were stifled by a narrow view of interests. Had this committee engaged in integrative bargaining, in a spirit of cooperation, the baseball strike might have been averted.

Attitudinal Structuring. There was little in the way of care taken by the principals to promote positive attitudes during the baseball talks. Rather than placing emphasis on accommodation, trust, mutual respect, and face-saving, the parties' actions seemed calculated to bring about the opposite. Consider, for example, some of the chief negotiators' comments that were reported in the print media. Following an unsuccessful negotiating session in 1980, Marvin Miller said: "They're acting like four-year-olds, the owners haven't made it to the 20th Century, they are not negotiating seriously, they won't move on anything and they won't listen."[103]

Ballard Smith, president of the San Diego Padres, provided this taunting gesture to the players in 1980:

> I've reached the point where I almost hope they do strike. I think a strike might be the only way to get the players back in touch with reality.... If there is a strike, it will be the players who will have to give in because it won't be the owners. Believe me, we're much better prepared for a long one than they are. You can't satisfy a ballplayer anymore. A lot of these guys make hundreds of thousands of dollars and all they do is complain. They don't care about the game. They don't care about the fans. All they care about is themselves.[104]

When mediator Moffett made a detailed written suggestion for ending the dispute, Grebey's reply was: "It's a setup. Marvin Miller wrote it."[105] Miller's reply was: "That's the worst lie he has told, and he has told many during these negotiations."[106]

These remarks, illustrate how very trying and frustrating negotiations can be and how they can provoke inflammatory rhetoric from normally calm participants. However, such commentary, even though it might contain elements of truth, is counterproductive to structuring the kinds of attitudes that lead to reasoned negotiations and settlement. They spark a one-upsmanship in which the target of the poisonous barb eagerly awaits the next opportunity to vilify his adversary through the media. Of course the media is delighted: Sharp criticism and its riposte make good copy and attract readers. But rather than promote agreement, this type of slur exacerbates the situation and may even move the parties farther apart. Few devices implemented during heated negotiations have done more to engender attitudes conducive to agreement than a news blackout.

Intraorganizational Bargaining. An interesting aspect of the baseball strike was the intraorganizational side. On this point the parties performed commendably. The owners bickered internally and put pressure on chief negotiator Grebey to change direction, but on the whole, they showed solidarity throughout the talks. This was due in part to the gag rule placed on the owners by Grebey and the knowledge that owners would be fined severely if they discussed negotiations in public. It also was due to the owners' belief in the righteousness of their cause: They were united by a desire to make money or at least not to lose it.

It may have surprised some observers that the players remained together as tightly and for as long as they did during the seven months of negotiations and strike. This solidarity seems attributable mostly to Marvin Miller, a remarkable labor leader. The players' respect for Miller and for all that he accomplished for them over the years allowed the MLBPA to present a strong, unified front that the owners were not able to breach.

STRIKE SETTLEMENT

As noted above, the only real basis for ending the baseball strike was for each side to give in toward the other's position and reach an acceptable compromise. Neither side wanted to lose the entire season because each would be damaged as would the sport in the public's eye. Arbitration was ruled out because neither party was willing to abdicate its control over the outcome of the settlement. The players had put their faith earlier in Judge Werker, who might have delayed the strike for a year, but that failed experiment with reliance on an outsider was the final step in launching the strike.

Several factors helped generate pressure for a settlement. Perhaps most important was that the duration of the strike was reaching the point where forfeiture of the season was imminent. If the season was cancelled, it was possible that the players would form a new league. Season ticket sales during the winter months would be hampered. The NLRB had already indicated a sympathy for the players' contention that since the owners had failed to turn over their financial data and they were not bargaining in good faith. Were the season to go down the drain, the union might turn again to the NLRB and the courts, with a spate of unfair labor practice and antitrust charges that could cause further delays, uncertainty, and costly litigation.

Also impelling a settlement was the increasing economic pinch. The owners' strike insurance policy was about to expire and the players had forgone seven weeks of pay. The fans were tired of the stalemate, and the professional football exhibition season was drawing near as an alternative public attraction.

Bridging the Gap

Negotiation meetings had been taking place at the Doral Inn in New York City, with a full complement of representatives on both sides and federal mediators. Two small but important changes were made for a negotiating session on July 31.[107] First, the bargaining scene shifted a few blocks away for a fresh start at the luxurious offices of National League President Chub Feeney. Second, the size of the negotiating teams was cut to a minimum. American League President Lee MacPhail, generally regarded as a conciliatory force among the owners, accompanied Grebey. Don Fehr, counsel for the MLBPA, accompanied Miller.

Other key representatives of the sides were gathered in individual caucus meetings, but the four principals were cutting the deal. Following sixteen hours of talks, an agreement to end the baseball strike was finally reached, subject to working out the details of contract language and ratification by the parties' constituencies.

Terms of the Settlement

Although the strike settlement agreement appears to be closer to what the players proposed in the spring than to the owners' position, both sides made significant concessions. In effect, the owners gained establishment of the principle of compensation for signing of premier free agents, while the players were able to mostly preserve a free-agency system that allows substantial mobility among teams. The new agreement included several key terms:

1. The premier free agents were ranked in two groups, Type A and Type B, based on performance over the past two years.
2. Type A players included the top 20 percent, and Type B players the next 10 percent. Ratings were determined by the leagues according to statistics such as batting average, on-base percentage, home runs, runs batted in, fielding percentage, assists, and except for catchers, total chances. Pitchers were rated on game appearances, innings pitched, games won and lost, earned run average, and strikeouts.
3. If a team signed a Type A free agent, it had to place all but twenty-four of its players in a compensation pool. When a team lost a Type A free agent, it received an additional amateur draft choice plus a choice from the compensation pool. The latter selection was not necessarily from the free agent's new team. Clubs losing a pool player were paid $150,000.
4. When a Type B free agent was signed by another club, the original team was allowed two additional choices from the amateur draft.
5. Up to five clubs could become exempt from the compensation pool by agreeing not to draft Type A free agents for three years.
6. Clubs that did not sign Type A free agents could protect twenty-six players from placement in the compensation pool.
7. If players who were not classified as either Type A or B (approximately 70 percent of the players) signed as free agents, compensation was an additional choice from the amateur draft.
8. Players who did not go through the free-agent draft before or who had twelve or more years of major league experience were exempt from the Type A and B rankings.
9. Players lost no service time as a result of the strike. Thus, the strike time counted toward the six seasons of major league play required for qualification as a free agent.
10. The basic agreement (signed in 1980) was extended for one year, so the new expiration date was December 31, 1984.

Experience with the application of these provisions in free-agent drafts is discussed later in this chapter.

Misguided Playoff Scheme

Play resumed in baseball with a rescheduled All-Star game on August 9 in Cleveland. The regular team schedule was continued on the following day. No lost games were rescheduled.

In an attempt to rekindle enthusiasm for the games, the owners voted to split the season and hold a second set of divisional races. The division leaders at the time that the strike broke off play in the first part of the season were declared automatically eligible for the postseason divisional playoffs leading to the World Series. These teams were the New York Yankees, Oakland A's, Philadelphia Phillies, and Los Angeles Dodgers.

Under the format originally devised by the owners, these teams would then play the winners of the second season in a three-out-of-five game playoff. However, the flaw in this scheme was that if a club won both halves of the season it would play the team with the second-best record over the full season. Paradoxically, this might cause a team to deliberately lose a game in order to gain an advantage. For instance, by contriving to lose a game to Team A, which won the first half of the season. Team X could help ensure that Team A would win the second half of the season as well. Team X could then qualify for the playoffs if its results were good enough to provide an overall record better than Team Y which was close to the division lead in the second season race. Team Y would thus be the victim of a deliberate loss by Team X to Team A.

To close the loophole in its playoff plan the owners altered the rules so that if a club won both halves of the season, the second playoff spot would go to the team with the second best record during the second half of the season. However, this was not the end of the playoff inequity. The Cincinnati Reds, with a record of 66 to 42, had the best overall winning percentage in baseball over the course of the entire season. But the Reds did not qualify for the playoffs because they did not win either half of the season outright. Also, the St. Louis Cardinals had the best overall record in their division, but they did not qualify for the playoffs because other teams finished ahead of them in the first and second halves.

Thus, the playoff scheme, even after it was patched up by the owners, was loaded with inequity to teams, players, and fans. Although there was talk of utilizing a split-season format again in future years, the notion was buried amid protest from all quarters. Even the owners, always looking for new ways to make money and heighten interest, realized that a permanent revision would violate the traditions and upset the rhythms of the season.

IMPACT AND AFTERMATH

During the fifty-day strike 713 games were cancelled. When the strike began on June 12, after about two months of play, attendance was at a record pace, about 1.14 million ahead of the total at the same time the previous year.[108] In the first two weeks after the resumption of play in August, average attendance dropped 11 percent from what it was at prestrike levels.[109] For the remainder of the season, attendance began to climb some but never reached the previous levels. Poststrike attendance averaged 19,255 in the National League and 17,884 in the American League, a reduction of 2,162 (about 10 percent) and 1,134 (about 6 percent) from the same period in 1980.[110] Television ratings dropped from 7.6 to 6.4 from a like period in the previous year on NBC's "Game-of-the-Week."[111]

Financial Losses

The owners saved on salaries and other expenses during the strike and were paid an estimated $44 million in strike insurance benefits. Major losses for the owners during the strike included the revenues from ticket sales (at an average of about $5 per ticket), concessions and parking, and radio and television income.[112] After subtracting the insurance reimbursement, the owners lost about $72 million from the strike, a deficit that was cushioned somewhat by their $15 million strike fund which was generated by income in past years.

The players lost an estimate $28 million in salaries.[113] Cities with major league teams lost approximately $10 million in tax income.[114] Satellite industries dependent on baseball probably lost into the hundreds of millions as a direct and indirect result of the strike.

The Bottom Line

In assessing the aftermath of the strike, the bottom-line numbers are that player salaries continued to rise, from an average $185,651 in 1981 to $241,497 in 1982 and on to $289,194 in 1983.[115] These increases of 20 to 30 percent are in the range that players' average salaries have been rising annually since the 1976 season, the first in which players were able to test their power in free-agent bargaining. If the owners' goal in the 1981 strike was to check the escalation of player salaries, it clearly fell short.

The other telling number is that major league baseball attendance set a record in 1982, at 44,585,000. This indicates that the fans cams back to the game and that except for the dropoff in attendance after the strike in 1981 the strike did not turn out to be a threat to the game's popularity and stability. Attendance also continued at this high peak in 1983 and 1984.

There was no real winner or loser in the baseball strike. The public's loss was only transitory. It may well be concluded that the strike was inevitable. Even if Judge Werker had delayed the strike for a year, it is unlikely that the parties could have resolved their differences without a strike. Some strikes simply must happen: The parties may even look forward to a test of their economic strength and staying power.

The agreement reflected a compromise. Since the players' association accepted the idea of compensation in excess of an amateur draft choice in early 1981, and in light of the owners' position referred to above, the agreement seemed to reflect more nearly the players' association position. Indeed, it would seem as though the Red Sox, through obtaining Carney Lansford, Mark Clear, and Rick Miller for Rick Burleson (about to become a free agent) and Butch Hobson, received more than the 1981 agreement compensation provisions require.[116] Moreover, players who received this compensation are drawn from a pool of participating clubs, an approach proposed by the players.[117] It took a strike of more than two months, however, to achieve this agreement—a factor that may not be lost on the players' association in future bargaining sessions.[118]

Although the 1981 agreement seemed closer to the players' position, some of the clubs have been rudely surprised by compensation. Two outstanding examples of this occurred in 1984. The first involved Tom Seaver, who had returned to the New York Mets after spending his middle years with the Cincinnati Reds. The Chicago White Sox were able to obtain Seaver as compensation for a lost free agent—producing outrage on the part of Mets' fans everywhere (an outrage based more on nostalgia for the Impossible Dream Mets of 1969 rather than Seaver's ability to make a significant difference in the pennant race of 1984).

The loss of Tom Belcher of the New York Yankees to the Oakland A's was more troublesome for both the Yankees and the Players' Association.[119] That the compensation agreement contemplated inclusion of minor league or newly signed rookies seems questionable. The Yankees argued that the protected lists were frozen as of January 16 and that therefore the players available for selection as compensation should be similarly frozen as of that time and should have been in this instance ineligible for selection by the Oakland A's. However, Commissioner Kuhn, in considering the matter in the decision discussed below, stated that in reviewing the bargaining history of the 1981 agreement, he could not conclude that

> it was the clear intention of the parties to create a frozen pool of compensation players. That would work well enough for a situation such as the expansion draft which occurs on a single predetermined date, but obviously difficult problems result when reentry draft players may be signed over a long period of time.

Belcher was an outstanding rookie prospect with years of good pitching in front of him. In contrast to the symbolism of the Seaver compensation, Belcher is the kind of player that clearly should have been protected.

Commissioner Kuhn has triggered a grievance[120] by awarding the Yankees a "special" additional selection in the June 1985 free-agent draft, although permitting the selection of Belcher by the A's to stand.[121] Moreover, the Commissioner concluded that the selection should be made following the conclusion of the first round of the regular phase of the free-agent draft and that $150,000 payment to the Yankees from the central fund as compensation for selection by Oakland should be reduced to $112,500, the amount of the bonus that the Yankees had paid to Belcher. The excess balance of $37,500 was to be refunded by the Yankees before the June 1985 free-agent selection.

As noted above, the Players' Association filed a grievance challenging the decision of Commissioner Kuhn on the ground that the draft selection, the compensation, and the conclusion that the equities favor the Yankees' position—but that nevertheless Belcher's selection was proper—all violate the basic agreement between the parties.

Yet it seems as though compensation has had little positive affect on the ability of players to improve their positions economically: Improvement has come about mainly as a result of salary arbitration and free agency. In the spring of 1983, the *New York Times* noted that the New York Yankees' payroll was $7.5 million. This meant that average annual guaranteed income per player was $558,754. At the bottom of the scale was the rookie standout, first baseman Don Mattingly, making the $35,000 major league minimum, and at the top, left fielder Dave Winfield, who earned $1,531,600 and who received an annual average of $2 million. Of the twenty-seven Yankees, twenty-one had contracts with a total guaranteed value of more than $1 million.[122] Even outside Yankee Stadium the compensation provisions of the collective bargaining agreement do not seem to have interfered with salary escalation. Today, the average player earns in excess of $300,000.

The Duty to Bargain

Employees in other industries may insist on bargaining to reduce workweeks because both wages and employment conditions are at issue. If baseball players, for example, were to bargain for a seven-inning game, they would be demanding a shorter work day. The players already have set the number of games they will play per season in their collective bargaining agreement. The clubs would argue that this interest is exclusively entrepreneurial and beyond the scope of bargaining—in part, because fans identify nine innings as integral to the product.

The owners' argument is weakened, however, in light of their record of alterations of baseball's structure. The owners, for instance, instituted the designated hitter rule (DH) in the American League—much to the consternation of baseball afficionados who delighted in late inning pinch hit strategy, which was inevitably linked to managerial judgments about the strength of the bullpen. Red Sox fans, for example, recall the final game of the 1949 regular season. The two teams entered the game tied for the league lead. Behind 1 to 0 after seven innings, Boston manager Joe McCarthy had to decide whether to allow his pitcher, Ellis Kinder, to bat. Kinder had limited the Yankees to four hits and the single run. McCarthy sent in a pinch hitter, and the choice proved disastrous. The Red Sox failed to score in their half of the eighth, and Kinder's first replacement, Mel Parnell, who had pitched the previous day, promptly allowed a Yankee home run. The second Red Sox replacement, Tex Hughson, allowed two more runs. Although Boston scored three times in the top of the ninth, that was not enough to win. The Yankees won the game 5 to 3, and the pennant, as Birdie Tebbetts fouled out to Tommy Heinrich to end it.[123]

The designated hitter rule altered key elements in the game—as did the lowering of the pitching mound to improve the hitter's chances. The players' associations argue that these rules affect both player performance, salaries, and longevity. In essence, aspects of the game that directly affect playing conditions, once immutable, are now being questioned. In the pitching mound example, where sore arms and shoulders can be the price of change, the argument for characterizing such matters as mandatory subjects of bargaining within the meaning of the National Labor Relations Act (NLRA) is even more persuasive.[124]

The recently announced plans of the owners to expand the playoffs in baseball again brings about a convergence between the integrity of the game as it is understood by the public as well as the players' obvious interest in limiting games—unless, that is, for compensation so substantial that it cannot be resisted.[125] But clearly, any attempt to blur and undermine further the significance of the pennant race cannot be viewed as a decision by the owners that involves a management prerogative or as an entrepreneurial judgment that is beyond the concern of the players' association.

Another issue that has triggered the tensions between managerial prerogatives and scope of bargaining for unions is the so-called 60-40 amendments to the league constitutions. These require each club to meet an asset-to-liability ratio of not less than 60 to 40. The clubs have maintained that such a ratio is required by serious financial difficulties experienced by a number of individual clubs and that the absence of such a rule would threaten the stability of the respective leagues. Specifically, losses in San Francisco and San Diego have prompted the National League to advance sizable sums of money to keep the clubs operating and in the American League, Seattle actually entered federal bankruptcy proceedings during spring training following a period in which the league advanced funds and appointed a custodian to oversee the club's financial affairs.

The clubs have maintained that the contractual language relating to measuring the prerogatives and the duty to negotiate tracks the statutory language of section 8(d) of the National Labor Relations Act. The association's concern is that the 60-40 rule will limit the amount of monies that are available to players. But the position of the owners has been that the nonbargainability of the 60-40 rule is consistent with Supreme Court authority such as *First National Maintenance* because the decision did not turn on labor costs and it can be implemented in a number of ways such as infusion of new capital from the club owners' personal assets, the increase of ticket prices, or improvement of marketing methods. In essence, the clubs' position is that it is not necessary to cut players' salaries in order to implement the rule.

The Players' Association takes the position that the 60-40 rule represents a banding together of a club that definitely affects and inhibits the conduct of negotiation for multiyear contracts, with which free agency is "virtually synonymous." Moreover, the players have taken the position that without the rise of player costs, the 60-40 rule would not have ever been adopted. The entrepreneurial concerns, which are exclusively those of the employer, are not involved here, contend the players, because the arbitrator would not be required to dictate the method of financing by the clubs if it sustained the grievance. Because the 60-40 rule is similar to salary caps, which are found in collective bargaining agreements such as those in basketball, it would be bargainable under the agreement.

NOTES TO CHAPTER 3

1. For a general source concerning the origins of baseball and the formation of the early leagues, see H. Seymour, Baseball: The Early Years (1980). Additional information can be found in L. Lowenfish and T. Lupien, The Imperfect Diamond (1980), and F. Menke, The Encyclopedia of Sports 46-68 (4th ed. 1969).
2. Constitution and Playing Rules of National League of Professional Base Ball Clubs (1876), reprinted in Spalding's Official Baseball Guide (1881).
3. *Id.* at art. 3, §1.
4. *Id.* at art. 5, §2.
5. *Id.* at art. 11, §1.
6. On some of the early restrictive devices employed by the baseball leagues, see R. Smith, Baseball (1947).
7. Constitution and Playing Rules of National League of Professional Base Ball Clubs (1876), reprinted in Spalding's, *supra* note 2, at rule 4 §§2-3.
8. *Id.* at rule 5, §15.
9. *Id.* at rule 5, §§5-6.
10. *Id.* at rule 7, §§5, 8.
11. According to Seymour, *supra* note 1, at 141, 154-56 (1960), litigation kicked off in 1882 when Cincinnati, of the newly formed American Association, sued Samuel Washington Wise for not honoring his contract. Furthermore, mentioned in the text is the Union Association. One of the

better-known pitchers of the early era, Tony Mullane, first agreed to jump to that league, then reneged. He also wound up in court.

12.   For detailed information on the Players' League, *see id.* at 228–29, 240–50; *see also* Lowenfish and Lupien, *supra* note 1, at 39–53 (1980).

13.   On the formation of the American League, *see generally* L. Allen, The American League Story (1962), and R. Smith, Baseball (1947).

14.   Allen, *supra* note 13, at 18.

15.   Seymour, *supra* note 1, at 314.

16.   *See* Chapter 2 for discussion of Philadelphia Base-Ball Club v. Lajoie.

17.   *See* Chapter 2 for discussion of American League Baseball Club of Chicago v. Chase, 86 Misc. 441, 149 N.Y.S. 6 (Sup. Ct. 1914).

18.   American League Baseball Club of New York v. Pasquel, 63 N.Y.S.2d 537 (1946).

19.   *See* Chapter 2 for reference to Gardella v. Chandler, 172 F.2d 402 (2d Cir. 1949), *rev'g* 79 F. Supp. 260 (S.D.N.Y. 1948).

20.   *See, e.g.*, Kowalski v. Chandler, 202 F.2d 413 (6th Cir. 1953).

21.   D. Honig, Baseball When the Grass Was Real 219 (1975).

22.   Several accounts relate the early attempts to form baseball unions. In particular, *see* J. Dworkin, Owners versus Players 25–39 (1981); P. Gregory, The Baseball Player: An Economic Study 182–207 (1956).

23.   Mike Witt of the California Angels joined this select group in 1984. Len Barker had last done it in the abbreviated 1981 baseball season. *See* Len Barker Pitches Perfect Game against Toronto, N.Y. Times, May 10, 1981, at 17, col. 4.

24.   *See* sources in note 22, *supra.*

25.   American League Changes Rule on Play-Off of Tie for Pennant, N.Y. Times, Dec. 11, 1956, at 52, col. 2.

26.   Brady, Player Rep Friend Raps Proposal That Athletes Form Labor Union, Sporting News, Aug. 3, 1963, at 4.

27.   Strike of '72, Harv. Busi. School, Case Report 9–677–200, 4 (1977).

28.   *See* Chapter 2 for Metropolitan Exhibition Co. v. Ewing, 42 F. 198 (C.C.S.D.N.Y. 1890); Metropolitan Exhibition Co. v. Ward, 9 N.Y.S. 779 (1890); and Philadelphia Base-Ball Club v. Lajoie, 10 Pa. Dist. Rpts. 309 (1901), *rev'd* in 202 Pa. 210, 51 A. 973 (1902).

29.   *See* Chapter 2 for Flood v. Kuhn, 407, U.S. 158 (1972); Toolson v. New York Yankees, 346 U.S. 356 (1953); and Federal Baseball Club of Baltimore v. National League of Professional Baseball Clubs, 259 U.S. 207 (1922).

30.   American League of Professional Baseball Clubs, 180 N.L.R.B. 190 (1969).

31.   Basic Agreement between the American League of Professional Baseball Clubs and the National League of Professional Baseball Clubs and Major League Baseball Players Association art. 5, D(6)–(8); art. 10 (Jan. 1, 1973) [hereinafter cited as 1973 Baseball Basic Agreement].

32.   The Hunter free-agency saga captured the media's attention, since baseball was a sport historically immune from antitrust. The following chronological reports highlight the unfolding of the drama: Koppett, A's Hunter

Ruled Free Agent, N.Y. Times, Dec. 16, 1974, at 51, col. 5; Koppett, Real Hunter Fuss Is on Bidding, N.Y. Times, Dec. 17, 1974, at 45, col. 5; Anderson, Catfish and His Country Lawyer, N.Y. Times, Dec. 19, 1974, at 63, col. 5; Koppett, Finley Hope Hangs by a Legal Thread, N.Y. Times, Dec. 20, 1974, at 47, col. 1; Finley Accused of Perjury, N.Y. Times, Dec. 24, 1974, at 13, col. 6; Smith, Dred Scott and Some Other Guys, N.Y. Times, Dec. 27, 1974, at 41, col. 2; Chass, Yankees Sign Up Catfish Hunter in Estimated $3.75-Million Deal, N.Y. Times, Jan. 1, 1975, at 1, col. 5; Chass, Hunter Salary Is "Only" $150,000, N.Y. Times, Jan. 9, 1975, at 43, col. 1. For an account of the established procedure to allow clubs to bid for Hunter's services, *see* B. Libby, Catfish: The Three Million Dollar Pitcher 7–41 (1976).

33.   In the matter of arbitration between American and National Leagues of Professional Baseball Clubs (Oakland Athletics) and Major League Baseball Players Association (James A. Hunter), Decision No. 23, Grievance Nos. 74–18 and 74–20, Dec. 13, 1974. Seitz, Impartial Chair of Panel.

34.   Great speculation centered around the origin of James Augustus Hunter's famous nickname "Catfish." The popular theory is that the owner of the Oakland A's, and Hunter's eventual adversary, Charles O. Finley, revived the name given Hunter as a child to make his star pitcher more colorful. The childhood story is supposedly that Hunter had been gone from home several hours, and his parents were worried and looking for him. Hunter wandered home on his own, carrying two catfish, and his parents thereafter called him Catfish. *See* H. Frommer, Sports Roots 35 (1979); The Encyclopedia of Sports Talk 51 (Z. Hollander ed. 1976). Doubt, however, is cast on this story by a conflicting account in a Hunter biography. Hunter contends that the appellation was a complete invention. Finley was looking for a nickname for Hunter and mentioned it in casual conversation to Hunter's brother, Pete, who recounted that Jim liked to fish and, as a boy, would eat only catfish. "That's it," Charlie said, "We'll call you Catfish. Catfish Hunter." Libby, *supra* note 33, at 52.

35.   Libby, *supra* note 32, at 157.

36.   Hunter Bids Told to Kapp Jury, San Francisco Chron., March 19, 1976, at 55, col. 5.

37.   Kapp v. NFL, 586 F.2d 644, 648 (9th Cir. 1978).

38.   K. Harrelson and A. Hirshberg, Hawk 187, 200–04 (1969).

39.   In the matter of arbitration between Major League Player Relations Committee and Major League Baseball Players' Association, Panel Decision No. 50 A & B, salary guarantee grievances (November 2, 1983).

40.   *Id.* at 5.

41.   The players involved are referred to in Arbitrator Goetz's opinion at 13–19.

42.   Professional Baseball Clubs, 66 Lab. Arb. & Disp. Settl. 101 (1975) (Seitz, Arb.).

43.   *Id.* at 102.

44.   *Id.* at 101–02.

45.   1973 Baseball Basic Agreement, *supra* note 31, art. 15.

46.   66 Lab. Arb. & Disp. Settl. at 102.
47.   *Id.* at 104.
48.   *Id.* at 106–07.
49.   *Id.* at 107–08.
50.   1973 Baseball Basic Agreement, *supra* note 31, art. 3.
51.   66 Lab. Arb. & Disp. Settl. at 110.
52.   *Id.* at 116.
53.   *Id.* at 117–18.
54.   For a discussion of the use of precedent in the arbitration of labor man-
       agement disputes, *see* E. Elkouri, How Arbitration Works 365–68 (3d ed.
       1973). In contrast to the judicial system, where the stare decisis concept
       renders prior decisions authoritative, prior arbitration awards are con-
       sidered "helpful" but not binding. Arbitrators emphasize the unusual cir-
       cumstances of each dispute they resolve:

   > A word as to arbitrators' opinions. Unlike judges who write opinions for the legal
   > profession and the people in general, arbitrators may write their opinions solely for
   > the parties before them. The opinions may serve an independent educational pur-
   > pose; and to serve that purpose, it must be adapted to the character of the particu-
   > lar parties. Accordingly, particular language, a simplification, an exaggeration, a
   > sermon, a "wise-crack," an emphasis, or an ellipsis which may seem out of place or
   > in bad taste for an article for general distribution may have been deliberately em-
   > ployed for the eyes of the particular parties; and conversely what may seem other-
   > wise proper may be out of place or in bad taste in the particular situation. Such, at
   > least, is the view of some umpires.

   H. Shulman and N. Chamberlain, Cases on Labor Relations 7 (1949).
       Precedential value is greater in a permanent umpireship where one arbi-
       trator resolves disputes for the duration of the agreement than under a
       relationship in which different arbitrators are selected on an ad hoc basis.
       See Shulman, Reason, Contract Law in Labor Relations, 68 Harv. L. Rev.
       999, 1019–21 (1955). The involvement of the judiciary in arbitration has
       meant the courts often are asked to determine whether an award applies
       to a particular controversy or whether a new dispute is presented by the
       facts, thus requiring invocation of an arbitration process in which preced-
       ent will not necessarily be followed. Oil, Chemical & Atomic Workers,
       Local 4–16000 v. Ethyl Corp., 644 F.2d 1044 (5th Cir. 1981); Boston
       Shipping Ass'n v. Longshoremen's Ass'n, 108 L.R.R.M. 2449 (1st Cir.
       1981). "Absent a provision in the contract to the contrary, the arbitrator
       could reasonably conclude that strict adherence to stare decisis would
       impair the flexibility of the arbitral process contemplated by the parties."
       Riverboat Casino v. Local Joint Executive Board of Las Vegas, 578 F.2d
       250, 251 (9th Cir. 1978).
55.   United Steelworkers v. American Mfg. Co., 363 U.S. 564 (1960); United
       Steelworkers v. Warrior & Gulf Navigation Co., 363 U.S. 574 (1960);
       United Steelworkers v. Enterprise Wheel & Car Corp., 363 U.S. 593
       (1960).
56.   532 F.2d 615 (8th Cir. 1976).

57. *Id.* at 620–21. According to the Eighth Circuit:

> We cannot say that Article XV, on its face, constitutes a clear exclusionary pro
> vision. First, the precise thrust of the phrase "this Agreement does not deal with
> the reserve system" is unclear. The agreement incorporates the provisions which
> compromise the reserve system [the incorporation of the uniform Players Con
> tract]. Also, the phrase is qualified by the words "except as adjusted or modified
> hereby." Second, the impact of the language "This Agreement shall in no way prej
> udice the position . . . of the Parties" is uncertain. Third, the "concerted action"
> which the parties agreed to forego does not clearly include bringing grievances.

58. *Id.* at 622–23.
59. *Id.* at 626.
60. *Id.* at 624.
61. *Id.* at 625.
62. *See* discussion in Chapter 5 of Mackey v. NFL, 407 F. Supp. 1000 (D. Minn. 1975), *modified* 543 F.2d 606 (8th Cir. 1976), *cert. dismissed* 434 U.S. 801 (1977).
63. 532 F.2d at 632.
64. This refers to language of Justice Holmes in Federal Baseball Club of Baltimore v. National League of Professional Baseball Clubs 259 U.S. 200, 208–209 (1922), discussed in Chapter 2.
65. 1973 Baseball Basic Agreement, *supra* note 31, art. 5, §D(6).
66. Basic Agreement between the American League of Professional Baseball Clubs and the National League of Professional Baseball Clubs and Major League Baseball Players Association art. 5, §E (Jan. 1, 1976), *reprinted in* Practicing Law Institute, Representing Professional and College Sports Teams and Leagues 125–29 (Patents, Trademarks and Literary Property Course Handbook No. 84, 1977) [hereinafter cited as 1976 Baseball Basic Agreement].
67. *Id.*
68. One of the most publicized gains from salary arbitration was the $700,000 award received by Chicago Cubs relief ace, Bruce Sutter. Sutter of Cubs Is Awarded $700,000 Pact by Arbitrator, N.Y. Times, Feb. 26, 1980, §C, at 11, col. 4. *See also* Chass, Arbitration Victory Gets Kemp $600,000, N.Y. Times, Feb. 24, 1981, §C, at 13, col. 5. Since the Sutter and Kemp awards, escalation in player demands in salary arbitration has been constant. In 1983 Fernando Valenzuela was awarded a million dollars through arbitration. In 1985 that amount was equalled by Wade Boggs and exceeded by the $1.2 million award to Tim Raines. For the late developments in salary arbitration, *see* Chass, Seven in Baseball Ask $1 Million and Up, N.Y. Times, Jan. 29, 1985, p. A21, col. 1; Chass, Salary Arbitration Becomes a Game Within the Game, N.Y. Times, Jan. 13, 1985, p. 3, col. 1; and Raines Wins $1.2 Million in Arbitration, Boston Globe, Feb. 22, 1985, p. 62, col. 1.
69. Memorandum of 1980 Baseball Agreement (May 23, 1980).
70. *See* Durso, Rich Getting Richer? High Cost of Survival, Sporting News, July 26, 1980, at 8, col. 1.

71. *See* Moore, Crisis in the Grand Old Game, San Francisco Chron., March 8, 1981, §C, at 1, col. 3.

72. Koppett, Yesterday: During the Brotherhood Revolt the Mood in Baseball Wasn't Fraternal, Sports Illustrated, June 1, 1981, at 89; and Sloane, Collective Bargaining in Major League Baseball: A New Ball Game and Its Genesis, 28 Labor L. J. 203 (1977).

73. Gipe, Yesterday: Ty Cobb's Anger Led to Baseball's First Strike, A Comedy of Errors, Sports Illustrated, Aug. 29, 1977, at W5–6; Walter, Baseball's First Strike Was as Rough as a Cobb, San Francisco Sunday Examiner & Chron., May 31, 1981, at C2.

74. J. Dworkin, Owners versus Players: Baseball and Collective Bargaining 32 (1981).

75. *Id.*

76. Loosening Up at Last, Time, March 29, 1976, at 66.

77. The Final Offer: Miller Will Seek Rejection, L.A. Times, March 17, 1976, pt. 3, at 1.

78. Kuhn Ends Lockout; Deadlock Remains, L.A. Times, March 18, 1976, pt. 3, at 1.

79. Data from L.A. Times, July 13, 1976, pt. 3, at 1.

80. Staudohar, Player Salary Issues in Major League Baseball, Arbitration J., Vol. 33 (1978) at 18.

81. Bill Campbell, a Boston Red Sox relief pitcher, is a classic example of the latter, but his excessive four- and five-inning relief stints on consecutive days may have been the culprit. There was never any doubt that Campbell was willing to earn his well-publicized salary. Elderkin, Baseball's Free Agents Pay Off, Except Sometimes When They Don't, Christian Science Monitor, July 2, 1980, at 14, col. 1.

82. Outfielder Dave Winfield supposedly has admitted that he would not go to the wall on long drives and fly balls because an injury might diminish his marketability. *Cf.* Yanks Signs Winfield for up to $25 Million, New York Times, Dec. 16, 1980, §A, at 1, col. 2. In contrast, Carlton Fisk, whose contract expired in 1980, risked injuring his throwing arm during the closely fought pennant race of 1978 and also on a cold April day in Milwaukee when he substituted for floundering Boston catchers. *See* Fisk Takes Risks and Wins, Sporting News, June 19, 1980, at 20, col. 1. *See generally* Fisk Going to Whitesox, N.Y. Times, March 10, 1981, §B, at 13, col. 4; Durso, Fisk Declared Free Agent; Cerone Wins Salary Arbitration, N.Y. Times, Jan. 25, 1981, §5, at 7, col. 1.

83. Nelson, The Baseball Strike, 39 Labor Center Rptr. 3 (July 1981).

84. For further discussion of this bargaining concept, see H. Northrup, The Case for Boulwarism, in R. Rowan, ed., Readings in Labor Economics and Labor Relations 149–60 (4th ed. 1980).

85. Fimrite, Yankee Stadium, Opening Day, 1980?, Sports Illustrated, March 3, 1980, at 60.

86. Newhan, Nobody Ready to Play Ball Yet, L.A. Times, Feb. 22, 1980, pt. 3, at 1.

87. Players Association Leaders OK Strike against Baseball, L.A. Times, March 5, 1980, pt. 3, at 1.

88. The lone dissenter was Kansas City Royals' utility infielder, Jerry Terrell, who held out because of deep religious convictions. *See* KC's Jerry Terrell Earns Spot in Baseball History, L.A. Times, April 4, 1980, pt. 3, at 1.

89. Owners Say New Proposal to Avert Strike, L.A. Times, March 19, 1980, pt. 3, at 1.

90. A summary of key provisions is provided in Chass, Plan for Compensation Study Is Basis of Pact, Sporting News, June 7, 1980, at 9.

91. Kaplan, No Strike Is a Real Ball, Sports Illustrated, June 2, 1980, at 48.

92. Staudohar and Smith, The Impact of Free Agency on Baseball Salaries, 13 Compensation Rev. 53 (1981).

93. For example, see Sports Illustrated, June 8, 1981, at 15.

94. Ruling Today May Delay the Strike, San Francisco Chron., May 27, 1981, at 1.

95. Labor Board Moves to Delay Baseball Strike, L.A. Times, May 28, 1981, pt. 3, at 1; Baseball Strike Off—for Now, San Francisco Chron., May 29, 1981, at 63.

96. Judge Throws Out Bid to Block Owner Moves in Baseball Strike, Wall St. J., June 11, 1981, at 6.

97. Data on these issues are from several sources, including L.A. Times, April 1, 1980, pt. 3, at 2, and Feb. 26, 1981, pt. 3, at 1; Oakland Tribune Today, Feb. 28, 1981, at D-4; and Wall St. J., June 15, 1981, at 16.

98. Excerpted from Casey on Strike, Wall St. J., June 15, 1981, at 22.

99. Baseball's Vanishing Season, Time, July 27, 1981, at 60.

100. Littwin, Boys of Summer, L.A. Times, July 27, 1981, pt. 3, at 1.

101. *See* N. Chamberlain and J. Kuhn, Collective Bargaining (2d ed. 1965).

102. *See* R. Walton and R. McKersie, A Behavioral Theory of Labor Negotiations: An Analysis of a Social Interaction System (1965).

103. Hall, The 3-2 Pitch, L.A. Times, April 1, 1980, pt. 3, at 3.

104. From the San Diego Evening Tribune, as quoted in Sports Illustrated, May 12, 1980, at 9.

105. Baseball's Vanishing Season, Time, July 27, 1981, at 60.

106. *Id.*

107. Descriptions of these changes are based on Kaplan, Let the Games Begin, Sports Illustrated, Aug. 10, 1981, at 14; Heisler, Baseball Can't Make Up Those 50 Days, L.A. Times, Aug. 1, 1981, pt. 3, at 1.

108. Players, Owners Far Apart—Talks End, San Francisco Chron., June 13, 1982, at 41.

109. Baseball's Sputtering Restart, Time, Aug. 31, 1981, at 54.

110. Data from the St. Louis Post-Dispatch, cited in Sports Illustrated, Oct. 5, 1981, at 19.

111. *Id.*

112. Pro-rated portions of local radio and television income would be deducted from the average of $1.86 million per team and from the national TV package averaging 1.6 million per team in 1981. Data from Kaplan, No Games Today, Sports Illustrated, June 22, 1981, at 20.

113. The Boys of Summer Return, Time, Aug. 10, 1981, at 44.
114. *Id.*
115. Figures released by Major League Baseball Players' Association.
116. Moreover, only players in 1981 are Type A players who may require major league player compensation. Also, the salaries negotiated by players who could have become free agents are in excess of what was negotiated in 1980. Chass, Free Agents Rewarded, New York Times, Nov. 12, 1981, at 26, col. 3.
117. Smith, Sneezing in the Draft, New York Times, Nov. 15, 1981, at 26, col. 1: "Some teams can dicker with Type A men with impunity. The Chicago Cubs, for instance, can be pretty sure that a team losing a Type A free agent would choose somebody else as compensation rather than the Cub's 25th player."
118. *See* Koppett, Owners' Goal Is Obvious: Soften the Union, Peninsula Times Tribune, July 13, 1981, §D, at 1, col. 1.
119. Grievance No. 84–16 (Major League Baseball Players' Association and the twenty-six major league clubs), September 24, 1984.
120. Decision in the matter of Timothy Belcher, Sept. 19, 1984, office of the commissioner.
121. *Id.*
122. Chass, What Price Glory: A $7.5 Million Payroll, N.Y. Times, April 11, 1983, at 31, col. 1. The salary arbitration in 1983 continued the upward economic mobility described above. Left-handed pitcher Fernando Valenzuela's $1 million per year was awarded against the Los Angeles Dodgers, topping the scale.
123. Yankees Whip Red Sox in Season Finale to Win 16th American League Pennant, N.Y. Times, Oct. 3, 1949, at 21, col. 1.
124. The Court, in 1981 in First Nat'l Maintenance v. NLRB, 49 U.S.L.W. 4769 (June 22, 1981), adopted what was previously only a concurring opinion of Justice Stewart that the design of the product is clearly a management prerogative. *Cf.* Fiberboard Paper Products Corp. v. NRLB, 379 U.S. 203 (1964). The issue in baseball, then, is whether the game is the product in the same sense that it cannot be bargained over except where safety issues are involved. *See* Gould, The Supreme Court's Labor and Employment Docket in the October 1980 Term: Justice Brennan's Term, 53 U. Colo. L. Rev. 1 (1981).
125. Plan to Expand Playoffs Leaves Union Unhappy, N.Y. Times, March 3, 1983, at 24, col. 5.

4 LABOR RELATIONS IN FOOTBALL

DEVELOPMENT OF THE PROFESSIONAL GAME

U.S. football was probably introduced in 1871 when a group of Harvard College students, with the permission of President Eliot, tried something variant from "the informal, unorganized kicking game" that had been banned by the Harvard faculty in the 1860s.[1] The ball the students produced was round, inflated, and made of rubber. Under the rules devised, the ball could be picked up at any time, thus introducing the use of hands as well as feet, and the holder could run with the ball. This was markedly different from the intercollegiate game that had been played since 1869 by teams from Rutgers, Princeton, Yale, and Columbia, which was more clearly a modification of the London Football Association rules of soccer.[2]

This description of the beginnings of U.S. football is, of course, not without controversy. Others would cite the earlier games as the true origins.[3] Still others would carry it all the way back to the fabled stories of Englishmen digging up the skulls of long departed Danes and using the grisly orbs for the earliest of sports.[4] Henry II of England (1159–89) had to contend with the vagaries of "futballe," finally banning it because his troops were more intrigued by the playing field than the fighting field, which was deemed to threaten national security.[5]

The bans against the sport extended throughout all levels of government. G. G. Coulton noted that at Acley, " 'it was enjoined upon all the tenants of the township than none should play at ball' [*ad pilam*]. This same prohibition is

often repeated and culminates in the injunction at East Merrington in 1382.
. . ."[6] According to Coulton, the sport in question was football, "and football
of the good old sort, one village pitted *en masse* against another."[7]

A Puritan writer, Philip Stubbes, described football as

> rather a friendlie kind of fyghte than a play or recreation . . . for doth not
> everyone lye in waight for his adversarie seeking to overthrow him and picke
> him on his nose. . . .[8]

Sir Thomas Elyot was even less kind:

> Foote-balle, wherein is nothing but beastlie furie and exstreme violence,
> whereof proceedth hurte, and consequently rancour do remain with them
> that be wounded.[9]

Finally, a verdict on the game from the time of Henry VI of England:

> A game, I say, abominable enough, and, in my judgment at least, more com-
> mon, undignified, and worthless than any kind of game, rarely ending but
> with some loss, accident, or disadvantage to the players themselves.[10]

Despite these cries of anguish over such a lowly sport, it continued through
the centuries, officially banned but generally played.

When James I formally lifted Henry's ban of 400 years,[11] the sport that
everyone had played covertly burst forth; and innumerable variations around the
world have come and gone in the past 400 years. In England, mainstays eventually became the sports of football (soccer) and rugby. U.S. football obviously
owes something to both sports, and then has added many ongoing refinements at
both the college and professional levels. In the New World, the game flourished
in the eastern part of the United States and only slowly gained footholds of loyalty elsewhere. Eventually, pockets in Pennsylvania led to large followings in
Ohio. It would have still been difficult ever to forecast that U.S. football would
become the sport it has or that U.S. football fans would rival in intensity football (soccer) fans in other parts of the world. But it occurred; and it was only a
matter of time until enterprising souls figured that there must be a way to make
money out of the sport's evident and growing popularity.

William (Pudge) Hefflefinger, a former Yale star athlete, is generally credited
to be the first football player openly paid for his services. He was brought in by
the Allegheny Athletic Association for a game in 1892 against the Pittsburgh
Athletic Club. Hefflefinger responded by running for the game's only touch-
down off a fumble recovery and walked away with $500 for his efforts.[12]

Pittsburgh was the first large city to have all-professional teams. Among the
earliest professional clubs were the Duquesnes of Pittsburgh, the Olympics of
McKeesport, Pennsylvania, and the Orange A.C. of Newark, New Jersey.[13] The
St. Louis Cardinals were formed in 1898 and are now the oldest continuing operation in professional football.[14] Teams organized in Canton and Massilon, Ohio,

in 1902 and 1903, and for the first time many former college stars joined the pro ranks.[15]

For years, college football coaches were among the most vigorous opponents of the professional games. Though pro teams managed to acquire an increasing number of college stars, the coaches, old grads, and other college interests were able to undermine the professional game. Attendance declined. Those interested in the professional game determined that a more formal league structure was necessary for survival.

The NFL: Early Struggles

George Halas remembered the words of his college coach, Bob Zuppke, "Why is it that just when you men are ready to learn something about playing football your career is ended? You have learned only the beginning in college. There is so much more."[16] Those were obviously the guides for Halas throughout his long and distinguished association with a league that began timidly and rockily. It was many years before it in any way resembled the industry it is today.

It was July 1919, in Canton, Ohio. Representatives from five existing professional teams met to form a new league. They called it the American Professional Football Association and determined that the cost of a franchise was $25. Canton, Columbus, Dayton, Rochester, and Akron were its five original members. By the start of the season, several other entries came forward.[17] The season was not like today's structured offerings. In 1919 and for several years after, there were no set schedule of games. Two teams agreed to play where they felt they could make money. Players changed clubs almost at will. And the shifting nature of the schedule allowed different clubs to claim the league championship for the same year.[18] For example, after the 1921 season, both the Buffalo All Americans and the Chicago Staleys claimed they were the champions. Buffalo's claim came because they beat Chicago 7 to 6 after both teams had gone undefeated. Chicago, however, got revenge in a postseason rematch, winning 10 to 7. Chicago then claimed the second game was the real determinant of the championship. Buffalo protested, but sentiment over the years has normally favored Chicago.[19] George Halas had his first championship.

Several times the league almost folded. It officially went out of existence after the 1920 season but was revived mainly through the efforts of Joseph E. Carr of Columbus, who headed the reorganization of the league into what became known as the National Football League. It was still a shaky enterprise, with one game between the New York Giants and the Chicago Bears drawing only eighty customers.[20] During the 1921 season, several teams disbanded, and others formed to begin play as the season progressed. As many as twenty-three different teams played all or part of that year. The league had great difficulty in luring collegians of all-American status, as these players demanded more than the club owners could pay. The clubs turned to lesser players, willing to play for the money available. During the period 1922 to 1932, there was a constant movement of franchises into and out of the league. NFL membership swelled to twenty-two teams in 1926 and dropped to eight during the 1932 season in the heart of the Depression.[21]

Despite fluctuations, the fortunes of the league slowly improved. Attendance climbed, and teams that had continually lost money began to show small profits. In turn, the league went after more famous collegians. The great breakthrough was the signing of Red Grange, the greatest halfback of the era, to a contract with the Chicago Bears. Grange quit the University of Illinois after their season ended and immediately played for the Bears in late November 1925. 38,000 turned out to watch a Thanksgiving Day game between the Bears and the Cardinals. Then the Bears were off on tour, with Grange and the Bears playing seven games in eleven days in St. Louis, Philadelphia, New York, and cities in the South and West. 70,000 viewed the Bears against the Giants in New York. Since this was the Giants' first year in the league, the turnout helped solidify the franchise in the United States' most populous city.[22] Although the league was not without its later struggles, a turning point was reached.

Red Grange left the Bears the following season when the club refused to give Grange a five-figure salary and a one-third ownership in the team, as demanded by Grange's manager, C. C. Pyle. Being the promoter he was, Pyle then leased Yankee Stadium in New York and petitioned for an NFL franchise. When the league refused him, Pyle formed the American Football League.

This first AFL lasted only a single season and was a financial disaster. Grange's New York Yankees and eight other clubs played in varying degrees of success through the season, but it was clear that the new league was doomed. A postseason championship game between the AFL champion Philadelphia Quakers and the NFL New York Giants, themselves only in the second year of existence, was won handily by the Giants, 31 to 0. While the league was a loser, Pyle had won his point. His New York Yankees, with Grange aboard, were admitted to play in the NFL the following season. Although the Yankees lasted only a couple of years, Grange stayed in the NFL until 1934, returning in 1929 to Halas and the Chicago Bears.[23]

When Grange retired, he wrote in a letter to Arch Ward, sports editor of the *Chicago Tribune*, words similar in sentiment to what Zuppke had told Halas years earlier:

> I say that a football player, after three years in college, doesn't know anything about football. Pro football is the difference between the New York Giants baseball team and an amateur nine. College players not only do not know how to play football, but they don't take as much interest in the game as the pros. In college you have studies to make up, lectures to attend, scholastic requirements to satisfy. In pro ball you are free from all this. . . . Pro football is smart. It is so smart you can rarely work the same play twice

with the same results. Competition is keen. There are no set-ups in pro football. The big league player knows *football*, not just a theory or system.[24]

As Grange reached the end of an illustrious college and professional career, the modern NFL was really just beginning. The mid-1930s in many respects were pivotal. Significant rules changes were introduced, most notably legalizing the forward pass from anywhere behind the line of scrimmage. Goal posts were put on the goal lines. And the league was divided into two divisions, leading to a championship playoff under regularized conditions at the end of the season.[25]

In 1935 the league lay the groundwork for introducing the amateur draft to professional sports, to begin in 1936. The first player ever drafted was Jay Berwanger, a quarterback from the University of Chicago, who was the first Heisman award winner. The choice was ironic. Not only did Chicago abandon football not many years thereafter, but Berwanger did not sign.[26] By this time, the NFL was getting a fair share of the top college players, but a number still saw their futures elsewhere. In 1936, as good news for the NFL, no franchise shifts occurred, which had rarely happened up to that point, and all teams played the same number of games.[27]

As discussed in Chapter 1, television has been kind to the NFL. Although it was hardly auspicious at the time, the first telecast of an NFL game was in 1939. The National Broadcasting Company beamed a game between the Brooklyn Dodgers and the Philadelphia Eagles from Ebbets field in Brooklyn. Only a handful of sets in New York City existed to pick up the game, but the first of several thousand telecasts had taken place.[28] There is no truth to the rumor that Howard Cosell was there to do the color commentary. The following season, the Mutual Broadcasting System paid $2,500 for the rights to televise the NFL championship, an interesting contrast to today's market, where a single sponsor pays $1 million for a thirty-second spot during a championship game.[29]

World War II caused disruptions: Rosters were reduced, and substitute players had to be found. In 1943 the Cleveland (later L.A.) Rams were allowed to suspend operations because their owners were in the service. By war's end, 638 players had served in the armed forces; twenty-one had died.[30]

Following the war, attendance and television revenues rapidly increased: Average attendance at regular season games exceeded 30,000 by 1947 and over 40,000 by 1958.[31] Since 1950 only one NFL franchise, the Dallas Texans, has failed. This team should not be confused with the Dallas Texans of early American Football League (AFL), which later became the Kansas City Chiefs. These NFL Texans were the Boston Yanks from 1944 to 1948, the New York Bulldogs in 1949, the New York Yanks from 1950 to 1951, and, finally, the Dallas Texans in 1952. The Texans' move to Texas largely was unheralded, and the episode is noteworthy only because it was the last failing NFL franchise not rescued by another buyer.[32]

The Los Angeles Rams became the first NFL team to televise all its games, for a fee of $307,000.[33] Though this experiment was abandoned when attendance dropped, precedent was set, leading to expanded television coverage with only the home viewing area blacked out. It also had the NFL in court as early as 1953 over its television and radio policies. Protection of the home gate was established firmly in *United States v. NFL*,[34] and it had continued, with modification, to the present.

By 1955 NBC was paying $100,000 to televise the title game,[35] a fortyfold increase over a relatively short time. When Congress granted antitrust immunity to the NFL to enter television contracts with networks on a leaguewide basis — despite a federal district court holding[36] that this would violate the earlier *United States v. NFL* decree — television and football became inseparable. It was also clear that others, both players and rival leagues, would attempt to get in on the action.

Competitor Leagues

The National Football League has been challenged by seven rival leagues. Four of the first five styled themselves by the same name, the American Football League, and the holdout in the first five (the fourth in the sequence) was barely more original; this was the All America Football Conference. Not until the 1970s (World Football League) and the 1980s (United States Football League) did creativity, in team names at least, take hold.

The first three American Football Leagues are little more than historical footnotes. The initial venture, mentioned earlier, was started by C. C. Pyle when the NFL would not admit him, his New York Yankees, and Red Grange. The league lasted a year, with only the Yankees surviving to join the NFL. The next two American Football Leagues did little better. Although each survived two years (1936–37 and 1940–41), neither produced any lasting franchises or memories. The latter league's timing was particularly poor, since World War II ended any chance it had to survive.[37]

At the conclusion of World War II came the fourth rival — the All-America Football Conference. The end of the war generated heightened interests in all of sports. The Mexican League bloomed briefly to challenge the majors in baseball,[38] and the Basketball Association of America, later to be called the National Basketball Association, was formed.[39] Both, along with the AAFC, started in 1946.

The AAFC was not a total failure. It played through four seasons, and three of its teams survived, joining the NFL for the 1950 season. All three — the Cleveland Browns, San Francisco 49ers, and Baltimore Colts — enjoyed periods of substantial success after joining the older league. It is of interest that, when the NFL and the 1960s AFL at length merged, two of the old AAFC teams (Cleveland and Baltimore) agreed to move over to the American Football Conference to balance the number of teams.

The AAFC produced fine players in its short tenure, including Otto Graham, Frankie Albert, George Ratterman, Y.A. Tittle, Joe Perry, and Lou Groza. The all-time rushing leader in the AAFC also has the distinction as the first black in a major professional sport league in the modern era. Marion Motley played all four years of the league's existence, rushing for 3,024 yards and scoring twenty-six touchdowns.[40]

Legally, however, the outstanding player from the AAFC was George Radovich. It was his later blacklisting by the NFL that led to the seminal case, discussed in Chapter 2, holding the NFL and, in essence, all professional sports leagues except baseball subject to the federal antitrust laws.[41]

The last American Football League, which began play in 1960, has been of course the most successful challenger to the dominance of the NFL. The new league immediately secured a network television contract with NBC, a move crucial to its survival. One of the AFL's first acts was to initiate an unsuccessful antitrust action, *AFL v. NFL*,[42] charging the established league with predatory practices in preying on cities that otherwise would have been sites of AFL franchises. Though the action failed, it served notice that the AFL was not to be taken lightly.

A number of players, both currently in the NFL and prized collegians, became involved in tugs of war between the two leagues. Several important lawsuits resulted, with a slight advantage going to the AFL.[43] In total, though the AFL was never far from the edge of financial defeat, it persisted long enough to convince the NFL that merger was desirable. This occurred when both camps sought congressional exemption from the merger prohibitions embedded in the federal antitrust laws. In maneuverings worthy of master politicians, the merger was obtained.[44] And the two leagues could come up with what some consider the greatest show on earth—the Superbowl.

Within only a few years, another group announced formation of the World Football League. The new league was woefully undercapitalized and almost from its first games exhibited dire financial trouble. Missed payrolls became routine. Not surprisingly, the league folded early in its second season. Only the Memphis Grizzlies and a couple of other franchises retained any semblance of viability. These teams combined, on paper, to form one entity and petitioned for admission to the NFL. The request was denied, leading to antitrust litigation. However, the NFL established in court its ability to pick and choose who should join its ranks.[45] Although there were a couple of other cases where the NFL or its clubs' exclusionary policies were overturned,[46] and one case where an attack on the WFL's attempts to sign NFL players failed,[47] in general the NFL won as many legal fights with the upstart league as it lost.[48] Of course, in the final victory—survival—the NFL was the undisputed champion.

The United States Football League announced it was opening for business in 1983. It did so with a couple of new wrinkles. One, it was to be a spring football league, culminating in a championship game in early July. Two, it would hold down payrolls, except that each team could pursue one or two stars from the college or pro ranks. By everyone's consensus, one target was bound to be Heisman Trophy winner, Herschel Walker.

On February 17, 1983, Herschel Walker, star running back of the University of Georgia Bulldogs, signed a contract to play for the New Jersey Generals of the USFL for an estimated $3.9 million for three years.[49] The contract represented the largest ever awarded a professional athlete directly out of college and the largest ever given to a professional football player.[50]

Initial reports as to whether a contract had been formed were conflicting. As an underclassman with one year remaining to his college eligibility, Walker was ineligible to negotiate a professional contract under both USFL and NFL rules.[51] Sources close to the negotiations said, however, that Jack Manton, an attorney acting as Walker's agent, initiated contract talks with the New Jersey Generals.[52] Reportedly, Walker signed with the agreement that he would have a twenty-four-hour grace period to change his mind.[53] According to these sources, Walker called off the deal a few hours later.[54] Even with this change of heart, however, if the reports were true, Walker was in violation of NCAA rules that forbid negotiations with professional teams and make the player no longer eligible to play college football if he negotiates.[55]

Though USFL rules forbid negotiations with college undergraduates, the USFL owners were willing to make a one-time exception because of Herschel Walker's importance to the fledgling league.[56] Chet Simmons, president of the USFL, also stated that, faced with lawsuits based on the league's denying a person the right to make a living, he considered it fruitless to challenge the arrangements made by Walker with the Generals.[57] The USFL made other inroads in obtaining college stars who would otherwise have played for the NFL. According to Dick Steinberg, New England Patriots director of players' development, the USFL signed seven players in 1983 that would have been selected in the top two rounds of the NFL draft.[58] By the second year the USFL was successful in acquiring approximately two dozen college players who would have been picked in the first three rounds in the NFL draft. The USFL also helped itself by obtaining quarterbacks from five NFL clubs.

More unsettling to the NFL was the Boston Breakers' signing of Dan Ross, even though he was still under contract with the Cincinnati Bengals.[59] Under his contract with the Breakers, Ross would complete his season with the Bengals and proceed to the Breakers thereafter.[60] Though prior to Ross's signing the USFL had taken a handful of NFL players, Ross was the first signed as a "future" and by far the best NFL player to cross over to the new league.[61]

The USFL was the principal topic of discussion when the NFL owners met in Palm Springs in late March 1983. Of great concern was the proposal by Ed DeBartolo, owner of the San Francisco 49ers, to purchase the Pittsburgh franchise in the USFL.[62] In their March 22 meeting, described as one of the most heated sessions NFL owners had had in years, twelve owners spoke against the purchase.[63]

On March 24, 1983, the owners agreed to continue their policy of not draft-ing underclassmen.[64] They agreed, however, to shorten the draft selection period to a single day to prevent USFL teams from approaching players not drafted in the initial rounds and from encouraging them to join the USFL.[65]

The NFL has also been successful in luring players under contract with the USFL. The San Diego Chargers became the first NFL team to raid a player from the rival USFL by signing Gary Anderson of the Tampa Bay Bandits on August 4, 1983.[66] In seeking an injunction against the Bandits from enforcing its contract, Anderson alleged that his agent, Jerry Argovitz, conspired to deliver him to the USFL so that Argovitz could receive a USFL franchise.[67] A U.S. District Court in Michigan also rescinded a contract between Billy Sims, Star running back with the Detroit Lions and the Houston Gamblers, made on July 1, 1983.[68] In his opinion Judge DeMascio held that Sims's agent, the same Jerry Argovitz, now a co-owner of the Houston Gamblers, breached his fiduciary duty to Sims when he negotiated a contract with the Gamblers.[69] The Court found that Argovitz's interest in the Gamblers led him to improper representation of Sims in negotia-tions with the Lions.[70] The Court found that Argovitz misrepresented the Lions' position to Sims in the negotiations and that Argovitz failed to secure the best offer he could from the Lions to encourage Sims to sign with the Gamblers.[71]

Despite such setbacks as the *Sims* case, the USFL clubs prevailed in other instances, such as where the Buffalo Bills of the NFL unsuccessfully sought to retain their running back, Joe Cribbs, under a right of first refusal. The court held that the right applied only to prevent Cribbs from moving to another NFL team and did not prevent his jumping to the USFL.[72] In addition to this legal victory, a publicity coup was scored when the USFL's Los Angeles Express signed Steve Young, of Brigham Young University and runner-up in the Heis-man Trophy voting, to a long-term, reported $40 million contract.[73] This came on the heels of the USFL's Pittsburgh Maulers' signing the Heisman winner him-self, Mike Rozier.[74] Clearly, the USFL was successful in luring some of the top names in the college ranks and a few of the established stars in the NFL. It was at a substantial price.

Within a few months, the salaries paid these players began to take their toll. Craig James of Southern Methodist University was signed to a multiyear con-tract by Washington of the USFL at over $700,000 a year. Hurt most of his rookie season, James was waived out of the league and signed with the New England Patriots at far lesser sums. He performed credibly for the Patriots during the 1984 NFL season. Mike Rozier and Pittsburgh virtually came to a parting of the ways. And the Los Angeles Express, which had doled out the huge sums to Young, was clearly in dire financial straits. In 1985, the USFL succeeded in signing Heisman winner Doug Flutie, but he was the only college player of notable stature to go with the new league for the 1985 season.

With such problems, the USFL determined to switch, then fight. The owners, although badly divided, voted to change to a fall schedule beginning in 1985.[75] A few weeks later, in November 1984, the USFL filed a $1.3 billion lawsuit against the NFL, alleging antitrust restraints by the NFL, particularly in the NFL's allegedly influencing the television networks not to deal with the USFL over any fall TV contracts.[76] The response by the NFL was that the legal action signified only that the USFL was in its waning days.[77]

In the meantime, the USFL players moved toward unionization. In a 1983 vote, two unions vied for the players' votes and neither obtained a majority, though the one backed by the NFLPA came within a few votes.[78] In 1984 the players approved the petition by the NFLPA to form the USFL Players' Association (USFLPA) with its own president and board of directors. Approved overwhelmingly by a 732 to 25 margin, the new USFLPA would be a part of the Federation of Professional Athletes.[79] Shortly after its certification, not accomplished without a fight, as described later in this chapter, the two sides set about attempting to negotiate a collective bargaining agreement. The process was a slow one, harkening back to the early troubles that the NFLPA had had with its leagues.

Origins of NFLPA

Although players' associations are now considered unions, achieving that recognition was a struggle. In the late 1950s, sports leagues other than baseball still had hopes of obtaining exemption from the antitrust laws. To improve its bargaining position, the NFL commissioner, Bert Bell, made the following statement to a House subcommittee:

> Accordingly, in keeping with my assurance that we would do whatever you gentlemen consider to be in the best interest of the public, on behalf of the National Football League, I hereby recognize the National Football League Players Association and I am prepared to negotiate immediately with the representative of that association concerning any differences between the players and the clubs that may exist. This will include the provisions of our bylaws and the standard players' contract which have been questioned by members of this committee.[80]

Despite the assurances given to the subcommittee in 1958, it was ten years before the NFL's first collective bargaining agreement. Once removed from Congress, Bell and his successor, Pete Rozelle, did not seem as willing to bargain as Bell had indicated. The players and their lawyers were also responsible, in part, for this delay. These individuals were afraid to declare that their organizations were unions. Creighton Miller, long-time counsel for the NFL Players' Association, generally resisted the union label.[81]

The NFLPA officially formed in 1956. After the rival American Football League began play, its players within a couple of years, in 1963, also organized, starting the AFLPA. As separate entities, the two unions pressed for collective bargaining within their respective leagues. The NFLPA experienced minimal success, despite Bell's statement to Congress. From 1956 to 1967 little progress was made toward reaching an overall agreement, though a small pension fund and some insurance coverage were established. In 1968 a breakdown in NFL negotiations led to the first full-scale, leaguewide strike in professional sports.[82] At issue was the owners' contribution to the pension fund. This contribution was the sole issue preventing the first collective agreement in football, and negotiations became difficult and heated. After reaching an impasse in negotiations, the players boycotted the preseason training camps. The owners retaliated with a lockout.

In the meantime, a memorandum of agreement was reached in the AFL between management and the union without any concerted outside action such as a lockout or strike. However, subsequent disagreements arose over the memo, and in fact the NFLPA reached accord with its league's owners before the AFLPA did. In 1970, after the NFL and AFL officially merged, the two unions likewise merged.

They merged just in time for the next round of collective bargaining negotiations, and here the newly combined union found itself facing a recognition problem from the league. Ed Garvey, executive director of the NFLPA, testified before a congressional special committee that the sixteen-club NFL had been the only employer signatory to the first collective bargaining agreement in 1968. In 1970, however, the owners refused to negotiate unless the NFLPA agreed to amend its certification petition by deleting the league as a joint employer. This refusal eventually resulted in the creation of the National Football League Management Council. Even this did not prevent a later breakdown in the negotiations, resulting in first a short lockout, then strike. It was not a long or bitter strike, but the boycott and resulting lockout influenced the parties' willingness to resume talks and reach an agreement. As a result, the NFLPA, as merged with the AFLPA, was recognized as the exclusive bargaining representative.[83]

In 1974, however, a football strike was definitely a failure—and nearly a disaster. The collective bargaining agreement had expired, and the owners and players were far apart, particularly over any changes in player mobility rules. The players voted to strike, and most of them did strike. Rookies were urged not to report to training camps, but many reported. Other aspiring professional players arrived on the scene and were labeled "scabs" by the striking players. Public sentiment was definitely antiplayer. The players' position weakened daily as more relinquished the fight and reported to preseason camp. After forty-four days, the strike ended in a whimper, and all players returned to camp under a fourteen-day moratorium that became moot when the players decided not to resume the strike at the end of the period.[84]

The union had suffered defeat; its members were in disarray. If the players through the union had not initiated a second line of attack, the union movement in football would have died. Although dissension racked the players' association, it still had the antitrust weapon. The decision in *Kapp v. NFL*[85] held early promise but was so diffuse that its ultimate effects were uncertain. This diffusion did not exist in *Mackey v. NFL*[86] and its companion case, *Alexander v. NFL*.[87] After an extended trial, the players scored an important triumph in *Mackey* and scored again in *Alexander*. The direct result of these cases was a multimillion dollar cash settlement[88] and the owners' promise to negotiate a new collective bargaining agreement.

COLLECTIVE BARGAINING AND THE
ANTITRUST LABOR EXEMPTION

The historical context for antitrust litigation in sports is considerably different than it has been for other industries. In industrial relations, the courts used the antitrust laws as a repressive weapon to thwart trade union organizations and their collective bargaining goals.[89] In contrast, trade unions or players' associations in professional sports have benefitted from the modern labor/antitrust cases. Despite the legal restraints otherwise imposed on the union, the courts have provided athletes an advantage in gaining credibility at the bargaining table and negotiating effectively over player mobility issues.

Background Cases

The antitrust cases begin with *United States v. Hutcheson*,[90] in which the U.S. Supreme Court held that if a union acts in its own "self interest" and does not combine with nonlabor groups, its conduct is immunized from antitrust liability.[91] This provision is the so-called statutory exemption to antitrust liability. Under this exemption, the Court invoked the policies of other modern labor legislation, such as the Clayton Antitrust Act[92] and the Norris-LaGuardia Act,[93] to interpret antitrust legislation in a manner compatible with some aspects of contemporary trade union behavior.[94] The Court thought that the *Hutcheson* rule would reconcile the competing policies of the statutes involved and concentrated on the antitrust laws, which prohibit practices designed to suppress or eliminate competition between firms, and the labor laws, which promote freedom of association among workers to foster the collective bargaining process and to remove labor cost competition between firms.[95]

In *Allen Bradley Co. v. IBEW, Local 3*,[96] the Court held that union/employer agreements aimed at boycotting unorganized local contractors and manufacturers and at barring the importation of equipment manufactured outside of the local area[97] were a combination that constituted a conspiracy to monopolize the trade. The Court noted that the labor and antitrust statutes sometimes promoted separate and competing policies. The policy of preserving a competitive business economy, for example, may conflict with the policy of preserving the "right of labor to organize to better its conditions through the agency of collective bargaining."[98] In *Allen Bradley*, the unlawful conspiracy was between labor and nonlabor groups and was aimed at controlling the market of goods and services.[99]

The next two major decisions, in 1965, represent the so-called nonstatutory exemption of antitrust liability where the union, through an agreement with an employer group, attempts to promote its interests and, in so doing, induces restraints in a product market. The first case was *UMW v. Pennington*,[100] in which a coal company cross-claimed in a suit by the trustees of the Welfare and Retirement Fund to recover royalty payments owed under the agreement. The cross-claim alleged an unlawful conspiracy between the UMW Welfare and Retirement Fund trustees and the large coal operators to violate the antitrust laws. The argument, essentially, was that the union agreed with the large coal operators to abandon its established stand against mechanized equipment and technological innovation in the mines in exchange for higher wages and royalty payments.[101] The union allegedly imposed a wage and benefit package that smaller operators could not meet. It was further alleged that the union engaged in a collusive bargaining agreement designed to drive such operators from the market.[102]

Justice White, writing for two other justices,[103] noted that national labor law sanctioned multiemployer bargaining. Such bargaining was held not to violate the antitrust laws in that a union might "as a matter of its own policy and not by agreement with all or part of the employers of that unit, seek the same wages from other employers."[104] Justice White, in contrast to Justice Goldberg's position in his separate opinion,[105] rejected the view that an agreement was immunized because its subject matter constituted a mandatory subject of bargaining for labor and management under the National Labor Relations Act (NLRA).[106] Despite the mandatory nature of the issues, the nonstatutory exemption would not prevail where the resulting agreement imposed terms on small employers that revealed the "predatory" intent of unions and large employers to injure the small employers. Additionally, if the agreement interfered with the union's ability to act in its self-interest,[107] it was unlawful. The *Allen Bradley* and *Pennington* cases dramatize a single, recurrent theme in sports cases. There is great judicial concern about possible injury to a third party not immediately involved in the union/employer relationship.

The second 1965 Supreme Court decision, *Amalgamated Meat Cutters, Local 189 v. Jewel Tea Co.*,[108] indicated that public injury due to product restraints could give rise to antitrust liability when trade unions negotiated such restraints. In *Jewel Tea*, an employer refused to sign a multiemployer collective bargaining agreement that litigated the number of hours per day that meat could be sold.

The Court, in finding no antitrust liability, weighed the legitimacy of the union's claim that the impact of the subject matter on employment opportunities significantly affected its members against the argument that the union's demands restrained product consumption and thus injured a third party. Because the union's interest in protecting its members' employment opportunities was "immediate" and "legitimate," the labor exemption was deemed applicable and immunized the union from antitrust liability. The third party in *Jewel Tea* was the consuming public, which could not purchase goods at convenient hours. In the sports case, the injured party is either the player, a competing league that is injured in its ability to attract players, or the consuming public. The peculiar relevance of *Jewel Tea* to the sports cases is best seen by reference to leading cases involving league-imposed restraints on player mobility.[109] Another important theme in *Pennington, Jewel Tea*, and their anticedents[110] is the statutory exemption,[111] which concerns a union's self-interest as a prerequisite to antitrust immunity. In *Jewel Tea*, the Court attempted to define self-interest. When the agreement is "intimately related to wages, hours, and working conditions"[112] and the union members' concern is "immediate and direct,"[113] an agreement "pursuant to what the labor unions deemed to be in their own labor union interests"[114] is appropriate.

The Sports Cases

The most important of the modern sport-labor cases is *Mackey v. NFL*.[115] Judge Larson, the trial judge in that case, concluded that the Rozelle Rule was an illegal combination or conspiracy and restraint of trade in violation of antitrust law and thus denied professional football players the right to contract freely for their services.[116] The Rozelle Rule permitted a player whose contractual obligation to a team expired to sign with a different club. The signing club was required, however, to compensate the player's former team. If the two clubs did not reach a satisfactory agreement, the commissioner had discretion to award compensation in the form of players or draft choices.[117] The gravamen of the *Mackey* complaint was that the unbridled discretion of the commissioner thwarted the free movement of players between teams in the NFL.

The district judge held that the Rozelle Rule constituted a form of group boycott or a refusal to deal with players—a per se violation of the antitrust laws.[118] The court also focused on the NFL's contention that the Rozelle Rule was part of the collective bargaining agreement and thus a labor exemption to the antitrust laws. In rejecting this contention, Judge Larson stated that the labor exemption was aimed at the collective bargaining process, which had not operated with regard to the Rozelle Rule. Stressing this point, Judge Larson noted that the NFL was a "weak union" when the first collective bargaining agreements were negotiated and, consequently, that no genuine collective bargaining had occurred.[119]

The Eighth Circuit Court of Appeals took a slightly different approach. That court rejected the NFLPA's argument that only employee groups were entitled to the labor exemption and that the defendant-owners therefore could not use the exemption to shield their behavior.[120] The court stated that

> Since the basis of the non-statutory exemption is the national policy of favoring collective bargaining, and since the exemption extends to agreements, the benefits of the exemption logically extend to both parties to the agreement. Accordingly, under appropriate circumstances, we find that a non-labor group may avail itself of a labor exemption.[121]

With regard to the labor exemption, the court noted that the parties bargained collectively over the Rozelle Rule. The owners relied on this fact to assert their immunity from antitrust liability. On the other hand, the plaintiff-players' association contended that the Rozelle Rule resulted from the clubs' unilateral action and that defendants therefore could not assert a "colorable claim of exemption." The court noted that there had been "little discussion" concerning the Rozelle Rule and that both sides failed to assert "concrete proposals."[122]

The players' bargaining representative attributed the failure to pursue modification of the negotiations to the fact that "negotiations have bogged down on other issues and the union was not strong enough to persist."[123] Nonetheless, the 1968 agreement incorporated by reference the NFL constitution and bylaws, of which the Rozelle Rule was a part. The agreement also explicitly provided that free-agent rules were not to be amended during its term. In the negotiations prior to the 1970 agreement, the players' association deliberately determined not to make the Rozelle Rule an issue. As noted above, there was limited discussion regarding the Rozelle Rule, although the agreement contained a "zipper" or "integration" clause that stated that "this Agreement represents a complete and final understanding on all bargainable subjects of negotiation among the parties during the term of this Agreement."[124]

By the commencement of the *Mackey* litigation, the 1970 agreement had expired. The Eighth Circuit noted that the players' association, "[s]ince the beginning of the 1974 negotiations . . . , [had] consistently supported the elimination of the Rozelle Rule. The NFLPA and the clubs have engaged in substantial bargaining over that issue but have not reached an accord."[125] The court reduced certain principles governing the "proper accommodation of the competing labor and antitrust interests involved here."[126] The court stated that

> We find the proper accommodation to be: First, the labor policy favoring collective eminence over the antitrust laws where the restraint on trade primarily only affects the parties to the collective bargaining relationship. . . . Second, federal labor policy is implicated sufficiently to prevail only where the agreement sought to be exempted concerns a mandatory subject of bargaining. . . . Finally, the policy favoring collective bargaining is furthered to the necessary degree to override the antitrust laws only where the agreement sought to be exempted is the product of bona fide arm's-length bargaining.[127]

The court rejected the district court's conclusion that the Rozelle Rule was a nonmandatory and illegal subject of bargaining.[128] The court noted that although the rule concerned interteam compensation, rather than "wages, hours, and other terms or conditions of employment," the district court found that rhe rule's effect was to restrict the player's ability to move from one team to another and [to depress] player salaries."[129] The court concluded that "Accordingly, we hold that the Rozelle Rule constitutes a mandatory bargaining subject within the meaning of the National Labor Relations Act."[130]

The court observed that the collective bargaining agreement not only referred to the issues in dispute but also contained a zipper (integration) clause, which presumably precluded any further bargaining during the contract period. The court further observed that there was no bona fide arm's-length bargaining; the provisions of the Rozelle Rule, unchanged since their unilateral promulgation, did not "insure to the benefit of the players or the union";[131] and finally, no "indirect benefit" could be found on the ground that the Rozelle Rule was a quid pro quo for pension benefits and the right to negotiate salaries individually.[132]

The circuit court, changing direction slightly, rejected the district court's conclusion that such a group boycott constituted a per se violation and adopted the rule of reason liability test. In so doing, the court expressed its view that the parties could avail themselves of the nonstatutory labor exemption when their collective bargaining agreement covered the controverted mandatory subjects of bargaining. The agreement was not the product of "bona fide arm's-length negotiations" and thus the nonstatutory exemption protection was not available.[133] The court stated that

> It may be that some reasonable restrictions relating to player transfers are necessary to the successful operation of the NFL. The protection of mutual interest of both the players and the clubs may indeed require this. We encourage the parties to resolve this question through collective bargaining. The parties are far better situated to agreeably resolve what rules governing player transfers are best suited for their mutual interests out of court. . . . However, no mutual resolution of this issue appears within the present record. Therefore, the Rozelle Rule, as it is presently implemented, must be set aside as an unreasonable restraint of trade.[134]

Prior to the Eighth Circuit's *Mackey* decision, the District Court for the District of Columbia, in *Smith v. Pro-Football*,[135] held that the draft system of allocating prospective professional football players to the clubs violated the antitrust laws and was not protected by the labor exemption. At the time this case was decided, the mechanics of the NFL draft provided that the team with the worst winning percentage chose first. Every team had one choice in each of the seventeen rounds of the annual draft. No team could negotiate with a player drafted by another team. As the court found in *Smith*, the "net result" was a series of restraints contained in the NFL constitution and bylaws that suggested that "if the player [could] not reach a satisfactory agreement with the team holding the rights to his services he [could] not play in the NFL."[136]

In *Smith* the district court noted the defendant's argument that the NFL draft was a mandatory subject of bargaining between the parties and, therefore, was immune from antitrust liability. The court correctly analyzed the labor/ antitrust cases as providing "no support whatever for the league's argument that arrangements related to mandatory subjects of collective bargaining, prior to their embodiment in an agreement, fall within the exemption merely because they related to mandatory subjects."[137] Indeed, as demonstrated earlier, the cases do not support this view, even when the subject matter is outlined in a collective agreement.[138] The court also concluded that the "unfettered" operation of the collective bargaining process is a prerequisite to the labor exemption: "[A] scheme advantageous to employers and otherwise in violation of the antitrust laws cannot under any circumstances come within the exemption unless and until it becomes part of a collective bargaining agreement negotiated by a union in its own self-interest."[139] The court noted that the draft was instituted prior to the time the association entered into a collective bargaining agreement. Since the plaintiff was drafted before the union's recognition agreement was in effect, the plaintiff's cause of action accrued before any exemption could dispose of his case.[140]

Despite the narrowness of the *Smith* holding, the court's discussion of the labor exemption, though dictum, is important. The court's position was that the subject matter must constitute a mandatory bargaining subject within the meaning of the NLRA.[141] The court referred to a Supreme Court case that established the propriety of mechanisms such as the hiring hall[142] for allocating employment opportunities among bargaining unit employees. The court also examined the similar role that seniority plays in collective bargaining agreements for industrial unions.[143] The court concluded that "each feature" of the draft would be considered a term or condition of employment. "It is clear that the union and the teams could collectively bargain in monetary compensation, benefits, incentives and guarantees to be paid to first year players as mandatory subjects."[144] The test, according to Judge Bryant, was whether the decision implemented with regard to mandatory bargaining subjects was "arrived at as a result of genuine, arms length bargaining and not . . . 'thrust upon' a weak players union by the owners."[145] The court complicated the analysis by stating that the agreement not be at the "behest" of nonlabor groups.[146] The court thought that the agreements at issue, unlike those in the major Supreme Court cases, operated solely to the employees' disadvantage. In the court's view, the employees were not "parties" to the agreement.

In declaring the draft a violation of antitrust law, the court also addressed the owners' arguments that competitive balance could not be obtained without the draft system and with a free market for player talent, the current balance would be "irretrievably destroyed" as players migrated to the richest teams and most glamorous cities.[147] The court found the evidence on this point "equivocal." On the one hand, a free market might indeed allow the wealthiest owners to purchase most of the player talent and cause the glamour of a particular city to attract a player to that city's team.[148] On the other hand, the court noted that many other factors were involved in a player's choice of location. The court stated that

> [the defendants] were unable to produce any credible evidence of a significant correlation between the opportunity to draft early in the draft . . . and improvement in team performance. In fact, the defendant's evidence in this regard indicates a correlation too low to be regarded as supporting their claim that the draft is essential to the survival of the league. For example, despite the existence of all the league's restraints on player movement, in the last three seasons, nine teams have captured 22 of the 24 spots available in the playoffs leading to the Super Bowl. This shows neither competitive balance in division races nor effectiveness of drafting by early-selecting teams.[149]

The court also declared that no "experiential" evidence existed

> to substantiate the owner's claim that in the absence of player movement restriction the best players would move to the small group of teams offering money, glamour, and success. Indeed the little empirical evidence available with regard to the movement of free agents and former World Football League players since the 1975 season ended does not show any such trend.[150]

The court concluded that the current system could not be protected by the rule of reason, since there were "significantly" fewer restrictive alternatives available.[151]

The Court of Appeals for the District of Columbia affirmed, with one member of the panel dissenting.[152] The appellate court, however, did not adopt all of the lower court's rationale. The appellate court concluded that the draft differed from a classic group boycott in that the plaintiff, an injured NFL draftee, was not a competitor or potential competitor for the NFL clubs' product market.[153] Accordingly, the draft could not be regarded as a per se antitrust violation.[154] The belief that the factors involved in the draft's formulation were beyond judicial expertise buttressed the court's view that the rule of reason should govern when considering the draft's compatibility with antitrust law.

On this basis, the court ruled that the trial judge's findings of fact should not be disturbed.[155] Judge Wilkey, writing for the majority, maintained that the draft had an anticompetitive effect that stripped college players of the opportunity to market their talents.[156] The NFL's contention that the need for competitive balance among the teams justified the draft was rejected on the ground that it affected not only the best players but also average players "who were, in a sense, fungible commodities."[157] The players, however, still could negotiate with only one team and might not play if they failed to reach agreement. Judge

Wilkey expressed no view on the labor exemption issue, which was not central to the outcome of the case.

The *Mackey* and *Smith* cases are of more than historical interest. The collective impact of these cases has been vital to the structure and processes of labor/management relations in the sports industry. While sports leagues have not seen the last of antitrust litigation involving the labor exemption, the players can no longer expect to achieve uniformly favorable results in such cases.[158] The *Mackey* and *Smith* courts were willing to invoke the labor exemption because the cases involved mandatory subjects of bargaining within the meaning of the NLRA. This characterization of the issues is appropriate given the ultimate relationship between the reserve and option clauses on one side and the wages and other income provisions on the other. The more restrictive the clauses, the more depressed the players' salary market. The proposition that a mandatory subject of bargaining is a prerequisite to the labor exemption, however, seems to be ill-founded. The Supreme Court has considered this issue relevant to the exemption question but has left open the possibility that legal nonmandatory subjects, which would have only a remote impact on the product market, might also qualify for antitrust immunity under the exception.[159]

In any event, whether the drafting of college or amateur players should be a mandatory bargaining subject is a more difficult problem because the individuals affected are outside the bargaining units. These individuals are, at the time of the bargain, applicants or potential applicants rather than members of the association or union. The economic impact of such players on the salary structure of veteran players is considerable. Rules increasing the bargaining power of draftees necessarily create upward pressure on salaries for all players in the bargaining unit.[160] As others have suggested, bargaining on these issues is analogous to bargaining about a hiring hall,[161] inasmuch as the procedure controls who enters the bargaining unit.

In this context, it is possible to analogize to the Supreme Court's holding that an employer may be refusing unlawfully to bargain by not discussing the contracting out of work from a bargaining unit. The rationale is that an intimate relationship exists between the contracting out of work and the conditions of employment in the bargaining unit.[162]

The problems of the duty of fair representation, while more complex for unions negotiating for nonunit employees, apparently can be solved. Justice Brennan, speaking for the Court in *Allied Chemical & Alkali Workers, Local 1 v. Pittsburgh Plate Glass Co.,*[163] stated that federal law "does not require a union affirmatively to represent non-bargaining unit members or to take into account their interests in making bona fide economic decisions on behalf of those whom it does not represent."[164] The Court concluded, however, that the relationship between incumbent employees and those individuals who had retired permanently from the bargaining unit was not sufficiently intimate to render pension and other retiree benefits a mandatory subject of bargaining within the NLRA's meaning. The Court refused to create any "affirmative" obligation.[165] In the draft case, no question of the duty to bargain is likely to arise because professional sports owners will now have a substantial incentive to negotiate with the associations. By virtue of their need to grasp firmly the labor exemption to avoid antitrust liability, negotiation on the subject would be a sine qua non for any collective bargaining agreement.

The troublesome part of the *Mackey* and *Smith* rationale is the so-called arm's-length or bona fide bargaining requirement. Judge Bryant and Judge Larson, the trial judges who presided in the two cases, attempted to measure the strength of the union that negotiated the contract. While the proposition that the clause in question was "thrust" upon a "weak union" was avoided studiously by the Eighth Circuit, both courts adopted similar approaches.[166] All these approaches are predicated on a misunderstanding of federal labor law policy and the realities of the collective bargaining process.

The failure of a union or employer to discuss, bargain, or do more than acquiesce to an established practice concerning a mandatory subject of bargaining generally has limited practical or legal significance. In *Mackey*, the parties negotiated a zipper clause as part of the collective bargaining agreement. This clause waived the union's right to bargain over any negotiable item.[167] To be sure, such clauses do not waive the right to bargain when management engages in unilateral conduct that alters existing employment conditions during the term of an agreement.[168] A more practical waiver aimed at the precise subject matter under dispute is required under such circumstances. This particular waiver requirement contrasts with *Mackey*, where the employer adhered to the status quo and the players sought the changes. Quite clearly, the union in *Mackey* waived its rights to bargain over the Rozelle Rule. The union's ability to extract concessions was limited so severely that it was willing to waive its right on all issues that it was not able to effectively address at the bargaining table.[169] The search for an arm's-length or bona fide bargain—or indeed any inquiry aimed at determining whether the union actually received its quid pro quo for the concession of the player mobility issues—ignores the reality that the quid pro quo exists only in the general sense expressed in the zipper clause. If the union had not negotiated the zipper clause and relinquished bargaining rights, it might not have had a collective bargaining agreement at all.

The heart of this phenomenon is obviously union restraint. Any rule that requires a bona fide or arm's-length bargain different from what the players achieved in *Mackey* is a rescue mission aimed at propping up a weak union (which has contractual provisions thrust upon it that it does not view to be in its self-interest). A quid pro quo for a concession on a particular issue or group of issues is not a prerequisite to good-faith bargaining under the NLRA. The Eighth Circuit adopted, in effect, a test that considered the strength or weakness of the labor organization involved. Under established labor law principles, *Mackey* seems to have been decided wrongly. The case gave needed muscle to the football players' efforts to establish collective bargaining, particularly in the wake of the abortive 1974 strike and subsequent events. The warning that "hard cases made bad law," however, cannot be ignored.

Emanations of *Mackey* were quite evident in the proceedings in *McCourt v. California Sports*.[170] *McCourt* had the added distinction of being the first major sports case to confront the labor exemption when the clause in controversy was specifically incorporated into the National Hockey League's collective bargaining agreement. At issue was what the Sixth Circuit characterized as a "modified Rozelle Rule."[171] This case is discussed at length in Chapter 8. It is noted at this point because of its contrasting style to *Mackey*.

The court in *McCourt* noted that the NHL and the players' association had signed their first collective bargaining agreement that provided that the standard players' contract and bylaws were "fair and reasonable terms of employment." The court stated that the district court, which found no quid pro quo for the relinquishment of free agent status for the players, had failed to take into account

> the well established principle that nothing in the labor law compels either party negotiating over mandatory subjects or collective bargaining to yield on its initial bargaining position. Good faith bargaining is all that is required. That the position of one party on an issue remains unchanged does not mandate the conclusion that there was no collective bargaining over the other issues.[172]

The court recognized that the players' association exerted great pressure at the collective bargaining table in presenting proposals for an alternate reserve system. The association also threatened to strike and to commence antitrust litigation. The Sixth Circuit concluded, however, that the players' association satisfied the arm's-length, bona fide requirement articulated in *Mackey* since it vigorously opposed or "bargained against" the reserve system.

The essential difference between the compensation procedure in *McCourt* and what was declared unlawful in *Mackey* was that a third neutral party, and not the commissioner, determined the compensation. The court's judgment about the procedure was appropriate because the parties focused on that procedure in their negotiations. It was not necessary that the association achieve a specific quid pro quo. The Sixth Circuit correctly viewed self-interest as not simply gaining or extracting specific concessions from the other party at the bargaining table. *Mackey* should have reached the same conclusion.

The disputed matter in *Mackey* was addressed in the collective bargaining agreement, and a zipper clause was negotiated that waived the union's right to bargain in the future on this subject as well as others. This waiver is compatible with modern collective bargaining and reflects a policy and practice that is recognized and promoted in these kinds of labor exemption antitrust cases.[173] A more stringent interpretation of self-interest and furtherance of the collective bargaining process is not in step with the contemporary trade union movement which negotiates collective bargaining agreements in the context of numerous established relationships.[174]

The matter is still not yet entirely resolved. The Eighth Circuit opinion in *Reynolds v. NFL*[175] indicates that there still may be a need for the judicial examination of player mobility under collective bargaining agreements. In *Reynolds* the court considered the allegation that the post-*Mackey* agreement was "more restrictive" than the Rozelle rule. It was noted, however, that almost as many players had played out their options in two years under the collective bargaining agreement's provisions as during eleven years under the Rozelle Rule.[176] *Reynolds* indicates a preference for bestowing the labor exemption on agreements negotiated in the wake of antitrust litigation,[177] but it leaves the door ajar for a case-by-case examination of the nature and effects of certain practices and procedures.

An even more formidable problem can arise in connection with negotiations the second or third time around, particularly when the parties are unable to resolve their differences and agree on a new collective bargaining pact. This delay is hardly an unlikely prospect in football, for example, where the NFLPA is seeking a substantial increase in salary percentage of total revenues[178] and promoting the novelty of wage seniority.[179] There is no obligation to reach a collective bargaining agreement, but only an obligation to intend, in good faith, to consummate such an agreement. The distinction has caused endless litigation and agony for labor law scholars.[180] The philosophy of the statute is at war with the view that collective bargaining agreements or any portion thereof may be imposed on private parties. While contract terms frequently survive the agreement's extirpation,[181] generally the terms may not if the parties reach an impasse in their bargaining. At that point, the employer may unilaterally, over the union's objection, institute an offer not inconsistent with its last position.[182] The issue then would become whether failure to agree waives the employer's protection from antitrust liability. The Eighth Circuit in *Mackey* was careful to note the following: "In view of our holding, we need not decide whether the effect of an agreement extends beyond its formal extirpation date for purposes of a labor exemption."[183]

A rule withdrawing immunity because the previous contract expired before a new agreement was reached is contrary to national labor law. The parties would be forced to enter into a collective bargaining agreement to avoid antitrust sanctions, when labor law is opposed to any such requirement. On the other hand, the employer cannot alter its stance subsequent to an impasse in negotiations and unilaterally impose a package different from what had been on the bargaining table. Such action would be a refusal to bargain and an unfair labor practice by the employer.[184]

While it might be fair to say that the union should "shape" the employer's unilateral imposition of employment conditions, to fashion a requirement that the employer's positions adopt some of the substantive content of the union's proposals would be inconsistent with federal labor law policy. What seems appropriate is that the employer's position emerged from the collective bargaining process. Good faith bargaining must occur, even to the point of impasse, regardless of the lack of substantive influence of the union's proposals in the negotiations. If an impasse occurs and the employer's unilateral terms are offered to the union, the employer should be deemed not to have violated any labor law. A union acceptance is not required to satisfy either the self-interest, bona fide, or arm's-length requirements in the collective agreement. To hold that the labor exemption is not available when the parties fail to renegotiate a contract after good faith bargaining is inconsistent with these principles.

Finally, there remains the situation where two leagues are competing for the same players. If new leagues appeared, a possible though not imminent occurrence, a new round of competition for players' services would ensue. Since player restraints affect parties other than the consuming public, the relevance of *Jewel Tea*[185] is limited in this context. In a one-league sport, the players or the public are assumed to be the product market, but the labor exemption antitrust cases indicate that the agreement will be scrutinized more carefully when third parties are involved. Nonetheless, problems affecting sports leagues' business practices remain, and with the advent of the USFL, further litigation is certain.

MODERN COLLECTIVE BARGAINING

Although the antitrust cases in football have discouraged restrictions on player mobility, the 1977 and 1982 NFL collective bargaining agreements are, ironically, two of the least effective agreements in professional sports on the issue of player mobility. This ineffectiveness begins with draft provisions of the agreement. Football's collective agreement provides that there will be 336 selections with special numbers for expansion teams,[186] or sign with the USFL. This provision attempts to accommodate those players who are not in the superstar category and who can negotiate freely with any team without affecting the competitive balance in the league. The 336 selections, however, funnel most of the viable candidates through the draft procedure and not through free agency. A player who is not signed with the club drafting him may be drafted by another team in an extra round. The only way to escape this provision is to play outside the United States.[187] If a player does not sign after the second round, he then may negotiate with any team without restriction. If a player has signed with a non-NFL team and wants to enter the NFL after two years, the NFL club that originally drafted him has a right of first refusal. Despite the *Yazoo Smith*[188] decision declaring the old draft illegal, the new draft, apparently insulated by the antitrust labor exemption, is far from an open one.

Option years are required for rookie one-year contracts and are permissible in all other instances. Despite the fact that the agreements seems to address a one-year option—the player is to receive 110 percent of the "salary provided in his contract for the previous year"[189] —arbitration award has held that players do not become free agents at the expiration of the option year. The NFLPA contended that the one-year-option interpretation would provide the clubs with a "perpetual option" on the player's service—the same position that was rejected in the *Messersmith* baseball award.[190] The clubs argued successfully that approval of the players' position ignored the detailed contractual language, referred to below, providing for both a right of first refusal and compensation in free agent situations. The arbitrator noted that the players were willing to agree to "restrictions and compensation" as part of an "overall procedure."[191] The arbitrator also noted that the parties had been careful to articulate contractual exceptions to the general rule that teams have both the right of first refusal and compensation if a player seeks to become a free agent.[192]

The most effective NFLPA argument was that the agreement's failure to enumerate in the agreement the compensation available to a player after his option year indicated that the parties did not intend for the team to retain his services. Moreover, with the invalidation of the Rozelle Rule in *Mackey*,[193] an appropriate approach to contract interpretation assumes that any limitations on free agency should be articulated clearly. Since the courts have held these player restrictions invalid absent the antitrust labor exemptions, any ambiguity should be construed in favor of the players. Indeed, in some respects, the association's position in the football option arbitration is more attractive than the baseball players' position in the *Messersmith* case. At the same time, however, the bargaining history of football did not reflect any explicit intention by the parties to confer free-agent status on players whose option year had expired, and the arbitrator refused to assume this duty absent an explicit provision to that effect.

Unlike baseball, any NFL player whose contract expires or who has played out an option year may seek free agency. The player's team, however, may match another team's offer through a right of first refusal. If a team matches the "principal terms" of the offer, a "binding agreement" with the player is created under the collective agreement.[194] (The 1982 negotiations are discussed in Chapter 5, and it seems clear that the NFL players' association was unsuccessful in its basic thrust.) If the right of first refusal is not exercised, the losing team received draft selections as compensation. The desirability of the draft choice is related to the amount of the free agent's offer.

Football players rarely move to new teams under the contractual free-agency procedures. The compensation deters most clubs from entering into serious bidding. As a result, average salaries, approximately $80,000 per year, are considerably lower than those in baseball or basketball. It is difficult, however, to assess the reasons for this differential. A greater number of football players are, in fact, fungible. Football differs from baseball in that a single player is less likely to affect a game's outcome because football is a more team-oriented sport. Moreover, there may not be an adequate economic incentive to sign free agents in football. Unlike baseball and perhaps basketball, it is doubtful that free agency boosts a football club's ticket sales. Even most losing teams are guaranteed a capacity crowd.[195] Consumer demand has made lucrative television and radio contracts available regardless of the presence of free agents and victories. Football enjoys full houses and an equal pay formula national television contract. Free agents in football, therefore, unlike the free agents in baseball, are an expensive and not necessarily attractive commodity.[196]

All of these considerations have led the NFLPA to emphasize demands based on a salary scale and a percentage of gross revenue rather than to address the free-agent issue in connection with the 1982 negotiations.[197] The high salaries paid to rookies apparently have increased the discontent among the rank and file.[198]

Guaranteed Contracts

The leading case dealing with this issue is *National Football League Players' Association v. Dante Pastorini, Jr.*[199] In the *Pastorini* case the quarterback had been under contract to the Oakland Raiders for the 1980 to 1983 seasons because of a trade between Houston and Oakland. Pastorini played with the Raiders until September 1981, when he was placed on waivers and released on the ground that his skill and performance were unsatisfactory. However, Pastorini had a guaranteed contract that obligated the Raiders to pay his salary even if his skill and performance were judged to be unsatisfactory.

Subsequently, Pastorini signed with the Los Angeles Rams, and at that point the Raiders informed Pastorini's attorney that the Raiders were no longer liable for further salary payments. Pastorini was released by the Rams and then played for the Philadelphia Eagles, and the Raiders contended that they were entitled to an offset of Pastorini's earnings during the time that he played with both the Rams and the Eagles against the guarantee set forth in the Raiders' agreement of 1981, 1982, and 1983.

Arbitrator Kagel noted that the wrongful discharge cases that invoke the duty to mitigate as an offset to terminated guaranteed contracts under common law have no applicability because Pastorini was not discharged but waived, as authorized by his contract. The Raiders, despite the waiver, had an obligation to pay. Kagel noted that when the league and management counsel wanted to provide an offset in the NFL player contract form, it had done so in a number of contexts—and it also provided for the termination of injury protection payments when a player signs with another NFL club or elimination of termination pay when the player resigns from another club. Accordingly, Kagel held that under the collective bargaining agreement and individual contract of employment, the Raiders were obligated to pay, but without an offset for payments received from the Rams and Eagles.

A second issue, which as we have seen, has its analog in baseball, relates to the continuation of salary payments during the 1982 stoppage. In this case,[200] as in baseball, the employers invoked the traditional distinction between pay and accrued benefits—the latter being held to be compensation, which the employer can lawfully refuse to award to strikers.

Here Arbitrator Kagel held that players, whether injured or not, could not receive payments under their individual contracts during the term of the strike. This is because the NFL Players' Association had negotiated the so-called Money Now clause, which provided immediate payments as an inducement to have the players return and to compensate them for losses incurred during the stoppage. Kagel rejected the view that the collective agreement, which modified the uniform player contract, could require the payment of both money now and payments to injured players during the strike. Although the union sought to eliminate injured players from the scope of the Money Now payment, Kagel concluded that the union had been unsuccessful in this regard. Accordingly, in contrast to baseball, where no Money Now provisions are negotiated during the strike, injured players receive nothing under their contracts, guaranteed or not, because of the dominance given to the collective agreements provision under the Court's *J. I. Case*[201] decision.

NOTES TO CHAPTER 4

1. F. Menke, The Encyclopedia of Sports 367 (4th ed. 1969) (hereafter cited as Menke).
2. *Id.*
3. A. Danzig, The History of American Football 7 (1956).
4. R. Treat, The Official Encyclopedia of Football 15 (7th ed. 1969) (hereafter cited as Treat).
5. *Id.*
6. G. G. Coulton, Medieval Village, Manor and Monastery 93 (1960).
7. *Id.* at 94.
8. *Id.* at 95.
9. M. Shearman, Football 6 (1904).
10. Knox and Leslie, eds., Miracles of King Henry VII 131 (1923).
11. Treat at 16.
12. Official 1978 National Football League Record Manual 113 (1978) (hereafter NFL Manual).
13. Menke at 427; NFL Manual at 113.
14. NFL Manual at 113.
15. Menke at 427.
16. Treat at 26.
17. *Id.* at 23. *But see* Menke at 427, who relies on 1920 as the official opening year. The difference between the two authors undoubtedly derives from the latter's rejection of the loose 1919 affiliation of clubs as constituting a real league.

    For another account of the early history of professional football, see T. Bennett, D. Boss, J. Campbell, S. Siwoff, R. Smith, and J. Wiebusch,

The NFL's Official Encyclopedic History of Professional Football 10–33 (1977) (hereafter Official History).

18. Treat at 29.
19. *Id.*
20. Menke at 428.
21. NFL Manual at 115–16.
22. *Id.*
23. *Id.*
24. Treat at 66.
25. Menke at 428; NFL Manual at 116.
26. Treat at 68. The second pick in the first draft, one Riley Smith, a quarterback, did sign with Boston and played five years in the NFL. *Id.*
27. NFL Manual at 116.
28. *Id.* at 117.
29. *Id.*
30. *Id.*
31. Menke at 429.
32. Official History at 241.
33. NFL Manual at 119.
34. United States v. NFL, 118 F. Supp. 319 (1953).
35. NFL Manual at 119.
36. United States v. NFL, 196 F. Supp 445 (1961). *See also* 15 U.S.C. §§1291–95 for the statutory authorizations that overcame the obstacles raised by the 1961 opinion in United States v. NFL.
37. *See generally* Treat at 564.
38. The Mexican League is discussed in Chapter 3.
39. The formation and early days of the Basketball Association of America, later the NBA, are discussed in Chapter 7.
40. For further on the All America Football Conference, *see* Treat at 564–68. As to Marion Motley's career rushing records, *see id.* at 566.
41. Radovich v. NFL, 352 U.S. 445 (1957).
42. 323 F.2d 124 (1963).
43. *See, e.g.,* Houston Oilers v. Neely, 361 F. 37 (1966); New York Football Giants v. Los Angeles Chargers Football 291 F. 471 (1961);Detroit Football Club v. Robinson, 186 F. Supp. 933 (1960); Los Angeles Rams v. Cannon, 185 F. Supp. 717 (1960). For a result in favor of an NFL club, at least to the extent of obtaining a remand, *see* Dallas Cowboys Football Club v. Harris, 348 S.W. 2d 27 (Tex. 1961).
44. The authorization for the NFL/AFL merger appears in language now contained in 15 U.S.C. §1291 (1976). Originally part of the Act of Nov. 8, 1966, Pub. L. No. 89–800, §6(b)(1), 80 Stat. 1515, it reads in pertinent part:

> In addition, such laws shall not apply to a joint agreement by which the member clubs of two or more professional football leagues, which are exempt from income tax under section 501(c)(6) of the Internal Revenue Code of 1954 [26 U.S.C. 501(c)(6)] combine their operations in expanded single league so exempt from income tax, if such an agreement increases rather than decreases the number of

professional football clubs so operating, and the provisions of which are directly relevant thereto.

15 U.S.C. §1291 (1976).

When it appeared this authorization might founder if introduced through normal legislative channels, it was appended to an Income Tax Investment Credit bill and presented to Congress through a Conference Committee report. Under this procedure, Congress was forced to either accept the entire bill or reject it. Despite opposition to the merger by certain influential members of Congress, the bill passed. H.R. Rep. No. 2308, 89th Cong., 2d Sess. 4, *reprinted in* [1966] U.S. Code Cong. & Ad. News 4372, 4377-78.

45. Mid-South Grizzlies v. NFL, 720 F.2d 772 (3rd Cir., 1983).

46. *See e.g.,* Hecht v. Pro-Football, 570 F.2d 982 (1977).

47. WFL v. Dallas Cowboys, 513 S.W.2d 102 (Tex. Ct. App. 1974).

48. The legal disputes often would involve specific WFL clubs and NFL players who had signed with those clubs, then later changed their minds. More often than not, the WFL club's obvious precarious financial state was the cause for a parting of the ways. In such instances, the player was relieved of any further obligations to the club. *See, e.g.,* Alabama Football v. Greenwood, 452 F. Supp. 1191 (1978); Alabama Football v. Wright, 452 F. Supp. 182 (1977); Alabama Football v. Stabler, 294 Ala. 551, 319 So. 2d 678 (1975). *See also* Matuszak v. Houston Oilers, 515 S.W.2d 725 (Tex. Ct. App. 1974).

49. Walker Reportedly Signed with USFL, Boston Globe, Feb. 19, 1983, at 25, col. 1. One year later, Walker was signed to an even more lucrative contract. Although the numbers do not sound as high as those for Steve Young (see note 73 and accompanying text), in actuality the contract may be a more valuable one. It deals much more in current payments, with very little deferred compensation. *See* Wallace, Walker Re-signs for Millions, N.Y. Times, March 19, 1984, at A21, col. 1.

50. Walker Reportedly Signed with USFL, Boston Globe, Feb. 19, 1983, at 25, col. 1.

51. *Id.*

52. *Id.*

53. *Id.*

54. *Id.*

55. *See* Principles for the Conduct of Intercollegiate Athletics, NCAA Constitution, art. 3, §1(a)(2).

56. USFL Defends Waiving Rule, Boston Globe, Feb. 24, 1983, at 53, col. 1.

57. *Id.* The USFL in fact was in court answering challenges to their eligibility rules. The league was ordered to allow a punter, Bob Boris, to be eligible to play in the league. He was subsequently signed by the then–Oklahoma Outlaws, and played for them part of the 1984 season before being released. *See* Boris v. USFL, No. CV 83-4980 LEW (Kx), Order re Plaintiff's Motion for Partial Summary Judgment, issued Feb. 28, 1984.

See also Janofsky, USFL Loses Antitrust Suit on Eligibility, N.Y. Times, March 1, 1984, at B17, col. 5.

58. Steinberg: USFL Snowed Draftees, Boston Globe, March 2, 1983, at 43, col. 1.

59. Bengals Say Ross Will Leave for Breakers in '84, Boston Globe, March 3, 1983, at 57, col. 1.

60. *Id. See also* Balzer, Dealing in Futures, Sporting News, March 28, 1983, at 46.

61. The signing of Dan Ross and other NFL players to future USFL contracts was not taken kindly by NFL owners, to put it mildly. Some suggested retaliation. *See* Modell: Let's Do unto the USFL as . . . , Boston Globe, March 6, 1983, at 51.

62. *See* DeBartolos Get Rebuke, Boston Globe, March 23, 1983, at 64, col. 3. The possible conflicts of ownership were not the only concerns to the NFL owners. Escalating player salaries, brought on by the USFL competition, suddenly loomed as another overriding problem. *See e.g.*, Eskenazi, Taylor Buys Out Generals' Pact, N.Y. Times, Jan. 18, 1984, at B9, col. 5; Gastineau Signed by Jets to $4 Million Contract, N.Y. Times, Feb. 29, 1984, at B9, col. 4; Miller, USFL Threat Pays Off for NFL's New Players, San Francisco Chron., June 24, 1983, at 77, col. 4; and Taylor Case Is Settled, N.Y. Times, Jan. 20, 1984, at A18. col. 5.

63. DeBartolos Get Rebuke, Boston Globe, March 23, 1983, at 64, col. 3.

64. NFL Split in Handling USFL Issue, Boston Globe, March 25, 1983, at 52, col. 1.

65. *Id.*

66. USFL Player Signed by Chargers, N.Y. Times, Aug. 5, 1983, at A16, col. 5.

67. *Id.*

68. Detroit Lions & Sims v. Argovitz, 580 F. Supp. 542 (1984).

69. The Court said: "For the reasons that follow, we have concluded that Argovitz's breach of his fiduciary duty during negotiations for the Gamblers' contract was so pronounced, so egregious, that to deny recision would be unconscionable." 580 F. Supp. at 544.

70. 580 F. Supp. at 548.

71. 580 F. Supp. at 545–46.

72. *See, e.g.*, Cribbs Is Absent as Camps Open, N.Y. Times, Jan. 24, 1984, at A23, col. 5; Judge Won't Bar Cribbs from Stallion Practices, N.Y. Times, Jan. 27, 1984, at A23, col. 5; Judge Rules for Cribbs, N.Y. Times, Feb. 24, 1984, at A20, col. 5.

73. Young Signs $40 Million Contract for 43 Years, Boston Globe, March 6, 1984, at 23, col. 1. As to other signings of players to the USFL at high salaries, *see* Some NFL People Feel USFL's Life Is Spent, Boston Globe, Feb. 19, 1984, at 61, col. 1.

74. The career of Mike Rozier in the USFL was surrounded with controversy from the beginning. It was first questioned whether he had signed before his college team, the University of Nebraska, played its final game, in the Orange Bowl. Later, there came reports that he had been paid while he was at Nebraska, purportedly from an agent. In the meantime, his struggles on

the field with his USFL team, the Pittsburgh Maulers, made for even greater strained relationships. Among many accounts, see Rozier Was Paid While at Nebraska, San Francisco Chron., Oct. 18, 1984, at 67, col. 6; Rozier Charges Denied, San Francisco Chron., Oct. 19, 1984, at 82, col. 1; and Cohn, Rozier Broke Stupid Rules, San Francisco Chron., Oct. 19, 1984, at 81, col. 1.

75. Outlook Is Mixed For USFL, N.Y. Times, April 22, 1984, §5, at 7, col. 4. The decision to move to the fall confirmed for many people that the USFL owners were badly divided and beset by internal problems that perhaps could not be resolved. The questions about the quality of ownership of many USFL franchises surfaced early in the league's history and did not abate over time. *See, e.g.*, Bisher, High Costs, Weak Leaders Seen as USFL Albatross, Sporting News, March 28, 1983, at 11.

76. *See* USFL "Discussing" Huge Antitrust Suit vs. NFL, San Francisco Chron., Oct. 6, 1984, at 44, col. 2; USFL Hits NFL with $1.3 Billion Suit, San Francisco Chron., Oct. 18, 1984, at 67, col. 1; Anderson, A "Grand Design" For Football Peace, San Francisco Chron., Oct. 24, 1984, at 53, col. 1.

77. A quote from Commissioner Pete Rozelle of the NFL: "You will know when they [the USFL] are on their last legs. They will bring a lawsuit against us. This (suit) will be how they try to keep the owners from jumping ship. They will hold out their suit as a way of getting their money back if they stay around." USFL Hits NFL with $1.3 Billion Suit, San Francisco Chron., Oct. 18, 19, 1984, at 67, col. 1.

78. *See, e.g.*, Balzer, Choosing a Union, Sporting News, May 2, 1983, at 56; USFL Vote on Union Due, N.Y. Times, Feb. 29, 1984, at B10, col. 1; Forbes, Union Taking No Chances on USFL Ratification Vote, USA Today, March 13, 1984, at 6C, col. 3; USFL Players Approve a Union, N.Y. Times, April 12, 1984, at B15, col. 1.

79. Other members of the Federation of Professional Athletes, which is an affiliate of the AFL–CIO, include the National Football League Players' Association, the North American Soccer League Players' Association, and the Major Indoor Soccer League Players' Association. The FPA is discussed briefly in Chapter 9.

80. Organized Professional Team Sports: Hearings on H.R. 5307, H.R. 5319, H.R. 6877, H.R. 8023, and H.R. 8124 before the House Subcomm. on Antitrust of the Comm. on the Judiciary, 85th Cong., 1st Sess. 2691–92 (1957–58) (statement of Bert Bell). George Halas, Chicago Bears owner and a founder of the NFL, concurred, with reservations, in this recognition. *See id.* at 2694–701 (statement of George Halas).

81. *See* Krasnow and Levy, Unionization and Professional Sports, 51 Geo. L.J. 749, 763 (1963). The authors cite correspondence they had with Miller in which he is extremely reluctant to talk in terms of the NFLPA as a union. *Id.* at 773 n.72.

82. *See* Hearings on Labor Relations in Professional Sports before the House Comm. on Education and Labor, 92d Cong., 2d Sess., H.R. 7152, at 12

(March 1972) (statement by Edward Garvey). *See also* J. Weistart and C. Lowell, The Law of Sports §6.01 at 779 (1979). The NFL experienced a three-day strike and subsequent seventeen-day walkout in 1970. *Id.* at §6.09, at 828.

83.   Hearings on Labor Relations in Professional Sports (see Note 82 above) (statement by Edward Garvey) at 12–14, 18. For a different recollection of the circumstances, see statement by Theodore Kheel, at pp. 74–75.

84.   *See* J. Weistart and C. Lowell, The Law of Sports §6.01 at 782–83 (1979). *See also* NFL Owner Offer Rejected by Players, N.Y. Times, Aug. 28, 1974, at 21, col. 1; Players Halt Strike 14 Days; Report to Camps Wednesday, N.Y. Times, Aug. 12, 1974, at 31, col. 1.

85.   Kapp v. NFL, 586 F.2d 644 (1978), *cert. denied*, 441 U.S. 907 (1979).

86.   Mackey v. NFL, 543 F.2d 606 (1976), *cert. dismissed*, 434 U.S. 801 (1977).

87.   Alexander v. NFL, U.S. Dist. Ct., Minn., 4–76, Civil 123. The *Alexander* case was settled, in light of the appeal of *Mackey* (note 86). Appeal of the *Alexander* settlement by dissatisfied players was unsuccessful. *See* Reynolds v. NFL, 584 F.2d 280 (1978).

88.   The settlement of the *Alexander* case resulted in the NFL paying to present and former NFL players a total of $13,675,000 and an additional $2,200,000 in legal fees. *See* Notice to Persons Who Are Now or Have Been under Contract to a Member Club of the National Football League at Any Time from September 17, 1972 to March 1, 1977, *reprinted* in Sporting News, May 21, 1977, at 17.

89.   *See, e.g.*, Coronado Coal Co. v. UMW, 268 U.S. 295 (1925); Duplex Printing Press Co. v. Deering, 254 U.S. 443 (1921); Loewe v. Lawlor, 208 U.S. 274 (1908).

90.   312 U.S. 219 (1941).

91.   *Id.* at 232.

92.   Clayton Act of 1914, §§1–26, 15 U.S.C. §§12–27 (1976).

93.   Norris-LaGuardia Act §§1–15, 29 U.S.C. §§101–15 (1976).

94.   312 U.S. at 234–36.

95.   *See, e.g.*, Apex Hosiery Co. v. Leader, 310 U.S. 469 (1940), where the Court stated:

> A combination of employees necessarily restrains competition among themselves in the sale of their services to the employer; yet such a combination was not considered an illegal restraint of trade at common law when the Sherman Act was adopted, either because it was not thought to be unreasonable or because it was not deemed a "restraint of trade." Since the enactment of the declaration in §6 of the Clayton Act that "the labor of a human being is not a commodity or article of commerce . . . nor shall such [labor] organizations, or the members thereof, be held or construed to be illegal combinations or conspiracies in the restraint of trade under the antitrust laws," it would seem plain that restraints on the sale of the employee's services to the employer, however much they curtail the competition among employees, are not in themselves combinations or conspiracies in restraint of trade or commerce under the Sherman Act.

Id. at 502–03 (citation omitted).

96. 325 U.S. 797 (1945).

97. *Id.* at 799–800.

98. *Id.* at 811.

99. *Id.* at 806.

100. 381 U.S. 657 (1965).

101. *Id.* at 656–60.

102. *Id.* at 660–61.

103. Chief Justice Warren and Justice Brennan joined Justice White. Justices Black, Douglas, and Clark joined in a concurring opinion. Justices Harlan, Stewart, and Goldberg dissented from the opinion but concurred in the judgment.

104. 381 U.S. at 664.

105. *Id.* at 697.

106. *Id.* at 664–65. *But see id.* at 710 (Goldberg J., dissenting).

107. *Id.* at 666.

108. 381 U.S. 676 (1965).

109. *See also* Nassau Sports v. Hampson, 355 F. Supp. 733 (D. Minn. 1972) (hockey); Denver Rockets v. All-Pro Management, Inc., 325 F. Supp. 1049 (C.D. Cal. 1971) (basketball).

110. It is unclear whether this constitutes a distinction between the sports cases and those in which it is alleged that employers violate antitrust laws where they boycott unionized employers. Carpenters v. Associated Gen. Contractors, 105 L.R.R.M. 3311 (9th Cir. 1980). *Cf.* Connell Construction Co. v. Plumbers & Steamfitters, Local Union 100, 421 U.S. 616 (1975).

111. *See* note 102 *supra* and accompanying text.

112. 381 U.S. at 689.

113. *Id.* at 691.

114. *Id.* at 688.

115. 407 F. Supp. 1000 (D. Minn. 1975), *modified*, 543 F.2d 606 (8th Cir. 1976), *cert. dismissed*, 434 U.S. 801 (1977).

116. *Id.* at 1007.

117. *Id.* at 1004.

118. *Id.* at 1009–10.

119. *Id.* at 1009–11. Inadequate finances and the organization's recent formation contributed to economic weakness and an inability to conduct a strike.

120. 543 F.2d at 612.

121. *Id.*

122. *Id.* at 612–13.

123. *Id.* at 613.

124. *Id.* at 612.

125. *Id.*

126. *Id.* at 614.

127. *Id.* (citations omitted).

128. *Id.* at 615.

129. *Id.*

130. *Id.*
131. *Id.* at 616.
132. *Id.*
133. "We find substantial evidence to support the finding that there was no bona fide arm's-length bargaining under the Rozelle Rule preceeding the execution of the 1968 and 1970 agreements." *Id.* at 616.
134. *Id.* at 623 (citations omitted).
135. 420 F. Supp. 738 (D.D.C. 1976), *modified,* 593 F.2d 1173 (D.C. Cir. 1978).
136. *Id.* at 741.
137. *Id.* at 742.
138. *See* notes 122 and 123 *supra* and accompanying text.
139. 420 F. Supp. at 742.
140. *Id.*
141. *Id.* at 743.
142. *Id.* at 743 (citing Teamsters Local v. NLRB, 365 U.S. 667 (1961)).
143. 420 F. Supp. at 743.
144. *Id.*
145. *Id.* at 743.
146. *Id.* at 744.
147. *Id.* at 745–46.
148. *Id.* at 746.
149. *Id.*
150. *Id.*
151. *Id.* at 747 n.6.
152. 593 F.2d 1173 (D.C. Cir. 1978). Judge McKinnon dissented in part and concurred in part. Judge McKinnon agreed with the majority's conclusion that the district court should not have found the draft to be a per se violation of the antitrust laws; he disagreed with the majority's holding that the draft was a violation of the rule of reason.
153. *Id.* at 1178–79.
154. *Id.* at 1182.
155. *Id.* at 1183.
156. *Id.* at 1185.
157. *Id.* at 1187.
158. *See* notes 188 and 198 *infra* and accompanying text.
159. *See* Amalgamated Meat Cutters, Local 189 v. Jewel Tea Co., 381 U.S. 676 (1965). *Cf.* Dolly Madison Industries, 182 N.L.R.B. 1037 (1970).
160. *See, e.g.,* Anderson, The NFL's Dangerous Trend, N.Y. Times, April 29, 1981, at 21, col. 1 (impact of Johnny Johnson's $1 million contract on veteran members of the Los Angeles Rams).
161. Jacobs and Winter, Antitrust Principles and Collective Bargaining by Athletes: Of Superstars in Peonage, 81 Yale L.J. 1, 8 (1971).
162. *Id.* at 15–16.
163. 404 U.S. 157 (1971).
164. *Id.* at 181 n.20.

165. *Id. Cf.* W. Gould, Black Workers in White Unions: Job Discrimination in the United States 191–200 (1977).
166. *See* Smith v. Pro Football, Inc., 420 F. Supp. 738 (D.D.C. 1976), *modified*, 593 F.2d 1173 (D.C. Cir. 1978); Mackey v. NFL, 407 F. Supp. 1000 (D.D.C. 1975), *modified*, 543 F.2d 606 (8th Cir. 1976), *cert. dismissed*, 434 U.S. 801 (1977).
167. 543 F.2d 606 n.13.
168. *See* GTE Automatic Elec. 240 N.L.R.B. 297 (1979) (employer unlawfully refused to negotiate with union regarding the implementation of a savings plan for unionized employees when plan was not available to nonunion employees and had not been conceived at the time the union signed the waiver clause); Western Foundries, 233 N.L.R.B. 1033 (1977) (board held that when an employer unilaterally implemented an employee profit sharing plan that excluded from its coverage those employees who were represented by a union board, despite the existence of a zipper clause, the employer violated §§8(a)(5) and (1) by refusing to bargain about this exclusion); Unit Drop Forge Division, Eaton Yale Towne, 171 N.L.R.B. 600 (1968), *modified*, 412 F.2d 108 (7th Cir. 1969) (where contract provided that parties agree upon changes in incentive plans, job change resulting in employees being transferred from incentive pay plan to hourly wage rate was subject to bargaining, despite general waiver clause). *See generally*, Cox and Dunlop, The Duty to Bargain Collectively during the Term of the Existing Agreement, 63 Harv. L. Rev. 1097 (1950).
169. *See* not 133 *supra.*
170. 600 F.2d 1193 (6th Cir. 1978).
171. *Id.* at 1194.
172. *Id.* at 1200.
173. Note, Labor Exemption to the Antitrust Laws, Shielding an Anticompetitive Provision Devised by an Employer Group in Its Own Interest: *McCourt v. California Sports, Inc.*, 21 B.C.L. Rev. 680 (1980). The author observed that

> In the Sixth Circuit's view, a union's failure to advance its interests because of the employers' hard bargaining does not mean that the labor exemption must be disallowed. Such a failure, the court notes, is "a part of and not apart from the collective bargaining process," the "ultimate objective" of which is an agreement accepted by the parties. Thus, examining the tenor of the *McCourt* opinion, the court's reluctance to accept the NHL's argument that the union interest, as well as the collective bargaining policy, had been advanced, and its interpretation of the significance of the new player benefits, it is submitted that, at least as far as the labor exemption is concerned, the Sixth Circuit views the integrity of the collective bargaining process as more important than the labor interests which a union may seek to further via that process.

Id. at 711.
174. *Id.* The author discussed the change in the labor movement and the way rational labor policy should shift to accommodate that change:

> The Court should respond to ... changes in congressional labor concerns by ascribing greater weight to the national policy favoring collective bargaining and

correspondingly less weight to that of advancing the interests of organized labor. This could result in a balancing test very similar to Justice Goldberg's, under which collective bargaining policy would be viewed as important enough to allow the labor exemption to protect *any* market restraint which results from bona fide, arm's length collective bargaining on mandatory subjects. If the Courts were to view unions and employers as bargaining equals, neither the origin of an anticompetitive provision, nor its effect on union interests would be relevant to the nonstatutory exemption issue. In addition, the *Mackey-McCourt* distinction between different types of market restraints would be unnecessary, since the Court would not require two labor policies to be advanced to protect a restriction which affects business competitors, but only one where no third party is affected.

Id. at 713.

175. 584 F.2d 280 (8th Cir. 1978).
176. *Id.* at 287.
177. As the court stated in its conclusion,

We emphasize today, as we did in *Mackey* . . . that the subject of player movement restrictions is a proper one for resolution in the collective bargaining context. When so resolved, as it appears to have been in the current collective bargaining agreement, the labor exemption to antitrust attack applied, and the merits of the bargaining agreement are not an issue for court determination.

Id. at 289.

178. *See* Forbes, Garvey, Players Want More When NFL Contract Expires, Miami Herald, March 1, 1981, §C, at 8, col. 1.
179. *See* Oates, Is NFL Ready for Equal Pay for All?, L.A. Times, July 22, 1979, §3, at 1, col. 2.
180. *See* H.K. Porter Co. v. NLRB, 397 U.S. 99 (1970) (exemplifies tension between "good faith bargaining" and the exercise of bargaining strength in "free collective bargaining"); NLRB v. American Nat'l Ins. Co, 343 U.S. 395, 404 (1952) ("the Act does not encourage a party to engage in fruitless marathon discussions at the expense of frank statement and support of his position. And it is equally clear that the Board may not, either directly or indirectly, compel concessions"); NLRB v. General Elec. Co., 418 F.2d 736, 758 (2d Cir. 1969), *cert. denied*, 395 U.S. 965 (1970) ("while the absence of concessions would not prove bad faith, their presense would . . . raise a strong inference of good faith"). *See also* Cox, The Duty to Bargain in Good Faith, 71 Harv. L. Rev. 1401 (1958).
181. *See, e.g.*, Nolde Bros. v. Bakery & Confectionary Workers, Local 358, 430 U.S. 243 (1977).
182. *See, e.g.*, American Fed'n of Television & Radio Artists v. NLRB, 395 F.2d 622 (D.C. Cir. 1968); NLRB v. United States Sonics Corp., 312 F.2d 610 (1st Cir. 1963); Schatzski, The Employer's Unilateral Act—A Per Se Violation—Sometimes, 44 Tex. L. Rev. 470 (1966).
183. 543 F.2d at 616 n.18.
184.. *See* NLRB v. Crompton-Highland Mills, 337 U.S. 217 (1949).
185. 381 U.S. 676 (1965).
186. Collective Bargaining Agreement between NFL Players Association and NFL Management Council, art. 13, §2 (March 1, 1977) [hereinafter cited

as NFL Agreement], *reprinted in* Representing Professional Sports, *supra* note 190, at 52.

187. Wallace, How Canada Provides a Lure for Many NFL Prospects, N.Y. Times, May 18, 1981, at 30, col. 1. *Cf.* Eskenazi, Ferragamo Gets Warm Welcome from Alouette Fans, N.Y. Times, June 7, 1981, at 26, col. 1.

188. *See* note 153 *supra* and accompanying text.

189. NFL Agreement, *supra* note 210 art. 14, §3, *reprinted in* Representing Professional Sports, *supra* note 190, at 59.

190. NFL Players' Ass'n v. NFL Management Council (Dutton) (May 14, 1980).

191. For a discussion of *Messersmith*, see notes 42–63, Chapter 3 and accompanying text.

192. NFL Players' Ass'n v. NFL Management Council, at 36.

193. *Id.* at 39–41.

194. *See* note 69–88 *supra* and accompanying text.

195. NFL Agreement, *supra* note 46, art. 15, §4, *reprinted in* Representing Professional Sports, *supra* note 190, at 61.

196. *See* Miller, The Not-So-Free-Agents, San Francisco Chron., Feb. 20, 1981, at 64, col. 1.

197. When the Philadelphia Phillies signed Pete Rose, the team's income from ticket sales and television contracts exceeded Rose's salary. Garvey, Why the NFL Snubs Free Agents, N.Y. Times, Aug. 12, 1979, §S, at 2, col. 1. In 1981 the Red Sox traded Rick Burleson and Butch Hobson. The team then suffered losses of television contracts that exceeded the anticipated salary expenditures for Fred Lynn and Carlton Fisk. Newhan, One Way to Avoid a $2 Million Tab, L.A. Times, Jan. 10, 1981, §3, at 1, col. 2. The same dynamics are not operative in football.

198. *See* The Coming Fight Over NFL Riches, San Francisco Chron., Apr. 21, 1981, at 47, col. 1; NFL Players Ask for Salary Scale, San Francisco Chron., June 12, 1981, at 83, col. 6. The players, however, seem to be divided on this issue. *See, e.g.,* Dickey, Disunity in the NFL's Player Union, San Francisco Chron., Aug. 19, 1981, at 61, col. 1; Miller, How the 49ers View the Next NFL Contract, San Francisco Chron., Aug. 14, 1981, at 71, col. 1. One virtue of a salary scale is that players would be compensated more adequately and without the need for free agency and consequent disruption of fan morale. Koppett, Fixed Pay Scale Might Benefit Fan, Sporting News, Nov. 28, 1981, at 12, col. 1. Anderson, The NFL's Dangerous Trend, N.Y. Times, April 29, 1981, §B, at 11, col. 4.

199. Opinion and decision of Sam Kagel, Arbitrator, May 30, 1984.

200. Opinion and decision of Sam Kagel, Arbitrator, San Francisco, January 11, 1984.

201. J.I. Case v. NLRB, 321 U.S. 332 (1944).

5 THE FOOTBALL STRIKE OF 1982

Shortly before the football players' strike of 1982, the possibility that players might strike stimulated national interest. The unfolding drama made good theater. Despite earlier skirmishes between the union and owners, some observers discounted these job actions because they were not sustained and had no impact on the regular schedule of games. Baseball had established a strike precedent in 1981, but that action was viewed as an aberration that could not happen again. These observers reasoned that the well-organized and tightly controlled National Football League (NFL), under the strong leadership of Commissioner Pete Rozelle, would not fall prey to the same shortcomings as baseball, that the National Football League Players' Association (NFLPA) was relatively weak and lacked solidarity, and that since players' careers were short, they had too much to lose from a strike.

Other observers worried that acrimonious labor relations had continued for too long between players and owners. While the players had lacked cohesiveness in the past, they might have gained commitment from baseball's example. The financial stakes were far higher than in the past, which could make football players more willing to gamble on the sacrifice called for by a strike. These observers also pointed to the wide differences that still remained between the parties in negotiations on substantive issues and the intense feelings of inequity experienced by players.

The football strike of 1982 lasted fifty-seven days and was the longest strike in the history of professional team sports. Numerous similarities can be found between the baseball and football strikes, and these similarities will be highlighted in this chapter. We are particularly interested in why the work stoppage occurred,[1] the dynamics of negotiations, and the outcomes. The strike and the terms of its settlement have crucial implications for the future of all professional team sports.

PREVIOUS JOB ACTIONS

The first suggestion of a football players' strike was heard in 1956, the same year the NFLPA was formed. Norb Hecker, co-founder of the union, and other players for the Washington Redskins were upset that they received no pay for expenses incurred during training camp.[2] In discussions with the owners the players' representatives sought $25 a week. When the owners refused to agree, players held secret meetings and decided to strike before the last preseason game between the Redskins and the Baltimore Colts. When these players refused to go onto the field for warmups, the Redkins' original owner, George Preston Marshall, threatened to play the game without the dissidents. Marshall's threat aborted the strike, and the players took the field without a promise of expense money.

A strike was again considered in 1959 during discussions between players and owners over a pension plan. Creighton Miller, a Cleveland attorney, was retained by the NFLPA as a negotiator, but he was not allowed to participate in bargaining talks with the owners, who were represented by NFL Commiosioner Bert Bell.[3] Frustrated by lack of progress in negotiations, Miller and Billy Howton, a player for the Green Bay Packers, considered calling a strike, but player solidarity was weak. Instead, players threatened a lawsuit challenging the NFL's reserve clause. As a result, Bell and the owners conceded on the pension plan, a significant achievement for the union. Howton, however, was traded to the Cleveland Browns before the start of the next season.

The First Walkout

The first full-scale, leaguewide strike in the NFL occurred in the fall of 1968. Issues in dispute included player freedom to change teams, minimum salary of $15,000, and a $5 million annual pension fund contribution by owners. The pension fund contribution became the key issue preventing the first comprehensive collective bargaining agreement in football, and negotiations became difficult and heated.[4] After reaching an impasse in negotiations, the players boycotted the preseason training camps. The owners then retaliated with a lockout. Only then, with battle lines firmly drawn, did the sides agree to talk. The ten-day strike and lockout ended in an agreement in which both sides compromised. It was not a long or bitter strike, but the boycott and resulting lockout influenced the parties' willingness to resume talks and reach agreement.[5]

Despite the 1968 agreement, issues continued to fester. In addition to increased pensions, the players made demands on postseason compensation and a grievance procedure. The first contract expired in January 1970, and, after fruitless negotiations, the players again struck training camps in July. During the three-day strike and subsequent seventeen-day lockout the players did not set up picket lines and made no attempt to keep rookies from attending training camps. Only about twenty veteran players reported to camp, apart from the Kansas City Chiefs' players, who were permitted to attend camps for one week to prepare for the College All-Star Game.[6] The strike and lockout ended when the owners conceded an estimated $19.1 million for four years, most of which was in the form of pension contributions.[7]

The 1974 and 1975 Strikes

When the 1970 agreement expired in 1974, the players again moved to shut down training camps. The 1974 strike was significant because its failure, due to erosion of player solidarity and lack of public support, left the union unable to negotiate a replacement contract for three years. Similar to the 1982 strike, the players in 1974 were negotiating during the formation of a new rival league, the ill-fated World Football League. It is also notable for being the second-longest football strike, lasting forty-two days.

The players in 1974 made sixty-three demands, including easing of curfews and other disciplinary rules. Particularly important points of contention were "freedom issues" such as elimination of the reserve list, option clause, and waiver system. The players' slogan became "No freedom, no football."[8] Focus was on elimination of the "Rozelle Rule," which allowed the NFL commissioner, Pete Rozelle, to award compensation (players, draft choices, money) to a player's former team when he signed a contract with a new team. The impact of the Rozelle Rule was to deny opportunities for players to sell their services to other teams.

When Ed Garvey appeared in the negotiations as executive director of the NFLPA, the players' position hardened. The executive director of the NFL Management Council was John Thompson, but chief negotiator for the owners was Theodore Kheel, a lawyer from New York with a background in labor/management relations as a mediator and arbitrator. Commissioner Rozelle was also fairly active in the dispute. He defended the rule bearing his name by noting that "if NFL players are given total freedom to negotiate their services, the league would be dominated by a few rich teams and would eventually lose both fan interest and revenue."[9]

Almost from the outset the strike appeared doomed. The owners invited rookies and free agents to training camps, and the NFLPA picket lines had little impact. Veterans began to dribble into camp, and after about a month an estimated 311 veteran players (out of 1,200) had crossed picket lines to join their teams.[10] Exhibition games were played and televised, but in nearly all cases fan attendance was very low. Several opinion polls showed that the fans favored the owners' position heavily. The strike collapsed quietly after forty-two days, with most of the issues still unresolved.

Three union leaders, Bill Curry, Kermit Alexander, and Tom Keating, were cut or sold by their clubs during the 1974 strike. The NFLPA filed unfair labor practice charges with the NLRB on this and other issues stemming from the strike. An NLRB administrative law judge determined that the three players should be offered reinstatement by their teams and that the owners violated the law by setting a preseason pay rate of 10 percent of a player's salary in 1974 without consulting the union.[11] Although this was something of a victory for the players, it was more of a rearguard action. It was clear from the failure of the 1974 strike that the owners had the upper hand.

This is evidenced further by the union's continuing lack of solidarity in the short-lived strike in 1975. Like the walkouts in 1970 and 1974, this strike began with high hopes but ended in frustration for the players. It centered mostly on a single team, the New England Patriots, and rebel player representative Randy Vataha.[12] Besides seeking to generate pressure on negotiating demands, such as an end to the Rozelle Rule, the strike characterized the players' impatience with lack of progress at the bargaining table.[13] Vataha and his teammates were trying to determine if the players really had a viable union.[14]

Joining the Patriots in voting to strike were four other teams.[15] One exhibition game was called off as a result of the strike, but eleven teams voted not to strike. The twenty-six teams in the league were acting independently, as mini-unions, which caused chaos and lack of a united front. Helpful in ending the dispute was the tireless mediation effort of W. J. Usery, director of the Federal Mediation and Conciliation Service. However, there was no change in the status of the Rozelle Rule as a result of the agreement, and the question of whether the players had a viable union was answered largely in the negative.

PRESTRIKE POSTURING

During the hiatus in the collective bargaining agreement, from 1974 to 1977, the NFLPA mounted a campaign to achieve its objectives through action in the courts. The court decisions that emerged from the union's efforts are discussed in Chapter 4. One of these decisions is particularly important to explaining the background of the 1982 strike. The *Mackey* case challenged the Rozelle Rule under the antitrust laws.[16] It alleged that the rule violated the Sherman Antitrust Act by denying players an opportunity to contract freely for their services. The court agreed with this contention, finding that the Rozelle Rule was an unreasonable restraint of trade because it acted as a prohibitive deterrent to player movement in the NFL.

As a result of the *Mackey* ruling, the NFLPA won a significant victory allowing greater mobility for players, not unlike the arbitration decision in baseball that overturned the reserve clause. However, rather than cementing most of their gains, as the baseball players did in their collective bargaining agreement following the negation of the reserve clause, the NFLPA arguably negotiated away too much of what they had gained. The 1977 collective bargaining agreement in football modified the system of reserve and compensation. Under that agreement, the player whose contract expired or who played out his option (usually where an unsigned player was paid 110 percent of his salary in the previous year) could seek to achieve free-agency status. The player's team had a right of first refusal in which it could match the offer of the bidding team and thus retain the player.[17]

However, the deterrent to signing free agents remained. If the team did not exercise its right of first refusal, the new team had to give up draft choices as compensation. Under the 1977 agreement compensation for free agents was too high to encourage player mobility. By 1981, for example, if a player made $80,000 to $129,000, the compensation required was a number-one draft choice; for players making more, compensation was two number-one draft choices in successive years. As a result of these contractual arrangements, only six of the over 500 NFL players who became free agents actually changed teams under the 1977 agreement.[18]

It is easy to see in retrospect that the NFLPA erred in abdicating its gains in the *Mackey* case by agreeing to a free-agency system that was too restrictive to encourage player mobility. Nevertheless, given the dominance in negotiations by the owners, and the players' eagerness for a collective bargaining agreement in the face of their lack of solidarity, it is not surprising that the union was unable to hold on to its winnings. The relinquishment became a sensitive point that would haunt Ed Garvey. Although he sought to explain away the significance of free agency for football players—and his arguments had merit—a stigma of failure remained. Responding to these charges must have inspired Garvey to his part in the truculence that became a hallmark of the 1982 negotiations.

Key Personalities

Garvey continued as chief negotiator for the union in 1982. The two protagonists in the lengthy negotiations and strike were he and Jack Donlan, executive director of the NFL Management Council. Other persons made significant contributions, particularly Gene Upshaw, president of the NFLPA, but the two chief negotiators had a direct hand in virtually all of the important decisions.[19] This factor did not portend smooth negotiations. Both Garvey and Donlan have strong tempers and are readily provoked into emotionalism.

Both Garvey and Donlan are of Irish ancestry, grew up in small towns, served in the army, held jobs during their higher education, and were employed in labor/management relations prior to their positions in 1982.[20] After graduating from law school in 1969, Garvey joined the Minneapolis law firm of Lindquist and Vennum. The firm later became general counsel to the NFLPA. Garvey left the firm to become executive director of the union in 1971.

Donlan for a time was employed by the U.S. Department of Labor and served as a mediator with the Federal Mediation and Conciliation Service. He left government service for employment as a labor negotiator at National Airlines. When National merged with Pan American, he became executive director of the NFL management council in 1980.[21] Despite their personal similarities, Garvey and Donlan had a particular antipathy toward each other that arose out of a steely commitment to their jobs.

Money Signals

Apart from Garvey's dismay at having given away free agency and the NFL's hiring of a tough negotiator in Donlan, there were other early signs of posturing for a strike. In 1981 the NFLPA proposed raising its annual dues from $670 per player to $1,122 but finalized the increase at $850.[22] This signaled the NFLPA's intention to build up a war chest in anticipation of a strike. Other important factors were the new television contracts and formation of the United States Football League.

By 1981 twenty million men between age 18 and 49 watched NFL games on television.[23] The money paid by advertisers for commercials on these games provided a revenue bonanza to the television networks. Under the NFL contracts with NBC, CBS, and ABC that expired in 1981, each of the twenty-eight teams in the league received about $5.8 million annually. In 1982 a new five-year agreement was reached in which the networks agreed to pay the teams an average of $14.2 million per season. This agreement guaranteed an enormous rise in team revenues, of which the players wanted a greater share.

An example of the profit potential caused by the TV contracts is provided by data from the Los Angeles Rams. The Rams probably have the highest gross income and costs of operation in the NFL. Their stadium in Anaheim has a capacity of nearly 70,000. Revenues from ticket sales and luxury boxes are conservatively estimated at $10 million. Adding television and other revenue would raise the total annual revenue figure to about $24 million.[24]

Although most teams do not disclose cost data, expenditures for the Rams in 1981 were made available to the NFLPA. These data, shown in Table 5-1, indicate operating expenses of about $14 million. While these expenses would rise in 1982, they would still be far less than total revenues with the new television money factored in.[25]

The NFL players' incentive to bargain tough and strike if necessary was also stimulated by the formation in 1982 of the United States Football League (USFL). Beginning in 1983 this new twelve-team professional football league

Table 5-1. Los Angeles Rams' Expenditures, 1981.

Players salaries	$ 4,200,000
Training camp	362,000
Offseason camp	23,000
Mini camp	28,000
Offseason training	157,000
Trainers	91,000
Equipment	186,000
Operating expenses[a]	5,317,000
Coaching expenses	1,470,000
Other payments to players	2,200,000
Total	$14,034,000

a. Includes travel expenses and salaries for non-football personnel.
Source: Data reported in L. A. Times, March 24, 1982, pt. 3, at 1.

played a twenty-game schedule from March through June, with a championship game in early July.[26] The USFL agreed to a two-year television contract with ABC for about $10 million per year.[27] The USFL's large bankroll from wealthy owners shook the NFL's monopoly control over football salaries. The rival league has had a marked effect on the salary structure in professional football because players can jump leagues after their contracts with NFL teams expire. The teams in both leagues are expected to increasingly do battle in bidding wars for new and veteran players.

Winter Meetings

Speculation about a possible players' strike intensified at the annual league meetings in Phoenix in March 1982. For the owners these meetings usually centered around rule changes and possible trades. In negotiating sessions shortly before the 1982 meetings, however, the players presented their demand for revenue sharing: They demanded that 55 percent of gross NFL revenues be placed into a fund for distribution to the players. (Details of this proposal are reviewed later in this chapter.) This radical departure from previous union bargaining approaches made negotiation strategy the primary topic of lively discussion among NFL representatives. For the first time head coaches were required to attend the meetings so that they could be apprised of the party line, and they were therefore thrust into a difficult "man-in-the-middle" role: They had to maintain consistency with the position of the owners who paid them, yet they needed to inspire confidence in the players they relied on to win games.

Announcements made by the owners to the press signaled their willingness to take a strike and their readiness to make contingency plans in anticipation of a strike. Donlan indicated that strike strategy possibilities included locking the players out of training camp and holding games with free agents and nonunion players. It was also revealed that the league had arranged a $150 million line of credit with banks to help clubs through a strike.[28] Strike insurance could not be obtained because carriers would not underwrite it in the wake of the baseball strike.

The NFLPA meetings in Albuquerque were significant because of the emergence of a new unity among players. An estimated 537 players attended, about a third of the total NFLPA membership.[29] They strongly endorsed the union's objective of negotiating a fixed percentage of the owners' gross income. In the past the union's public relations efforts were shown to be greatly inferior to the NFL's. The union therefore hired the Kamber Group of political consultants to handle their press relations and help build a favorable public image. The NFLPA was especially wary of the mistakes made by the union leadership in the air traffic controllers' strike in 1981, such as failure to communicate its position effectively to the public and to members of the union.[30] Urging players to attend the NFLPA meetings reflected this strategy. Also, in an attempt at enhancing its public image the union passed a resolution asking owners to lower ticket prices because of their rich television contracts.

Probably the most important decision reached at the NFLPA meetings was a commitment to strike if the bargaining demands on percentage of gross revenues were not met. This commitment was ratified by all twenty-eight player representatives.[31] Thus, both sides gave clear indication at the winter meetings of their intention to permit a strike unless their differences could be resolved. Given the disparity in the positions of the parties on the issues in negotiations, a strike seemed more likely than not.

In weighing the likelihood of success of a strike, unions are acutely aware of the past, especially the immediate past, and the degree to which other strikes achieved their purposes. The strike foremost in the minds of the NFLPA was the baseball strike of a year earlier.[32] As noted in Chapter 3, the two most important bottom-line results derived from the baseball strike were that baseball salaries continued their rapid escalation and fan attendance came back to record levels. The baseball players' lasting solidarity allowed them to maintain a favorable contractual arrangement and showed NFL players that they might achieve good results as well; if only they could hold fast. In this sense the baseball strike of 1981 was a major cause of the football strike in 1982.

ISSUES IN DISPUTE

In conventional labor negotiations the parties make their demands early, and the settlement results from compromise on these original issues. In football, however, the parties, especially the union, made significant changes in the proposals as negotiations proceeded. In some cases the changes involved not simply a modification in the initial position but a revised approach affecting the basic structure of the demands. This made negotiations complex. Unconventional negotiating methods lead to distrust and frustration among participants, and this distrust contributed to the frequent breakdowns in talks that eventually led to the strike.

Opening the Books

Prior to 1982 the NFLPA and the NFL management council staged a battle of words, unsubstantiated by hard data, over the percentage of the owners' gross revenue that was being paid to players. For 1981 the figure estimated by Donlan was 48 percent, while Garvey put it at 28 percent.[33] Although the actual percentage cannot be precisely estimated, compensation to players probably accounted for about one-third of NFL revenues.[34] In any event, the percentage that football players received in 1981 was less than players received in baseball and even further behind the proportion that basketball players received.[35]

In January 1982 Donlan sent a letter to Garvey offering to allow the players to inspect the financial books of NFL owners.[36] Donlan indicated that the union could choose a senior auditor from any Big Eight accounting firm to work with Arthur Andersen and Company on a "1981 pro forma combined statement of all NFL member clubs."[37] The audit was to begin in April and be completed in July. Garvey interpreted this letter to mean that the NFL would open its books, but Donlan later indicated he had no authority to do so.[38] Instead, Donlan said the clubs had been examined by Arthur Andersen and Company, which compiled an "anonymous audit" showing profit and loss for an "average team"; the union was not allowed to see the league's books or those of any individual club.[39]

The owners' position was upheld in an unfair labor practice charge brought by the union with the NLRB, although the NLRB's general counsel ordered the NFL to provide the union with information it requested on broadcast contracts, player salaries, and details of worker's compensation as to whether team doctors have financial interests in the clubs.[40] This battle is important because it points to the union's initial position on salaries, calling for 55 percent of gross revenues. The union could not justify this radical demand because it had no conclusive facts on the current percentage of gross revenue received by players.

55 Percent of Gross

The NFLPA's primary negotiating demand at the outset was that the NFL set aside 55 percent of annual gross team revenues for distribution to the players. Management was unalterably opposed to the idea.[41] If the union's proposal were accepted it would approximately double average salaries in 1983 from the 1982 level of $90,000. This estimate is based on the increases in revenue from new television money and higher ticket, parking, and concession charges. However, a few highly paid players, such as quarterbacks, might actually suffer a salary

Table 5-2. Proposed Allocation of Percentage of Gross.

Pool Item	Percentage
Base wages	70.0
Incentive bonuses[a]	15.2
Residual pool[b]	10.3
Playoff pool	4.5
Total	100.0

a. For top performers, Pro Bowl selection, team performance, and downs played.
b. Salary adjustments for previously negotiated contracts over proposed scale, administrative costs, and severance pay.
Source: National Football League Players' Association.

decline because of the equal distribution of revenues among players regardless of position.

Apparently the origin of the union's idea for the percentage of gross came in part from management itself. The sharing of television revenues equally among teams is a kind of corporate socialism created by the NFL's economic cartel. The union's proposal that the NFL distribute a fixed portion of television and other revenues to players on an equal basis is similarly socialistic. Also, the union's scheme would consolidate its power by taking over individual salary negotiations for the players and eliminating their agents. The percentage of gross concept had further precedent in the agreement negotiated by the Screen Actors' Guild with the television and motion picture industries after a lengthy strike in 1980. That union won a percentage of 4.5 percent of gross income from distribution of films used by pay television and in home video discs and cassettes. This pattern was later extended to film writers and directors.

When the NFLPA's demand of 55 percent of the gross was announced in January 1982, it did not specify how the fund would be operated, but the union indicated that monies would be distributed for salaries, insurance, pensions, and disability payments. Distribution was to be based on a uniform sliding scale, depending on years of service and number of downs played—regardless of position. Thus, offensive linemen would receive the same basic salary as quarterbacks. For incentive, those players chosen for the Pro Bowl would receive an extra $50,000 apiece; a portion of the gross revenue pool would be used to create a jackpot for players on teams that make the playoffs. About six months after the initial proposal, the union specified how it proposed to divide the percentage of gross revenue. This distribution is shown in Table 5-2.

Wage Scale

Because it was unable to make any progress on its percentage of gross demand, the NFLPA modified its position eight months after the initial proposal. Al-

Table 5-3. Experience Breakdown, 1982.

Years Experience	Players	Percentage	Average Salary
1	387	24.8	$ 55,120
2	220	14.1	67,647
3	197	12.6	72,976
4	147	9.4	87,657
5	173	11.1	97,920
6	118	7.6	112,065
7	84	5.4	125,993
8	62	4.0	144,667
9	55	3.5	142,309
10	39	2.5	142,366
11	28	1.8	182,995
12	19	1.2	183,752
13	15	1.0	156,693
14	10	0.6	166,001
15	5	0.3	206,506
16	2	0.1	217,500
17	1	0.1	264,000
	1,562	100.0	$ 90,102

Source: From a study initiated by and reported in Sporting News, Nov. 22, 1982, at 35.

though the demand for a fixed percentage of total revenue was dropped, the union continued its demand that certain revenues be earmarked for distribution to players and that compensation be based largely on seniority. This latter practice, known as a wage scale, is common in U.S. industry. Ironically, the owners had themselves proposed in 1975 that a general salary range be established for various positions with adjustments for length of service.[42] By 1982, however, they no longer favored the idea.

If management accepted a wage scale, it would meet one of the union's main concerns. Under the previous system of compensation the union negotiated an umbrella agreement setting minimum wage and benefit levels. Individual players negotiated salaries, usually through agents, with their teams. The average career length in the NFL is 4.2 years. But this figure is deceptive in that the median is less: As shown in Table 5-3, half of the league's players were in or above their third season, while half were in or below their third year. Also, the median salary of $75,000 was significantly less than the average of $90,102.

According to the NFLPA, the previous salary system underpaid many players, such as linemen, and encouraged teams to replace older players with younger ones making less money. This claim is supported by the data in Table 5-3. The union reasoned that establishing a wage scale to compensate players based on seniority rather than position would discourage the incentive to cut older play-

Table 5-4. Average Salaries by Position, 1981-82.

	1981	1982
Quarterbacks	$131,206	$160,037
Defensive linemen	85,683	92,961
Running backs	83,496	94,948
Receivers	75,968	85,873[a]
Offensive linemen	74,596	85,543
Linebackers	70,753	85,205
Defensive backs	68,753	79,581
Kickers	60,861	65,779

a. Data for wide receivers only.

Source: National Football League Management Council.

ers.[43] It would also eliminate the inequity of players who occupy glamorous positions making substantially more than players who do not, yet who perform the same work. This inequity is illustrated in Table 5-4.

Management's objection to the wage scale was that the previous system was working well and should continue. The owners worried that pay by seniority would reduce incentive to perform at peak levels, even though the union's revised proposal continued to have performance bonuses for players. They further objected that quarterbacks are more skilled than linemen and should be therefore paid more. The wage scale had some attraction to the owners in that it might eliminate troublesome agents representing players, but there were two other sticking points. One was that they would still have to pay players low in seniority but high in talent far more than scale because of bidding for players by the Canadian Football League and U.S. Football League.[44] Second, the union's wage-scale demand provided for distribution of $1.6 billion to players over four years through a fund administered independently of the owners. Apart from objecting to the size of the dollar amount for distribution, the owners were unwilling to give the union control of player payrolls.

Free Agency

As noted earlier the NFLPA negotiated away in 1977 the free-agency gains made by players in the 1976 *Mackey* case. The union's reason was that free agency had little value to football players. This rationale is based on the economics of football, compared to other professional team sports, and relies on two assumptions: (1) Owners have little incentive to sign free agents because of their uncertain impact on winning games, and (2) revenues are secure regardless of team personnel.

Table 5-5.   Teams with Highest Average Salaries, 1981.

Denver Broncos	$106,028
Pittsburgh Steelers	104,282
Cincinnati Bengals	100,058
Chicago Bears	95,311
Oakland Raiders	92,170

Source: National Football League Players' Association.

The first of these assumptions is probably valid. As shown in Table 5-5, the highest average salary for players in 1981 was paid by the Denver Broncos. (The lowest average salary, at $64,859, was paid by the Kansas City Chiefs.) Of the five highest-paying teams in the NFL, only Cincinnati was successful enough in its performance on the field to make the playoffs in 1981. The other high-paying teams may have compensated more for past success. In any event, it appears that there is little correlation between high salaries and winning football teams. Unlike other professional sports in which team sizes are smaller and personal performance is magnified, individual football players have less impact on overall team success.

The second assumption, that revenues are secure regardless of player contributions, has some validity. Stadiums are usually sold out for games, and television revenues, divided equally among teams regardless of performance, are guaranteed. However, a study determined that the difference to NFL clubs between winning and losing averages $170,000 a game.[45] It is easier for a winning team to assure a sellout crowd at stadiums, and they are generally able to charge higher ticket prices. Although football owners may have less incentive to win than their counterparts in other sports, they crave personal glory from success of their teams on the field. This can be a powerful incentive to bid for players, however elusive it may prove to be in terms of results. This is suggested by the large salaries paid to Tom Cousineau (Cleveland Browns) and Renaldo Nehemiah (San Francisco Forty-Niners) in 1982, who signed as free agents but without the usual contractual restrictions on free-agency compensation.

In the 1982 contract negotiations the NFLPA made two principal demands on free agency: (1) All cut players would automatically become free agents and not go through waivers, and (2) a player would become a free agent every three years unless he voluntarily agreed to stay with his team. The union did not place a high priority on achieving these demands, however, and chose instead to emphasize the 55 percent of gross and later the wage scale. Management opposed free agency by citing the damaging effects it had on the financial structure of baseball and basketball. The only group that favored free agency was the agents representing players, but they were not a party to the contract negotiations between the NFL and union.[46]

Pensions

As noted above, pensions were a pivotal issue for players in earlier negotiations and led to strikes in 1968 and 1970. Football player pensions are low compared to other professional team sports and cover only players active after 1958. In 1982 the players sought a reduction of vesting (entitlement to a pension payment on retirement) from four years to three, full benefit payment at age 50 instead of 55, with early retirement at 40, and a doubling of retirement benefits.[47] A fund was sought for distribution to old-timers.[48]

A comparison with baseball points up the relative disparity of football pensions. In the 1980 agreement baseball players received vesting after only one day of service (vesting required four years previously).[49] Baseball pension contributions were also raised to $15.5 million annually through 1983. Total contributions were $64.2 million from 1976 through 1981.[50] In contrast, for the same period the football pension contributions were $45.9 million, with $8.2 million received in 1981.[51] In addition to pension increases and other issues explained in this section, the NFLPA made demands concerning player safety, insurance, and choice of physician. The union wanted a four-year contract.

DYNAMICS OF NEGOTIATIONS

The owners did not make their first proposal until mid-July. It included a kind of wage scale based on a raising of minimum salaries. Rookies, for example, would receive at least $30,000, and fifth-year players $50,000. A reduction in the amount of compensation for free agents was proposed by the owners, based on the amount the individual players' signed for. The forty-eight-page proposal also addressed postseason compensation and numerous other issues, but not the 55 percent of gross. The owners wanted a five-year agreement to coincide with their television contracts. Although the owners' initial offer would have provided considerable economic enhancement over the old contract, the parties were separated by a wide gulf on the total amounts of money, and even more so on the financial allocation and control.

Exhibition games were played on schedule. Players sought to demonstrate their solidarity by having members of opposing teams join hands prior to the start of these games. This action rankled the owners, who considered fining the players but took no counteraction. Four days prior to the start of the regular season the owners made an offer reputed to contain more than $600 million in "new money."[52] This offer was broken down into $40 million for benefit increases, $126 million in "career adjustment" bonuses for veteran players, and $475 million for salary increases that would raise salaries by 15 percent per year. Career adjustment bonuses would pay players $10,000 for each year of service from 1977 to 1982 and an additional bonus of $10,000 per year from 1983 to

1986. However, this part of the offer was regarded by the union as flawed. With the typical player's short career, relatively few would actually get the full retroactive amount, and "bonuses" in the future might be used by owners as an offset to pay.[53] As a result, the offer was promptly rejected by the union.

Shortly after the start of the regular season the NFLPA dropped its demand on 55 percent of gross, in favor of the wage scale. The union's total demand was for $1.6 billion, with $1.06 billion coming from half of the clubs' total revenues from television.[61] When this revised proposal was rejected by the owners, the union announced its intention to strike between the second and fourth weeks of the season. A strike after the third game seemed most likely because players would then be assured credit toward their pensions for a full year's service.

The Strike Begins

On September 21, 1982, following the Monday night game between the Green Bay Packers and New York Giants, the players went on strike. At this point in the schedule, two weeks of the season had been completed. At the outset of the strike Ed Garvey characterized it as an "unfair practice strike" rather than an "economic strike," an important legal distinction.[55] This unofficial characterization by Garvey was made in case the owners tried to replace strikers and perhaps seek decertification of the union, as had occurred in the air traffic controllers' strike. Were the strike actually determined to be an unfair labor practice strike, the strikers would have job rights and the union would be protected from decertification.

Optimism that the strike would be short was justified by the notion that both sides appeared close to $1.6 billion in their total proposals, at least insofar as their statements to the media were concerned.[56] However, a closer look indicated that over $1 billion of the owners' offer was a *promise* to pay individual contracts (the owners rejected the union's wage scale) not yet negotiated, and the total money was to be for five years. The players, on the other hand, wanted a *guarantee* of $1.6 billion with a wage scale, over only four years. Thus, the parties' positions were farther apart than they appeared to be.

Immediately following the start of the strike, the owners announced that players were not to be paid for further games on the schedule, club facilities were closed to players, and medical treatment was not available at club facilities although the clubs would pay for medical treatment elsewhere. All monies lost by season ticket holders would be refunded.[57] Early in the strike nearly all players gathered at fields in local high schools and colleges to practice, but as the strike wore on most of the players went home and performed their conditioning exercises on an individual basis.

Reacting quickly to the strike, the television networks scrambled to come up with substitute fare for Sundays and Monday nights. Initially, ABC showed movies, CBS reran games from the prior season, and NBC showed live games from the Canadian Football League. CBS switched to coverage of small-college football games and later to boxing. Neither the Canadian nor the college games attracted much viewer interest.

Management Initiatives

Most of the repositioning during the strike was by the NFL Management Council, a movement in part due to prodding by mediators who assisted the parties in bargaining. (The use of mediation during the strike is discussed later in the chapter.) Although the owners' stance became increasingly generous, even to the point of moving close to the NFLPA's overall money demands, the animosity of the chief negotiators toward each other was so substantial and the distrust so great that compromise seemed almost impossible. The owners made what appeared to be a significant concession a week into the strike. Although they continued to insist in this offer that salary contracts between players and teams be negotiated on an individual basis, the $1.6 billion the players wanted was guaranteed. The owners sought to provide this assurance by stating that if at the end of five years the $1.6 billion had not been spent, the difference would be distributed to the players in the form of bonuses.[58] However, the offer was contingent on the union dropping its wage-scale demand and was for five years rather than the four-year contract the union wanted.

Following three weeks of intermittent talks in which the union did not accept the money guarantee, the owners decided to withdraw the offer.[59] They reasoned that the guarantee was based on five years of uninterrupted revenues and that the substantial drop in revenues because of the continuation of the strike necessitated a readjustment in management's position. At the end of October, on the fortieth day of the strike, the owners modified their offer again. They proposed a package of $1.28 billion—for the four years that the union wanted—but with the union allowed to control the distribution of only $50 million of the total package.[60] The money package would be guaranteed from 1983 through 1986 but not for 1982 because of lost revenue from the strike. The union's response to this offer was a demand for $1.1 billion for three years.

Frustrated by rejection of its latest proposal, on the forty-fifth day of the strike the owners tried a new tack by offering a $60,000 bonus to players who had played at least three games into their fourth season. This proposal, which became known as "money now," would be payable when a new collective bargaining agreement was signed. By this time the owners had accepted the idea of a wage scale, with $30,000 minimum salary and $10,000 increments for each year in the league, although the money that would fund the wage scale was nowhere near what the union wanted. In mid-November the owners raised their total money offer slightly—to $1.313 billion for four years—and indicated to the union that this was the final offer.[61]

Use of Mediation

Mediation is a voluntary impasse resolution procedure designed to assist the parties to move closer in negotiations. Mediators are usually neutral third parties who seek to achieve compromise by creative thinking and persuasion: They do not have the power to compel a settlement. Thus a strike may continue despite use of mediation. Mediation was helpful in resolving the baseball strike (discussed in Chapter 3), and, as noted earlier in this chapter, it was productive in ending the 1975 football strike.

The first signs that mediation might be used in the 1982 dispute came long before the strike, in late August. At that time the NFL Management Council requested assistance in negotiations from the Federal Mediation and Conciliation Service (FMCS).[62] The FMCS prefers to have mediation welcomed by both parties, since if each accepts the service it is more likely to be successful. The NFLPA, however, was not receptive to the idea because Ed Garvey felt it was premature to involve a mediator when management had not yet made a serious offer.[63] Perhaps Garvey was also wary because he knew that his adversary Jack Donlan had formerly been a mediator with the FMCS. Mediation was put on the back burner until October, when the NFLPA suggested a list of prestigious private citizens from which a mediator might be selected.[64] Typical of the position reversals that characterized negotiations by both sides, Donlan rejected the idea because he was not consulted about the list beforehand, some of the persons lacked mediation skills, and he preferred a mediator form the FMCS.

A few days later the parties agreed to consult Kay McMurray, director of the FMCS, about finding a mediator. Shortly thereafter the parties agreed on McMurray's suggestion of Sam Kagel. Kagel, a seventy-three-year-old lawyer from San Francisco, had a long career as a private mediator and arbitrator. Over the years he had been called in to attempt to resolve disputes in the longshore, newspaper, public school, hospital, food, and many other industries. Kagel was also known as a battler, however, and some observers questioned the wisdom of having him mingle with Donlan and Garvey.[65]

Almost from the start on October 12, Kagel ran into difficulty with the strong personalities negotiating for each side. He wisely ordered a news blackout, but it was violated as anonymous quotations from participants in the talks were cited frequently in the media. Kagel was helpful in clearing up noneconomic issues and kept the talks on all issues moving along at a brisk pace, which had been conspicuously lacking before he entered the scene. Kagel was critical of the union's position on a central fund out of which salaries would be paid.[66] Yet he could not budge the parties on this and other key economic issues. After twelve days of mediation, Kagel left Hunt Valley, Maryland, where the talks were being held, to return to San Francisco.[67] This allowed the parties to renew their strength and reassess their positions away from the heat of the bargaining table.

Kagel returned to Maryland a few days later for eight more days of intensive mediation but was again unable to break the impasse. He returned home again on November 6, with an offer to return if the parties were prepared to change their positions.[68] Kagel's reputation for toughness and irascibility was well deserved. He drove the parties hard in bargaining toward mediating the settlement and gave as good as he got in the chaotic atmosphere of the football talks. Some observers continued to criticize Kagel's choice as a mediator on grounds that the last thing the stalled talks needed was another feisty personality. His tough actions may have fueled on already raging fire, or the timing simply may not have been right for a settlement. Perhaps the chief negotiators needed more time to expend their wrath toward each other. Perhaps the pinch of the strike had to hurt sufficiently before settlement could come, no matter who was in the role of mediator.

At the request of the union, Kay McMurray picked up the mediator's role about a week after Kagel left the talks. By this time the positions of the parties had softened, particularly in light of growing restiveness of the players and owners over the lack of progress at the bargaining table. With McMurray's efforts to bridge the gap and later those of still another mediator, Paul Martha, a settlement was finally reached.

STRIKE ANALYSIS

The power theory of Chamberlain and Kuhn and the behavioral theory of Walton and McKersie, applied to the baseball strike analysis in Chapter 3,[69] are discussed in this section as they apply to the football strike.

Power Applications

Effective use of power in negotiations means getting the other side to agree to your terms. Various tactics that can be used for offensive and defensive purposes in enhancing power. These tactics can be drawn on to increase the other party's cost of disagreeing with you and thus force an agreement. The positive side of the scale—trying to get the other party to agree with you by making it less costly—involves compromises that induce rather than force agreement. Regrettably, hardly any examples of inducement emerged from the football negotiations and strike. Instead, power was mostly generated by raising costs of disagreement through offensive and defensive weapons. Similar to the baseball strike of 1981, the power equation in football was pretty evenly distributed on both sides. Inability of either side to tilt power significantly in its favor is a major factor explaining the long duration of the football strike.

Owners. The "money now" offer made by the owners in the sixth week of the strike was thoughtfully calculated to break the players' resistance to a settlement. Termed a "bribe" by the union leadership, the $60,000 bonus, essentially for four-year veterans and above, came at a time when players had already forgone considerable income as a result of the strike. It almost certainly was an important factor in ending the walkout, as eligible players contemplated the sizable carrot of up-front cash. Although its precise impact is difficult to determine, this imaginative proposal is a good example of how to reduce the other side's disinclination to come to terms by taking positive action.

Offensive power tactics were not used to much effect by the owners. They threatened to fine players for joining hands at exhibition games to show solidarity, but their overreaction to this gesture by the players led to their retreat from the threat of fines. Along with Commissioner Rozelle, the owners also sought to manipulate public opinion in their favor during the strike by carefully orchestrating statements to the print and broadcast media. In past strikes the public showed overwhelming sympathy for the owners' position. This was partially offset in the 1982 strike by the players' more astute public relations.

In the final analysis the public's reaction was more akin to "a plague on both your houses" than an indication of support for either party. Despite the enormous popularity of the game, as the strike wore on fans displayed a surprising lack of interest in the outcome. Therefore, pressure from the public was not a factor that either side could use effectively against the other to increase power. Another offensive power tactic that might have been used by the owners was the lockout, but they forswore a lockout during the exhibition games in order to keep the option open for the regular season. If they were serious about a lockout then, the players beat them to the punch with the strike.

Defensive power tactics were put to somewhat better use by the owners. Their $150 million line of bank credit provided a cushion for the strike, although there is no evidence that any loans were actually made by the owners. At the least, the credit provided psychological assurance. Two other possibilities were considered by the owners but never effectuated. One was using free agents to play games, unattractive because of the paucity of free agents and unsigned rookies. The other was to invite players to return to camp. This might have been a viable option had the strike continued much longer, since player support for the walkout was beginning to wane. Perhaps the most effective defensive power tactic of the owners was that payments under the 1982 television contract continued during the first two weeks of the strike. This was thoughtfully arranged by Commissioner Rozelle in the contract with the networks and provided considerable economic insulation to the owners during the strike.

Players. Similar to the owners, the players showed hardly any willingness to induce agreement through compromise. The union's intransigence is best illustrated by its clinging to the chimerical 55 percent of gross demand for over eight months. Given the radical nature of this demand compared with past practice, and the devastating effect it would have on owner finances, the players must have realized its futility. Some observers thought at first that the 55 percent of gross was a smoke screen and that the notion would be relinquished quickly after its shock impact on the owners had been achieved. That the union stuck with the demand for so long was in part due to the owners' delay in putting a money offer on the table. When the union finally dropped the demand, shortly after the start of the regular season, it was replaced with the wage scale. In its original form as proposed by the union, the wage scale was nearly as controversial as the 55 percent of gross. Indeed, the wage scale continued to be tied to revenue sharing (from television) and posited control of allocation by the union. At this point the union's time for striking was running out, yet it gave the owners little incentive to maneuver toward a compromise that could have averted a strike.

From their arsenal of offensive tactics the players relied chiefly on the ultimate weapon of the strike. There was some talk during the strike of the players forming a new league, and wholesale player signings with the new USFL were considered. But these were more in the nature of options in case the season was cancelled and were not serious offensive tactics.

The NFLPA brought several charges of violation of federal labor law before the NLRB in 1982 in an attempt to increase its power leverage. These unfair labor practice claims were used partly as offensive tactics and partly as defensive ones. Although they did not significantly affect the strike outcome, they are an interesting part of the mosaic. Three such actions are notable. The first charges, brought early in 1982 to force the owners to open their books were described earlier in this chapter. Although the union was able to gain release of some data, it could not force full disclosure on employer finances. The NLRB may have been reluctant to become further embroiled in the dispute at this time because of its failure to head off the baseball strike (see Chapter 3).

A second incident occurred in early September when Sam McCullum, player representative for the Seattle Seahawks, was put on waivers pending release by the team. Seahawk players signed a petition calling for McCullum's reinstatement and threatened to strike over the incident.[70] Trying to avoid a premature work stoppage, the NFLPA ordered the Seahawks not to strike. An unfair labor practice charge was filed with the NLRB by the union on grounds that McCullum was put on waivers because of his union activities. The NLRB ruled that the Seattle club had violated the law and gave the club an opportunity to settle the matter with McCullum before it would issue a complaint.[71] In the meantime, McCullum was picked up on waivers and signed a contract to play for the Minnesota Vikings.

The third situation stemmed from the initial NLRB charges on opening the books. Several allegations of unfair labor practices were made concerning failure to bargain in good faith, including that the owners did not make any monetary proposals until July and had not responded with counterproposals since then. In October the NLRB general counsel, William Lubbers, upheld the union's contentions. In effect, this meant that the owners could not legally continue to refuse to bargain over the wage scale by insisting on negotiating salaries individually with players.[72] As a result of the NLRB's ruling, the owners subsequently made a proposal that would have allowed union control over some monies for a wage scale. However, as with the baseball players' union, the NFLPA was never able to use the NLRB to much advantage in increasing its power through offensive and defensive tactics.

All-Star Games. One other defensive tactic used by the union deserves mention. Shortly after the strike began, the NFLPA announced that a series of twenty all-star games would be played over a nine-week period beginning October 10. If successful, the games would provide player revenues, as a replacement for the nonexistent strike fund, and would satisfy fan interest. An agreement was signed by the union with Turner Broadcasting Company, an Atlanta-based cable network owned by Ted Turner, to televise the games.

When the owners took legal action in state courts to prevent players from participating in these games, the union filed suit in federal court charging that the clause in player contracts precluding them from engaging in activities where there was risk of injury was unenforceable because of the expiration of the collective bargaining agreement in July.[73] Federal District Court Judge John Penn, ruling on the union's request for an injunction to stop the owners' interference, decided that any legal attempts by the owners to block the games would have to be brought before his court. At the same time, however, Judge Penn declined to issue the injunction.[74] Still, the decision was a victory for the players, and when the NFL was initially unable to get it overturned by the U.S. Court of Appeals, the first two all-star games were on.

The first game was played in Washington, D.C., on October 17, and the second in Los Angeles the following night. Both were televised nationally on the Turner cable network and by some local independent stations. However, the games attracted only about 9,000 and 5,000 fans, respectively, and the promoters reportedly lost money.[75] Several of the best-known players refused to participate in the games because of fear of injury and possibly also retribution by owners.[76] A few days after the games, the U.S. Court of Appeals voted 2 to 1 to overturn district court Judge Penn's decision that players could be sued for participation in all-star games only in federal court. The appellate court ruled that the NFL could sue players in state courts.[77] Lacking the money to defend players in lawsuits across the nation, the NFLPA decided to cancel further scheduled all-star games. Failure of these games meant that the players could not rely on outside support during the strike. Although the union arranged for loans of up to $20,000 for each player, many players took jobs. The ill-fated experiment also foiled any plans of Ted Turner to steal a march on the major television networks in case a new players' league was formed out of the all-star games.

Miscalculation. Power is intangible and sometimes transitory. It is based on an estimate of what one side thinks the other's power is. Based on the players' lack of solidarity in the past, the owners misjudged their power in 1982. Had they realized the strength of the players' commitment, they would probably have made more generous offers earlier. For their part, once they perceived their solidarity, the players began to overestimate their strengths and failed to accurately gauge the owners' ability to withstand a strike. Had each party known of the other's resolve it might have acted to prevent a strike or at least to have limited its duration.

SETTLEMENT

By mid-November negotiations were on the verge of total collapse, and cancellation of the season seemed imminent. Serious divisions were occurring in the ranks of both players and owners. Intraorganizational pressures moved both sides to a final attempt to resolve the impasse.

Terms of the Settlement

In the end the players dropped their demands for 55 percent of television revenues and control over the allocation of a central fund, the principal sticking points in the negotiations. They also relinquished their demand for a three-year contract and settled instead for five years. The union agreed to drop charges before the NLRB. Free agency was liberalized some, but players will not enjoy significant freedom of movement under the new rules because compensation must still be made with draft choices. The owners maintained the previous system of individual player negotiations on salaries. There was no change in pension plan vesting. (Settlement terms are summarized in Table 5-6.)

The players' gains were mostly economic. The overall package included $1.28 billion over four years plus about $320 million for 1982, for a total of $1.6 billion over five years. A wage scale established minimum salaries that increased during the life of the agreement. Based on seniority, these minimums started at $30,000 for rookies and ended at $200,000 for sixteen-year veterans (see Table 5-6). The players gained $60 million in "money now" seniority bonuses, the first time such bonuses were awarded in professional sports. Another new concept implemented was the establishment of severance pay based on seniority. Improvements in pensions and insurance totaled about $60 million. The union also won the right to approve agents negotiating contracts on behalf of veteran players. Players can send disputed rule changes involving safety to arbitration. Although the union did not get a fixed percentage of income or control over its allocation, it did achieve a money guarantee. If the owners' player compensa-

Table 5-6. Summary of National Football League Settlement Terms.

Total Money

$1.6 billion over five years, including 1982.

Salaries

Rookies: $30,000 in 1982, $40,000 in 1983 and 1984, $50,000 in 1985 and 1986. Minimums rise in $10,000 increments per year of experience (e.g., twelve-year veteran minimum of $140,000 in 1982). The top minimum salary is $200,000.

Bonuses

Total of $60 million in immediate bonuses based on seniority: $10,000 for rookies, $20,000 for second-year players, $30,000 for third-year players, and $60,000 for four-year players and above.

Severance Pay

Starts at $2,000 for players with at least two years' service; $20,000 for three-year players, $60,000 for four-year players, up to $140,000 for twelve years or more. All past years of service are credited in determining severance pay.

Playoff Money

Wildcard games $6,000 per player, division playoffs $10,000, conference championship games $18,000, Super Bowl winners $36,000, losers $18,000; Pro Bowl winners $10,000, losers $5,000.

Agents

A rookie may retain the agent of his choice. All veterans must have agents approved by NFLPA. With the player's approval the union itself can negotiate individual salaries.

The Draft

Continued through 1992. If a player is drafted but joins another league, his NFL team retains exclusive bargaining rights for four years (up from two years in 1977 agreement).

Free Agency

Team that loses a third-year player earning a minimum of $110,000 would receive one first-round draft choice (down from two first-round choices in 1977 agreement).

---

tion costs do not total $1.28 billion from 1983 through 1986, they will have to make up the difference.[78]

Ratification

Ratification of the agreement by the owners was made without incident. Although the union's executive board voted 6 to 1 against the agreement, the player representatives voted 19 to 6, with three abstentions, to send it to the players. Ed Garvey initially predicted that the players would reject the settlement. They were to be given the choices of (1) voting to accept, (2) rejecting but continuing to play, or (3) resuming the strike. However, the player vote was postponed while some details of the agreement were cleaned up, such as the union's right to reopen the contract if the NFL renegotiated its current television contracts. A second vote by the player representatives of 19 to 9 recommended that the players approve the agreement.

When the players finally voted, it was to either accept or reject the agreement. They accepted by a 3 to 1 margin, although a majority of players on two teams, the Chicago Bears and Detroit Lions, voted against ratification. The agreement was finally signed by the parties on December 12.

Assessment

Who won the fifty-seven-day football strike? No clear-cut verdict is acceptable to everyone. As with most strikes a good argument can be made that both sides lost. Surely the public was a loser because it was deprived of entertainment, although some fans probably did well to reassess their slavish commitment to the game. Certain player agents, who may become disenfranchised, suffered a setback. But in assessing the overall outcome a strong case can be made that the owners prevailed. They held the line well enough on free agency and defeated revenue sharing and allocation of a central fund that were the players' most important goals. In effect, the owners preserved the prior system for another five years.

The players came away with a seemingly impressive $1.28 billion guarantee. But given the probable expenditures that the owners will have to make on player compensation, regardless of the collective bargaining agreement, the guarantee becomes more of a Pyrrhic victory for the union. During the long strike it gained little more than what the owners offered in early September. Apart from the virtually meaningless money guarantee, the union acquired minimum salary increases, bonuses, severance pay, and increases in pensions and insurance, totaling about $250 million.[79] This money represents only about 22 percent of the owners' increase in revenue under the five-year television contract. In short, the 1982 agreements should make ownership of an NFL franchise far more profitable than it was under the old labor and television contracts.

AFTERMATH

Poststrike play in the NFL resumed on November 21 with games originally scheduled. One makeup game was added to the schedule. Counting the two games played prior to the strike, the regular season in the NFL was nine games. Instead of the ten teams that normally qualified for the playoffs (six division champions and four wild-card entries), the number of teams qualifying for post-season play was increased to sixteen. The Super Bowl was played on January 30 as originally scheduled.

Financial Impact

Although it is not possible to make an exact accounting of the total cost of the strike, it was at least several hundred million dollars. Direct income forgone from the missed seven regular season games was about $210 million for owners and $63 million for players.[80] Businesses dependent on NFL play lost even greater amounts of income from withheld expenditures by fans on concessions, gambling, hotels, restaurants, transportation, and the like. There were certain income offsets, but nearly all individuals and organizations with a direct economic stake in the game lost money.

Players. Players were paid for the nine regular season games but forfeited income for the seven games lost. Based on an average salary of $90,000, the average player lost $5,625 for each missed game, or a total of $39,375. However, this loss is offset by income from outside work that some players performed during the strike, bonuses paid as part of the strike settlement, and playoff money for players on the six extra teams that qualified for postseason play.

Owners. All teams lost money during the strike, averaging about a $5 million deficit.[81] But this estimate is deceptive because in the aftermath of the strike some teams suffered far more substantial declines in ticket sales than others. Owner incomes were cut from forgone games and television monies. These direct revenue losses were offset by savings on player salaries and other expenses that stopped with the strike. Teams also received substantial interest payments on monies held from season ticket sales.[82] Although the owners received about $60 million from their television contracts during the first two weeks of the strike, this money is an offset to 1983 payments from the networks, which were reduced accordingly.

Other Business. The total business loss suffered in cities with NFL franchises differed because of stadium sizes and because games in some cities bring in greater proportions of visitors from outlying areas who spend more money on travel, lodging, and food. Most league cities lost an average of about $1 to $2 million per week in hotel and restaurant revenue from the strike.[83] Approximately the same amount was lost by concessionnaires. The NFL on Sundays is the biggest single-day betting attraction in the United States, and the strike hurt the gambling industry badly, especially in Las Vegas. Television revenues fell because the high rates charged advertisers for NFL games could not be maintained for alternative fare and some advertisers dropped out entirely.

Fan Reaction

Similar to the fan reaction in the aftermath of the baseball strike, football's poststrike attendance dropped significantly. Empty seats from tickets not sold or not used averaged only about 6 percent in 1981 and in the games prior to the strike; after the 1982 season resumed, empty seats rose to about 27 percent.[84] Cooler public attitudes toward football were also reflected in television ratings. For the first four weekends after the strike ABC and CBS were down 16 percent from the same period in 1981, and NBC was off 4 percent.[85]

The players were humbled by the strike but worked hard after it was over to restore their image. Ed Garvey departed as the NFLPA executive director, to be replaced by more conciliatory leadership, under ex-NFL player Gene Upshaw. The owners also marshaled their considerable public relations resources to win back the fans and meet the challenge of the newly formed USFL. While salaries escalated, the league recovered, as baseball did from its strike. However, the football strike was an unfortunate experience that hopefully will not likely be repeated in any professional team sport for a long time. No one wants so see strike three.

NOTES TO CHAPTER 5

1.   There is a certain incongruence in goals of workers as they attempt to deal with management. This was certainly the case with football players in the NFL, as the discussion in this chapter illustrates. Some of the bases for the incongruence is discussed in basic textbooks on organizational psychology, including Ernest J. McCormick and Joseph Tifflin, Industrial Psychology (6th ed. 1974), and Fred Luthans, Organizational Behavior (2d ed. 1977). Regarding the unique problems faced by football players, see Fugett, The Fear Factor in Pro Football's Contract Talks, N.Y. Times, Sept. 5, 1982, at 55; Hoffer, Psychologists' View: Football Players Going on Strike – Of All Things!, L.A. Times, Sept. 22, 1982, pt. 3, at 5; and Vecsey, The Pro Football Players Move into an Early Lead, N.Y. Times, Sept. 26, 1982, at 55.

2.   Cooney, Hecker Recalls '56 Strike Call, Sporting News, Oct. 11, 1982, at 12.

3.   Coughlin, Why Coach Was Erased from Photo, Sporting News, Oct. 18, 1982, at 60.

4.   Berry and Gould, A Long Deep Drive to Collective Bargaining: Of Players, Owners, Brawls, and Strikes, 31 Case W. Res. L. Rev. 745 (1981).

5.   Ibid.

6.   This information on the 1970 strike and lockout is from San Francisco Chron., June 30, 1974, sec. C, at 6.

7.   Gustkey, History of Acrimony and Abuse Resurfaces in Squabbles of '82, L.A. Times, Sept. 21, 1982, pt. 3, at 4.

8. Underwood, Summer of Their Discontent, Sports Illustrated, July 29, 1974, at 20.

9. Statement by Commissioner Pete Rozelle, quoted in Kennedy, Star-Struck Canton, Sports Illustrated, Aug. 5, 1974, at 12.

10. Data from Sports Illustrated, Aug. 12, 1974, at 11.

11. NFL Owners Cited in Labor Row, L.A. Times, July 2, 1976, pt. 3, at 2.

12. *See* Kennedy, Pat's Rabbit Who Turned Tiger, Sports Illustrated, Sept. 29, 1975, at 55.

13. Paul, Growing Threat of Pro Football Strike Irks Fans and Worries Clubs, TV and Odds-Makers, Wall St. J., Sept. 18, 1975, at 34.

14. No Gain, Time, Sept. 29, 1975, at 62.

15. These teams were the New York Jets, New York Giants, Detroit Lions, and Washington Redskins. *See* NFL Players Set Pact; Weekend Games Are On, Wall St. J., Sept. 19, 1975, at 12.

16. Mackey v. National Football League, 543 F.2d 644 (8th Cir. 1976), *cert. dismissed*, 434 U.S. 801 (1977). For further discussion of the *Mackey* case, see Strauss, Sport in Court: The Legality of Professional Football's System of Reserve and Compensation, 28 U.C.L.A. L. Rev. 252–90 (1980).

17. Staudohar, Professional Football and the Great Salary Dispute, 61 Personnel J. 674 (1982).

18. Data from Sports Illustrated, Feb. 1, 1982, at 7.

19. For a brief profile of the other participants, see Felser, Cast of Characters, Sporting News, Oct. 11, 1982, at 25; and Morrow, Upshaw: Leader of Raiders and NFLPA, Sporting News, Nov. 8, 1982, at 49.

20. Portions of this profile are from Oates, At Stake in This Fight Are Millions, and the NFL Season, L.A. Times, Feb. 21, 1982, pt. 3, at 3; and Boyle, The 55% Solution, Sports Illustrated, Feb. 1, 1982, at 30.

21. In his job as chief negotiator for the NFL in 1982, Donlan worked with the council's executive committee, which included Chuck Sullivan, New England Patriots; Mike Brown, Cincinnati Bengals; Leonard Tose, Philadelphia Eagles; High Culverhouse, Tampa Bay Bucaneers; Jim Kensil, New York Jets; and Dan Rooney, Pittsburgh Steelers.

22. In December 1982, after the strike, the union raised its annual dues from $850 to $1,200.

23. The $2 Billion Understanding, Time, April 5, 1982, at 80.

24. Staudohar, Professional Football and the Great Salary Dispute, 61 Personnel J., 676 (1982).

25. These estimates are based on a full season for 1982, which did not occur because of the strike. Ticket prices for 1982 were increased by most teams. This raised the average ticket cost from $10.50 in 1981 to about $15 in 1982. *See* The $2 Billion Understanding, Time, April 5, 1982, at 80.

26. Johnson, Whole New League, Whole New Season, Sports Illustrated, May 24, 1982, at 82.

27. Data reported in Wall St. J., May 27, 1982, at 5; and Axthelm, et al., They're Playing for Keeps, Newsweek, Sept. 20, 1982, at 71.

28. McDonough, Battle Brewing in NFL, Boston Globe, March 25, 1982, at 47.

29. Litsky, Players Union Focuses on Antitrust Issues, N.Y. Times, March 28, 1982, at 53.

30. Nyhan, NFLPA Learned from PATCO, Boston Globe, Sept. 24, 1982, at 42.

31. L.A. Times, March 25, 1982, pt. 3, at 5.

32. *See* Linderman, Sport Interview: Gene Upshaw, Sport, January 1982, at 16.

33. Estimates by Donlan and Garvey vary in published accounts. Donlan's estimates ranged from 44–48 percent and Garvey's from 28–31 percent.

34. A 32 percent figure was reported in the Wall St. J., Feb. 2, 1982, at 1.

35. *See* Monopoly Pays Off in the Business of Sports, Bus. Week, Oct. 13, 1980, at 147.

36. McDonough, NFL: We'll Open Up the Books, Boston Globe, Jan. 23, 1982, at 30.

37. *Ibid.*

38. NFL Says the Players Can't See the Books; Garvey Hollers Foul, L.A. Times, Feb. 19, 1982, pt. 3, at 4.

39. *Ibid.*

40. NLRB Orders NFL to Disclose Contracts to Players, L.A. Times, April 9, 1982, pt. 3, at 12.

41. For a statement of the positions of the chief negotiators on the 55 percent of gross demand, see Garvey, Why Players Want Altered Salary Plan, N.Y. Times, Feb. 18, 1982, at 25; and Donlan, Why Owners Must Maintain Their Control, N.Y. Times, Feb. 14, 1982, at 25.

42. NFL Asks Individual Salary Negotiations, L.A. Times, Oct. 3, 1975, pt. 3, at 7.

43. It's Fourth Down in the NFL's Labor Bowl, Bus. Week, Sept. 27, 1982, at 27.

44. Scorecard, Sports Illustrated, Oct. 11, 1982, at 19.

45. This study is reported in Sports Illustrated, Oct. 11, 1982, at 19.

46. For statements by agents in favor of free agency, see McEwen, Woolf: Players May Strike, But for Wrong Reasons, Tampa Tribune, May 15, 1982, at 1C; and Leader, Agents Back NFL Strike, Not Garvey, San Francisco Sunday Examiner & Chron., Oct. 3, 1982, at C1, C11.

47. Boyle, The 55% Solution, Sports Illustrated, Sept. 27, 1982, at 32.

48. *See* Steadman, The NFL Fails to Take Care of Its Own, Sporting News, Nov. 15, 1982, at 39; and Another Weekend Is All But Shot, L.A. Times, Sept. 29, 1982, pt. 3, at 2.

49. Balzer, Charts Show Inequities in NFL Salaries, Sporting News, Nov. 22, 1982, at 35.

50. Balzer, Pro Football Focus, Sporting News, Oct. 25, 1982, at 50.

51. *Ibid.*

52. Figures reported in Sports Illustrated, Sept. 20, 1982, at 11.

53. Klein, Do You Care If Football's Suspended?, Wall St. J., Sept. 22, 1982, at 28; and Madden, Hasselbeck: Chances of Strike Now 100 Percent, Boston Globe, Sept. 9, 1982, at 70.

54. McDonough, NFL Strike: Owners Stop Pay, Close Down Facilities, Boston Globe, Sept. 22, 1982, at 65; and NFL Players Abandon 55% Demand: Talks Broken Off Anyway, L.A. Times, Sept. 18, 1982, pt. 3, at 1.

55. NFL Players' Panel Has Called a Strike Over Football Pact, Wall St. J., Sept. 21, 1982, at 16.

56. Madden, Surveying the Strike, Boston Globe, Sept. 26, 1982, at 61.

57. For details of these actions by the NFL Management Council, see McDonough, NFL Strike: Owners Stop Pay, Close Down Facilities, Boston Globe, Sept. 22, 1982, at 65; and Oates, Owners Talk of Employing Free Agents, L.A. Times, Sept. 22, 1982, pt. 3, at 1.

58. Owners Strike Out with Latest Offer, L.A. Times, Sept. 27, 1982, pt. 3, at 1.

59. The offer withdrawal is discussed in Janofsky, Owners Withdraw Guarantee, N.Y. Times, Oct. 20, 1982, at B11; NFL Owners Retract $1.6 Billion Package, San Francisco Chron., Oct. 20, 1982, at 57; and NFL Loses Fifth Week; $1.6 Billion Offer Is Withdrawn by Owners, L.A. Times, Oct. 20, 1982, pt. 3, at 1.

60. Reported in Eskenazi, NFL Owners Make New Offer, N.Y. Times, Nov. 1, 1982, at C1; and Modified Version of Salary Fund in New NFL Offer, San Francisco Sunday Examiner & Chron., Oct. 31, 1982, at C2.

61. NFL Owners Say Latest Proposal Is Final Offer, San Francisco Chron., Nov. 15, 1982, at 45.

62. Barnes, NFL Asks Mediators to Intervene, Washington Post, Aug. 27, 1982, at D1.

63. *Ibid.*

64. The list included Arthur Goldberg, former Supreme Court Justice; Archibald Cox, chairman of Common Cause; John Dunlop, Willard Wirtz, and Ray Marshall, all former Secretaries of Labor; and Rev. Theodore Hesburgh, president of Notre Dame University. *See* Janofsky, NFL Rejects a Proposal to Have Private Mediator, N.Y. Times, Oct. 8, 1982, at B15.

65. For a profile of Kagel, see Katz, A Mediator Who Builds Confidence, N.Y. Times, Oct. 13, 1982, at B9.

66. Janofsky, Mediator Leaves Talks in NFL, N.Y. Times, Oct. 24, 1982, sec. 5, at 1; and Stellino, NFL Name-Calling Yields to Bargaining, Sporting News, Nov. 8, 1982, at 45.

67. Shinoff, Kagel Here: "Talks Need Pause," San Francisco Sunday Examiner & Chron., Oct. 24, 1982, at C3.

68. Kagel Quits; Season May Be Over, San Francisco Sunday Examiner & Chron., Nov. 7, 1982, at C1.

69. *See* Neil W. Chamberlain and James W. Kuhn, Collective Bargaining (2d ed. 1965); and Richard E. Walton and Robert B. McKersie, A Behavioral Theory of Labor Negotiations: An Analysis of a Social Interaction System (1965).

70. Seattle Asked Not to Strike, Boston Globe, Sept. 11, 1982, at 28; and Janofsky, McCullum: 'Didn't Want Me Around,' N.Y. Times, Sept. 12, 1982, at C5.

71. L.A. Times, Sept. 18, 1982, pt. 3, at 5.

72. *See* L.A. Times, Oct. 22, 1982, pt. 3, at 4; Oct. 28, 1982, pt. 3, at 1; and Oct. 29, 1982, pt. 3, at 6.

73. Janofsky, Union Files Suit against NFL, N.Y. Times, Sept. 24, 1982, at B11.

74. Janofsky, Legal Ruling Aids Pro All-Star League, N.Y. Times, Oct. 7, 1982, at B17.

75. Attner, NFL Fans Ignore Players' All Star Games, Sporting News, Nov. 1, 1982, at 47.

76. An insurance policy of $2.5 million per player was supposedly arranged with Lloyd's of London, but it was reported that this deal fell through and was replaced by insurance with State Mutual of Worcester (Mass.) for $250,000 per player. *See* McDonough, NFL Aims for Games Next Week, Boston Globe, Oct. 15, 1982, at 33.

77. Barnes, Court Decision Causes Players to Cancel Games, Washington Post, Oct. 21, 1982, at E1.

78. Money will be distributed if costs fall below established figures in any one year—$240 million in 1983, $260 million in 1984, $290 million in 1985, and $320 million in 1986.

79. Klein, After the Football Strike: The Won-Lost Column, Wall St. J., Nov. 28, 1982, at 28. *See also* Zimmerman, The Strike: The Winners, The Losers, and Who Did What to Whom, Sports Illustrated, Nov. 29, 1982, at 19–22; and Ray, Players Ask: Was Long Walkout Worth It?, Sporting News, Nov. 29, 1982, at 41.

80. Zimmerman, The Strike: The Winners, The Losers, and Who Did What to Whom, Sports Illustrated, Nov. 29, 1982, at 19.

81. Data reported in Sports Illustrated, Dec. 27, 1982, and Jan. 1, 1983, at 19.

82. *See* Miller, The 49ers' Grub Stake, San Francisco Chron., Nov. 5, 1982, at 69; and Cherwa, How NFL Teams Made Money during the Strike, L.A. Times, Nov. 13, 1982, pt. 3, at 1.

83. *See* Ray, While Packers Take Hike, 7,500 Fans Have a Party, Sporting News, Oct. 4, 1982, at 2; and Leader, What the Walkout Is Costing the League Cities, San Francisco Sunday Examiner & Chron., Oct. 31, 1982, at C2.

84. Estimates based on numerous published sources.

85. Data from Sports Illustrated, Dec. 27, 1982, and Jan. 1, 1983, at 19.

6 LABOR RELATIONS IN BASKETBALL

THE EVOLUTION OF THE NBA AND THE NBPA

According to a few intrepid sports historians an 1893 outing in Herkimer, New York, was the earliest professional basketball game. Others claim that the earliest game was played in 1896 in Trenton, New Jersey, where each player was paid $15 and the captains of the teams $16 for the game.[1] Those early years saw many attempts to capitalize on this American-invented, peach-basket-descended sport:[2] There was the National Basketball League (1893-1903); the Philadelphia League (1903), later expanded into the Eastern League, which included clubs from Pennsylvania, New York, and New Jersey; the Central League, which joined the Philadelphia connection; the Hudson River League (1909): the New York State League (1911); the Western Pennsylvania League (1912); the Pennsylvania State League (1914); the Inter-State League (1915); the Metropolitan Basketball League (1921); the first American Basketball League (ABL) (1926-31); finally culminating in the Basketball Association of America (BAA) (1946), which merged with the National Basketball League in 1949 to form the National Basketball Association that exists to this day.[3]

Although there had been earlier notable teams, such as the Buffalo Germans, who ruled the floors around the turn of the century, and Ed Wachter's Troy (N.Y.) Trojans in the early teens, not until the late teens did two well-known teams create stars still remembered in basketball annals. The New York Whirlwinds were relatively short-lived but good while they lasted. Their rivals became even better. Starting out as the New York Celtics (1914-17), they became the Original Celtics in 1918 but still played out of New York. When the two teams clashed in a best of three series in 1921, the match had to be called after two games because emotions among players and fans ran too high. The series never resumed, and each team walked away with a victory.

The Whirlwinds faded, but the Original Celtics kept going, becoming clearly and indisputedly the powerhouse team of the 1920s. Led by Dutch Dehnart, Nat Holman,[4] Pete Barry, and their big man, 6' 5" Joe Lapchick,[5] they toured the country, winning game after game and rarely losing. Ironically, the Celtics helped undo the American Basketball League. They were too good. They joined the league in 1929 and were soon so overpowering that owners lost money because of the demise of fan interest. Cries of "Break up the Celtics" were answered when the league dispersed the Celtics players to different teams (which would be an interesting exercise today in light of the spate of antitrust suits that have been successfully pursued for far less drastic acts). Even the breakup did not save the league: The American Basketball League folded in 1931, and the old Original Celtics players followed other pursuits. (Joe Lapchick and Nat Holman, of course, became highly successful coaches, both in colleges and the pros.)

The American Basketball League was resuscitated in 1933 and lasted until 1946, the year the BAA was founded. The ABL, however, never quite recaptured its former renown, though a couple of its teams, the Philadelphia Sphas and New York Jewels, were strong. Ironically, neither was as good as one team that could not get admitted to that or any other league: the all-black Renaissance Big Five (known as the "Rens").[6]

Another league that preceded the founding of the BAA and later the NBA was the National Basketball League (NBL). Unlike the ABL, the NBL played in smaller cities, which helped keep it minor league. Even so, it might have survived in Oshkosh, Flint, Hammond, Toledo, and some larger cities had it not lost four franchises to the BAA in 1948. When these four departed, particularly the Minneapolis Lakers and their budding star, George Mikan, the league could only capitulate to the BAA. The following year, six more teams moved from the NBL to the BAA, the NBL folded, and the now-named NBA was fully underway.

The NBA had started in 1946 with teams such as the Celtics (Boston), the Knicks (New York), the Warriors (Philadelphia), the Ironmen (Pittsburgh), the Huskies (Toronto), the Steamrollers (Providence), and the Bombers (St. Louis).[7] Within a few years others appeared: the Pistons (Fort Wayne) (sometimes called the Zollner Pistons), the Lakers (Minneapolis), the Royals (Rochester) (later the Cincinnati Royals, the Kansas City Kings and today, the Sacramento Kings), the Nationals (Syracuse) (today the Philadelphia 76er's). These seven are the only NBA teams that can trace their history to the 1940s.

With the advent of the 1949–50 season, several teams moved from the old National Basketball League to form a third division of the NBA: the Sheboygan Redskins, the Waterloo Hawks, the Anderson Packers, the Denver Nuggets (no connection to today's franchise), the Indianapolis Olympians, and the Tri-Cities Blackhawks (Moline, Davenport, Rock Island). The team that survived from that short-lived division was the Blackhawks, which lived as the Hawks (Milwaukee to St. Louis, and ultimately to Atlanta). In that 1949–50 season the Tri-Cities had a young but already seasoned coach named Arnold "Red" Auerbach.

Crumbling franchises, peripatetic clubs, and transient owners have too often plagued the NBA. While such patterns have not totally disappeared, there are signs that they are abating. Even so, as recently as the events leading to the latest collective bargaining agreement, reached in 1983, several franchises were thought headed for extinction. This has not yet proved to be the case, thanks to a new direction in collective bargaining, the purchase of several weak franchises by "new money," and a new potential for tapping new revenue sources. Before examining the league in the context of these recent events, particularly developments in labor relations and collective bargaining, we turn to other themes that must be understood in order to fairly assess today's National Basketball Association: These include the history of rival leagues, the growth of the National Basketball Players' Association (NBPA), the persistent dominance of black players in the NBA, and the perceived problems plaguing professional basketball in the 1980s.

Rival Leagues

The "new league and expansion" fever hit professional sports in the late 1950s, and basketball was seen as a growth-potential sport. Although the NBA was by no means a solid success in 1961, it was attractive enough so that people wanted to share in its action. Abe Saperstein, founder and owner of the Harlem Globetrotters, was the moving force behind the new league – the American Basketball League (ABL). It was named for two earlier failed ventures and did little better.[8] Although its eight original teams survived the first season with only one casualty, the league folded early in its second year. It was notable for one of its stars, a young player named Connie Hawkins, who had left the University of Iowa after his freshman year because of alleged involvement in point-shaving scandals:[9] He averaged a heady 27.5 points per game in the league's one full season.

The rival league faced inevitable charges of predatory practices and resulting litigation. In *Central New York Basketball v. Barnett*,[10] the young star guard for the Syracuse Nationals, Dick Barnett, was restrained from abandoning his contractual obligations with the Nats and jumping to the Cleveland Pipers of the ABL. (See Chapter 2 for discussion.) The case is mentioned at this point to illustrate the upheaval that rival leagues can have on the established order.

At least two effects are generally observed when a rival league emerges. The initial effect is that players are presented with the prospects of higher salaries: New teams need familiar names with gate appeal. Although the new owners' judgments as to the value of the names may be misplaced and overblown, increased salaries are offered and accepted. Even if the league fails, the short-term increased salaries help to revise and up-grade the salary scale. Such was the case in the 1960s in the wake of the late ABL.[11]

Following closely in this effect is the heightened confidence that players gain because of the increased salaries they can command. They express increased interest in organizing in order to better present their views. When there are rivals and increased riches, unions benefit. The agents and attorneys who represent athletes on an individual basis are beneficiaries as well. The appearance of rival leagues in several professional sports, beginning roughly around 1960, greatly spurred the development of players' associations and the rush to represent by agents and lawyers.

Clearly the National Basketball Players' Association was a beneficiary of the rival leagues in the 1960s. It was helped by the ABL, and it was aided even more by the appearance of yet another rival league in the later 1960s, the American Basketball Association. The ABA was a legitimate challenger to the NBA. Some of its franchises were better financed, and it approached the task of taking on an established league in a realistic fashion. Nevertheless, the ABA had its share of speculators who knew little more about basketball than that a basketball was round, attested to by their quickly disappearing, shifting, shaky franchises: the Anaheim Amigos, the San Diego Conquistadors, the Minnesota Muskies, the Memphis Sounds.[12] But the ABA's legacy was complex: It gave more to basketball than the red, white, and blue ball[13] and the three-point play.

The American Basketball Association started with the 1967–68 season. The old Laker, George Mikan, was its first commissioner, and Connie Hawkins, still barred from the NBA because of the point-shaving stigma, was its leading scorer, just as he had been six years earlier in the ABL. His team, the Pittsburgh Pipers, were the first-year champions, Hawkins leading the league with a 26.8 point per game average. He was joined on the Pipers by Artie Heyman, another NBA cast-off who had to win his lawsuit with a minor league club before he was allowed to join the ABA.[14] The ABA was hardly an instant success, but it was still hanging on nine years later when the NBA took in four of its clubs and helped pay off the others so that a one-league system for professional basketball could be restored.

In the meantime, some significant legal action had commenced, most notably the *Oscar Robertson* litigation,[15] brought by several NBA players under the auspices of the Players' Association. (This case is examined later in the chapter.) It has been cited by the players a number of times to test actions undertaken by the league. The presence of the ABA also resulted in the usual number of contract-jumping cases, a variety of antitrust threats, and other labor problems.[16]

In testimony before a 1972 congressional committee conducting hearings on bills that would have authorized the merger of the ABA and the NBA, a leading opponent of such authorization was the executive director of the NBPA, Larry Fleisher.[17] The NBA players, led by Oscar Robertson, clearly supported Fleisher in opposition to any merger.[18] While the ABA players were evidently more equivocable, since their league was showing signs of weakness and possible collapse by that time, the ABA players, under the leadership of their president, Zelmo Beaty, were also not in favor of a merger absent certain conditions.[19] As it developed, the merger was never approved by Congress, in large part because the two leagues, and the NBA in particular, backed away from seeking such a bill when it became apparent it would be approved only if a number of provisions unacceptable to the leagues were attached to the merger authorization.[20]

In testimony given that same year (1972) before another House committee, in hearings on unfair labor practices and proposed strengthened remedies under the National Labor Relations Act, Fleisher testified at some length on what the rival ABA had meant to NBA players.[21] He noted the differences in negotiating over collective bargaining issues before the ABA came into existence and since that time. Before 1967 the NBA had no collective bargaining agreement nor did any professional sport. In addition, Fleisher noted that the NBA required no minimum salary, no pension, no health or accident insurance, no life insurance, and not even a trainer for road games.[22] The players had proposed an insurance plan that would cost each team the sum of $1,500 per year. This was rejected.[23]

Fleisher also noted that whenever he made any requests or inquiries to the league management it took several months to get a response. In 1965 Fleisher had been barred from a meeting of the league's board of governors where he sought to present his requests.[24] Of course, these were Fleisher's words and his memories; it is likely the NBA people remembered things differently. These were Fleisher's and the players' perceptions, however, and their point was that things changed dramatically after the ABA appeared: The owners were willing to talk and made considerable improvements in working conditions. By the time the ABA expired when four of its clubs entered the NBA in 1976, the players were in a much stronger position than they had been before the ABA made its appearance. Indeed, Fleisher credited the threat that the ABA posed as the chief inducement to obtaining from the NBA owners in 1967 the first collective bargaining agreement in sports.[25]

Founding of the NBPA

The existence of a rival league to aid the growth of the union movement in the NBA was one of several events that were overtaking basketball. Increased television exposure and resulting television revenues produced a euphoria about the future of professional sports. It also triggered concern about what should be done to prepare for the future bonanza that would be realized from television and other riches. Players in all sports in the 1960s concluded that mere organization into loose players' associations was not enough: Actions had to capitalize on collective strength. This feeling did not immediately manifest itself in massive shows of united action within the National Basketball Players' Association. Activities were more subtle, but volatility lay just below the surface.

As with other sports unions, the NBPA did not rush to declare itself a full-fledged union. It skirted the issue and was slow to assert itself. It was a low-key, basically one-person affair, and that person was Larry Fleisher, operating the union out of his law office.[26] The union seemingly operates in much the same fashion today, which is somewhat misleading. Though Fleisher has added a minimal amount of staff assistance, the union is as it has been for over twenty years— the extension of the personality of its executive director, Larry Fleisher. Probably more than in any sports union, however, the players participate in the actual operation of the union and the determination of its future. Even then, there is still the suspicion that when it comes down to the final line, one man decides. Many of the union's player leaders have also been clients of Fleisher, hiring him as their agent for individual contract negotiations,[27] which does little to alter his image as the ultimate power.

The same situation prevailed in the 1960s. Larry Fleisher, the Harvard Law graduate, gave direction to the union's initial efforts. If unionization, whatever it was, was to occur, Fleisher would have to make it happen. He would have to bring the league into the negotiating rooms and forge the first collective bargaining agreement. It was not an easy task, and he undoubtedly was aided by the creation of the American Basketball Association. But the union was formed.

The NBPA's initial approaches stuck to basic labor issues: minimum salary, pension fund, insurance benefits, and other standard wage and condition of employment requests. Although the matter of restraints on player mobility was raised, the owners maintained that restraints were not subject to bargaining; they persisted in this position for at least three years.[28] Only threats of litigation and the existence of a competitor league softened their stance.

During the slow movement toward collective bargaining, the players became increasingly assertive. Indeed, the first indication that NBA players might strike for their rights came in 1964. Upset over the owners' position regarding contributions to be made to the newly established player pension fund, the players threatened to boycott the league's All-Star Game. The players delayed the start of the contest for several minutes until, in a locker room confrontation, they received guarantees that the owners would take positive action.[29] Interestingly, that has been the only occasion on which the NBA players have had to take such action. While players in other leagues have taken job actions and the NBA referees have picketed to voice their demands, the NBA players have enjoyed a comparatively peaceful existence. They have had to threaten; but except for delaying an All-Star Game for a few minutes, they have not had to walk.

The NBPA in the 1960s did not resort to litigation, although this posture changed in the 1970s in cases such as *Robertson*.[30] The union did not seek the protections of the NLRB either, despite what would appear to have been solid grounds for doing so under any of a number of unfair labor practice allegations, including refusal to bargain over what were clearly mandatory bargaining issues. The union's leader, Fleisher, did not press matters before the board because he felt that his players were in a tenuous position and that to proceed that boldly might have backfired.[31] That was the 1960s.

In addition to the NBPA's one-man leadership, two other aspects of its development are worth noting: star participation and black participation. The athletes themselves were not simply involved: The top players in the league were also among the leaders in the union. Oscar Robertson, John Havlicek, Paul Silas, and Bob Lanier held important union positions. Lanier was particularly important in the 1982 and 1983 negotiations. The others were leaders at strategic times in the past. This was a positive force in gaining respect for the union.[32] Whether top players as union leaders has created other problems, such as causing a tilt toward bargaining over issues more important to the top players than to others in the league, is evaluated later in this chapter. At this point it can be said that no clear conclusions can be made of overriding favoritism. If there have been leanings, they have been subtle and have arisen out of complex circumstances.

Also in reference to the union leadership is the number of blacks who have been at the top of the union ranks. Blacks play a unique role in the NBA as athletes, and their role in the NBPA is significant as well.

Race and the NBA

Chuck Cooper broke the color line in the NBA by signing with the Boston Celtics for the 1950–51 season. He arrived in Boston at the same time as Red Auerbach. Joining Cooper within weeks as the second black signed to an NBA team was Nat "Sweetwater" Clifton of the New York Knicks. It was more than coincidence that the Knicks' coach, Joe Lapchick, and Auerbach were the first two to have blacks on their rosters. Auerbach wanted the best players available and later traded a popular Ed Macauley and Cliff Hagan to ensure himself the draft rights to Bill Russell.[33] Lapchick had toured the country in the 1930s with members of the Original Celtics, playing game after game with the powerful all-black Rens.[34] While the breach of the color barrier in the NBA did not have the high drama that accompanied the Jackie Robinson saga in baseball two years earlier, the move was not without consequences denoting racism. Not all in the NBA family took the moves kindly or silently. The same was true of fan reaction.[35]

Both Cooper and Clifton had substantial NBA careers. Cooper remained with the Celtics for four years, then played two more years, partly with the St. Louis Hawks and a short time with the Fort Wayne Pistons. His first year with the Celtics was his best in terms of scoring average (9.3 points per game over sixty-six games).[36] Clifton almost matched Cooper's first-year statistics, appearing in sixty-five games and averaging 8.6 per game. Overall, Clifton surpassed Cooper, enjoying a solid seven-year career with the Knicks, generally hovering around the 10-point average per game, and being one of the team's better rebounders. He wound up his career with one year with the Pistons, who had by this time moved to Detroit. Despite the prowess of these two pioneers, though, it was indeed true that the NBA and basketball fans in general had not "seen nothin' yet." What was to come was the flow of super-talented black ballplayers.

For those such as Auerbach and Lapchick who knew the game, the fact that there were not only good but great black players was no surprise. The Renaissance Big Five—the Rens—had organized in Harlem in 1922, under Bob Douglas, who somehow kept them together for more than twenty years. Not admitted to any league, they barnstormed and became without question the dominant team in the 1930s. Between 1932 and 1936 they compiled 473 wins against only 49 losses, this against the best competition they could find. In 1933-34, they were 127 and 7, enjoying an 88-game win streak at one stretch. Perhaps just as amazing is that during the early 1930s they were basically a seven-man machine, year after year: It was Clarence "Fats" Jenkins, Bill Jenkins, John "Casey" Holt, James "Pappy" Ricks, Eyre "Bruiser" Saitch, Charles "Tarzan" Cooper, and, the biggest man on the squad, Wee Willie Smith. As a unit, they were elected to the Basketball Hall of Fame in 1963.[37] Other black teams developed as the game popularized in the large metropolitan centers and routed ample talent into the NBA.[38]

The eventual ascendancy of blacks in the NBA can be traced by studying the league's champion teams.[39] Neither Cooper nor Clifton enjoyed this success. Cooper played on the Celtics before their golden years, and while Lapchick, with Clifton on the team, took the Knicks to three straight championship playoffs (1951 to 1953), no champion rings were garnered. First the Rochester Royals and then the Minneapolis Lakers, twice, were too tough. The distinction of being the first blacks on an NBA champion, therefore, was left to Earl Lloyd and Jim Tucker on the 1954-55 champion Syracuse Nats. Lloyd had contributed to the Nats' efforts throughout that year, playing in seventy-two games at an 8.9 points per game average. Tucker was less a factor, a 5.3 average in just twenty regular season games but was there at the end for the playoffs and the championship.

When the Boston Celtics won the first of their many titles, in 1957, Bill Russell was the only black on the team, though his lone presence was hardly insignificant. Over the next several years, with the Celtics winning year after year (except 1958), the Celts generally had three or four blacks on the squad, until the 1963-64 season when there was five (on a twelve-man squad). By then the Jones boys (K.C. and Sam) had joined Russell to be part of the nucleus of the great Celtic teams. Then, for the 1964-65 campaign and another gold ring in April 1965 the majority switched. For the first time, a champion had a majority of blacks, six to five, as Willie Naulls, Satch Sanders,[40] and John Thompson (later the successful coach at Georgetown University) joined Russell and the

Joneses. The numbers were still in the ascendancy from that point. It was seven of twelve in 1965–66, as Woody Sauldsberry came aboard, and two years later, with some shifts in personnel, eight of twelve Celtics were black, led by now Coach Bill Russell. This was also the last year of the dynasty, with no team since that year winning even back-to-back NBA titles, let alone approach the Celtics record of eight in a row (1959–66) and eleven of thirteen between 1957 and 1969.

Other NBA champions have been even more heavily black than the Celtics. The highest numbers belong to the Golden State Warriors in 1974–75, with Rick Barry and Jeff Mullins being the only whites, and the Washington Bullets in 1977–78, where Kevin Grevey and Mitch Kupchak were the exceptions. In both instances, therefore, ten of the twelve-man squad were black. Today, blacks are over 70 percent of the players in the league overall, an estimated 80 percent starters,[41] and probably as high as 95 percent of the true stars in the league.[42] The NBA is quite possibly the U.S. industry most dominated by blacks, at least in terms of those realizing the greatest percentage of the financial returns from that industry.

Despite more black coaches, head and assistant, being employed in the NBA than in other professional sports, they are still a distinct minority.[43] Moreover, there are exceedingly few black front office executives. The league front office is very white as well. Perhaps this will change, but progress, if it can be termed that, is painfully slow. In dealing with a union dominated by blacks, even though its director Larry Fleisher is white, management may have found a new type of color barrier.

Also disquieting is the inevitable image the NBA projects to black youth. To play in the NBA is the goal of millions of black youngsters. They see the NBA as the one way they may succeed. But among blacks, as with whites, the odds against making it into the league are still overwhelming: Most black aspirants are not going to make it.[44]

There are always ironies to be found, and the matter of race in the NBA has more than its share. A final twist is that the team that was there first, the Celtics, has in recent years been one of the whitest in the NBA. This is strictly relative, of course, as their many fine black players (Maxwell, Parish, first Archibald, then Dennis Johnson) have helped key recent NBA championships in 1981 and 1984. But the Celtics were the last NBA champion team to have a majority of whites on the squad, for the 1981 championship.[45]

ECONOMICS OF PROFESSIONAL BASKETBALL

Economic stability has always been a concern in the NBA, more so than it has been in either the National Football League or major league baseball (discussed previously). While the NBA experiences some of the same economic realities as the National Hockey League (discussed in Chapter 7), there are variations between these two leagues as well. As with all other professional team sports leagues, the NBA relies largely on gate receipts and broadcast revenues for its chief sources of income; but certain variables dictate that the NBA has its own idiosyncratic economic structure. This results partly from conditions endemic to the sport and partly from circumstances created over time by the league's owners and players.

In any assessment of the current financial base of the NBA, as well as its potential for future development, certain factors dominate. An NBA club has few players on its payroll, but the salary structure developed over the years puts the per player average salary at or near the highest in professional sports.[46] Arenas where the games are played have limited capacities. Even when sold out, which assuredly is not the norm for most games, the arena income yields only a fraction of the needed gross. There must be other revenue, and radio, national and local television, and now cable contracts may be the sources that will be not only maintained, but expanded. These financial realities demand a close examination of league/club revenues and player salaries. Economics has become critical in labor relations and collective bargaining in the NBA. Understanding economic fundamentals helps explain why certain important issues in collective bargaining have been addressed as they have.

League and Club Revenues

Teams in the NBA play in arenas that vary in seating capacity from as low as 11,000 to the 30,000-plus in the multipurpose Kingdome in Seattle and Silverdome in Pontiac, Michigan.[47] Disparities in arena size and in enthusiasm for teams varies from city to city and inevitably result in significant differences in attendance. In 1983–84 three clubs (Boston, Los Angeles, and Detroit) had in excess of 600,000 home attendance for their forty-one regular season home games. Four clubs (Atlanta, Chicago, Cleveland, and San Diego) had less than half that figure, all totaling under 300,000 for the same forty-one games.[48] Attendance revenues varied significantly, particularly since there is no sharing of the gate between the home and visiting teams.

Overall, attendance in the NBA in 1983–84 hit an all-time high, for the first time exceeding ten million for the regular season.[49] Moreover, some clubs in trouble but a year or two earlier made dramatic resurgencies. The Detroit Pistons, playing in the Silverdome, showed the greatest turnaround. In 1980–81, the Pistons were at the bottom of the league in attendance at 132,565 for the regular season (and they did not make the playoffs). In 1983–84 they increased over fourfold and led the league in attendance at 652,865, a remarkable change, spurred in no small measure by the additions of such players as Isiah Thomas and Kelly Tripucka and increasingly good fortunes on the basketball floor. They were not alone. While still losers on the court, the Indiana Pacers increased attendance by better than 100 percent in the one-year span between 1982–83 and

1983-84,[50] probably because of new ownership and better marketing. Overall league attendance was up 25 percent in 1983-84 from what it had been three years previously in 1980-81.[51] Even so, the disparities in gate receipts continue, and as fortunes swing, formerly financially sound clubs may find themselves in trouble.

Fortunately for the NBA there are few players on a club payroll. With only twelve players per squad, the number of paychecks to meet each month is small compared to the NFL or major league baseball. But as is discussed later, this is not the total picture. Deferred compensation obligations and other salary commitments inflate the figures and require additional sources of revenue. The main prospects are broadcast contracts.

Much of the NBA's financial worries could be solved if it had network television contracts that approached those for the NFL or major league baseball. The NFL is currently on a five-year $2 billion contract that brings $400 million to the league each year, or basically $14.2 million per club. Major league baseball has also embarked on a new era in televised sports, signing a contract with two networks that in combination garners some $1.125 billion over the course of the contract, netting revenues of $7 million per club per year. The NBA story, however, is hardly as fortuitous. Its current network contract is $88 million over four years, or just under $1 million per year per club.[52]

The NBA catches up a bit, at least vis-à-vis the NFL, when local broadcast revenues are factored into the overall broadcast revenue picture. Since the NFL in one form or another does network telecasts of all its games, there are no regular season or playoff games left for local broadcasts. The locals look only to radio and preseason telecasts. Even these net about $1 million per year per NFL club, but compared to the network payments of $14.2 million per club, this is not a major revenue source. For NBA clubs, at least the fortunate, the local broadcast revenues are crucial, much more so than in the NFL. A club's $1 million share per year from the network contract does not pay even one player's salary for several of the NBA superstars. Much more is needed. In addition to a national cable contract entered in 1984, local revenues, particularly with the onset of cable and pay systems, are perceived to be the salvation. Whether this proves to be true or not remains to be seen. Certainly, cable should be a boon to the NBA, as it is proving to be to baseball as well. The question is how large the pie will be.

One great problem facing the NBA, as well as major league baseball, is that the disparity between the television haves and have-nots is substantial and is not improving. This gap interferes with opportunities to compete in such important areas as the free-agent market. In the NBA, local broadcast revenues range from piddling to impressive, from well under $1 million to highs of $4 or $5 million.[53] While the recently instituted NBA salary cap is designed to alleviate disadvantages created by such disparities (as is discussed later in this chapter), it is doubtful whether the cap is the full answer. Some other measures may be needed, and increased revenue sharing may ultimately be the only solution. This will not come without intense opposition from the well-financed clubs, however, and must be considered a last resort at this point.

Thus, at present and for the foreseeable future, the NBA has three factors that signal monetary problems when it comes to generating revenue. One is the difference in arena sizes, which limits some clubs' potentials more than others. Second are differing degrees of enthusiasm and thus support for a club, regardless of arena size. Third are the disparities in television revenues, perhaps spelling greater problems for the league than either of the first two factors.

Salaries

The top NBA players, and some not so top, have been made financially secure for life. At salaries near or in excess of $1 million per year, often in up-front cash, it is only a matter of prudent handling of these finances that should be of concern. While only a few players actually exceed the $1 million per year mark (still under ten players as of the 1984–85 season),[54] the fact that these few have topped the milestone, and that several others follow not that far behind in the $500,000 to $1 million range,[55] suggest that, at least for the chosen, the NBA is a path to riches.

In truth, it is hardly slave labor at the bottom. The NBA minimum salary for 1984–85 was $65,000[56] and will climb. The average salary for all players in the league was $340,000.[57] If a player can stay in the NBA for a few years, whether or not a star, the good money will be there. From the players' perspective, for those who make it, the making is marvelous.

Leaguewide average salaries, of course, tell only part of the story. Further breakdowns team by team are often revealing. For example, for the 1983–84 season, before the full implementation of the maximum and minimum team salaries (discussed later in this chapter), the total expenditures by teams on salaries varied significantly. It was reported that the Indiana Pacers total payroll was under $1.5 million,[58] which was less than Larry Bird or Moses Malone individually earned. At the high end for teams was the Los Angeles Lakers with an imposed maximum team salary of $5.2 million,[59] which was probably exceeded because of various exceptions allowed under the new collective bargaining provisions.

While there is a definite positive correlation between a team's revenues and its salary obligations, there are exceptions. The most notable was probably the Cleveland Cavaliers, which, for the 1981–81 season, had salary obligations of $3.7 million and a *total* gross from all sources of only $2.8 million. When other operating costs were added to salary expenditures, the Cavaliers had an operating loss of $5.1 million for that one year.[60] While much of this could be attributed to the folly of the Cavaliers' then owner, Ted Stepien, and his headlong rush into the free-agent market, the situation, while extreme, has not been singular. Although few teams may have spent more on salaries than was their total gross, there have been many who have committed to such high salary levels as virtually to assure overall losses.

The reasons for such arguable excesses are complex, in part related to player market pressures, in part perhaps to an owner's ego, in part to honest, though probably negligent, miscalculations. It is difficult to ascribe excessive salary commitments to one cause. There are usually multiple factors at work. But the fact that many NBA teams lose money consistently has been a reality. Tax depreciation allowances and other bookkeeping measures undoubtedly present a bleaker picture than the net effects justify. Even so, if not losing money outright, certain NBA clubs have committed to present and deferred salaries at levels that have saner heads in the league worried.

LEGAL FRAMEWORK

The 1976 NBA collective bargaining agreement, attended as it was by the absorption of four surviving American Basketball Association teams into the older league and the consequent demise of the ABA, signaled a new beginning. It did not, at the same time, free the NBA of all its problems, either legal or business. Some of the more pressing ones were at least assuaged. Others simply would not go away. The final section of this chapter will examine the step-by-step progress of the league in terms of collective bargaining, as it moved from 1976, to the next agreement in 1980, to the institution of special prearranged procedures in 1981, to the revolutionary amendments of 1983. All of these steps, however, must be examined in the context of modern law and of league economics. We have discussed the finances. Now we need to add the legal framework as it has evolved principally through litigation, but of late through labor arbitration.

Litigation

As with the other leagues, the NBA has felt the effects of the fearsome three-some: contracts, antitrust, and labor. Each has taken unique twists in the NBA, and other legal areas have found interesting interpretations through first the courts and then in arbitration.

We begin the analysis with a touch of whimsy. Partly because a basketball team fields only five players at a time and partly because basketball players have been proficient both on the ball court and in the law court, we present as an introduction to the fields of litigation and arbitration our choices for an all-NBA all-litigators team, chosen roughly on weighting our ratings two-thirds for the importance of the legal nature of the complaints involved and one-third for perceived playing prowess.

Table 6–1.   All-NBA Litigators.

First Team	Second Team	Honorable Mention
Rick Barry (captain)	Connie Hawkins	Billy Cunningham
Rudy Tomjanovich	Julius Erving	Bill Walton
Spencer Haywood	Wilt Chamberlain	George McGinnis
Dick Barnett	Lou Hudson	Jack Molinas
Oscar Robertson	Art Heyman	Marvin Webster
		Paul Silas

Space does not permit a full explanation of law court and basketball court exploits of all these players, but a few remarks about the legal areas in which each has been most notable must be made. Leading with our strength, we go immediately to the captain, Rick Barry, of the San Francisco Warriors, Oakland Oaks, Washington Capitols, New York Nets, back to the Warriors (now Golden State), and on to Houston Rockets fame. While not every team switch involved legal problems, most did.

Rick Barry joined the Warriors in 1965 and immediately led the team in scoring his rookie year, at a 25.7 point per game clip. He followed this in 1966–67 with a 35.6 average, tops in the NBA.[61] Then it happened. The ABA formed, Barry forsook the Warriors to pursue a new career and additional dollars in the newly formed league, and his old club toppled from first to third place in the NBA's Western Division the following year. Barry's choice of teams in the ABA was the vaunted Oakland Oaks. Only one obstacle stood between Barry and immediate realization of his goals—an option year under his contract with the Warriors. In the initial legal action, he was preliminarily enjoined from playing for the Oaks, but at full trial on the merits a year later, the injunction was lifted because by that time the option year had expired.[62] The court refused to extend an injunction beyond the contract term, falling in line with usual precedent where courts are extremely loath to extend injunctive relief in cases of employment contracts beyond the contract term unless the contract had specified that such could be done. No such provisions appear in NBA contracts, unlike the extension provisions in an NFL form contract.[63]

By the time Barry was ready to play for the Oaks, the Oaks were ready to call it quits in Oakland. Undoubtedly an incentive in Barry's contract that called for bonuses if gate receipts reached certain levels was never realized.[64] The destitute Oaks departed quietly and headed across country to become the Washington Capitols. This created a problem for Barry, who did not want to go. His heart was in San Francisco, or at least the Bay area, and he tried to sign again with the Warriors. Once more, injunctive relief was sought, this time by the Capitols. Barry unsuccessfully claimed that the Capitols should have invoked against them the "clean hands" doctrine, whereby a party can be denied equitable relief if that party has engaged in conduct in relation to the circumstances under question that is illegal, immoral, or in other ways repugnant to the court. Barry's claim was that the Capitols' predecessor, the Oaks, were nefarious creatures, even though Barry of course had earlier fought to join them under the circumstances he now contended constituted unclean hands. Now that the Oaks had moved, he did not want to go. The court, however, refused to attribute the sins of the assignor to the assignee,[65] thus reaching a result opposite to that in Lou Hudson's case,[66] one of our all-NBA litigators second-team stalwarts. The two cases are interesting contrasts, but do little to enlighten on just when unclean hands are transmissible.

Even this second bout did not end Barry's litigation career. Still in the ABA, he was later traded to the New York Nets. By this time, he was committed to return to the Golden State Warriors (as they were now called) at the end of his then-current contract. When that time arrived, however, he had changed his mind again. Fresh from an ABA championship with the Nets, Barry's heart was now in New York. Threatened litigation, however, had him hit the trail back to the Warriors. There he helped lead them to an NBA championship.[67] Then it was off again—this time hitting the free-agent trail within the NBA. Barry now left litigation, temporarily, and shifted to arbitration.

Barry's career ended with the Houston Rockets, but not without a red glare bursting. When he signed with Houston, his old club, the Warriors, and his new, the Rockets, could not agree on the compensation to go from Houston to Golden State for the latter's loss of Barry's services. Under the compensation rules then in existence (discussed later in this chapter), after a hearing, Commissioner Larry O'Brien decreed that Houston must award to Golden State either Houston's young guard John Lucas and $100,000 cash *or* the Rockets' 1979 first-round draft pick and $350,000.[68] Golden State could choose; and it opted for Lucas and the lesser amount of cash. Rick Barry finished his career with Houston, helping garner no more league championships but remembered as the last of the pros to use the two-handed, underhand free throw, as the all-time free throw leader with a career mark of .893,[69] and, of course, as one hell of a legal in-fighter.

Rick Barry's legal career underscores the continuing importance of contract actions in both the courts and now in arbitration. Except for one brief excursion as a defendant in a tort action,[70] Barry stuck to contracts, joining others who merit selection on the NBA litigation squad, including Dick Barnett,[71] Lou Hudson (mentioned above),[72] Wilt Chamberlain,[73] Art Heyman,[74] Billy Cunningham,[75] and Julius Erving.[76] Each deserves special analysis, but for now their marks must simply be noted and passed over in favor of the heavy antitrust hitters among the NBA players. Among these are two giants: Spencer Haywood and Oscar Robertson, one on his own, the other as a representative of that new breed, the sports union man.

The *Haywood* case[77] brought to an end, in the NBA at least, the four-year rule that decreed that a player could not enter the professional ranks until his college class had graduated. It must be carefully noted that there was no requirement that the player have graduated, only that he had been kept out of the league the appropriate length of time. Spencer Haywood caught the public's eye in the summer of 1968. His sensational performance in the Olympics that year had immeasurably helped an undermanned U.S. team, doing without the services of such as Lew Alcindor (Kareem Abdul Jabbar), Elvin Hayes, and Wes Unseld, all of whom passed on the opportunity. The United States emerged with the gold medal, its unbeaten Olympics record unblemished.[78] Haywood enjoyed a brief career at the University of Detroit, then headed well ahead of graduation into the ABA. A couple of years later, with his college class still not graduated, Haywood wanted to switch to the NBA. One team was glad to oblige, but the NBA said no.

The *Haywood* suit charged the league with an illegal boycott of his services. It was probably not so much that the league really felt he should be excluded; it was more that the league did not want to alienate the colleges by relaxing its rules. The U.S. District Court hearing the case had no such qualms, ruling that a boycott did indeed exist and that the league's rule was a per se violation of the antitrust laws. The case was not appealed, which led the NCAA evidently to feel that the NBA had not vigorously pushed for retention of the rule. This led to strained relations between the colleges and the NBA that have persisted, to a degree, to the present time. In the meantime, Haywood was free to enter the NBA, the league set up a procedure by which other college-eligible players could declare "hardship" and be subject to the draft, and later, dropping the hardship requirement, the league streamlined its procedures whereby today a simple declaration of availability, filed by a certain date, is enough to allow any player to be eligible for the draft. Over the years since *Haywood*, approximately 100 players have chosen this option. Magic Johnson and Isiah Thomas have been notable successes. Others have foundered and quickly disappeared.[79] Any rule of this nature has mixed blessings. As a final irony, since the centers in the NBA have not been the heaviest hitters in the courts, Spencer Haywood has been moved from his natural power forward position and placed here in the pivot on the all-NBA all-litigators squad.

Oscar Robertson instigated an entirely different situation. Robertson did not take on the NBA as an individual; He was a leader in the NBPA and put his name at the top of the list of many NBA players who sought to head off what was perceived as multiple legal infractions by the league. In truth, it was a labor-inspired suit, maintained by the players' association. Whatever its origin, *Robertson vs. NBA* spanned multiple hearings[80] before the U.S. District Court in which it originated and before a special master appointed by the court to determine whether actions by the league were in accord with the later so-called *Robertson* settlement.[81]

The issues have been complex in both the original *Robertson* case and in hearings arising out of the later *Robertson* settlement. The original case was directed at several of the restraints employed by the league to limit player movement from one team to another. The complaint was also aimed at thwarting a merger of the NBA and the ABA, protesting the monopoly of professional basketball that would result. Preliminary restraining orders indicated to the league that it would have to deal with the players if it was to proceed with merger plans and still maintain some of its restrictions on player mobility. With the *Robertson* settlement, approved by the court, the merger could at length go forward, but significant concessions were made to the players, including a new collective bargaining agreement in 1976 and an oversight function retained by the court and its special master, which by the settlement was to continue for the following decade. The resolve of several legal disputes in the NBA in recent years has been unlike that in the other leagues, because of the *Robertson* case and settlement. It is an ongoing procedure, witnessed by the unsuccessful 1984 attempt by rookie Leon Wood (like Haywood, of Olympics fame) to challenge the provisions in the 1983 salary cap provisions that significantly limit rookie player salaries.[82] The salary cap is discussed at length toward the end of this chapter. Significant here is that there are means of testing what the NBA as a league does in its operations vis-à-vis players, and the testing is one where immediate access to the court under the *Robertson* provisos is assured.

One other instance of litigation should be mentioned because its ultimate effects were later raised in a collective bargaining context. This was the case brought by Rudy Tomjanovich against the owners of the Los Angeles Lakers, and the companion case brought by his employers, the Houston Rockets, also against the Lakers. Under contested circumstances Tomjanovich joined a melee that had brought a game between the Rockets and Lakers to a halt. Not known as a fighter, Tomjanovich claimed he rushed to the milling group to act as peacemaker. Whatever his intent, Tomjanovich was greeted by a devastating blow to the jaw by Kermit Washington of the Lakers. The jaw was shattered and could be repaired only by extensive surgery and lengthy rehabilitation. In truth, both players were probably not quite the same after that incident.

Tomjanovich and the Rockets did not sue Washington. Instead, suit was instituted against Washington's employer, the Lakers. Tomjanovich's claim was that the employer was responsible in this instance for the act of the employee because the Lakers had knowingly put a dangerous instrumentality on the floor, in that the Lakers knew or should have known of Washington's violent tendencies. The Rockets sued over the loss of Tomjanovich's services. Only Tomjanovich's suit got to trial, in a spectacle that had the videotape of the blow shown over and over to a parade of witnesses to test if this accorded with their memory of the incident. Obviously, the intent was to impress the jury as to the great degree of violence and injury that was involved. The jury was suitably impressed, awarding Tomjanovich in excess of $3 million in damages, more than the amount requested by his lawyers. With only a slight reduction by the trial judge, the award was affirmed. The Lakers then paid Tomjanovich rather than fight further and then quickly settled with the Rockets.[83]

The case is extensive in its implications. It underscores how this supposed noncontact sport exists continually on the edge of injury and violence. Injury is a way of life in the NBA, as multiple-injury arbitrations attest. Violence often erupts between players and at times between players and spectators. The league must be concerned and has taken steps to increase penalties for fighting. This was shown by the levying of $30,000 in fines for a single incident involving Larry Bird and Julius Erving and ultimately almost all of the Celtics and '76ers in their first meeting of the 1984–85 season.[84] On the other hand, a possible deterrent to players was removed by provisions in the 1980 collective bargaining agreement, wherein all teams in the NBA agreed they would not sue another team's player for injuries inflicted on that team's player.[85]

Arbitration

Not all legal disputes head for the courts. This has become particularly true as collective bargaining agreements have placed more and more emphasis on the resolution of disputes through arbitration. The result has been the displacement of litigation in multiple instances and the creation of a mini-legal system with its own procedures and precedents. The NBA has witnessed this type of development. Arbitration has become an important, some would argue indispensable, way of handling legal and business affairs in the league.[86]

Since the arbitrations are extensive and voluminous, little more than high-lighting can be attempted here. Relevant are labor grievances by the players concerning contract interpretations relating to options, termination of the contract, salary disputes, and rights to renegotiate. A few of the most important awards should be mentioned.

One involved the great center for the Warriors, 76ers, and Lakers, Wilt Chamberlain.[87] The man who scored 100 points in one game[88] and averaged 50 points per game over one long NBA season[89] did not score well in arbitration. In a contract long on complexity and short on clarity, the question revolved around whether the Lakers had complied with the contract in terms of certain monies owed Chamberlain. This was essential in order for the team to bind Chamberlain to an additional year under the contract. The real issue was whether Chamberlain could be prevented from forsaking the NBA and taking residence as player/coach for the ABA's San Diego Conquistadors. The arbitrator ruled against Chamberlain, and his future with the Conquistadors, at least the immediate one, was limited to that of coach. This was a situation that proved not to be satisfactory to either the San Diego club or to Chamberlain. He lasted but a year. Wilt later claimed that the Lakers were conspiring to prevent his dealing with other NBA clubs and initiated antitrust litigation. This became intertwined with the *Robertson* settlement, and ultimately Chamberlain's legal efforts came to naught.[90] Had he pressed forward, there is little doubt that the man who once pulled down fifty-five rebounds in a single game would have had to be named to our all-litigator (arbitration) first team.[91] As it is, he must be content with the second squad.

Other noteworthy arbitrations involved lesser luminaries when it came to basketball exploits. Again, this is relative. Given the high skill level required of any NBA player, we are drawing fine lines between the great players and the near-great. Even so, it may take the hardiest of NBA fans to recognize all but a couple of the principals that follow:

The *Ken Charles* arbitration[92] challenged the notion that a player could have his contract terminated at the complete will of the club. Charles maintained he was cut because of his club's economy and youth movements, and not for lack of requisite skills as provided as grounds for termination under section 20 (b) (2) of the NBA uniform player contract. Because of statements made to Charles by the coach at the time of termination, and because of statements made by the front office and owner to the press, the arbitrator agreed with Charles. The arbitrator held that Charles was not released because his skills were no longer competitive. The club was really after cheaper, younger talent, and there was nothing in the NBA contract allowing that as a grounds for termination. Needless to say, after the *Charles* decision, coaches and front office were warned to be more circumspect about their statements to a player or to the media.

Bob Love played in the NBA for several years, compiling a solid if unspectacular record.[93] At one point, he demanded a renegotiation of his contract, claiming that club representatives had earlier represented that he could renegotiate if he had a good season. Whether an oral promise had been made or not, the arbitrator said in effect that unless it was in writing, it was not enforceable. Acknowledging that there are questions as to just how much precedential value an arbitration decision has, the arbitrator nevertheless went further and explained that he would regard all such renegotiation demands in this same vein.[94] The league and union have added one other twist. If a player, dissatisfied with his present contract, refuses to perform in the last year of his contract unless the contract is renegotiated, that player shall not become a free agent at the end of that season.[95] If the last year is not performed, the contract is in effect extended. That has not deterred threats of sit-outs by players, but players generally drop their threats before they lose their potential for free-agent status.

The two final arbitrations here discussed involve salary grievances, one where a player's contract was terminated and the other where the salary was reduced. In the first arbitration, Rudy Hackett claimed that the Denver Nuggets did not pay all that was due him. Hackett had originally signed a one-year contract for his rookie season in the NBA, with half of the salary being guaranteed whether he was retained by the team or not. Hackett and his contract were transferred to the Nuggets for the start of the NBA season. He soon was cut, having been paid what was owed him up to that point. Denver made no claim that it was relieved of all salary responsibility for the remainder of the one-half guaranteed. However, the club did claim that when Hackett later signed and played with another

NBA club, his salary from the new club should be taken in mitigation of the obligations owed him. The arbitrator disagreed. He held that a guarantee was an absolute one and that such monies were considered to be earned. Regardless of what Hackett did after his contract was terminated, he had earned the full amount guaranteed. There was no mitigation.[96] The *Hackett* award was also addressed in later collective bargaining negotiations, which modified the full impact of the decision.[97] The main point, then, is that arbitration decisions on individual grievances may well suggest to the two sides, labor and management, that changes in how contracts operate may be desirable. Whether or not the two sides agree on a law approach, arbitration has been the impetus for a hard look at the practice through the labor relations processes.

This leads, at length, to the *Ben Poquette* arbitration,[98] an interesting counterpoint to both the *Charles* and the *Hackett* decisions. Poquette signed a non-guaranteed contract with the Detroit Pistons. As the preseason drew to a close and the opening of the regular season was at hand, the Pistons informed Poquette that they would like to keep him on the team but did not feel they could pay him what was stipulated in his contract. To stay on the squad he would have to agree to a salary cut. This he did and was seemingly content just to remain in the NBA. It was not he who later protested the Pistons' action. The players' association claimed that the Pistons were in violation of the collective bargaining agreement and the uniform players' contract. The matter went to arbitration with the union, not the player, taking the lead. The decision, however, went in favor of the club. The arbitrator held that this was not like cutting a player for economy reasons, as in the use of Ken Charles. Thus, whether a club took its actions for "skill" reasons or not was irrelevant. The two parties were free to renegotiate, and there was no obvious legal impediment to this occurring.

While losers on this particular occasion, the NBPA nevertheless asserted in this and other arbitrations that its role in the labor grievance process may well exist apart from the interests of the individual player.[99] It is a role of vigilance that seeks to assure that clubs adhere to the dictates of the collective bargaining provisions and of the player contract as it is incorporated into those provisions. The union is not always successful in its grievances, but it has won important victories and undoubtedly will remain a key participant in the future.

THE PRESENT AND THE FUTURE

The discussion of economics earlier in this chapter underscores how the league, and the clubs and players with it, have been swept along by the big-dollar philosophy that has become so prevalent in professional sports. In 1971, when salary levels in the NBA topped the $50,000 per year average,[100] it was felt that a new era had dawned. By 1976, for the first time in any professional sport, the average player salary hit the six-figure range, $109,000.[101] In that respect and others 1976 was a pivotal year for the NBA. It marked the beginning of the current era, one that has seen salaries escalate at an even faster pace.

Two other events in 1976 must be mentioned. First, the NBA and ABA owners agreed that four ABA teams could enter the NBA and that the ABA could disband. The merger, however, had to go before the *Robertson* court for approval, which was obtained with several stipulations attached. Second, the NBA and the National Basketball Players' Association reached terms on a new collective bargaining agreement, a pact that had some of its most essential and far-reaching terms tied in with the *Robertson* settlement. The court was to monitor league practices for the following ten-year period. In addition, the collective bargaining agreement included provisions for what was to happen on the very important issues of player mobility. These provisions were designed to cover the following eleven years, an unusually long time for one agreement to cover.

1976 — Providing for Free Agency

The 1976 agreement included one important feature that immediately drew the most attention. This was the provision for what was to occur when a player had fulfilled all obligations to a club under his then-existing contract. In line with prior practices, he was a free agent; but there have always been limits on free agency, and the 1976 provisions spelled out what these were to be for several years to come.[102] The league and union agreed on a two-step process. The first was to provide that an initial five-year period, until the end of the 1981 season, would deal with compensation for free-agent signings to be handled in one fashion and that from 1981 until the end of the 1987 season that a second system would be utilized. After 1987 there are to be no restrictions on the signing of free agents unless the league and union choose to renegotiate their agreement.[103] This will undoubtedly precipitate intense infighting, which is discussed in the last subsection of this chapter. But first we examine the compensation system that was in effect from 1976 to 1981 and the right of first refusal, which replaced that system in 1981 and which will remain in effect at least until 1987.

The system put into effect for the initial five-year period provided that a team that signed another team's veteran free agent (where the player had performed to the end of his contract) must compensate the team that lost him in the form of draft choices, current NBA players, cash, or some combination of the three. If the two clubs, the old and the new, could not agree on a system of compensation, then the matter was to go to arbitration. The commissioner of the NBA was to sit as arbitrator, hearing the case and issuing his decision.[104] The compensation system, in other words, was very close to that used in the NFL under the old Rozelle Rule, a system declared illegal in the *Mackey* litigation.[105] Here, however, the system was the result of collective bargaining and seemingly insulated from antitrust attack by the labor exemption.[106]

During the five-year period when this system was operative, there were a number of free-agent signings, and a number of times when the two clubs could not agree on the compensation. One instance, where Rick Barry left the Warriors for the second time to sign with the Houston Rockets, was mentioned earlier. Other notable free-agency compensation awards involved such notable players as Leonard "Truck" Robinson, [107] Jamaal Wilkes,[108] Bill Walton, [109] and, as discussed below, Marvin Webster.[110]

One important question was whether a compensation award made by the commissioner could be challenged, not in terms of a wholesale antitrust attack but under the *Robertson* settlement, since the inquiry was whether the commissioner had acted in a manner inconsistent with that settlement. Under *Robertson*, it will be recalled, the NBA players had brought an antitrust action to invalidate restrictions on player mobility and other alleged illegal league activity, including the possibility of merger with the ABA. The U.S. District Court, utilizing the services of a master, retained jurisdiction over the parties to enforce the terms of the settlement and the consent judgment. The settlement provided that the district court accept the special master's findings of fact, unless found clearly erroneous, and the master's recommendations for relief, unless based on clearly erroneous factfindings, an incorrect application of law, or an abuse of discretion.[111]

Marvin Webster, a center with the Seattle Supersonics, signed with the New York Knicks after completing his contract obligations with the Sonics. The Sonics and the Knicks were unable to agree on compensation. The commissioner then awarded a compensation package to the Sonics consisting of (1) the contract for New York player Lonnie Shelton, (2) a New York first-round draft choice, and (3) $450,000. The players' association attacked the commissioner's adjudication as a "penalty" and therefore in violation of the agreement. The Knicks also protested the award.[112]

The special master concluded that the commissioner's award was, in fact, "excessive" but concluded that the award could not be set aside unless there was intent on the part of the commissioner to make the team losing the player more than whole or that the award was so "clearly excessive" that it could be attributed to improper intent or "gross error of judgment." Accordingly, the master denied plaintiffs' petition to set aside the award. Additionally, the master ruled that in future proceedings the Players' Association could not present evidence that had not been previously presented to the commissioner. Finally, the master ruled that both teams—the one that had signed and the one that had lost the player—were proper parties in the proceedings before him.[113]

District Judge Carter reversed the master's rulings.[114] Judge Carter granted the player's petition that the award was a penalty and set it aside. He concluded an award that was "excessive" was a penalty and, despite the commissioner's broad discretion in fashioning a "final" award, the master and ultimately the court were mandated to set aside an excessive award as a penalty. Judge Carter's ruling was appealed to the Court of Appeals for the Second Circuit, which upheld the District Court's basic view that it had "virtually plenary authority to determine whether the substantive standards of the agreement had been observed."[115] But the court, speaking through Judge Newman, adopted a standard intermediate between that of the District Court and the master, rejecting Judge Carter's view that any compensation that exceeded the worth of a player beyond an "insignificant" amount was a penalty. This would have left the commissioner with no discretion and would therefore be inconsistent with the settlement agreement. Said Judge Newman:

> While we do not wish to inject mathematical certainty into an area that requires some flexibility, we would not think the Special Master would be unwarranted in concluding that an award becomes a penalty when it exceeds the fair value of the player by approximately 20 percent to 25 percent.[116]

The court opined that it would not have been "displeased" if the parties had determined that the compensation issue was to be immunized from judicial scrutiny. But since they did not, the court would consider it. While the "nuances" of basketball skills are not problems considered by the federal judiciary with regularity, the court noted that it was frequently called on to resolve disputes relating to the value of property and personal services.[117] In so doing, the court took account of the fact that the commissioner was not impartial in player/club disputes. This undoubtedly influenced its decision to proceed. The wisdom of this might be questioned, particularly when one considers such complexities as were presented in the *Bill Walton* compensation award, but this was rendered largely moot by a shift to the NBA's use of right of first refusal.

1980 – Draft, No-Trade, Deferred Compensation, and Television Revenues

While the arbitration system for free-agent compensation was still in effect and anticipation was building as to what the shift to a right of first refusal would mean, other provisions of the 1976 collective bargaining agreement had to be negotiated once again. Thus, in 1980, a new agreement was reached that revamped certain provisions of the 1976 agreement and addressed new concerns, while at the same time, because of the prior agreement, not changing the free-agent compensation procedures.[118] Several of the 1980 provisions should be discussed, including the continuation of the amateur draft and new provisions mandating what can and cannot be amended in a UPC related to curtailing no-trade provisions in individual player contracts, limiting deferred compensation, and attempting but not succeeding in settling the thorny question of who owns what rights in potential new sources of revenue, particularly those generated by the rapidly developing new technologies.

The 1980 collective bargaining agreement left intact most of the provisions relating to the draft of eligible amateur athletes.[119] A team that drafts a player is the only team with which the player may negotiate, provided the club makes a tender offer before September 5 immediately following the initial draft. If an offer is not extended, a highly unlikely situation where any high-round draft pick is concerned, the player is free to negotiate and sign with any team on the September 6 following the draft. However, if a drafted player signs with another professional team outside the NBA, the drafting team retains exclusive rights to negotiate with the player in the future.

The provision on a player signing outside the NBA was a carryover from the 1976 agreement and the *Robertson* settlement. Before 1980 the provision had precipitated yet one more resort to the special master appointed by the court under *Robertson*. The players' association initiated a complaint on behalf of player Dave Batton, who had been drafted in the third round by the New York (now New Jersey) Nets in 1978 but had signed instead with Pallacanestro Gabetti Cantu of the Federazione Italiana Pallacanestro (the Italian Basketball League). Batton now sought to deal with NBA teams other than the Nets. In support of Batton's position, the NBPA contended that Italian basketball teams and leagues were not professional within the meaning of the *Robertson* settlement. The major argument was that the Italian league was considered amateur by the International Amateur Basketball Association (FIBA), which ruled on eligibility of players for the Olympics and other international amateur competition. This was despite the fact that players in the Italian League were openly paid quite handsomely. Batton himself received $45,000 plus bonuses for a one-year stint.

The special master rejected the attempts by the NBPA to have FIBA's actions as controlling. The master instead turned to the dictionary definition of *professional* and concluded that Batton indeed fell within that definition, as did the Italian league. He found no evidence that, in reaching agreement as to when a club could continue to retain rights to a drafted player, there was ever any intent to vary the commonly understood definition of professional. That FIBA considered the Italian league amateur, probably in violation of its own standards, was unpersuasive and, ultimately, irrelevant.[120]

The 1980 provisions relating to the draft thus basically carried forward the *Robertson* settlement terms, including, it must be assumed, the rationale of the *Batton* holding. As noted earlier, the *Haywood* case had expanded the category of players eligible for the draft, and indeed the 1980 provisions state that a player is eligible once his high school class has graduated. This was the path taken by a few players, notably Moses Malone and Darryl Dawkins. Thereafter, however, if a player enters college and has not been drafted prior to that event, the player is not again eligible for the draft until his college class graduates, unless he takes the affirmative step of renouncing his intercollegiate eligibility. As noted, several players have done so over the past decade, with decidedly mixed results.

As to the individual player contracts, several innovations, even today unique to the NBA, were instituted in the 1980 agreement. One was to specify exactly what parts of the uniform player contract could or could not be amended.[121] Indeed, the agreement mandates, in most instances, what the amending language has to be.[122] *Allowable amendments* was a term and concept new to professional sports, signaling an attempt to get away from disparate language in contracts that too often contained ambiguities that made later disputes all too likely. One practice that the "allowable amendments" concept did not curtail, however, is individually drafted language for special covenants related to bonuses, loans, extra insurance, and other additional benefits.[123]

Another issue addressed in the 1980 agreement was the question of limitations on the ability of a club or of the commissioner, in a free-agent compensation award, to assign a player contract to another club. During the 1970s player agents increasingly pressed for and obtained the so-called no-trade provisions in their clients' individual contracts. Clubs were finding it hard to make deals; and Commissioner O'Brien was particularly exorcized by the situation, feeling it made equitable compensation awards in the arbitration proceedings then in effect extremely difficult. Consequently, management sought and obtained the concession from the players' association that player contracts entered after the effective date of the 1980 collective bargaining agreement could not contain any restrictions on the assignability of the individual player contract.[124] This restriction has continued, with only a slight alteration in 1983 that allows a player to obtain a one-year no-trade when he signs an offer sheet with a new club.[125] If the old club exercizes the right of first refusal, it is bound as well by the one-year no-trade provision. After the implementation of the prohibitions in 1980, no-trades became rare as pre-1980 contracts concluded, until, for the 1983–84 season, only one NBA player retained a no-trade clause. This was Leonard "Truck" Robinson of the New York Knicks.[126] Ironically, Robinson was not with the Knicks when he negotiated the no-trade provision. He came via trade, having waived the no-trade rights in his player contract.[127]

Another concern to many owners in the league was the practice of several clubs to commit to long-term payments to players through deferred compensation arrangements. Some clubs were obligated for substantial sums for as much as twenty years in the future. Since it was felt that at least certain clubs would not control themselves, the league obtained from the NBPA the right to institute imposed limits on deferred compensation in future player contracts. Under the 1980 agreement, the league could restrict such compensation from as little as 50 percent of the salary to as much as only 5 percent.[128] This was reviewed in the 1983 negotiations, and the memorandum of agreement amending the 1980 accord settled on a 30 percent limit on deferred compensation in any given player contract.[129]

Money concerns, largely pressed by the players, dominated another issue that largely resulted in a stalemate. The two sides could not agree on the ultimate solution but did agree to postpone other legal actions for a period of years. The dispute concerned certain types of actual and potential revenues that could be anticipated flowing to the NBA, particularly those arising from new technologies. The NBPA had earlier contested the rights of others, including cable companies, to transmit the images of the NBA players. The suit was instituted by NBA players who were union leaders, headed by the then NBPA president, Paul Silas.[130] In effect, the 1980 provisions caused the *Silas* litigation to be withdrawn. In the agreement, the players' association, for itself and for present and future NBA players, covenanted not to sue over certain rights before the conclusion of the 1986–87 playoffs.[131]

As to the merits of the issue, the NBA and the players' association in effect said that they were postponing the eventual showdown. This was stipulated in the 1980 agreement; it was repeated with slightly different shadings in the 1983 memorandum, which stated that[132]

> The NBA and the Players Association disagree as to whether the NBA or any Team has the right to use, distribute, or license any performance by the players, under this Memorandum or the Uniform Player Contract, for Pay TV, Cable TV, any form of cassette or cartridge system, or other means of distribution known or unknown. By entering into this Memorandum, the parties specifically reserve any rights, legal or otherwise, on this point that they may own.

In addition to the covenant not to sue, provided in the 1980 agreement, the 1983 memorandum stipulates that the NBA and its teams do have the rights to use, distribute or license any performance by players during the term of the memorandum.[133]

The sum of the succession of events that question rights to market player performance in certain ways, beginning with the *Silas* litigation, suggests that both sides are holding back—for now. But if and when the big money from pay and cable television and other new technologies becomes a reality, the fighting will resume.

1981—The Right of First Refusal

With the several changes in 1980 in the way of doing business in place, there was great anticipation as to what would happen when the arbitration over free-agent compensation awards gave way to a right of first refusal, without any additional compensation to the old club if it decided not to match the new club's offer. Several on management's side were actually predicting that a right of first refusal would act to halt salary escalation, if not depress salaries a bit.[134] Others were not as sanguine about that possibility, feeling there were owners who could not resist the temptation to raise the stakes. If the threat of having to give substantial compensation to the player's prior club was removed, it might entice owners to put even more into salaries.[135]

It was curious that the NBA and the players' association had spelled out an eleven-year scheme for free-agent compensation and that one system would operate for five years and a significantly different system would replace the first. It is fairly clear that the owners were persuaded to provide for compensation on a transitional basis, with the later switch to a right of first refusal, for several reasons. The owners wanted all issues settled so that the demise of the American Basketball Association could take place. They were willing to gamble on the effects of the new free-agent schemes because of the alternatives. There was still the threat of severe liability in the *Robertson* case. There was the hope that the elimination of the ABA would depress rookie salaries immediately and eventually reduce the entire salary level in the NBA. There was also the view that the initial compensation provisions, in effect between 1976 and 1981, would deter player mobility and thus limit salary increases.

The owner strategy, then, was that the compensation procedures in effect the first few years would give the clubs breathing room necessary to enter long-term individual contracts with their players and stagger them so that a common expiration date would not act to place clubs under excessive pressure. There was also the hope that the advent of broad-based cable television would mitigate expenses attributable to increased player salaries. It was not a bad strategy, but it did not work. Only the escape from potential liability in *Robertson* proved to be tangible and undisputed. The ABA's departure did not appreciably lower salaries,[136] and as discussed earlier, the compensation provisions did not depress the free-agent market. Substantial numbers of players left their old clubs and sought new fortunes. Despite the players' association fears that the compensation awards by the commissioner would discourage clubs from offering lucrative contracts, as expressed in such as the *Webster* and *Walton* cases, free agency did produce player movement, and the awards seemed not to deter. Thus it developed that the contemplation of a right of first refusal became regarded, perhaps wistfully, as a welcome respite from the old procedures. However, this hope quickly faded.

The first few months after the right of first refusal went into effect were a catalyst. The dealings of Ted Stepien of the Cleveland Cavaliers set the tone. His announcement that he was going after top players at almost any price caused owner groans to turn to shrieks of outrage.[137] Stepien's immediate dealings were unsettling to say the least, but it is the aftermath of those dealings that are most instructive. Clubs have dealt with the right of first refusal in several ways.

Stepien's initial foray was to extend an offer to Otis Birdsong, a high-scoring guard on the Kansas City Kings. The offer was a multiyear contract that called for a slightly escalating base salary, beginning at $900,000 per year, with several incentive clauses. One in particular would pay Birdsong substantial amounts each year in which attendance climbed above a certain figure. Jeff Cohen, the newly appointed general manager of the Kings, had tried to head off Birdsong's free agency by earlier offering Birdsong a contract in the $600,000 to $700,000 range over several years. Birdsong's lawyer, Bob Woolf, had turned down all such offers, feeling that Birdsong should try the free-agent route in this, the first year of first refusal. When at first the offers did not come, Woolf was uneasy; but in stepped Stepien, and the free-agent maneuver netted Birdsong many extra hundred thousands of dollars.[138]

Ted Stepien did not get the services of Otis Birdsong. But then, neither did Jeff Cohen and the Kings. Cohen was instructed by his owners that there was no way that the Kings could afford that salary. Thus, Cohen matched Stepien's offer, but then Cohen immediately traded Birdsong to the New Jersey Nets, salvaging what he could from the situation. The Kings obtained Cliff Robinson in the deal, but no one would suggest that, in other circumstances, a Birdsong-for-Robinson trade would have been consummated. A gun to his head, Cohen did what he could.[139]

Stepien was not through with Kansas City. His next move was to extend a huge offer to Scott Wedman, who signed the $700,000 per year offer sheet and proferred it to Kansas City. In another maneuver that has become a standard way to handle such moves, Kansas City agreed not to match the offer in return for Cleveland's assigning to Kansas City a future high-draft pick.[140] Before he was through, Stepien was to expend his number-one draft choices time after time in this fashion, not just to obtain free agents, but in trades as well. When Stepien at length sold the club in 1984, having squandered millions of dollars, the club's draft picks had vanished as well as Stepien's personal fortune. This was so much the case that the new owners, for a price, were able to persuade the league to allow Cleveland special first-round slots.[141] In the meantime, Scott Wedman toiled for a time with Cleveland, his $700,000 salary easing the pain of playing for a team that was still at the bottom of the standings. Wedman eventually was traded to the Boston Celtics, but only after Stepien agreed to continue to pay almost half of Wedman's salary.[142]

Stepien's final 1981 foray into the free-agent market was another wonder, luring James Edwards away from the Indiana Pacers under a multiyear contract in excess of $700,000 a year. When faced with matching the offer or losing Edwards, the Pacers said good-bye. Edwards played only a few short years (or were they long?) in Cleveland, then was traded to the Phoenix Suns.[143]

Not all dealings under the right of first refusal have had the sound and fury of the Stepien deals. But certainly the right of first refusal acted as a goad to ever-increased salary escalations in 1982 and 1983. It was not just the actual free-agent market that was affected; it was also the spectre of the market that drove clubs to negotiate new contracts early with their own players and thus dissuade the players from testing the free-agent waters. It took only a couple of free-agent deals like the one that Philadelphia offered Moses Malone to persuade teams they had best act quickly with their star players.[144]

By this time, many provisions in the 1980 agreement were reaching a termination date, and salaries in the NBA averaged in the high $200,000s and were climbing. The owners were issuing proclamations of financial doom. Several clubs seemed headed for extinction. Many declared the right of first refusal was going to have to be tempered.

1983 – The Salary Cap

On June 1, 1982, the collective bargaining agreement between the NBA and the players' association expired, and the players entered the 1982 – 83 season without a contract. The old agreement provided that if no new agreement was reached by its expiration date, the old agreement would stay in force until a new agreement was settled. Unlike other sports leagues in recent years, it was not the players who were adamant with new demands. The owners wanted changes. The owners' initial demands included that (1) NBA rosters were to be reduced from twelve to ten players; (2) the players, not owners, should pay for pension funds and insurance; (3) guaranteed contracts and deferred payments were to be eliminated; (4) first-class travel was to be eliminated; and (5) the owners would get a percentage of the players' sneaker contracts.[145] These demands hardly got matters off to an auspicious beginning. Above all, the players were "ripped" by the owners seeking a share of the "sneaker action."

In light of these demands, the players' association came up with its own list: (1) guaranteed contracts; (2) television revenue; (3) increased pension and medical benefits, as well as increased playoff shares and meal money; (4) reduction of the eighty-two game schedule; and (5) increased team rosters from twelve to fifteen.[146] Point and counterpoint.

As negotiations moved into late October, the chief stumbling block in negotiations seemed to be the owners' demand for the elimination of the players' benefits (such as pension and medical). Larry Fleisher, for the NBPA, refused to accede to the league's demands and asserted that "the owners are trying to turn back the clock and take away benefits the players have accumulated in 15 years."[147] The reason for the owners' demand was that the average NBA team loses $700,000 and that seventeen of twenty-three were losing money.[148]

Commissioner Larry O'Brien announced that an entirely new player compensation structure had been proposed. While refusing to elaborate, O'Brien threatened that if negotiations with the players' association were unsuccessful, the NBA would implement several cost-saving measures, such as reduction of rosters and elimination of fringe benefits. Fleisher countered by accusing the NBA of not acting in good faith.

In early November 1982 O'Brien stated that if there was no evidence of progress in the talks within two weeks the owners would implement the threatened cost-saving devices. When Fleisher and the players' association gave no intention of giving in on any of these points (benefits, rosters, sneaker percentage), a strike in late November seemed possible.[149] But then the owners and players began talking again, and both parties seemed interested in a "new approach" to payment, although neither O'Brien nor Fleisher would reveal exactly what the "new approach" was. While Fleisher indicated it was too early to talk about a strike, he claimed that the players' association had become more solidified in the wake of the NBA's threats of cost-saving sanctions. Further, while the owners claimed that seventeen of twenty-three lost money in the previous year, Fleisher made a request to look at the NBA's books to see exactly what the financial picture was.[150] But by November 14, 1982, the owners appeared ready to back down from their demands as long as the talks continued and the players continued playing.[151]

On February 16, 1983, Fleisher set April 1 as the deadline for a new agreement. While not characterizing this as a strike threat, Fleisher did indicate that a walkout was among the options. Fleisher acknowledged that the April 1 date, seventeen days before the start of the playoffs, was chosen to pressure the owners into action. It was at this time that O'Brien revealed what the new approach to compensation was: The owners proposed a limitation on team salaries (that is, a salary cap, estimated by different sources to be from $1.6 million to $4 million), in exchange for giving the players a fixed percentage of league revenues.[152] While Fleisher agreed in principal with the concept, he felt it would erode the *Oscar Robertson* settlement of 1976, which had set the stage for the right of first refusal, in which a free agent's club had fifteen days to match any other offer. Fleisher also claimed that if the salary cap was agreed, the players' association would demand that it should not go into effect until 1987, the year the *Robertson* settlement would expire. This delay, according to Fleisher, would protect rookies and players soon to be free agents. The owners, on the other hand, wanted immediate implementation of the salary cap.[153]

By late February these major issues dominated: (1) the effective date for implementing the salary cap the players' association wanted delayed to 1987, in accordance with the *Oscar Robertson* settlement (the NBA owners pushed for immediate implementation); (2) the percentage of the league gross revenue to be allocated the players (the players sought 55 percent, while the owners proposed 40 percent); and (3) the dollar cap to be used as an alternative to a percentage. The players did not seem to be making any suggestions at this time, but indicated that the owners' offer of $1.6 million was unacceptable.[154]

In early March Fleisher walked out on a negotiation after only twenty-four heated minutes, where he more directly indicated the players' intention to strike on April 1 unless a settlement could be reached.[155] Three days later the NBA countered by saying that if the players did strike, the players scheduled to become free agents in June would be deemed to have forfeited this right and would not be permitted to negotiate with other teams. Further, the NBA said it would suspend all deferred payments, insurance policies, and other fringe benefits.[156]

Undeterred, Fleisher continued to warn of the impending strike. He also claimed that a $1.6 million cap would be disastrous, and reaffirmed his commitment to delaying the cap until 1987. The owners felt that a four-year delay would put several clubs out of business.[157] Even so, by March 25 the owners had conceded a great deal in terms of revenue percentage for players. The owners now offered 50 percent (up from 40 percent), while the players' association had come down 2 percent, down from 55 percent to 53 percent. But now another issue surfaced: exactly what constitutes gross revenue. While both sides agreed that television revenue and gate receipts should be considered revenue, the owners refused to put income from parking, concessions, and exhibition games.[158] Three days later, both sides indicated they were far apart and that a strike was imminent.

This may have been a smoke screen. Clearly, the talks became more serious and the parties closer to an agreement. Both the NBA and the players' association indicated a possibility that a strike could be avoided. Fleisher conceded that he would agree to let the salary cap go into effect for the 1984-85 season, three years earlier than he had earlier stipulated. The players still asked for a $3.8 million cap, and the owners offered only $2.8 million.[159]

On the eve of the threatened strike, March 31, 1983, the sides announced they had reached agreement. Details were few, but the strike was averted. Reports indicated that a minimum team salary would be part of the package, rumored to be 3 million dollars. There was immediate speculation as to the potential harm this would have on some clubs with current payrolls well below that figure. The Indiana Pacers, for example, had a 1982-83 payroll in the neighborhood of only $1.4 million. Other reports talked about the implementation of a maximum that would use an "either/or" approach, namely a percentage or a set dollar cap, whichever was higher. It was also obvious that several other provisions, probably exceptions to a cap, would be added to the agreement.[160]

In truth, while the parties had an agreement in principle as of March 31, much work was necessary before the actual terms were finalized. Hindsight perhaps suggests even more work was needed. The provisions were in many instances sketchy and not internally consistent. The final agreement forged was one that added several features not necessarily in existence as of March 31. While the ideas were there, what would make them work took further deliberation. At length, through, the final result is a new approach for the sports industries, provocative in its concepts.[161] The famous salary cap needs explication; it is not a simple concept.

It is fair to say that the 1983 provisions are not air-tight examples of drafting. This is hardly surprising. The novel approaches, supplemented by numerous exceptions, have tried to anticipate all contingencies. It is obvious the drafters were only partially successful in this regard. For those intimately involved in working under the cap, understanding the 1983 collective bargaining provisions is almost a full-time job.

The basic concept in the cap is that each club will be bound to a certain amount each year, which it can expend on player salaries. Although it at first appears from the document that this team maximum is to be determined in one of two ways, there are in reality four alternatives. Two apply supposedly to most clubs, binding all to one or the other.[162] The other two are individually accrued, based on a club's special circumstances. Under the first two alternatives, those applied as an "either/or" to clubs, all clubs will have a maximum team salary of no less than $3.6 million for the 1984-85 season, or 53 percent of gross revenues, whichever is more. Although the percentage will remain the same for the succeeding two years, the dollar amounts will rise to $3.8 million in 1985-86 and $4.0 million in 1986-87. The 53 percent of the gross, if that is utilized, is not based on a team's individual earnings. It is based on total league gross for the prior year, extrapolated by an additional percentage into the following year, then divided by the number of teams in the league (twenty-three). If that figure—the extrapolated league gross divided by the number of teams—exceeds the set dollar cap, then this higher figure becomes that year's maximum team salary for all affected teams.

We say "all affected teams" because it is apparent from the agreement that many teams will not have their caps calculated under the percentage-versus-set-dollar-cap method. These teams will each have its own maximum team salary. The 1983 memorandum of agreement begins by singling out five teams (Lakers, Knicks, Nets, 76er's, and Sonics) that were already over the $3.6 million mark at the end of the 1982-83 season. It was stipulated in the agreement that these clubs would be placed under immediate caps, all of which were above $3.6 million and ranged from a low of $3.75 million (Nets) to a high of $5.2 million (Lakers).[163] It was also stipulated that these clubs could keep those caps, with certain exceptions, in succeeding years as well.[164] So these clubs knew they could remain above the supposed cap, if they so chose. Others were also given the opportunity to emulate the spending five.

The final alternative measure for a team's maximum team salary came at the end of the playoffs for the 1983-84 season. It was then that the "official" team maximum was determined for all clubs, except the five mentioned above, which had their caps established a year earlier.[165]

The establishment of the maximum team salary supposedly brings into final effect the salary cap, and it is obvious that many of the teams will be above the percentage of the gross or the set dollar cap supposedly mandated for the league. For one thing, clubs did not hesitate to sign their own players to long-term contracts that would, in total for the team, establish a lofty maximum team salary.[166] For example, the Boston Celtics was not one of the five teams who had an immediate cap imposed at the conclusion of the 1983 season. They were free to deal, and deal they did. After signing Kevin McHale, Larry Bird, and Cedric Maxwell to new pacts, it is clear that their top six players alone (the three named, plus Parish, Johnson, and Ainge) command in combined salaries in excess of $5 million.[167] As explained below, no team is precluded from paying its own players grandiose sums, cap or no cap. In the Celtics' case the signings, except for the late agreement with Maxwell,[168] helped establish a team maximum that the Celtics can carry with them for some years to come, with only slight variations over time. The 53 percent of the gross or the $3.6 million limits mean almost nothing to that club and many others similarly situated.

That is only the beginning. In dealing with the team maximum, there are numerous other considerations. Once a team maximum is established, there are multiple transactions that must still be analyzed. The questions that arise concern how a team changes personnel. When a player retires, is cut, traded, or signs with another team as a free agent, then what? This is where the operation of the cap gets complex. The highlights will be summarized, but are not a substitute for the full document.

It is provided that any team with a total team salary at or over the maximum team salary established for that club may still sign players that will have the net effect of driving that team's salary even higher over its cap. The principle exception is that a team is always able to resign one of its own players who has become a veteran free agent.[169] A club can do so either by matching the offer sheet that a player signs with another club or by proceeding to sign the player to a new contract, even where no offer sheet from another club has been tendered or signed. What a club cannot do vis-à-vis its own players is resign them to increased amounts that take effect during the original term of the player's contract.[170] In other words, if a player has one year to go on his current contract at $500,000 for that remaining year *and* if the club is at or over its team maximum, then in fashioning a new agreement with that player, the club cannot pay increased monies, salary or bonus, to the player during the running of his contract for that year. What can be done is to sign the player to increased amounts to begin to be paid after the time when his current contract expires.

Other exceptions to the maximum team salary are at times even more esoteric. If a player is injured, there are two different possible responses for a team at or over its cap. The club may replace the player on a short-term basis by continuing to pay that player and sign a replacement player at the league minimum salary (on a pro-rata basis for the period in which the substitute is on the roster). If the injury is long-term, extending for example through the remainder of that season, the injured player must continue to be paid, and a substitute can be signed at no greater than 50 percent of the injured player's salary.[171] Since this will often be above the minimum salary and since that is an amount that goes on top of the club's pre-existing salary obligations, it can be seen that, for a period of time, the club's actual salary obligations will be above the club's supposed team maximum. Injuries being the reality they are in the NBA, many clubs often may be spending above their caps because of these exceptions to the team maximum provisions.

Where a club's veteran free agent signs with another club and the old club does not match the offer through its right of first refusal, the old club can replace the lost free agent at 100 percent of what the player *last* made.[172] Where a player is traded, he can be replaced, either through the trade or otherwise, by a player or players that make no more than 100 percent of what the traded player made.[173] On the other hand, if a player is waived or retires, then the waived or retired player can be replaced only at 50 percent of that player's contract.[174]

All of these seem straightforward enough, but in practice the complications become immediately apparent. Some clubs change personnel frequently, particularly in the off-season. It may not be readily apparent just who is replacing whom. In addition, a reality of life in professional sports is that there are always new bodies waiting their turns. A few will succeed; many will not. All will give it a try until they are cut. Clubs look at numerous aspirants, all of whom are under contract, however temporarily. The response under the 1983 provisions allows a club to increase its roster to twenty during the off season, without regard to its maximum team salary. However, the new players can be signed only to "make good" contracts, meaning that these are totally without guarantees, bonuses, or salary before the first day of the season.[175] Then if this player does make good, the team has to make room for him on its twelve-man roster and must change its salary commitments in other respects to be able to afford to pay the player what was promised him under the "make good" contract.

There is one other set of provisions that affect the newcomer, in this case those who have just been drafted. If a team is at its maximum team salary, it can sign the rookie to something other than a "make good" contract. It can even be one that is guaranteed. But the maximum salary that can be paid the rookie is the league minimum,[176] except for first-round picks, who can be signed at $75,000. In addition, the contract can be for only one year and cannot contain an option clause. The rookie in this category, therefore, gets hurt in salary for the year, since at least first rounders will command a higher salary for that year. But the potential benefit is that the rookie becomes a free agent at the end of the one year and can deal with all clubs, subject only to the old club's right of first refusal.

The provisions as to rookies have several consequences, many of them potentially discriminating to the rookie who finds himself drafted by a club at or over its maximum. First, it is arbitrary as to what players end up having to deal with a team that can offer the player only the minimum, as opposed to a player, perhaps taken later in the draft, who can immediately sign a multiyear deal at a far higher salary. The first drafted player may in fact never be able to catch up with the others below him, leading to justifiable criticism that there is unfortunate arbitrariness in how the rookie provisions impact. Second, if a player signs for the one year, there is hardly a guarantee that his free-agent status at the end of that year will garner him sufficient rewards to offset his earlier minimum contract. Few rookies break into the NBA with the style and effect of a Larry Bird, Magic Johnson, Isiah Thomas, or Michael Jordan. There may be a lot of bench time that first year; and the player emerges from his rookie season still an unknown quantity. If anything, since he was not an instant success, his market value may be less than it was a year earlier. Finally, with more and more clubs at or over their team maximum, the ability to make offers to any free agent, either one who has just completed the rookie year or a real veteran, may be curtailed. Thus, the rookie who has to sign cheap may be severely disadvantaged.

This led one drafted collegian, Leon Woods, to challenge the 1983 provisions as they related to his situation. Woods distinguished himself in the 1984 Olympics and was a high first-round draft pick of the Philadelphia 76er's. The Sixers however were at their maximum, imposed a year earlier per terms of the agreement. For some months, the Sixers said they could offer Woods only the mandated minimum. Woods and his agent balked, then filed suit in U.S. District Court under the *Robertson* settlement. Although the 76er's eventually made roster changes that allowed Woods to obtain a multiyear contract above the minimum, the basic issue was not mooted and went before the special master. The master ruled against the position advocated by Woods, holding that the special provisions for rookies must be considered in light of the entire 1983 agreement. He could not find that the specified protested provisions, in that context, were violative of the terms of the *Robertson* settlement.[177]

Thus, with the salary cap in place, for a few years at least, the process is now on-going as to the effects this new system will have on the financial base of the clubs and players. While it is premature to discern the ultimate effects, certain trends have appeared. First, it was apparent in seeking this approach that the clubs were gambling short-term increases in salary against long-term leveling. Since in 1983 numerous teams were under what would apparently be the minimum team salaries that would be imposed, these clubs were going to have to spend more. This has occurred, and average player salary levels rose in both 1983 and 1984. In that sense, some analysts have said, "What cap? It's a joke."[178] This reaction may be mistaken. The final proof will come as players become free agents in the next two to three years and try to extract continuing high offers from either new clubs or their old teams.

The second trend, then, deals with free agency. Although one year's experience is insufficient to allow more than speculation, it appears that more and more players are going to find that the combination of the cap and the right of first refusal depress the free-agent market. Larry Fleisher complained this occurred in 1984 and asserted that clubs were using the cap as a camouflage and that the cap should not be causing the paucity of offers that symbolized the free-agent dealings in 1984.[179] Only two NBA players were really able to use effectively the free-agent system between the 1983–84 and 1984–85 seasons. These were Pat Cummings and Kelly Tripucka. Cummings obtained what many regard as more than a substantial offer from the New York Knicks, some $600,000 per year over several years.[180] Tripucka resisted Detroit's attempts to cut back on its initial offer to him and extracted from Cleveland a very impressive seven-year offer at basically $900,000 per year. While Cummings's old club, Dallas, did not match the offer and Cummings moved, Detroit did match Cleveland's offer, keeping Tripucka. This was with rancor, as the Pistons expressed outrage at what they thought was something other than a good-faith attempt by Cleveland to actually obtain Tripucka's services.[181] Since Cleveland committed itself to pay the substantial sums, should Detroit not match, this attack is questionable. It does, however, suggest what may have become a philosophy about the right of first refusal, now enhanced by the salary cap.

There is a widespread perception that clubs will match other clubs' offers most of the time. This then leads clubs to question how much they should become involved in approaching other club's free agents. If most clubs match, then the only real effect is that each club is driving up the other club's salaries, without benefitting anyone other than the player. Thus, the only time that a club may be enticed to extend an offer sheet is where (1) it is willing to offer exceedingly high amounts in terms of that player's perceived value and (2) it believes that the player's old club will either not match or will want to match and deal the player, probably to the club extending the offer. If these assessments become prevalent, the owners' attempts at decreasing overall the free-agent market in the NBA may become a reality. It is not clear this has happened, but there are positive indicators, such as the 1984 off-season. This is almost certain not to become a circumstance as extreme as exists in the NFL, where free-agency movement is virtually nonexistent. The "star" quality of certain NBA players almost undoubtedly will be too strong for an owner in a given circumstance to resist making the huge offer in hopes the old team will not match. But these instances may become exceedingly few compared with what has occurred the past few years. If so, this will but add intrigue and zest to the next round of collective bargaining NBA style.

1987—World War III?

The NBA has had an interesting history in labor relations. Its record is idiosyncratic, greatly influenced by Larry Fleisher. Management has been of a high quality, beginning with current Commissioner Stern, and it may be that management should be credited with a major victory emerging from the 1982–83 negotiations. That victory should not necessarily be viewed as at the expense of the players, at least not as a group, but as a step that may get the league finally moving toward firmly established and continuing financial stability.

The current state is in many respects only as strong as its structure; and the structure rests in large part on the provisions of the collective bargaining agreement of 1980, as amended in 1983. Those provisions have time yet to run, but will expire eventually.

In a statement concerning current labor relations and prospects for the future, Larry Fleisher foreshadowed what is to come by suggesting that 1987 will be World War III in the NBA.[182] Fleisher was undoubtedly referring to two occurrences to come in 1986 and 1987: The current collective bargaining provisions expire, and the *Robertson* settlement terminates. The salary cap, draft, right of first refusal, and the host of other provisions will be up for grabs. Clearly, the battle is not over yet.

NOTES TO CHAPTER 6

1. Z. Hollander, ed., The Modern Encyclopedia of Basketball 211 (1969) (hereafter cited as Hollander I).
2. F. Menke, ed., The Encyclopedia of Sports 150–52 (4th ed. 1969) (hereafter cited as Menke). This source is of particular interest, in that it includes James Naismith's own recollections of how the game began.
3. General background on the early professional leagues can be found in Hollander I at 211–19, and in Menke at 172–73. *See also* Z. Hollander, ed., The NBA's Official Encyclopedia of Pro Basketball 1–32 (1981) (hereafter cited as Hollander II); and Z. Hollander, ed., The Encyclopedia of Sports Talk 75 (1976).
4. J. Lapchick, 50 Years of Basketball 21 (1968):

    Holman came out of New York's East Side and was gifted in all phases of the game. A pass-master and an artist at feinting and faking, he was a wizard at drawing fouls. He came to the Celtics from the New York Whirlwinds. During his playing days he studied at Savage Institute and got a degree in physical education. . . . Holman averaged ten points a game as a player, often half the points the Celtics scored in winning a game.

5. In Joe Lapchick's own accounts of the early days, he dwells particularly on the Original Celtics. Lapchick started playing professionally with the New York Whirlwinds at $7 a game. By jumping from one team to another, and playing one coach against another, he was able, within a couple of years, to command as much as $75 a game, an amount almost unheard of in those early days. Lapchick joined the Original Celtics in 1923 and, with the team's other stalwarts, proceeded to dominate the game for several years. At one stretch, the Original Celtics won 194 of 205 games. *See* J. Lapchick, 50 Years of Basketball 10–26 (1968).
6. *See* Hollander I at 218–19; and Hollander II at 33–36. *See also* R. Lapchick, Broken Promises 141 (1984).
7. The other original entries in the BAA in 1946, all long defunct, were the Chicago Stags, Cleveland Rebels, Detroit Falcons, and Washington Capitols. Arnold "Red" Auerbach coached the Capitols in the first year of the league. *See* Sporting News, Official NBA Guide 1984–85, at 430–32 (1984) (hereafter cited as NBA Guide). In general, for a year-by-year, team-by-team record on the NBA, see NBA Guide.
8. *See* Hollander I at 378.
9. For an excellent account of Connie Hawkins's career, including his time at the University of Iowa leading to his dismissal from the University, and his

later lawsuit against the blacklisting by the NBA, see D. Wolf, Foul! Connie Hawkins Story (1972), particularly 85-121, 333-50. On the earlier 1951 scandals, see Menke at 150.

10.   181 N.E.2d 506 (Ohio 1961).

11.   Dick Barnett's own experience when a rival league appears is testimony to the effect on player salaries that is likely produced. Barnett had earned $8,500 for the 1960-61 season. Knowing of the competition, his NBA club, the Syracuse Nats, were willing to raise that to $11,500. The ABL suitor, the Cleveland Pipers, went above to $13,000. Compared with modern-day salaries, these sums are miniscule; but in terms of percentage raises for the players, in Barnett's case almost 50 percent in one year, the increases were significant. *See* 181 N.E.2d at 514.

12.   Other ABA teams that hardly live brightly in the memories of basketball buffs would include such as Miami Floridians, New Jersey Americans, New Orleans Buccaneers, Pittsburgh Condors, San Diego Sails, and Washington Capitols. *See* NBA Guide at 108. Of course, some of these teams had longer lives under other names in other locales. In all, one estimate puts total losses by ABA clubs during the league's existence at $50 million. *See* Hollander II at 278.

13.   The ABA was proud and possessive of its red, white, and blue ball. Indeed, the league tried to protect it as its exclusive property under a trademark theory, but was unsuccessful in this attempt. *See* American Basketball Ass'n v. AMF Voit, 358 F. Supp. 981 (1973).

14.   Connecticut Professional Sports Corp. v. Heyman, 276 F. Supp. 618 (1967).

15.   Robertson v. NBA, 389 F. Supp. 867 (1975).

16.   *See, e.g.*, Munchak Corp. v. Cunningham, 457 F.2d 721 (1972); ABA Players Ass'n v. NBA 404 F. Supp. 832 (1975); Washington Capitols Basketball Club v. Barry, 304 F. Supp. 1193 (1969); Munchak Corp. v. Riko Enterprises, 368 F. Supp. 1366 (1973); Minnesota Muskies v. Hudson, 294 F. Supp. 979 (1969); Lemat Corp. v. Barry, 80 Cal. Rptr. 210 (1969).

17.   Hearings on the Antitrust Laws and Organized Professional Team Sports, Including Consideration of the Proposed Merger of the American and National Basketball Associations, House Comm. on the Judiciary, 146-50 (July-Sept. 1972) (testimony of Lawrence Fleisher) (hereafter cited as 1972 Merger Hearings).

18.   *Id.* at 317-18 (statement of Oscar Robertson).

19.   *Id.* at 146 (report on sentiments of Zelmo Beaty, president of ABA players' association, concerning the proposed merger).

20.   *See* Authorizing the Merger of Two or More Professional Basketball Leagues, and for Other Purposes, report No. 92-1151, Senate Comm. on the Judiciary, 92d Cong., 2d Sess. (Sept. 18, 1972).

21.   Hearings on Labor Relations in Professional Sports, House Comm. on Education and Labor, 92d Cong., 2d Sess., H.R. 7152, at 65-67 (March 1972) (statement by Lawrence Fleisher) (hereafter 1972 Labor Hearings).

22.   *Id.* at 66.

23.   *Id.*

24. *Id.*
25. *Id.* at 67.
26. Larry Fleisher has represented the NBPA since 1962. *See id.* at 65. *See also* Powers, He's Running the Break: Meet Larry Fleisher, Point Guard for the NBA Players, Boston Globe, March 29, 1983, at 53, col. 3.
27. *Id.*
28. 1972 Labor Hearings at 67.
29. NBA Players Threaten Strike in Dispute Over Pension Plan, N.Y. Times, Jan. 15, 1964, at 34, col. 3.
30. Robertson v. NBA, 389 F. Supp. 867 (1975).
31. 1972 Labor Hearings at 68.
32. *See, e.g.*, NBA Talks Called Hopeful, N.Y. Times, March 30, 1983, at B7, col. 4; A Costly Meeting, N.Y. Times, March 30, 1983, at B11, col. 3.
33. Little needs to be said about the impact that Bill Russell had on the Boston Celtics and the NBA. As noted in the text, between 1956 and 1969, the Celts were NBA champions eleven of thirteen years, exactly coinciding with the thirteen-year career of Russell. During that time, he was NBA MVP five times, and appeared in eleven All-Star games. The last three years, Russell was also the coach of the Celtics. His first season as coach (1966–67) saw the Philadelphia Warriors cause one of the rare interruptions in the Celtics' string of championships; but the Celts rebounded to capture the flags the next two years. When Russell resigned as a player in 1969, he also resigned as the Celtics coach, though he did later return to the NBA to coach the Seattle Sonics for four years (1973–77). *See* Hollander II at 331, 337, 501.
34. Joe Lapchick had nothing but praise for the talents of the Rens, as was true with other members of the Original Celtics. Lapchick went so far as to call the Rens' Charles "Tarzan" Cooper the best center he had ever seen. *Id.* at 36. Lapchick's son, Richard, recalls that the surviving members of the Rens all attended his father's funeral, another aspect of the respect existing between the old basketball competitors. R. Lapchick, Broken Promises 120 (1984).
35. For an account of the anonymous "hate calls" that Joe Lapchick received when he added Nat Clifton to the Knicks' roster, see R. Lapchick, Broken Promises 125 (1984).
36. *See* NBA Guide 411.
37. *See* Hollander I 218–19. *See also* Hollander II at 373. In addition to the Rens, three other "teams" have made it to the Hall of Fame in Springfield, Massachusetts. These are the Original Celtics, Buffalo Germans, and The First Team (the eighteen students from Dr. James Naismith's physical education class, who participated in the first basketball game in December 1891, at the Springfield Armory YMCA). *Id.* at 372–73.
38. The contributions of the Harlem Globetrotters as an alternative for black players in the earlier days must be noted. *See* Menke at 151, 153–54.
39. *See* NBA Guide at 206–432. These pages contain the year-by-year reports on the NBA, including the league champions.

40. Thomas "Satch" Sanders actually joined the Boston Celtics in 1960, playing a consistent forward for them for thirteen years. Sanders returned to the Celtics as head coach for the latter part of the 1977–78 and first part of the 1978–79 seasons. He also coached the Harvard University basketball team. On his professional career, see Hollander II at 331, 501.

41. Ryan, Race: How Big a Factor?, Boston Globe, March 29, 1982, at 29, col. 1.

42. One measure of stardom is being named to the All-NBA first or second teams at the conclusion of the season. In the four seasons beginning with 1980–81 and running through 1983–84, only two white players have made the ten-man honor roll. Larry Bird was first team all four years, and Jim Paxson of Portland was second team in 1983–84. *See* NBA Guide at 100. If one expands the term "star" a bit more, white players do somewhat better. For the 1984 All-Star Game, of the twenty-four players named to the two squads, eight were white. *Id.* at 101.

43. *See, e.g.*, Marantz, Celtics Were Integration Model, yet . . . , Boston Globe, Aug. 5, 1979, at 60, col. 1; Ryan, Race: How Big a Factor?, Boston Globe, March 29, 1982, at 29, col. 1. As of 1984, two blacks were in the NBA front office. For the twenty-three NBA clubs, two head coaches and one general manager were black.

44. *See generally* the discussion of the black athlete and his chances of a professional career in R. Lapchick, Broken Promises (1984). *See also* D. Wolf, Foul! Connie Hawkins Story (1972).

45. The NBA roster size for the 1980–81 season was eleven players. For the playoffs and eventual championship, the Celtics had six whites and five blacks on their squad. That is somewhat misleading, in that, for much of the regular season, it was six blacks and five whites. But Wayne Kreklow (twenty-five game appearances) replaced Terry Duerod (thirty-two games) in the stretch run. Duerod nevertheless participated with the Celtics in their victory celebration following their four games to two championship win over the Houston Rockets. *See* NBA Guide at 247, 253.

46. Papanek, There's an Ill Wind Blowing for the NBA, Sports Illustrated, Feb. 26, 1979, at 20; Harvey, 82 Games Are Just Too Many, L.A. Times, Feb. 11, 1983, pt. 3, at 1, col. 1.

47. *See* Shirley, Sports Has Become More Than a Game, It's Serious Business, L.A. Times, March 29, 1983, pt. 3, at 1, col. 5. *See also* attendance data released each year by the NBA.

48. Figures cited in text are based on statistics released by NBA offices. For 1983–84 attendance figures, *see also* NBA Guide at 232.

49. *Id.*

50. *Id.*

51. *Id.*

52. Craig, TV's Slow Fade, Boston Globe, March 30, 1982, at 31, col. 1.

53. *Id.*

54. According to one report, the following earned $1 million or more for the 1983–84 season: Larry Bird, Mitch Kupchak, Moses Malone, Kareem Abdul-Jabbar, Ralph Sampson, Jack Sikma, Otis Birdsong, and Kevin McHale. Rosen, ed., The Sport 100, Sport, March 1984, at 125. Added to

those, because of contracts taking effect for 1984–85, would be Magic Johnson and Isiah Thomas, joining the million-dollar class.

55. For the 1983–84 season, those NBA players in the $500,000 to $1 million range include Marques Johnson, Alex English, Bernard King, Calvin Natt, Bob McAdoo, Gus Williams, James Edwards, Julius Erving, Bill Walton, and Scott Wedman. Added to that list should be Robert Parish. As of the 1984–85 season, additional signings brought Kelly Tripucka, Pat Cummings, and Cedric Maxwell into the very high-priced category. See Rosen, *supra* note 60.

56. The minimum NBA salary is set forth in Memorandum of Understanding between the NBA and Players' Association, June 6, 1983, art. 3, §C(11)(a) (hereafter cited as 1983 Memorandum). The minimum salary will rise to $70,000 in 1985–86 and $75,000 in 1986–87. *Id.*

57. *See* Goldaper, Salary Cap Helps to Reshape NBA, N.Y. Times, Oct. 26, 1984, at 24, col. 1.

58. Harvey, Jury Is Still Out on Who Won, L.A. Times, April 1, 1983, pt. 3, at 1, col. 6.

59. *See* 1983 Memorandum, art. 3, §B(2).

60. *See* Stricharchuck, Ted Stepien Learns Pro Basketball Is an Expensive Hobby, Wall St. J., Feb. 16, 1983, at 1, col. 3; Shaughnessy, Owners Have League in an Overlapping Grip, Boston Globe, March 28, 1982, at 77, col. 1.

61. NBA Guide at 347. For statistics on 1965–66 season, *see id.* at 351.

62. Lemat Corp. v. Barry, 80 Cal. Rptr. 240 (1969).

63. *See* National Football League Uniform Player Contract ¶16.

64. Attendance bonuses for Rick Barry described in Washington Capitols v. Barry, 204 F. Supp. 1193 (1969).

65. *Id.*

66. Minnesota Muskies v. Hudson, 294 F. Supp. 979 (1969).

67. The San Francisco Warriors were NBA champions in 1975. In an upset, they swept the Washington Bullets 4 to 0 in the championship finals. Rick Barry was second in the NBA regular season in scoring average, finishing behind Bob McAdoo. NBA Guide at 297–303.

68. Golden State Warriors & Houston Rockets (Rick Barry), Sept. 1, 1978. Decision by Commissioner Lawrence O'Brien.

69. Rick Barry's career free-throw shooting percentage of .893 barely edges out that of Calvin Murphy (.892), a Houston Rockets teammate on Barry's last NBA stop. The .893 mark included Barry's stats in the ABA, as well as the NBA. The NBA includes the ABA performance records for statistical purposes. *See* NBA Guide at 119. Through 1984, Barry was also seventh in all-time scoring (again including ABA records) with 9,695 points, and was tenth in scoring average with a career mark of 24.8 per game. *Id.* For a capsule career summary on Rick Barry, *see* NBA Register at 273.

70. Brenner v. Barry (N.J. Sup. Ct. No. L-19708-79). Among others named as co-defendants in the suit were Barry's teammates, Moses Malone and Calvin Murphy. The suit was settled before trial.

71. Central New York Basketball v. Barnett, 181 N.E.2d 506 (Ohio 1961).

72. Minnesota Muskies v. Hudson, 294 F. Supp. 979 (1969).

73. In the Matter of the Arbitration between California Sports & Wilton N. Chamberlain, Dec. 4, 1973, reported in 61 L.A. 1066; Robertson v. NBA, 556 F.2d 682 (1977) (Wilton Chamberlain et al., objectors-appellants); Robertson v. NBA, 622 F.2d 34 (1980) (Wilton N. Chamberlain, appellant).

74. Connecticut Professional Sports v. Heyman, 276 F. Supp. 618 (1967).

75. Munchak Corp. v. Cunningham, 457 F.2d 721 (1972).

76. Erving v. Virginia Squires Basketball Club, 468 F.2d 1064 (1972).

77. Denver Rockets v. All-Pro Management, 525 F. Supp. 1049 (1971).

78. *See* Hollander I at 409. For a complete record on basketball in the Olympics, through 1968, see *id.* at 407–10.

79. After the *Haywood* decision, the immediate years that followed (1971 to 1975) saw many players go "hardship," opting for an early NBA career. Of the 120 who applied for eligibility, however, only eighty-three were actually drafted by an NBA club and only sixty-seven ever had any type of NBA career. When the "hardship" requirement was dropped and an "early eligibility draft" was substituted, the numbers dropped. Between 1976 and 1983, only fifty-nine applied, forty-three were drafted, and thirty-eight actually played in the NBA. *See* The Chronicle of Higher Education 25 (May 16, 1984).

80. Among numerous instances where the *Robertson* matter has been before the court, see, among others, 625 F.2d 407 (1980); 622 F.2d 34 (1980); 557 F.2d 953 (1977); 556 F.2d 682 (1977); 479 F. Supp. 657 (1979); 413 F. Supp. 88 (1976); 404 F. Supp. 832 (1976); 389 F. Supp. 867 (1975); 72 F.R.D. 64; 1979–1 Trade Cases ¶16,524; 1977–1 Trade Cases ¶61,324; 1976–1 Trade Cases ¶60,777; Slip Opinion, N.S. Dist. Ct. (S.D.N.Y.) No. 70 Civ. 1526 (RLC), May 6, 1981; Slip Opinion, U.S. Dist. Ct. (S.D.N.Y.) No. 70, Civ. 1526 (RLC), Dec. 19, 1978.

81. Robertson v. NBA, 72 F.R.D. 64 (1976), *aff'd*, 556 F.2d 682 (1977).

82. Thomas, Wood Suit Challenges the NBA Salary Cap, San Francisco Chron., Sept. 22, 1984, at 47, col. 1.

83. *See, e.g.*, NBA: Jury Gets Rudy T. Case, Boston Globe, Aug. 13, 1979, at 50, col. 1; NBA: Tomjanovich Seeks 1m in Damages against Lakers, Boston Globe, Aug. 7, 1979, at 34, col. 1; Rudy T. Given $3.3, Boston Globe, Aug. 18, 1979, at 22, col. 2.

84. *See, e.g.*, Shaughnessy, NBA views Tapes of Boston Brawl, Boston Globe, Nov. 11, 1984, at 56, col. 5; He Ought to Know an Elbow, L.A. Times, Nov. 15, 1984, pt. 3, at 2, col. 1.

85. Collective Bargaining Agreement between National Basketball Association and National Basketball Players' Association, Oct. 10, 1980, art. 19, §5 (hereafter cited as 1980 Agreement).

86. All professional team sports leagues that have collective bargaining agreements also provide for arbitration of most types of player (employee) grievances. Such provisions for NBA players are set forth in 1980 Agreement, art. 19.

87. In the Matter of the Arbitration between California Sports & Wilton N. Chamberlain, Dec. 4, 1973, reported in 61 L.A. 1066.

88. Wilt Chamberlain's 100 point NBA game occurred on March 2, 1962, against the New York Knicks. Wilt was with the Philadelphia Warriors at the time. However, the game was played in neither New York or Philadelphia; the teams met on the neutral site of Hershey, Pennsylvania. Chamberlain scored his 100th point with forty-six seconds left in the game, won by the Warriors 169 to 147. One other mark attained by Chamberlain that night was contrary to his later reputation as a wretched free-throw shooter; he was 28 for 32 from the line. He also had 25 rebounds. *See* NBA Guide at 127. The 169 to 147 mark was not the highest scoring NBA game. That belongs to the three-overtime affair on Dec. 13, 1983, with the Detroit Pistons beating the Denver Nuggets, 186 to 184. *Id.*

89. Chamberlain averaged 50.4 points per game for the 1961–62 NBA regular season, by far the highest single season average. NBA Guide at 367.

90. Robertson v. NBA, 556 F.2d 682 (1977) (Wilton Chamberlain et al., objectors-appellants); Robertson v. NBA, 622 F.2d 34 (1980) (Wilton N. Chamberlain, appellant).

91. Chamberlain hauled in 55 rebounds on November 24, 1960, ironically against Bill Russell and the Boston Celtics. Russell is next on the single-game rebound chart. In fact, he holds the second through fourth best marks, with 51, 49, and 49 rebounds. For the top ten single-game marks, it is all Chamberlain and Russell. And for the top twenty games, only Nate Thurmond with one entry (42 rebounds) breaks the monopoly. For their careers, Chamberlain finished with 23,924 rebounds, Russell with 21,620. *See* NBA Guide at 112, 116.

92. In the Matter of Arbitration between National Basketball Ass'n (Atlanta Hawks) & National Basketball Players' Ass'n (Ken Charles) (Seitz, Arb.) (June 22, 1978).

93. Bob Love played eleven years in the NBA, most of them with the Chicago Bulls. His career scoring average was 17.6 points per game. *See* Hollander II at 477.

94. In the Matter of the Arbitration between National Basketball Ass'n (Chicago Professional Sports Corp: Chicago Bulls) & National Basketball Players' Ass'n (Robert E. Love) (Seitz, Arb.) (Feb. 6, 1975).

95. 1983 Memorandum, art. 4, §C:

> A player who withholds his playing services during the last season of his Player Contract shall be deemed not to have "complet[ed] his Player Contract by rendering the playing services called for thereunder." Accordingly, such player shall not be a Veteran Free Agent and shall not be entitled to negotiate or sign a contract with any other professional basketball team unless and until the Team for which the player last previously played expressly agrees otherwise.

96. In the Matter of Arbitration between National Basketball Ass'n (Denver Nuggets) & National Basketball Players' Ass'n (Rudy Hackett) (Seitz, Arb.) (Sept. 27, 1977).

97. *See* 1980 Agreement art. 17, for the club's right of set-off where the player subsequently signs with another NBA club.

98. In the Matter of Arbitration between National Basketball Ass'n (Detroit Pistons) & National Basketball Players' Ass'n (Ben Poquette) (Seitz, Arb.) (July 24, 1978).

99. *See* the discussion of the individual versus the collective interests in Chapter 8.
100. The average NBA player salary first topped the $50,000 mark in 1971. At that time, the NFL was second in average salaries among the four major league sports. By 1980 basketball was still first at $190,000, but football had faded to a distant fourth at $78,657. *See* Inside Sports, Aug. 31, 1981, at 58, 69; *see also* Inside Sports, July 31, 1980, at 19.
101. *Id.*
102. Agreement between the National Basketball Association and the National Basketball Players Association, April 29, 1976 (hereafter cited as 1976 Agreement). Provisions relating to the college draft, option clauses, compensation rule and right of first refusal are all contained in 1976 Agreement, art. 16.
103. *See* 1980 Agreement, art. 22, §2(a).
104. 1976 Agreement, art. 16, §1(c)(1).
105. Mackey v. NFL, 407 F. Supp. 1000 (1975), *modified*, 543 F.2d 606 (1976), *cert. dismissed*, 434 U.S. 801 (1977).
106. *See* discussion of the antitrust labor exemption in Chapter 4.
107. In the Matter of Atlanta Hawks & New Orleans Jazz (Leonard Robinson compensation) (decision by Commissioner Lawrence F. O'Brien) (Oct. 3, 1977).
108. In the Matter of Golden State Warriors & Los Angeles Lakers (Jamaal Wilkes compensation) (decision by Commissioner Lawrence F. O'Brien) (Sept. 14, 1977).
109. In the Matter of Portland Trailblazers & San Diego Clippers (Bill Walton compensation) (decision by Commissioner Lawrence F. O'Brien) (Sept. 18, 1979); Robertson Class Plaintiffs, Report of the Special Master (S.D.N.Y. July 7, 1980); Modified Opinion and Award of the Commissioner (Aug. 15, 1980); Walton & Webster (S.D.N.Y. Sept. 17, 1980).
110. In re Robertson Class Plaintiffs, 479 F. Supp. 657 (1979), *aff'd in part*, 625 F.2d 407 (1980).
111. Robertson v. NBA, 72 F.R.D. 64 (1976), *aff'd*, 556 F.2d 682 (1977).
112. In re Robertson Class Plaintiffs, 479 F. Supp. 657, 661–62 (1979).
113. *Id.* at 662.
114. *Id.*
115. Robertson Class Plaintiffs v. NBA, 625 F.2d 407, 412 (1980).
116. *Id.* at 413.
117. *Id.* at 414.
118. The previously agreed on procedures were incorporated into the 1980 Agreement in art. 22, including §1(c), Compensation Rule, and §1(d), Right of First Refusal.
119. 1980 Agreement, art. 22, §1(a).
120. Robertson Class Plaintiffs (David Batton), Report of Special Master, Feb. 12, 1981; *see also* N.Y. Times, Feb. 13, 1981, at A18, col. 5.
121. 1980 Agreement, art. 1, §1(b).
122. 1980 Agreement, exhibits AA-1 — AA-19.
123. 1980 Agreement, art. 1, §1(b).

124. 1980 Agreement, art. 14.
125. 1983 Memorandum, art. 4, §A, *amending* 1980 Agreement, art. 14.
126. *See* The Last Clause, N.Y. Times, Jan. 24, 1984, at A22, col. 2.
127. Leonard "Truck" Robinson was with the Phoenix Suns when he signed what proved to be the last of the NBA no-trade clauses. He moved via trade from the Suns to the Knicks after the 1981–82 season, in exchange for Maurice Lucas. Robinson had earlier been involved in a free-agent compensation case when he left the Atlanta Hawks to play for the New Orleans Jazz. *See* Note 107. *See also* NBA Register at 170.
128. 1980 Agreement, art. 15.
129. 1983 Memorandum, art. 4, §P, *amending* 1980 Agreement, art. 15. *See also* Powers, The Time Bomb That Could Break NBA Banks, Boston Globe, April 3, 1983, at 90, col. 1.
130. Silas, Lanier & Lee v. Manhattan Cable Television, 79 Civ. 3025 (S.D.N.Y. filed June 8, 1979).
131. 1980 Agreement, art. 18, §2.
132. 1983 Memorandum, art. 4.
133. *Id.*
134. *See, e.g.*, Looney, The Start of a Chain Reaction, Sports Illustrated, Feb. 16, 1976, at 18; Littwin, NBA Owners: They're Taking a Second Look at First Refusal, L.A. Times, July 10, 1981, pt. 3, at 1, col. 1.
135. Newman, Can the NBA Save Itself?, Sports Illustrated, Nov. 1, 1982, at 38; Dickey, The NBA's Predicament, San Francisco Chron., Oct. 14, 1982, at 61, col. 2.
136. The surviving ABA teams joined the NBA in 1976. At that time, the average NBA salary was $109,000. It then rose to $125,000 in 1977, $145,000 in 1978, $160,000 in 1979, and $180,000 in 1980. *See* 2 Inside Sports 19 (July 31, 1980).
137. *See* These Agents Are Hardly Free, Sports Illustrated, June 8, 1981, at 30.
138. *Id.*
139. Johnson, Birdsong Is Playing Down His Million-Dollar Salary, Boston Globe, Oct. 26, 1981, at C7, col. 1. One of the victims of the early forays in the right of first refusal was Jeff Cohen, mentioned in the text, the then newly arrived general manager for the Kansas City Kings. With a number of his players becoming free agents, and his owners taking a hard line on what salaries could be afforded, Cohen found himself in a "no-win" situation. A year later, he was out of a job. *See* Boston Globe, May 9, 1982, at 68, col. 2.
140. Littwin, They're Taking a Second Look at First Refusal, L.A. Times, July 10, 1981, pt. 3, at 1, col. 1.
141. Two New Owners in NBA, Boston Globe, May 10, 1983, at 57, col. 6; The NBA's Charity Case, Sporting News, May 23, 1983, at 6.
142. When Scott Wedman was traded to the Boston Celtics, the Cleveland Cavaliers received Darren Tillis, the Celtics' first-round pick the year before, plus some badly needed cash. However, the Cavaliers had to continue to pay approximately $300,000 per year of the amount still owed on Wedman's contract. Later, it was confirmed by the Celtics front office that the

old contract was rescinded and two new ones, one with the Celtics and one personally with Ted Stepien, were substituted. In that manner, if the Cavs folded, the Celtics were not responsible for the remaining obligations. This information based on interview with Jan Volk, then executive president and counsel for the Celtics. As of summer 1984, Volk assumed the position of general manager of the Celtics.

143. *See* Goldaper, Salaries and Trades Top Menu, N.Y. Times, May 31, 1981, §5, at 7, col. 2; Stepien Takes the Stand, Boston Globe, June 2, 1981, at 53, col. 1.

144. *See* Shirk, Malone Sent to 76ers, Boston Globe, Sept. 16, 1982, at 49, col. 5; Shaughnessy, Will Moses Lead NBA into Ruin?, Boston Globe, Sept. 19, 1982, at 50, col. 3; Up, Up and Away in NBA, Sporting News, Sept. 27, 1982, at 6; Goldaper, Malone's Season Worth $2.9 Million, N.Y. Times, June 8, 1983, at B7, col. 5.

145. *See* Hoop Scoop, Sporting News, Oct. 11, 1982, at 51.

146. *Id. See also* Muniz, NBA Sides Far from Agreement, Hartford Courant, Oct. 12, 1982, at D1, col. 4.

147. Goldaper, NBA Owners Will Be Briefed on Talks, N.Y. Times, Oct. 20, 1982, at B11, col. 1.

148. Goldaper, NBA Studies New Pay Plan, N.Y. Times, Oct. 21, 1982, at B23, col. 4; Progress, Impasse Plan in NBA Negotiations, San Francisco Chron., Oct. 21, 1982, at 71, col. 1.

149. Harvey, Has NBA Finally Achieved Parity with NFL?, L.A. Times, Oct. 27, 1982, pt. 3, at 1, col. 2; Harvey, Another Strike Looms, L.A. Times, Nov. 2, 1982, pt. 3, at 3, col. 1.

150. Mitchell, NBA Studies New Pay Plan, Sporting News, Nov. 8, 1982, at 26.

151. Shaughnessy, Owners Won't Rock the Boat during Stalled Negotiations, Boston Globe, Nov. 14, 1982, at 44, col. 1.

152. Goldaper, Players In NBA Issue Deadline, N.Y. Times, Feb. 17, 1983, at B13, col. 1; NBA Players' Union Sets April 1 Contract Deadline, L.A. Times, Feb. 17, 1983, pt. 3, at 16, col. 1.

153. Shaughnessy, NBA Management Takes the Offensive, Boston Globe, Feb. 17, 1983, at 52, col. 5; Goldaper, Schulman Dares NBA Union to Strike, N.Y. Times, Feb. 18, 1983, at A24, col. 1; Muniz, NBA Says Union Reneged, Hartford Courant, Feb. 18, 1983, at F4, col. 4.

154. Harvey, The Disagreement in the NBA, L.A. Times, Feb. 22, 1983, pt. 3, at 1, col. 4.

155. Goldaper, NBA Talks Recess after Brief Session, N.Y. Times, March 2, 1983, at B11, col. 1; Players Put NBA on Strike Notice, L.A. Times, March 2, 1983, pt. 3, at 5, col. 1.

156. NBA Cautions Free Agents over Strike, Boston Globe, March 6, 1984, at 48, col. 3; A Threat to Free Agency, N.Y. Times, March 6, 1983, at 4, col. 5; NBA Takes Step to Deter Strike, L.A. Times, March 6, 1983, pt. 3, at 4, col. 1.

157. McDonough, NBA Ship of Fools Near Rocks, Boston Globe, March 17, 1983, at 49, col. 1; Shaughnessy, Players Mean It—Fleisher, Boston Globe,

March 13, 1983, at 65, col. 1; Douchant, Hoop Scoop, Sporting News, March 14, 1983, at 19.

158. NBA Owners Shoot for a 50% Solution, but Players Reject It, L.A. Times, March 25, 1983, pt. 3, at 6, col. 1; Muniz, Painting a Picture of Doom, Hartford Courant, March 28, 1983, at D1, col. 6; Shaughnessy, Players, Owners in Sea of Madness, Boston Globe, March 27, 1983, at 65, col. 3.

159. NBA Talks Called Hopeful, N.Y. Times, March 30, 1983, at B7, col. 4; Harvey, Drossos Isn't Spurring a Settlement, L.A. Times, March 29, 1983, pt. 3, at 2, col. 1; Harvey, NBA Strike No Longer "Inevitable," L.A. Times, March 30, 1983, pt. 3, at 1, col. 5.

160. Goldaper, Pro Basketball Strike Averted with Accord on 4-Year Pact, N.Y. Times, April 1, 1983, at A19, col. 5; NBA Averts Strike with Salary Cap, L.A. Times, April 1, 1983, pt. 3, at 1, col. 1.

161. *See generally*, as to the provisions on Maximum Team Salary, Minimum Team Salary, and related issues, 1983 Memorandum, art. 3.

As to general analysis of the agreement, written around the time of the conclusion of the negotiations, *see, e.g.*, Raskin, NBA's New Contract: A Statesmenlike Settlement, N.Y. Times, April 3, 1983, §5, at 2, col. 2; Shaughnessy, NBA Agreement Leaves Questions, Boston Globe, April 1, 1983, at 31, col. 3; Harvey, One Man, One Vote, One Strange Point of View, L.A. Times, April 5, 1983, pt. 3, at 6, col. 1; Mitchell, Equality Goal in New NBA Pact, Sporting News, April 11, 1983, at 34; Rosenbaum, How Owners Benefit from NBA Contract, San Francisco Chron., April 6, 1983, at 64, col. 1; Harvey, Jury Is Still Out on Who Won, L.A. Times, April 1, 1983, pt. 3, at 1, col. 1; Dickey, Winners, Losers of NBA Deal, San Francisco Chron., April 1, 1983, at 65, col. 1; Elderkin, Pro Basketball's "Landmark" Decision and What It Means, Christian Science Monitor, April 11, 1983, at 18, col. 1.

162. 1983 Memorandum, art. 3, §C(1).

163. *Id.* at §B(2).

164. *Id.* at §B(3)(4).

165. *Id.* at §C(2)(a).

166. Among some of the bigger names in the NBA who have signed new contracts without testing their market value as free agents, Larry Bird, Magic Johnson, Isiah Thomas, and Julius Erving would be four notables. *See, e.g.*, Shaughnessy, A Seven-Year Hitch for Bird, Boston Globe, Sept. 29, 1983, at 45, col. 5; Pistons Sign Thomas to $10 Million Pact, N.Y. Times, March 13, 1984, at D25, col. 1; Green, Magic's New Numbers Are $25 Million for 25 Years, L.A. Times, June 26, 1981, pt. 3, at 1, col. 1.

167. The contracts for Bird ($1.8 million), McHale ($1.0 million), and Maxwell ($800,000) total $3.6 million for just those three. Parish, Johnson, and Ainge in combination command approximately another $1.6 to $1.8 million. The grand total for the six, therefore, is in the $5.2 to $5.4 million dollars for year. Among the six, some get part of that in deferred, but others, like Bird, are paid in straight dollars, nothing deferred. Of course, as far as calculation of a team's maximum salary is concerned, deferred

monies are counted toward current obligations. 1983 Memorandum, art. 2, §B(3).

168. The team maximum for the clubs, including the Celtics, was determined by their salary obligations existing at the end of the playoffs in June 1984. Since Cedric Maxwell did not sign until October, his salary was not included in the Celtics' team salary. *See* 1983 Memorandum, art. 3, §C(2)(a).

169. *Id.* at §C(2)(b). But note limitations, *id.* at §2(e)(i).

170. *Id.* at §C(8).

171. *Id.* at §C(2)(g)(i) and (ii).

172. *Id.* at §C(2)(b)(ii).

173. *Id.* at §C(2)(d).

174. *Id.* at §C(2)(c).

175. *Id.* at §C(14).

176. *Id.* at §C(2)(f). *See also id.* at §C(11)(b).

177. Wood v. NBA, 1984–2 Trade Cases, ¶66, 262 (1984). *See also* Boston Globe, Sept. 16, 1984, at 50, col. 2; Thomas, Wood Suit Challenges the NBA Salary Cap, San Francisco Chron., Sept. 22, 1984, at 47, col. 1.

178. *See, e.g.,* Kurlanzik, Salary Caps in the NBA: Paper Tigers, Hartford Courant, June 17, 1984, at E17, col. 1.

179. Goldaper, Salary Cap Helps to Reshape NBA, N.Y. Times, Oct. 26, 1984, at 24, col. 1.

180. Of the sixty-three free agents who were potentially looking for offers from other clubs during the summer of 1984, only eleven were presented with offer sheets. Tripucka and Cummings topped the list, though others, such as Vinnie Johnson of the Pistons, also got sizable, if not spectacular offers. *Id. See also* Goldaper, Salary Caps Cloud NBA's Free-Agent Market, N.Y. Times, March 26, 1984, at C3, col. 1.

181. May, Tripucka Changed Positions, Not Cities, Hartford Courant, Nov. 2, 1984, at E1, col. 2.

182. Remarks by Larry Fleisher at conference sponsored by American Bar Association, Common Concerns in Professional and Amateur Sports, New York City, March 9, 1984.

7 LABOR RELATIONS IN HOCKEY

Hockey has not enjoyed the popularity that baseball, football, and basketball have in the United States, but it is still very much in the mainstream of labor relations in professional sports. Although U.S. hockey has lacked a national television contract, it is an exciting game, especially live at arenas. Youth hockey is thriving in the United States and has long been popular in Canada.

Once hailed as the sport of the 1970s,[1] professional hockey's failure to boom has made it the stepchild of the U.S. sports industry. It has fallen victim to over-expansion and a violence that has been especially acute. Hockey's most dramatic form of violence is fighting, a phenomenon supposedly inherent and sponta-neous to players in heated competition, but hockey's violence often becomes conscious and contrived. Some observers have even likened hockey to profes-sional wrestling and Roller Derby, the so-called silly sports. Although this anal-ogy is undeserved, it points up a credibility gap that hockey faces.

GAME, LEAGUE, PLAYERS, AND UNION

In some respects hockey labor relations are conducted at the highest level found in professional sport. Unlike baseball, football, and basketball, labor and man-agement in hockey have pursued their objectives with peaceful tactics and will-ingness to compromise. Cooperation between the parties has headed off strike threats and resulted in negotiated agreements that accommodate the uniqueness of the sport and exemplify a labor relations system that may apply to other sports.

The Game

An early form of hockey was first documented in 1740 when French explorers sailing up the St. Lawrence River observed Iroquois Indians hitting a hard ball with sticks and, as legend has it, punctuating their action with shouts of *"Hogee"* (It hurts!).[2] Another, more likely, theory has it that the game takes its name from the stick called *hockey* after the shepherd's staff known as *hoquet* in Old French.[3] Ice hockey appears to have originated in Canada as early as the 1830s,[4] with the first game played under standard rules in Montreal in 1875.[5]

Today, hockey is played on boarded ice rinks of varying sizes. Typical is the rink of the Detroit Red Wings at the Joe Louis Sports Arena, which measures 200 feet by 85 feet.[6] The two far ends of the rinks have curved corners, similar to a race track. There are six players on the ice from each side, except when teams play shorthanded as a result of penalties: The forward line consists of a center and right and left wings; the other players are two defensemen and a goalie. Free substitutions are allowed, and every minute or two, fresh players take the ice, even as play continues. Goals are scored by shooting the puck with the stick into a fabric net that has steel goal posts six feet apart and four feet high. Pucks are six-ounce disks with a solid inch of vulcanized rubber, three inches in diameter.

Because players skate at speeds approaching 30 MPH and shoot the puck at speeds up to 120 MPH, hockey is sometimes called the "world's fastest game." Play is not continuous, however, since zone violations or penalties stop play. For example, a player is not allowed to skate over the blue line, designating the attacking zone, ahead of the puck. This prevents players from stationing themselves near the opponent's goal to await a long pass, as occurs in basketball. Penalties stop play for various infractions such as tripping, boarding, high-sticking, and fighting. Games are divided into three twenty-minute periods.

National Hockey League

Professional hockey originated in the 1900s. Shortly thereafter, the Stanley Cup, established in 1893 as the top prize among the amateur teams in Canada, became the symbol of supremacy in professional hockey. The first professional hockey team, known as Portage Lakes, was formed in 1903 by J.L. Gibson, a dentist from Houghton, Michigan, who imported players from Canada.[7] Soon after, other professional teams were formed in Calumet, Michigan, Sault Sainte Marie (both the Michigan and Ontario cities of that name), and Pittsburgh. These cities formed the first professional league in 1904, known as the International Professional Hockey League.[8]

Another early league was the National Hockey Association, and when this league expired in 1917, the National Hockey League (NHL) was formed. Of the four teams that initially constituted the NHL, only the Montreal Canadiens survived without acquiring a new name or location. The Montreal Wanderers had to withdraw during the first season when their arena burned down.[9] The Toronto Arenas failed to finish the second season but were reorganized the following year as the St. Patricks and in 1926 became the Maple Leafs. The Ottawa Senators played until 1931, were then disbanded for a year, and played again from 1932 to 1934 before finally collapsing.

For the first decade of its existence the winner of the NHL competed in playoffs for hockey supremacy with the winner of either the Pacific Coast Hockey Association (PCHA) or the Western Canada Hockey League (WCHL). By 1926 the PCHA and WCHA had dissolved, and the NHL was expanded to ten teams with two divisions;[10] however, several franchises folded during the Great Depression. At the end of the NHL's first twenty-five years, in 1942 to 1943, only six of the fifteen teams that had been in the league during this period still survived.[11] By this time the NHL was firmly established, with two Canadian clubs (Montreal and Toronto) and four United States teams (Boston, New York, Chicago, and Detroit). The league remained in this form until 1967, when expansion began. (See Table 7-1.)

Expansion was well justified when the NHL doubled from six teams to twelve in 1967. But additional expansions to fourteen in 1970, to sixteen in 1972, to eighteen in 1974, and to twenty-one in 1979 have strained economic capacity and diluted quality of play. Similar to baseball and basketball, which have lengthy regular seasons followed by extended championship playoffs, quality of play has also lagged from players' physical exhaustion. The number of games played by each team in the NHL has steadily increased over the years to its current level of eighty games in the regular season.

The NHL annually drafts amateur players who will reach at least age 18 by January 1 of the following season. Beginning with the team that had the worst record in the preceding season and continuing through the team with the best record, each team selects one player in each round. Drafting procedure is not materially different from that in other professional sports. Unlike other sports, however, eligibility for the draft is not related to college or high school graduation: Most amateur hockey is played in leagues sponsored by the NHL, and these leagues are not affiliated with schools.[12] Once drafted, the player is the exclusive property of the team that selects him.

The principal minor leagues in professional hockey are the American Hockey League, Western Hockey League, and Central Professional Hockey League. There are numerous amateur teams, among the best of which in Canada play in Junior A leagues such as the Ontario Hockey League. The International Hockey League and Eastern Hockey League are amateur or at best semipro.

Unlike professional football and basketball leagues, whose players come mostly from colleges, a system that avoids the need for maintaining a farm system, the NHL must invest significant amounts of money in the system of minor

Table 7-1. National Hockey League Teams and Date Franchises Awarded, as of 1983.

Team	Date of Franchise
Montreal Canadiens	2-22-17
Toronto Maple Leafs	2-22-17
Boston Bruins	11- 1-24
New York Rangers	5-15-26
Chicago Black Hawks	9-25-26
Detroit Red Wings	9-25-26
Los Angeles Kings	6- 5-67
Minnesota North Stars	6- 5-67
Philadelphia Flyers	6- 5-67
Pittsburgh Penguins	6- 5-67
St. Louis Blues	6- 5-67
Buffalo Sabres	5-22-70
Vancouver Canucks	5-22-70
New York Islanders	6- 6-72
Calgary Flames[a]	6- 6-72
Washington Capitals	6-11-74
New Jersey Devils[b]	8-25-76
Edmonton Oilers	6-22-79
Hartford Whalers	6-22-79
Quebec Nordiques	6-22-79
Winnipeg Jets	6-22-79

a. The Calgary Flames' franchise was transferred on June 24, 1980, from the Atlanta Flames, which had received a franchise on June 6, 1972.

b. The New Jersey Devils, which began operation in the 1982–83 season, received their franchise by transfer from the Colorado Rockies, which had, in turn, received their franchise through the Kansas City Scouts, a team originally enfranchised on June 11, 1974.

Source: Compiled from data in National Hockey League, 1982–83 Official Record Book 97 (1982)

leagues and amateur hockey. Nearly all the Canadian Junior A amateur teams as well as minor league teams are owned outright or have a sponsorship agreement with individual NHL clubs. Hockey is more akin to baseball in this respect.

The president of the NHL is John A. Ziegler, Jr., who succeeded Clarence S. Campbell, president from 1946 through 1977. A graduate of the University of Michigan Law School, Ziegler is the first American to serve as league president. Prior to this appointment he served as an executive with the Detroit Red Wings and as chairman of the NHL board of governors, a policymaking group that has representatives from each club.

Players

For much of the NHL's history team rosters were filled almost exclusively by Canadian players. It was rare for a team to have an American player, even

Table 7-2. Birthplaces of National Hockey League Players.[a]

	Number	Percentage
Canada	773	80.1
United States	112	11.6
Other countries	80	8.3
Total	965	100.0

a. These are players listed on official NHL rosters, and include players that may not actually be a member of a nineteen-member team during the season.

Source: Data compiled from team rosters in National Hockey League, 1982–83 Official Record Book 34–75 (1982).

though most of the NHL teams were based in the United States.[13] In the past decade there has been a growing influx of U.S. and European players into the league. Team rosters continue to be dominated by Canadians, but not nearly as much as before. Hockey's growth as an international sport, improved organization and coaching in the United States, and the lure of attractive salaries account for much of this change. League expansion has been important, too, as teams fish in an increasingly depleted Canadian talent pool.

As shown in Table 7-2, approximately four-fifths of the players on NHL rosters during the 1982–83 season were born in Canada. Most of these players hail from the provinces of Ontario, Manitoba, Quebec, Alberta, and Saskatchewan. Players born in the United States comprised 11.6 percent of the roster personnel. Minnesota is the most heavily represented state, with Massachusetts, New York, and Michigan also making significant contributions of players. About 8.3 percent of the players are from other countries, with Sweden, Finland, and Czechoslovakia by far the most common countries of origin.

Talented young hockey players in Canada seldom view college education as a top priority. Their sights are set on NHL play, and formal education takes a back seat to play in the Junior A leagues. While completion of high school is not uncommon, relatively few of the Canadian NHL players have attended college. In contrast, U.S. players who aspire to NHL careers usually attend college, and U.S. schools provide a feeder system to the NHL on a smaller scale but similar to football, basketball, and baseball. Those Canadian players who pursue higher education often do so by concurrently playing for U.S. college hockey teams.

The exodus of Europeans to play in the NHL began in 1973 when the Toronto Maple Leafs signed two Swedes, Borje Salming and Inge Hammarstrom. There was concern that because of the nonviolent style of play in Europe, these players would not be physical enough to cope with the tough, body-checking environment in the NHL. But the Europeans proved they could survive and even flourish in the league.[14] The European connection also had a special interest because players could be signed as free agents without going through the draft.[15] Some of the best players in the NHL today are European, including Salming,

Peter and Anton Stastny, Anders Hedberg, and Kent Nilsson. Although their hockey and cultural transition has been difficult, they have adapted well and even brought some change to the NHL style of play.[16] More NHL teams are blending the physical play of North American hockey with the smooth skating and playmaking of the European amateur game.[17]

NHL Players' Association

There are several attempts in the 1950s to organize NHL players. But despite their tough image on the ice, hockey players are probably the most docile of professional athletes when it comes to fighting with owners over pay and working conditions. By 1957 the NHL had a minimum salary of $7,000, or $100 a game for the then-existing seventy-game schedule. Players have a great love for their game and many were willing to play at or near the minimum salary. Each attempt to organize players was stymied by the owners. Some players who agitated for a union were traded to other teams.

At this time the ownership of league teams was anachronistic by modern standards. Owners were sole masters of their fiefdoms. James D. Norris and his family owned two of the six clubs outright, the Chicago Black Hawks and Detroit Red Wings, plus had effective control of the New York Rangers through ownership in Madison Square Garden. This gave the Norris family three of the six votes on the NHL board of governors and created unique opportunities for self-dealing in players through trades and keeping salaries low. Most NHL player contracts provided a dual salary arrangement, specifying one salary for NHL play and another salary for play with an affiliated minor league team.[18] This meant that if a player was sent down to the minors, even for a short period, he was paid during that time at the lower salary level.

The sparking incident for establishment of the initial players' association involved a television contract. In 1956 the six NHL teams presented a total of ten televised games on Saturday afternoons under a contract with CBS. These games received a favorable audience response, so the next year the contract with CBS was expanded to twenty-one games. Under these arrangements the individual club owners received all television receipts for home games, and the players received nothing.[19] The television deals angered the players, who formed a players' association in 1957.

The president of the association was Ted Lindsay, known as Terrible Ted for his feisty play. The union hired J. Norman Lewis to represent it in dealings with the owners. Lewis had been successful in getting a share of television revenues from World Series and All-Star games earmarked for the baseball players' pension fund. The hockey players thus wanted television proceeds distributed to their pension fund. When the owners took evasive action, Lewis filed a $3 million antitrust suit in federal court.[20] The lawsuit was settled when the owners gave the players additional monies for their pensions. These pension increases were funded from television revenues but were guaranteed regardless of future TV monies.

Despite achieving a significant victory in early dealings with the owners, the fledgling players' association could not sustain its momentum. Several additional attempts to break through on money issues were thwarted by the owners. Unable to generate sufficient player interest and organizational power, the players' association ceased to function effectively. It was not until a decade later that a reconstituted union became a viable entity.

The proposed expansion of the NHL in 1967 gave the players a unique opportunity to seek recognition from the league.[21] By this time the players, especially star players, had greater leverage in their bargaining positions. R. Alan Eagleson, a Toronto lawyer who had recently negotiated a precedent-setting contract for Bobby Orr with the Boston Bruins, was named executive director of the new National Hockey League Players' Association (NHLPA). Eagleson signed up large numbers of players for membership in the union. He was in major part responsible for turning the tide toward increased player power in dealings with the owners. League expansion also helped the union because a larger league required broader, more enlightened policies for governing players. In June 1967 NHL owners signed a recognition agreement formally acknowledging the union. Under the terms of that agreement the owners recognized the NHLPA as the representative of the players for purposes of handling their relationships with the individual clubs.

All players who have signed contracts with NHL clubs are eligible for membership in the NHLPA. Among the union's objectives are:

1. To establish improvements in conditions of employment;
2. To provide information and assistance to NHL players and engage in activities to advance and safeguard their welfare;
3. To develop such projects and enterprises that will bring further benefits to members as individuals or to the NHLPA as an entity.[22]

A key difference in the operation of the NHLPA involves the role of its executive director, Alan Eagleson. In addition to his function as chief negotiator in collective bargaining, Eagleson handles contract negotiations on salaries and acts as a financial advisor for about a third of the league's players.[23] He has also negotiated contracts for international competition involving NHL teams, which began in 1972 with the celebrated games between the Russian nationals and an all-star team of NHL players. Although criticized by a few players for conflict of interest in his multiple functions as NHLPA executive director,[24] Eagleson is admired by most players because of the economic gains he has brought them.

EARLY AGREEMENTS

Shortly after the NHLPA was formed, negotiations were held in the spring of 1967 to test its strength. Three gains were achieved by the union at this time: (1) Players would receive $100 per exhibition game between NHL teams, (2) per diem expenses were increased from $10 to $15, and (3) players on the six existing teams (but not the expansion teams) must be signed prior to training camp.[25] The latter achievement was especially important because prior to this time unless a player had a long-term contract, he was in limbo until a salary contract could be reached, and a training camp injury could weaken his bargaining power.

Continuous Negotiations

Until 1975 there was no collective bargaining agreement in hockey in the conventional sense. In other professional team sports and in North American industry as a whole, there is a long-standing practice of negotiating contracts for multiyear terms. Three-year agreements are the norm, but occasionally contracts extend for five years or more. These contracts are interpreted and applied on a day-to-day basis, with disputes that arise resolved through the contractual grievance procedure.

In the early years of formal labor/management relations in hockey, collective bargaining occurred in the same manner as in other sports, except that negotiations took place more frequently. Responsibility for bargaining was vested in a joint committee of representatives known as the Owner–Player Council. From 1967 through 1974 this group met annually to discuss matters raised on an agreed agenda. Agreements reached in these negotiations were recorded in formal minutes. The total of the actions taken over time by the council formed the contractual arrangement. From time to time the formal minutes of the meetings were consolidated and printed in total.[26] Thus, hockey had a built-in system for revising the contract, causing its provisions to change frequently.

This continuous bargaining system ran counter to generally accepted principles of labor relations. On the surface it appeared risky in that greater frequency of negotiations would suggest increased exposure to strikes over substantive issues. Paradoxically, the practice of continuous bargaining proved effective in certain circumstances, such as the newly created formal relationship between labor and management. It allows the parties to revise the contract readily in situations where discussions of initial provisions are not successful. Continuous negotiation facilitates adaptation to changing economic or legal conditions. It can even forestall strikes in the sense that the parties are not dealing with multiple complex issues at one time, as is the case when a long-term contract expires.

No work stoppages occurred in hockey during the period of continuous nego-tiations, and labor relations were not characterized by the acrimony found else-where. While this may have been due to factors other than negotiation practice, there is no evidence that it produced negative results.

Revised Bargaining Structure

Negotiations in 1975 led to the first "collective bargaining agreement," in the usual context in which such agreements are viewed. That is, the agreement was for a fixed term of five years. However, vestiges of continuous bargaining re-main. The Owner-Player Council continues to exist, and meetings have been increased from annual to semiannual talks, once during the season and once dur-ing the off-season.

Although the 1975 agreement was initially designed to last five years, major changes were made in 1977. At this time it was decided that the duration of the contract would be extended to 1982. However, in 1979, when the NHL merged with the World Hockey Association, further changes were made through negotia-tions. It was agreed that the contract would remain in effect until 1984 but that the union was permitted to reopen the terms of the 1979 contract after three years by giving one-year's notice. The NHLPA exercised this reopener right. Thus, negotiations resumed in 1981, which resulted in the signing of a new five-year agreement in 1982.

This unconventional pattern of long-term agreements, punctuated by reopen-ers and continuous revisions by the Owner-Player Council since 1975, has cre-ated frequent changes in contractual arrangements. We next consider key areas of post-1967 agreements, deferring review of the 1981–82 negotiations and agreement to later in the chapter.

Salary Arbitration

In 1969 a Task Force on Sports in Canada was critical of the reserve clause found in the standard players' contract since 1958.[27] Known as paragraph 17, this provision tied the player to his team in much the same way that players were controlled by the old reserve clauses in baseball, football, and basketball. Salaries were to be determined by "mutual agreement" under Paragraph 17, with disputes over salaries submitted to the president of the NHL for final decision. This system of salary determination allowed the players little power. In 1969 the NHLPA got the NHL to agree to salary arbitration.

Under this arrangement, as originally constituted, disputes over what a player should be paid under Paragraph 17 were submitted to arbitration with each side choosing an arbitrator and the two selectees trying to reach a decision. If these arbitrators were unable to agree they would select a third arbitrator who would then decide the issue. This initial salary arbitration procedure remained in effect until 1971 when the Owner-Player Council agreed to modify the system on a one-year trial basis so that Paragraph 17 salary disputes would be decided by a single arbitrator. Edward J. Houston of Ottawa was chosen as the permanent arbitrator or "umpire" of salary disputes. Later agreements continued to provide for the single umpire, but, as before, his jurisdiction extended only to salary disputes over the option year provided in the standard players' contract.

Evidence that can be presented by the parties to the arbitrator includes:

1. The overall performance, including official statistics prepared by the League (both offensive and defensive) of the Player in the previous season or seasons.
2. The number of games played by the Player, his injuries or illness during the preceding season.
3. The length of service of the Player in the League and/or with the disputant Club.
4. The overall contribution of the Player to the competitive success or failure of his Club in the preceding season.
5. Any special qualities of leadership or public appeal not inconsistent with the fulfillment of his responsibilities as a playing member of his team.[28]

The procedure for salary arbitration in hockey is similar to that in baseball. A key difference between the two is that baseball provides for final-offer arbitration, where the arbitrator must choose the offer of either the player or the club, without being able to compromise between the two positions. In hockey, a conventional method of arbitration is used in which the arbitrator has latitude in determining any salary he feels appropriate.

In the first year that salary arbitration was available there were twenty instances of its use, mostly related to the Oakland Seals, a team owned by Charles O. Finley.[29] It is interesting to note that in the early days of arbitration of baseball salary disputes, several of the cases were brought by members of the Oakland A's, a team then also owned by Finley. Until the commencement of the World Hockey Association in 1972, there were about fifteen salary arbitrations per year,[30] and since that time approximately eight to ten cases per year have been arbitrated.[31]

Hockey players have not used salary arbitration as frequently as their baseball brethren. (See Chapter 3.) There is no apparent reason for this disparity. Indeed, one might expect that baseball, with its final-offer feature making arbitration an all-or-nothing proposition, would have fewer cases on a per capita basis. Analysis of hockey's salary arbitration is hindered by the strict control of the NHL and NHLPA on releasing salary data resulting from arbitrations. It can be concluded that hockey players find salary arbitration a less attractive alternative from an economic standpoint. But whether this is the result of low salaries being determined by arbitrators or other factors is not clear.

Free Agency

Free agency has been a controversial issue in all major team sports. Prior to 1972 free agency was not allowed in hockey. With the formation of the World Hockey Association, NHL players challenged the reserve clause in their contracts by jumping to the new league. Because limited free agency was santioned by the courts, in 1973 the NHL owners decided to replace the perpetual reservation system with a one-year option clause in standard player contracts, beginning with the 1974–75 season. This meant that teams could hold players for only one year after their contracts expired.

The option system, allowing for free agency, was incorporated into the 1975 collective bargaining agreement. The 1975 agreement presented a novel dual-option procedure designed to aid the player and the club.[32] The first half of the option provides that during the last year of a player's contract, the club may request that he sign a termination contract. If the player signs such a contract, his contract is extended for a year, but after this he becomes a free agent. If the player elects not to sign the termination contract he is unconditionally released before the next season begins. If the club does not tender the termination contract, it is required to offer a standard player contract with the same terms as the previous contract, including Paragraph 17, which allows the procedure to occur again.

The second part of the option is that the player may exercise certain rights regardless of the club's actions. He may request that the club tender an option contract. Although this contract is new, the terms remain the same, except that the contract is extended until the following year when the player becomes a free agent. Thus, after the club offers the player either a termination or new standard player contract, the player essentially may refuse either of these by requesting a one-year extension of the old contract. However, if the club offers a termination contract the player cannot then request an option-year contract. If neither party exercises its rights, the parties are required to enter into a new agreement under a standard player contract, with the same terms except that salary is to be determined by arbitration.

Equalization

If a player becomes a free agent and signs with another club, an "equalization" process goes into effect for determining compensation due clubs that lose free agents. In the event that the old and new clubs cannot agree on the compensation, the dispute is submitted to an arbitrator. Each club presents its opinion on the appropriate compensation level. The submitted figures are not required to have been subject to discussion or negotiation between the clubs. The method of decision used by the arbitrator is to select between the two final offers, without amendment or compromise. Thus the equalization procedure in hockey for determining compensation for signing free agents uses the same method as in baseball, except that in baseball the final-offer method is used for establishing player salaries in non-free-agency situations.

The equalization procedure, contrived as a result of the court decisions allowing free agency, was confusing to players and clubs alike. After a few years it became apparent to the players that it did not work to their advantage. Clubs were discouraged from signing free agents by the uncertain and potentially heavy penalty of equalization.[33] At the time of the merger of the NHL with the World Hockey Association in 1979, negotiations took place in which the union tried to change equalization in its favor. Although the union was unable to gain a change in the rules, it did achieve a provision for reopening equalization discussions after two years. Helping to salve the players' chafing over equalization were increases estimated at $10 million in pension, insurance, and playoff monies.[34]

Only three arbitration cases were decided on equalization from 1974 until 1982 when the procedure was changed. It should be emphasized that the 1975 equalization rules continue to apply to players under age 24 or with less than five years of professional experience. In the first case, Gary Sargent, a defenseman for the Los Angeles Kings, became a free agent in 1978 and signed with the Minnesota North Stars. When the two teams could not agree on equalization, the matter was submitted to arbitration. The arbitrator awarded the Kings three players: Rick Hampton, Steve Jensen, and Dave Gardner.[35] In the second case, the Kings lost another player to free agency, goalie Rogatien Vachon, who signed with the Detroit Red Wings in 1978. As compensation the arbitrator awarded a talented young Detroit forward, Dale McCourt, to the Kings. This decision prompted McCourt to file suit to prevent his removal from the Red Wings, but the arbitration award was upheld in court, as detailed later in the chapter. The third arbitration occurred in 1981 when it was determined that the compensation for Greg Millen, a goalie signed by the Hartford Whalers as a free agent, was to award two players to the Pittsburgh Penguins, Pat Boutette and Kevin McClelland.

Grievance Arbitration

Prior to 1975 the final determination on all grievances was made by the president of the NHL. With the negotiation of a comprehensive collective bargaining agreement in that year, the union gained provisions for the submission of certain grievances to arbitration, which remain in effect. Two general types of disputes are covered by grievance arbitration: (1) disputes between a player and club involving the propriety or imposition of discipline and (2) disputes over the interpretation or application of the terms of the collective bargaining agreement or club rules.

Although disputes regarding the propriety of discipline are subject to arbitration, questions concerning the severity of discipline are not. The latter disputes, as well as those involving interpretation of the standard players' contract, continue to be acted on finally by the president of the NHL.

WORLD HOCKEY ASSOCIATION

When the NHL expanded its franchises from six to thirteen during the period from 1967 to 1970 (see Table 7-1), a hoped-for by-product was to reduce the likelihood of any projected new rival league. Entrepreneur Gary Davidson had other ideas. This maverick promoter, who placed his stamp on rival leagues in other sports, such as the American Basketball Association and World Football League, viewed the diminished caliber of play in the NHL as an indication that a new league could provide similar entertainment. The NHL standard player contract was on shaky legal ground, and enough established NHL players could be lured away to provide star quality.

Formation

The World Hockey Association (WHA) was incorporated by Davidson and Dennis Murphy in June 1971, and they set out to develop and sell franchises. By the 1972–73 season the WHA was ready to take the ice with twelve teams, and with eventual championship playoffs to determine the winner of the Avco Cup.[36] The new league recommended to its teams that they include on their rosters six players graduating from the Junior A amateur leagues, a minimum of six professional players from the minor leagues, and five other professionals, preferably NHL players.

WHA teams did not realistically expect to sign many NHL players because of their anticipated reluctance to challenge the standard player contract by becoming embroiled in litigation. However, as a result of successful lawsuits by a few NHL players that allowed them to jump leagues, the WHA was able to pirate seventy-eight NHL players out of a total of 340 signed for the inaugural season.[37] Important to fan recognition, some of the NHL players signed were superstars, notably Bobby Hull, Bernie Parent, Derek Sanderson, Gerry Cheevers, and Johnny McKenzie. Rosters were also stocked with some promising amateur players, such as Wayne Gretsky who signed with the Edmonton Oilers.

More than any other player, Bobby Hull gave the WHA instant respectability. Known as the Golden Jet for his blond hair and dashing play, Hull was one of the brightest stars in sports. He was the first NHL player to score over fifty goals in a season, and became the most exciting player in the league over his fifteen seasons with the Chicago Black Hawks. In order to get Hull to play in the WHA, its teams placed about $100,000 each in a fund, with the rest of the monies to be paid by the Winnipeg Jets.[38] As a result, Winnipeg was able to sign Hull to a ten-year contract worth $2.75 million, and the new league got off to a surprisingly good start.[39] Franchises that cost only $25,000 when the league was formed shot up in price to an estimated $200,000.[40] The WHA looked like a winner.

Operation

Hull's signing touched off a dollar war for all hockey players that caused average salaries to escalate. Ticket prices were hiked to meet rising costs. After the initial excitement of viewing major league hockey in new cities wore off, attendance problems appeared, with crowds averaging only about 5,200 at games.[41] The strength of individual teams varied widely, and the overall caliber of play showed signs of shoddy skating and passing. Franchises were sold and resold. It became clear that the potential for expansion of high-quality professional hockey was wildly overestimated.

After three years of WHA operation, player salaries began to drop in both leagues. Salaries fell an average of 10 percent in the NHL to $70,000, and 15 percent in the WHA to $45,000.[42] However, the period of salary deescalation did not continue for long, as a renewed cycle of competitive bidding for players brought pay back up to record levels. The WHA was never a serious rival to the NHL, but it drained the resources of all hockey by overexpanding and spreading talent thin. The WHA increasingly took on an image of a second-rate league, and many top amateur players shunned it in favor of the NHL. Some of the better WHA players who had previously jumped leagues signed back with NHL teams.[43] The only way out for the WHA, which was edging close to total bankruptcy by 1977, was to merge with the NHL. Initially unwilling to even consider entering into merger talks with the upstart league because of fear of litigation and low regard for the overall quality of the WHA, the NHL grudgingly sat down to try to unravel the problems of consolidation.

Merger

After two years of beleaguered talks and three previous rejections by the NHL board of governors, the two leagues merged on March 30, 1979. Spurred by political pressure from a merger motion in the Canadian House of Commons, the NHL finally voted 14 to 3 to bring into the league four WHA teams: the Edmonton Oilers, Quebec Nordiques, Winnipeg Jets, and New England (now Hartford) Whalers.[44] By this time the WHA, which had once expanded from twelve to fourteen teams, was down to only six. With resales of numerous franchises and bankruptcies of others over the seven years of the WHA's existence, a total of thirty-two teams lost an estimated $50 million.[45]

Table 7-3.   Conference and Divisional Alignment in the National Hockey League, 1982-83.

Prince of Wales Conference

Patrick Division	*Adams Division*
New York Rangers	Montreal Canadiens
Philadelphia Flyers	Boston Bruins
Pittsburgh Penguins	Buffalo Sabres
New York Islanders	Quebec Nordiques
Washington Capitals	Hartford Whalers
New Jersey Devils	

Campbell Conference

Norris Division	*Smythe Division*
Toronto Maple Leafs	Los Angeles Kings
Chicago Black Hawks	Vancouver Canucks
Detroit Red Wings	Calgary Flames
Minnesota North Stars	Edmonton Oilers
St. Louis Blues	Winnipeg Jets

The merged WHA teams were allowed to retain all players whose rights were not held by NHL clubs, plus two goalies and two skaters. Other players reverted to NHL teams that held property rights to them. The NHL teams established lists of protected players, including fifteen skaters and two goalies. Players left unprotected by NHL clubs were eligible for drafting by WHA teams, with the stipulation that no NHL team would lose more than four players. The exchange of players through these drafting procedures found the NHL clubs getting more quality players than they gave up to the WHA teams. Each of the four WHA teams had to pay a $6 million fee for entrance into the NHL.[46] The two teams that were not granted entry into the NHL were the Birmingham Bulls and the Cincinnati Stingers. For the loss of their franchises and players and probably also to head off potential antitrust action, these teams were paid an estimated $2.8 million and $3.5 million, respectively, by the four clubs that merged.[47]

From a Canadian perspective, the merger accomplished something that four previous expansions failed to do: bring the NHL to three additional Canadian cities, Edmonton, Quebec, and Winnipeg, doubling the number of Canada-based teams in the league.[48] There has been since the merger a realignment of teams within the four divisions of the two NHL conferences to stimulate regional competition. For example, Montreal was shifted from the Norris to the Adams Division to create a divisional rivalry with Quebec. The alignment of the NHL as of the 1982-83 season is shown in Table 7-3.

LEGAL ISSUES

Formation of the WHA in 1971 threatened the NHL's hegemony over players. Most of the players signed by WHA teams were subject to a reserve clause though their NHL, minor league, or amateur team. One of the anomalies of hockey prior to 1973 was that player contracts at all levels of the sport contained perpetual reserve clauses that acknowledged the NHL and its associated minor leagues as the sole and exclusive governing bodies in professional hockey.[49] When players signed with the WHA, lawsuits were filed by NHL teams claiming that the players breached their reserve clauses. Resulting court decisions generally favored the players. The following sections review these cases as well as others that pertain to antitrust issues.

WHA Cases

In the *Cheevers* case,[50] two star players for the NHL's Boston Bruins signed contracts with WHA teams: Gerry Cheevers with the Cleveland Crusaders and Derek Sanderson with the Philadelphia Blazers. Although the contracts with the Bruins had expired by the time the players were scheduled to begin play in the WHA, both player contracts with the Bruins contained a perpetual reserve clause, or so-called Paragraph 17. This provision in the standard players' contract stated:

> 17. The Club agrees that it will on or before September 1 next following the season covered by this contract tender to the Player personally or by mail directed to the Player at his address set out below his signature hereto a contract upon the same terms as this contract save as to salary.
>
> The Player hereby undertakes that he will at the request of the Club enter into a contract for the following playing season upon the same terms and conditions as this contract save as to salary which shall be determined by mutual agreement.[51]

In addition to the reserve clause, the standard player contract that Cheevers and Sanderson signed also gave the Bruins the right to enjoin players through court injunction for playing hockey for another team. In defense against the injunction sought by the Bruins in federal court to prevent the players from jumping leagues, the players contended that Paragraph 17 violates the Sherman Antitrust Act by causing an unreasonable restraint of trade. As a counterargument to this point the Bruins noted that hockey player contracts are not subject to federal antitrust laws, and that the existence of a valid collective bargaining agreement provided further immunity.

Relying on the rationale of the U.S. Supreme Court in the baseball case of *Flood v. Kuhn*,[52] the U.S. district court emphasized that the only professional sport with immunity from the antitrust laws is baseball. Thus finding the Sherman Act applicable to hockey, the court went on to note that hockey's reserve clause was not arrived at through collective bargaining with the players' union. Because the Bruins were found to have a healthy and profitable business, which defection of the two players would not affect significantly, the court refused to issue the injunction. It could find no "irreparable harm" to exist.[53] Although the court in *Cheevers* did not strike down the technical validity or further use of the reserve clause in hockey, it did allow the two players to jump leagues despite the existence of a reserve clause in their contracts.

Shortly after *Cheevers* was decided another case came up involving the same basic issue of whether to issue an injunction to prevent a player from jumping leagues.[54] Ted Hampson, after being traded from one NHL team (Minnesota North Stars) to another (New York Islanders), signed with the Minnesota Fighting Saints of the WHA. The district court found that there was justification for issuing the injunction on grounds of irreparable injury to the plaintiff by losing the unique services of a valuable player, contrary to the district court (but not the appellate court) ruling in *Cheevers*.

However, the court in *Hampson* reached the same outcome as *Cheevers* because it felt that other factors outweighed this irreparable harm. These factors included the determination that the player and his new team would be substantially impaired if the injunction were issued. Moreover, the public interest would suffer. In this sense the court viewed the new league as increasing competition with the NHL, which was a healthy economic development and stimulated public interest. Consequently, the court refused to issue the injunction. Another player thus slipped through the tangled web of the reserve clause and freely contracted with a team in the WHA.

The next federal court case on Paragraph 17 is the most important because it unequivocally strikes down the perpetual reserve clause.[55] Several players were involved in the suit. District Court Judge Higginbotham seemed less impressed with the public interest than his colleague in *Hampson*. With tongue in cheek he poetically observed that "the basic factors here are not the sheer exhilaration from observing the speeding puck, but rather the desire to maximize the available buck."[56]

Judge Higginbotham noted that the Supreme Court had never ruled on whether hockey is subject to the antitrust laws. However, in his view hockey did not enjoy the same immunity that baseball did. Accordingly, the issue became whether the NHL violated the antitrust laws by trying to preclude players from joining WHA teams by enforcing the reserve clause in player contracts that expired in 1972. The court determined that the NHL violated the Sherman Antitrust Act, section 2, and granted injunctive relief to the WHA teams involved in the suit. The key reason for this finding was that the reserve clause in players' contracts was never reached as a result of good-faith collective bargaining between the NHL and NHLPA, a point made earlier by the district court in *Cheevers*. As Judge Higginbotham put it:

> [T]he owners have never been willing to modify it [the reserve clause] except as to the arbitration of salary. There is no indication that for any of the benefits offered the players that the owners would have been willing to modify the reserve clause in lieu of the other benefits given. Thus in that context there does not appear to have been any "collective bargaining" on the reserve clause except as to arbitration of salary. Further, the arbitration of salary did not in any respect modify the perpetual nature of the reserve clause.[57]

However, not all of the federal court decisions were decided in favor of the players.[58] Garry Peters was another player who signed with the WHA. Similar to the other players involved in litigation, he had not signed a contract with his NHL club for 1972–73. The NHL's Boston Bruins took the position that they could extend the contract into perpetuity or at least for the three-year duration of the collective bargaining provision on arbitration of player salary disputes.

The district court found that because Peters had signed a contract for 1971–72 with the Bruins that contained the reserve clause language, the contract created an option for the Bruins that allowed them to extend Peters's service obligation for one year. Thus, language from Paragraph 17 of the standard players' contract that the club had a renewal option for the following year was taken literally by the court as an established contract right of management. The court enforced this right by refusing to allow Peters to jump leagues. However, by limiting the option year to one rather than three years or perpetuity as the Bruins wanted, the court acknowledged the susceptibility of the reserve clause to legal challenge.

McCourt Case

The *McCourt* case has the distinction of being the first major sports case to confront the labor exemption of the antitrust laws when the clause in controversy was specifically incorporated into the league's collective bargaining agreement.[59] At issue was what the U.S. Court of Appeals, Sixth Circuit, characterized as a "modified Rozelle Rule" for professional hockey.[60] Thus the court made considerable reference to the *Mackey* case involving professional football, discussed in Chapters 4 and 5 of this book.[61]

Plaintiff Dale McCourt signed an NHL standard players' contract to play for three years with the Detroit Red Wings, for which he was to be paid $325,000. In his rookie year with the team, McCourt was the leading scorer. Rogatien Vachon had been the Los Angeles Kings' star goalie for six years when he became a free agent. After rejecting a substantial offer from the Kings, Vachon signed a contract with the Red Wings. This contract subjected the Red Wings to an equalization payment under the NHL bylaws as incorporated in the collective bargaining agreement. As discussed earlier in the chapter, this compensation procedure utilizes a final-offer method under which each team places a final offer before an arbitrator who then selects one of the parties' positions without compromise.

The Sixth Circuit accepted the *Mackey* criteria as the applicable law in deciding whether the arbitration procedure violated antitrust law as an impediment to player mobility. The court also accepted the proposition that the restraint "primarily affected" hockey players and that the subject matter was a mandatory bargaining subject under the NLRA.[62] The Sixth Circuit in *McCourt* stated:

> The court in *Mackey* held under the circumstances before it that such arm's-length bargaining was missing. So did the district court here. The underlying facts in the two cases, however, are quite different.
>
> In *Mackey* it was shown that the National Football League Players Association, at least prior to 1974, had stood in a relatively weak position with respect to the clubs. The Rozelle Rule had remained unchanged in form since it was unilaterally promulgated in 1963, even before the Players Association was formed. The Eighth Circuit specifically found that the Rozelle Rule was not bargained over in the negotiations leading to the 1968 or 1970 collective bargaining agreements. . . .[63]

The court noted that the NHL and the players' association had signed their first collective bargaining agreement that provided that the standard players' contract and bylaws were "fair and reasonable terms of employment." The court stated that the district court, which found no quid pro quo for the relinquishment of free-agent status for the players, had failed to take into account

> the well established principle that nothing in the labor law compels either party negotiating over mandatory subjects of collective bargaining to yield on its initial bargaining position. Good faith bargaining is all that is required. That the position of one party on an issue remains unchanged does not mandate the conclusion that there was no collective bargaining over the other issues.[64]

The court recognized that the players' association exerted great pressure at the bargaining table in presenting proposals for an alternate reserve system. The association also threatened to strike and to commence antitrust litigation. The NHL agreed that the entire collective bargaining agreement could be voided if the NHL merged with the WHA. Such nullification might be necessary if the merger would depress the salary market and make the reserve system "too onerous" because of the players' loss of competitive advantage.[65] The trial court found that the players' association had received new benefits that were not "directly related" to the negotiation of the reserve clause.[66] The Sixth Circuit concluded, however, that the players' association satisfied the arm's-length, bona fide requirement articulated in *Mackey* because the players vigorously opposed or "bargained against" the reserve system.

An essential difference between the compensation procedure in *McCourt* and what was declared unlawful in *Mackey* was that a neutral third party, and not the commissioner, determined the compensation. The court's judgment about the procedure was appropriate because the parties focused on that procedure in their negotiations. It was not necessary that the association achieve a specific quid pro quo. The Sixth Circuit correctly viewed self-interest as not simply gaining or extracting specific concessions from the other party at the bargaining table. *Mackey* should have reached the same conclusion.

Other Antitrust Cases

Two other cases involving antitrust issues in professional hockey should be noted briefly. In the first case, Ken Linseman, a nineteen-year-old amateur player, challenged a WHA regulation preventing persons under age 20 from playing professional hockey.[67] (The NHL had the same rule.) Linseman had been drafted and signed by the WHA's Birmingham Bulls despite the regulation. The day after the draft the WHA president informed the Bulls that the choice of Linesman was null and void because of the age limitation.

The challenge to this rule was brought under the Sherman Act, claiming that an illegal restraint of trade had occurred. The U.S. District Court relied on the precedent established in the *Haywood* case from professional basketball (discussed in Chapter 6).[68] It found that Linseman was entitled to relief because the damage he would suffer by enforcing the age regulation would cause irreparable injury to his playing career. The court characterized the regulation as a "concerted refusal to deal" with Linseman solely because of his young age. As a result of this decision the WHA and NHL reduced the minimum age at which players can play professional hockey to 18.

In the second case, a hockey player who had previously lost an eye playing hockey sued the NHL on grounds that its refusal to allow him to play violated the Sherman Act.[69] The U.S. Court of Appeals held that the reason for the NHL's bylaw preventing a one-eyed hockey player from playing for a member club was safety, not anticompetitive. Even though the player had a specially designed safety mask, it was not sufficient protection of himself or other players at risk because of his blind side during the rough physical contact.

ECONOMIC ISSUES

As in other professional team sports, hockey owners operate as a cartel. They reach agreements on virtually all phases of the business, including distribution of franchises, movement of players, scheduling, ticket prices, and rules of play. Owners' prerogatives through league and individual control are countervailed by the players and their union in areas of mutual concern, primarily pay and work-

Table 7-4. Average Salaries in the National Hockey League.

1967	1972	1975	1977	1979	1981	1983
$19,133	$44,109	$74,000	$96,000	$101,000	$110,000	$125,000

Source: 1967, 1972, and 1977 data from Kennedy and Williamson, Money: The Monster Threatening Sports, Sports Illustrated, July 17, 1978, at 46. Later years estimated by the authors based on various sources.

ing conditions. However, management rights are largely insulated from encroachment by outside interests, and teams enjoy considerable freedom to regulate the economic environment. Canada-based teams are at a financial disadvantage compared to teams based in the United States in that the tax laws of Canada do not permit player depreciation. But this is more than offset by the popularity of the sport in Canada, which has made its professional hockey franchises among the most successful financially.

Salaries

At the time the NHLPA was formed in 1967, hockey players were substantially underpaid. Buoyed by the union and by the appearance of lawyers and agents, players acquired professional bargaining assistance. With superstar Bobby Orr's signing by the Boston Bruins, league expansion, and a national television contract, hockey entered an age of affluence. As shown in Table 7-4, average salaries more than doubled from 1967 to 1972. Then, with bidding wars inspired by WHA competition, NHL salaries kept rising rapidly through about mid-decade. Pay of hockey superstars became as high as that in any sport. A case in point is Brad Park. In his four seasons with the New York Rangers his salary rose from $10,000 to $40,000.[70] Then in 1972 the Cleveland club of the WHA started negotiations to lure Park away from the Rangers. The result was a five-year contract at an estimated $200,000 per year to keep Park in New York.[71]

As economic problems caused by overexpansion became more apparent, average salaries in the NHL actually decreased for brief periods in 1974 and 1976. Since then they have continued to rise but not as rapidly as during the 1970s and at a slower pace than in other professional sports. The NHL still experiences attendance problems as a result of overexpansion, which act as a drag on salaries.

Attendance

Table 7-5 shows average attendance at NHL games for several years. The relative decline since 1973 is due to overexpansion and the dilution in overall quality of play that it spawned. It also reflects the preoccupation with violence that be-

Table 7-5. Attendance at National Hockey League Games.

Year	Total Number of Games	Total Attendance	Average Attendance
1972–73	624	8,574,651	13,741
1973–74	624	8,640,978	13,847
1974–75	720	9,521,536	13,224
1975–76	720	9,103,761	12,644
1976–77	720	8,563,890	11,894
1977–78	720	8,526,564	11,842
1978–79	680	8,333,609	12,255
1979–80	840	10,533,623	12,540
1980–81	840	10,725,134	12,768
1981–82	840	10,710,894	12,751
1982–83	840		

came more pronounced with league growth, to the dissatisfaction of many fans who enjoy a purer form of hockey.

Over the years fan attraction to hockey has been stimulated by some outstanding players and teams. Beginning in the 1930s with Howie Morenz, the NHL has had players with truly remarkable skills. Mere mention of their names evokes memories of flashing skates and booming shots: Maurice "Rocket" Richard, Gordie Howe, Bobby Hull, Bobby Orr, and the latest member of the pantheon, Wayne Gretsky. In the 1981–82 season Gretsky had the most prolific scoring output in the history of the league with the Edmonton Oilers, producing 92 goals, 120 assists, and 212 total points—all NHL records.[72] He eclipsed the old records by such wide margins that some observers feel he is one of the finest athletes ever in any sport. Wherever Gretsky plays he usually fills the arena.

Great teams have also hyped attendance. The Montreal Canadiens built their strength through sponsorship of minor league hockey and rights to French-speaking draft choices. Although the days of Montreal's domination of professional hockey are over, because of depletion of minor league talent and revised drafting rules, the team's appearance in league cities is still much anticipated by fans.

When the NHL had only six teams attendance was at or close to 100 percent of capacity. With twenty-one teams today, more fans see NHL hockey but fewer stadiums are full. Attendance dropped to about 70 percent of capacity in the NHL in 1976.[73] Since then attendance has gone up some, but most arenas are nowhere near full. At about $10, average ticket prices are fully developed. The relative stability of player salaries in recent years reflects this economic squeeze. In addition, the recession of the early 1980s hurt attendance. Despite a moderation in expenses, several teams are in dicey financial straits. It was estimated in 1983 that even if the St. Louis Blues were to fill their stadium (capacity 18,000) for every game, they would still lose money.[74] It may not be possible for the NHL to sustain its current level of twenty-one teams in future years.

Television

As noted earlier in the chapter, regular telecasts of professional hockey in the United States began in 1956 under a contract between the NHL and CBS. It was not a profitable enterprise for the network, which lost money on the sport nearly every year.[75] In the early 1970s NBC began presenting games on television, but it too had little success in attracting viewer interest. The turning point in the NHL's finances came in 1975 when the U.S. national television contract was not renewed because of low ratings.

Although hockey is an exciting spectator sport when seen live, television diminishes its appeal. It is particularly hard to relate to the televised game if one has not previously played hockey or viewed it live. Instant replays help the television audience, but this advantage is offset by the smallness of the puck and difficulty of providing smooth coverage with cameras during the fast action of helter-skelter play. The demise of hockey on U.S. television brought mutual recriminations from the parties, with the networks contending that the NHL moguls refused to cooperate in scheduling and marketing, while the NHL owners retorted that they did not want the networks telling them how to run their sport.[76] Both sides had good arguments. The NHL did refuse to provide the best game for viewing each week, but the hockey owners are commendable in not allowing the networks to manipulate their game, a problem that has shown up with regularity in other professional team sports.

Games are still televised regularly in Canada under contracts with independent stations, and some are shown in the U.S. on cable networks. But the revenues derived from sale of hockey broadcast rights are piddling compared with those of football, baseball, and basketball. In this regard hockey has been described as "like an urchin with its nose pressed to the picture tube."[77] Hockey may again come back to U.S. major network television. The game is not wholly unadaptable to the medium. Far more U.S.-born players are in the NHL today. Coverage of the exploits of the U.S. Olympic hockey team in Lake Placid, New York, sparked viewer participation. A change from three periods to two halves of play might help stimulate interest in television, which has difficulty "filling" between periods. However, this would radically alter the game as it has been played for so long.[78] Instigation of overtime to help end the inconclusiveness of tie games may be an attractive alternative. So would "cleaning up the game" by ending its unnecessary brawling.

1981–82 NEGOTIATIONS

Labor relations in hockey have been characterized by informality and high levels of trust between the parties. Hockey players are far less militant than those in other team sports in terms of supporting overall league interests through accommodation at the bargaining table.[79] As noted above, as a result of the 1979 negotiations that renewed the agreement on equalization, the union was allowed to reopen negotiations on this issue in 1981. Meanwhile, committees were formed by the players and owners to observe and assess the area of free-agent compensation. The next sections examine the dynamics of negotiations resulting from reopening the contract on equalization by the NHLPA.

Issues

Preliminary discussions were held in 1980 between the owner and player committees on free agency. As detailed earlier in the chapter, the existing system of equalization provided that teams signing a free agent negotiated a payment of players, draft choices, or cash to the team that lost a free agent, with disputes resolved through final-offer arbitration. The player committee's initial position was for total free agency with no compensation or equalization required for teams that lose players. The owners' proposal called for a scale for determining equalization payments for free agents, based on draft choices, that was similar to the practice in professional football. For example, a first-round draft choice would be awarded for players in the $80,000 to $100,000 salary range, with greater compensation required for players with higher salaries and less compensation for players with lower salaries.[80] Owners were also to be given a right of first refusal for players making less than $80,000. The owners' proposal would have caused little change in compensation levels from what had occurred under the existing equalization arrangement. Unable to reach agreement in these exploratory talks, the union decided to formally exercise its option to reopen the contract.

As a result of reopening, another issue emerged: overtime. Under the point system that determines team standings in the NHL, a win counts two points and a tie counts one. Tie games are better than losses, and some teams, especially when playing on the road, play cautiously toward the end of an even game lest a tie slip away. However, viewing a tie is unsatisfying to most spectators because of its inconclusive outcome. Overtime was used briefly in the NHL during World War II but was discontinued in 1942. In 1980 the owners voted to institute a five-minute overtime period.[81] The NHLPA refused to go along with the change because it had not been consulted. When the players could not reach a consensus among themselves, the matter was postponed. It is unusual for a union in sports to have a voice in determining playing rules like overtime. The players finally decided they wanted overtime, but the issue foundered during discussions of what the union would get in return for agreeing to it. Thus, overtime hung in limbo while its fate was determined in negotiations.

Another issue was the length of the agreement. The union wanted a two-year agreement, which would allow renegotiation if new free-agency rules did not work out to the players' benefit. The owners wanted a seven-year contract.

Moving toward Compromise

Although the positions of the parties were far apart on equalization, positive attitudes between the negotiators were evident throughout the months of bargaining that finally led to agreement. Cooperation between the principals in hockey sharply contrasts with the rancor that has characterized labor relations in certain other professional sports. Instead of vilifying one another in the print and broadcast media, the chief negotiators in hockey exercise great care to show respect for the other side and willingness to compromise. The following statements are typical:

> *Eagleson* — Each side understands the strong position of the other side. But we realize total free agency with no compensation is a difficult thing for the owners to swallow.

> *Ziegler* — The NHL doesn't consider the elimination of compensation a satisfactory response to the owners' proposals, although the owners are not wedded to a specific plan.[82]

Speaking five months later, following a bargaining session, the negotiators said:

> *Eagleson* — There was a greater appreciation on the players' part of the owners' problems and there was a greater appreciation on the owners' part of what the players' problems are. Hockey is the only sport where there is a partnership of owners and players.

> *Ziegler* — This meeting is probably one of the most productive and encouraging we've had at the owner–player level in a long time. The views on the (two) positions are still strong, but the attitude on how to solve them is so good that it's great to be in this game.[83]

Both sides had strong arguments, suggesting that a one-sided result was unlikely. The owners had invested substantial monies in the development of players and wanted to protect as many as possible from free agency. About half of the NHL teams were losing money, and some might have to go bankrupt, sell, or relocate if star players were lost with little compensation. Liberalized free agency would provide an impetus to salary increases for all players that would further aggravate the owners' financial plight. NHL owners were particularly aware of the effect that free agency had on baseball.

The players, on the other hand, felt that the old system of equalization discouraged free agency and thus kept salaries down. Because of the depreciation in value of the Canadian dollar vis-à-vis the U.S. dollar, many players were anxious to move as free agents to U.S.-based teams. Another source of concern was that the average age of a NHL player dropped from 28 to 25 as a result of the draft of eighteen-year-olds, cutting a player's career down from an average of eight to only four or five years.[84] Greater mobility of free agents would help offset the trend toward shorter careers by boosting salaries during the time spent in the league. However, the players realized that if they pushed their demands too far, to the point of bankrupting teams, it would create an increase in the supply of players that could decrease average salaries.[85]

The first indication of a possible strike over free-agency compensation came when Eagleson went to England to visit Lloyd's of London about obtaining strike insurance.[86] Having insured the baseball owners during their earlier strike, Lloyd's was not receptive to taking the risk again. A newspaper poll found that thirteen of fifteen NHLPA team representatives would vote for a strike if a new collective bargaining agreement could not be achieved.[87] However, the strike talk was more in the nature of tactical maneuvering than contemplation of a reality. No one really wanted a strike. Optimism that an agreement would be worked out remained at a high level.

In early August 1982 a major barrier to agreement was broken when the union conceded that it would accept the inclusion of an established player in compensation for a free agent.[88] As to length of the contract, the union raised its offer from two years to three, and the owners lowered their proposal to six years from seven. The overtime issue was never in doubt since both sides appeared to want it. With the start of training camps less than six weeks·away, the pace of negotiations quickened.

NEW AGREEMENT

Although both sides compromised substantially on their initial positions, the players conceded more than the owners. The final agreement, reached on August 17, 1982, was for five years, with each party having the right to terminate at the end of the fourth year by giving one-year's notice. The players agreed to waive their objections to overtime, giving the NHL the right to institute up to a ten-minute overtime period without further approval by the NHLPA.

Free-Agent Compensation

The new agreement on free-agent compensation includes the following features:

1. If a player age 33 or over changes teams as a free agent, no compensation is required.
2. If a free agent is under age 24 or has less than five years of professional experience, the old system of equalization applies.
3. Compensation for other free agents is based on the salary offer of the new team. For players offered up to $85,000, no compensation is required.

    $85,000 to $99,999: a third-round draft choice.

    $100,000 to $124,999: a second and a third-round draft choice.

    $125,000 to $149,999: a first-round draft choice or player from new club (excluding a protected list of eight players).

    $150,000 to $199,999: a first- and a second-round draft choice or a first-round choice plus a player (protected list of six players).

    $200,000 and above: two first-round draft choices, or a first-round choice plus a player (protected list of four players).

4. A right of first refusal, under which the previous club can retain the player by matching the offer of the new team, applies in all cases except for offers under $85,000 and where the old system of equalization is in effect.[89]

Likely Impact

The revised system of free-agency compensation thus provides for draft choices from the amateur draft and player choices from the free agent's old team. In determining the number of players that the old team can protect (either eight, six, or four players depending on the salary offer), the free-agent player himself must be included among the players being protected.

A majority of the NHL players who sign as free agents will require compensation of a second- and a third-round draft choice from the amateur draft. However, the most marketable free agents will require even greater compensation. It is unlikely that the new rules will cause a rash of free-agent signings because the compensation levels are fairly steep. Moreover, players under age 24 or with less than five years of professional experience (including minor leagues) are still covered by the old equalization rules, which did not provide much player mobility. This will protect clubs from losing budding stars.[90] The new system combines certain elements of rules developed in professional football (compensation based on salary), basketball (right of first refusal), and baseball (protection of certain players from selection as compensation). While few players are expected to change teams under the new rules, players should have a stronger voice in salary negotiations with their clubs.

Uniqueness

Although hockey's collective bargaining agreement is tailored to fit the exigencies of the sport, it contains several features found in other major sports agreements. Hockey is unique because labor and management do not follow the adversary win/lose relationship that characterizes other sports and much of North American industry. Instead, the model that has developed in hockey is more akin to integrative bargaining in which the parties seek solutions to common problems. Resolving these problems in a spirit of cooperation and accommodation results in agreements that are to the mutual advantage of the parties by promoting the long-run health of the game.

It is refreshing to see that attitudes in sports bargaining can be structured toward trust, respect, and face saving. Absence of hostility and recrimination has made it easier for the parties to come to reasoned agreement without impasse and strikes. The use of outside mediation has not been necessary in hockey because the parties have learned to solve their own problems at the bargaining table. They do not parade their dirty linen before the news media. The labor relations system in hockey is not perfect, however: the players have shown a greater sense of compromise than the owners, who have contributed to their own problems by overexpansion. Players, motivated by human avarice, exacerbated the economic crunch by playing one league off against the other in the days of the WHA. Violence grew uncontrollably at NHL games because the league did not act decisively enough in dealing with miscreants. But the problems hockey faces cannot be laid at the doorstep of labor relations.

NOTES TO CHAPTER 7

1. Greenfield, The Iceman Arriveth: Hockey Is the Sport of the Seventies, Esquire, Oct. 1974, at 160–61, 274.
2. Isaacs, Checking Back: A History of the National Hockey League 17 (1977).
3. *Id.*
4. Despite hockey's origin and popularity in Canada, lacrosse is the country's national sport.
5. Richard Beddoes, Stan Fischler, and Ira Gitler, Hockey: The Story of the World's Fastest Game xi (1969).
6. National Hockey League, 1982–83 Official Guide 13 (1982).
7. Isaacs, Checking Back: A History of the National Hockey League 30 (1977).
8. *Id.*
9. Brian Conacher, Hockey in Canada: The Way It Is 2 (1970).

10. National Hockey League, 1982–83 Official Record Book 94 (1982).

11. Brian Conacher, Hockey in Canada: The Way It Is at 2.

12. Lionel S. Sobel, Professional Sports and the Law 251 (1977).

13. A few of the exceptional American-born players prior to the last decade achieved distinction in the NHL. Often from the Iron Range of Northern Minnesota, they include Frank Brimsek, Sam LoPresti, John Mariucci, and Tom Williams. In 1973 a United States Hockey Hall of Fame was established in Eveleth, Minnesota.

14. *See* Gammons, The Swedish Invasion, Sports Illustrated, Oct. 18, 1976, at 38–41.

15. Duffy, The "Inter" National Hockey League, Boston Globe, Oct. 3, 1981, at 25.

16. Matheson, It's Tough Going for Europeans in NHL, Sporting News, Feb. 7, 1983, at 29.

17. European Pros Change NHL Style of Competition, Oakland Tribune, Dec. 19, 1982, at F-7.

18. Phinizy, The Eagle and His Fat Flock, Sports Illustrated, Oct. 21, 1974, at 61.

19. Parker, The Hockey Rebellion, Sports Illustrated, Oct. 28, 1957, at 19.

20. *Id.* at 20.

21. Isaacs, Checking Back: A History of the National Hockey League 203–04 (1977).

22. Summarized from Constitution of the National Hockey League Players' Association. This constitution, initially written in 1967, was revised in 1975. A copy of the revised constitution was furnished the authors by the NHLPA in 1983.

23. Phinizy, The Eagle and His Fat Flock, Sports Illustrated, Oct. 21, 1974, at 56.

24. Player Mike Milbury of the Boston Bruins has been particularly critical of Eagleson. *See* Rosa, The Eagleson Issue, Boston Globe, Jan. 8, 1980, at 25; and Singelais, Milbury Raps Eagleson, Boston Globe, Jan. 10, 1980, at 41.

25. Conacher, Hockey in Canada: The Way It Is 89, 94 (1970).

26. This procedure is explained in a letter from Clarence S. Campbell to Paul D. Staudohar, Sept. 7, 1974.

27. James B. Dworkin, Owners versus Players: Baseball and Collective Bargaining 264 (1981).

28. Collective Bargaining Agreement between National Hockey League Players' Association and National Hockey League (August 1, 1981), Exhibit 2, sec. A, 7(b), at 42.

29. Letter from R. Alan Eagleson to Paul D. Staudohar, June 13, 1974. The Oakland club later became known as the California Golden Seals.

30. *Id.*

31. Data provided the authors by S.G. Simpson, director of operations of the NHLPA, March 28, 1983.

32. Description of this system is based on Berry and Gould, A Long Deep Drive to Collective Bargaining: Of Players, Owners, Brawls, and Strikes, 31 Case W. Res. L. Rev. 790 (1981).

33. Frayne, Two Worlds of Sharpened Bats and Blunted Blades, Macleans, June 30, 1980, at 38.

34. Rosa, Players OK NHL Merger, Boston Globe, June 7, 1979, at 47.

35. Merry, Kings Get Compensation for Sargent: 3 North Stars, L.A. Times, July 15, 1978, pt. 3, at 1, 4.

36. The original WHA franchises were located in Edmonton, Winnipeg, Ottawa, and Quebec, Canada, and in Boston, New York, Cleveland, Chicago, Minneapolis-St. Paul, Houston, Los Angeles, and Philadelphia.

37. Isaacs, Checking Back: A History of the National Hockey League 224 (1977).

38. Mulvoy, Hockey's Turn to Wage a War, Sports Illustrated, June 19, 1972, at 26.

39. Bobby Hull's Millions, Newsweek, July 10, 1972, at 85.

40. Mulvoy, Hockey's Turn to Wage a War, Sports Illustrated, June 19, 1972, at 27.

41. On Thin Ice, Time, Dec. 10, 1973, at 78.

42. Mulvoy, A Seller's Market, Sports Illustrated, Oct. 20, 1975, at 31.

43. Gammons, A Matter of Dollars and Sense, Sports Illustrated, Nov. 29, 1976, at 28.

44. O'Hara, The Hand Is Offered, the Ring Is Kissed, Macleans, April 2, 1979, at 24.

45. Davis, A Nowhere Ride, Sports Illustrated, May 28, 1979, at 44.

46. Id.

47. L.A. Times, March 31, 1979, pt. 3, at 4.

48. Quinn, Now it's a Game for All Seasons, Macleans, Oct. 15, 1979, at 42.

49. Sobel, The Emancipation of Professional Athletes, 3 W. State U. L. Rev. 195 (1976).

50. Boston Professional Hockey Ass'n. v. Cheevers, 348 F. Supp. 261 (D. Mass.), remanded 472 F.2d 127 (1st Cir. 1972).

51. Quoted from 348 F. Supp. at 264, and Nassau Sports v. Peters, 352 F. Supp. 870 (1972).

52. 407 U.S. 258 (1972).

53. The U.S. Court of Appeals in remanding Cheevers disagreed with this conclusion. See 427 F.2d 127, at 128.

54. Nassau Sports v. Hampson, 355 F. Supp. 733 (D. Minn. 1972).

55. Philadelphia World Hockey Club v. Philadelphia Hockey Club, 351 F. Supp. 462 (E.D. Pa. 1972).

56. Id. at 466.

57. Id. at 485.

58. Nassau Sports v. Peters, 352 F. Supp. 870 (E.D. N.Y. 1972).

59. McCourt v. California Sports, Inc., 600 F.2d 1193 (6th Cir. 1979). Discussion of this case is from Berry and Gould, A Long Deep Drive to Collective Bargaining: Of Players, Owners, Brawls, and Strikes 31 Case W. Res. L.Rev. 769–71 (1981). See also Miller, The National Hockey League's Faceoff with Antitrust: McCourt v. California Sports, 4 Ohio State L.J. 603–26 (1981). Detailed discussion of the labor exemption can also be found in Chapter 4.

60. 600 F.2d at 1194.
61. Mackey v. National Football League, 543 F.2d 644 (8th Cir. 1976), *cert. dismissed*, 434 U.S. 801 (1977).
62. 600 F.2d at 1197-98.
63. *Id.*, at 1198.
64. *Id.*, at 1200.
65. *Id.*, at 1202.
66. *Id.*, at 1202-03.
67. Linseman v. World Hockey Ass'n, 439 F. Supp. 1315 (D. Conn. 1977).
68. Denver Rockets v. All-Pro Management, 325 F. Supp. 1049 (C.D. Cal. 1971).
69. Neeld v. National Hockey League, 594 F.2d 1297 (9th Cir. 1979).
70. Kahn, Sports, Esquire, March 1974, at 32.
71. *Id.*
72. National Hockey League, 1982-83 Official Guide at 223.
73. Gammons, A Matter of Dollars and Sense, Sports Illustrated, Nov. 29, 1976, at 29.
74. Statement by Emile Francis, General Manager of the Blues, in Sporting News, Feb. 7, 1983, at 6.
75. Mulvoy, It's Gotta Be Orr—Or Else, Sports Illustrated, Oct. 19, 1970, at 29.
76. Maslow, Hockey on Thin Ice, Saturday Review, Dec. 10, 1977, at 70.
77. Kennedy and Williamson, Money: The Monster Threatening Sports, Sports Illustrated, July 17, 1978, at 75.
78. In the old National Hockey Association, forerunner of the NHL, the game consisted of two thirty-minute periods until 1910, when it was changed to three twenty-minute periods. National Hockey League, 1982-83 Official Record Book, 99.
79. *See* Hessler, Players Keeping NHL Alive, Buffalo Courier Express, Aug. 11, 1982, at C-1.
80. Rosa, NHLPA Refuses Owners' Proposal, Boston Globe, Feb. 6, 1980, at 26.
81. Fayne, Overtime Has Come, to Talk of Benefits and Things, Macleans, Sept. 22, 1980, at 42.
82. Quotes of Alan Eagleson and John Ziegler, Jr., in Keese, Agreement Is Sought on Free-Agent Issue, N.Y. Times, Feb. 8, 1981, at 55.
83. Quotes of Alan Eagleson and John Ziegler, Jr., in Rosa, NHL Players Optimistic, Boston Globe, July 10, 1981, at 30.
84. Rosa, NHL Draws Battle Lines, Boston Globe, June 3, 1981, at 37; and Hockey Has Its Problems, the NHLPA's Boss Admits, Hamilton (Ontario) Spectator, Feb. 27, 1982, at 20.
85. Strachan, Chilly Strike Rumors Invade Midsummer Idyll, Toronto Globe & Mail, July 17, 1982, at S2.
86. Proudfoot, Hockey Players Taking First Step toward a Strike, Toronto Star, Oct. 22, 1981, at D-2.
87. We'd Strike, Players Warn, Hamilton (Ontario) Spectator, Feb. 27, 1982, at 20.

88. Campbell, NHL Players Bend on Compensation, Toronto Globe & Mail, Aug. 5, 1982, at 11.
89. This summary is based on information provided the authors by the NHL and NHLPA.
90. Greenberg, NHL Devises an Agreement for Everyman, Philadelphia Daily News, Aug. 18, 1982, at 66.

8 UNRESOLVED ISSUES FACING SPORTS UNIONS

Certain problems pertaining to sports labor unions cut across all professional team sports. These issues have been peripherally considered earlier. We need at this point to analyze them in greater detail. The issues relate to definition of the unit for collective bargaining purposes, to the exclusivity granted a union in its bargaining efforts, and to the problems of balancing the interests of the collective (union) and the individual (player). Part of our discussion centers on lessons learned from a defunct league, the North American Soccer League. Even so, while the league may have faded, the importance of the legal rulings arising from that league's labor travails persist.

THE UNIT

Employees of any "labor organization" may file a petition calling for a vote to select their representatives in the collective bargaining process. If the employees are petitioning for representation and an election concerning a "labor organization" within the NLRA's meaning, and if 30 percent of the employees in the appropriate unit vote to have a board conducted election, the board must hold an election for workers in an appropriate unit or grouping.[1]

In professional sports, if a majority of players in the unit who vote in the Board conducted election cast their ballots in favor of the union or association, the board certifies the union as the exclusive bargaining agent for the unit. Sometimes craft or skilled workers may sever themselves from the unit.[2] It has been suggested that superstars or players representing an occupational minority in sports (such as pitchers in baseball, quarterbacks in football, and goalies in hockey) ought to separate from the broader unit and bargain collectively for themselves. The board is not likely to allow this separation. While most players in these positions have maintained a separate sense of identity—a criterion that the board considers in determining whether an occupational group should become its own unit[3]—other criteria, such as the integration of their tasks with the functions of the enterprise and the qualifications of a union experienced in representing them, make severance seem unwise.

Another persistent issue is whether the appropriate unit or grouping of players for collective bargaining purposes should be defined according to club or league. This classification is particularly important, since many decisions are made on a leaguewide basis, specifically through the commissioner's office. When the NFLPA petitioned the board for a leaguewide unit, naming the commissioner as the employer's representative, the NFL was induced to negotiate a consent agreement. This agreement provided that a newly created entity, the NFL Management Council, would serve as employer, thus eliminating any reference to the commissioner.[4]

The issue is important because the commissioner purportedly acts as a neutral arbitrator. This position as an impartial protector of the game's integrity would be seriously undermined if he were regarded as a representative of the employer. It would be impossible for the NFLPA to negotiate regarding player mobility, in the form of reserve and option provisions, because these decisions are made by the league or commissioner. The same rationale applies to the draft and rules relating to circumstances under which players may be waived and traded. Approval of the standard player contract often comes from the commissioner's office, which is often involved in disciplinary matters.[5]

North American Soccer League[6] was the first sports case to confront the issue. The board held that the league and the clubs constituted a joint employer. Although the individual clubs also might be deemed an appropriate unit on a club-by-club basis, the joint employers were an appropriate unit within the meaning of the NLRA. The board particularly was influenced by the following factors: The commissioner conducts the annual college draft and establishes the conditions under which a college player may be signed to a professional contract; the commissioner may disapprove the assignment of a player to another club if, in his opinion, the agreement contains terms not in the league's best interest[7] or if either party is guilty of conduct detrimental to the league or the sport; the commissioner's approval must be obtained for any player's waiver, and the commissioner will not approve the contract termination if he determines that the league's interests will suffer; and, under the standard player contract, the player must comply with the applicable provisions of the league constitution, regulations, and bylaws.[8] In addition, the board found that the clubs had considerable autonomy in certain aspects of their employment relationships because numerous modifications were allowable under the standard player contract. The clubs and the league, therefore, were regarded justifiably as joint employer.

Whether the NSPA could be regarded as a "labor organization" within the NLRA's meaning also was addressed. The owners contended that the NSPA did not intend to act as an exclusive bargaining representative, since individual salaries still were negotiable. The board concluded that simply because agents bargain on important salary items, a players' association is not deprived necessarily of labor organization status.[9]

The board has been confronted with similar issues in the United States Football League.[10] Here the regional director, confronted with the argument that a unit should not be established on a leaguewide basis, noted that the league retains "considerable authority and control over the labor relations of the member-clubs."[11] In arriving at this conclusion the regional director noted that the clubs utilize a standard player contract prepared by the league in consultation with member clubs and that that contract authorizes the commissioner to arbitrate disputes between a player and the club, the formula for compensation for playoff games and an agreement to be bound by league rules relating to waiver.

Noting that the control over labor relations is a critical factor in determining whether a joint employer relationship exists, the board held that *United States Football League* was a fact situation "almost identical" to that set forth in the *North American Soccer League* case. In both cases the board noted that the commissioner exercised "a significant degree of control and influence over the clubs including the terms and conditions of employment of the players."

Another issue arising in the United States Football League case was whether, by virtue of its affiliation with the National Football League Players' Association, the United States Football League Players' Association was entitled to bargain with the employer. The argument put forward by the USFL was that the bargaining relationship with a competitor of the employer here created a conflict of interest for the labor organization. But the regional director concluded that in other cases where such conflict had been found there was access to confidential information that was in the possession of one of the competitors. Said the regional director:

> There is insufficient evidence on the record to show that the Employer herein intends to reveal to the Petitioners any confidential information. Second, this case involves the legitimacy of Petitioner USFLPA/FPA as the statutory 9(a) representative and not an unfair labor practice proceeding involving the duty to bargain with certain representatives. While the Board has held that under certain circumstances a union may be disqualified from representing employees if the union itself is a competitor of the employer, no case has been cited or found which precludes a labor organization from representing employees of competing employers.[12]

Finally, an issue that has been confronted in a number of cases emerged in *United States Football League*: that is, the question of whether free agents are to be included within the appropriate unit for bargaining purposes. The board in

Major League Rodeo, Inc.[13] had held that employees with no reasonable expectation of reemployment were not properly within the unit. The employees in question were free agents. A similar conclusion was reached by the regional director in a case involving the major Indoor Soccer League Players' Association where agents were excluded. But in the United States Football League the board refused to exclude free agents "who have played out their USFL contracts, . . . [inasmuch as] the League has just started and not completed its first season [and therefore] no such players yet exist."[14]

EXCLUSIVITY

Over a forty-one-year period, the courts and the board followed the Supreme Court's lead in a series of cases. These decisions established the union's preeminence as exclusive bargaining representative and have collectivized practically all portions of the employment relationship where a union has been selected by a majority of the employees. The Court, fashioning a corollary to the broad authority given the union as exclusive agent, has held that the union has a duty of fair representation to all workers in the bargaining unit—whether union or nonunion. The union must bargain and negotiate on behalf of its players without hostility, bad faith, or discrimination.[15] Although the meaning of these words is ambiguous,[16] the union apparently has broad discretion in negotiating collective bargaining agreements and may recognize legitimate differences between different occupational groups.[17] Just as a union may negotiate a hiring hall or seniority provision in the collective bargaining agreement without violating its duty of fair representation, it also may negotiate maximum and minimum salary levels. Baseball and basketball owners have had a particular interest in this approach.[18] Although this policy seems to have been abandoned, the NFLPA has been advocating wage and occupational seniority—provided that the percentage of football revenues allocated to player incomes is at least doubled.[19] The extent to which high-salaried quarterbacks, for instance, would accede to such limitations is highly problematic.

Issues arising out of the North American Soccer League have posed unusual labor issues to professional sports. In *J.I. Case v. NLRB*,[20] the leading decision relating to the exclusivity doctrine, the employer executed individual contracts with approximately 75 percent of his work force. The employer initially relied on these contracts as a bar to a representation proceeding, but the board directed an election, which the union won. The union then was certified as the exclusive bargaining representative for all the employees in the appropriate unit. When the union sought to bargain with the employer, management offered to negotiate on matters not affecting any rights under the individual contracts. All other matters would be open for negotiation as the contracts expired. The union alleged that this refusal to bargain collectively constituted an unfair labor practice under the NLRA. The board agreed and ordered the company to cease and desist from giving effect to or extending the contracts in question and from entering into new contracts. The board further ordered the company to bargain on the subject matter of the individual contracts. The Circuit Court of Appeals enforced this order, and the Supreme Court affirmed.[21] The Court's rationale bears on some of the problems faced in the sports cases.

The Court noted that the negotiation of the collective agreement did not constitute an employment contract since no individual was employed under its terms. The labor contract created no obligation to employ particular individuals. The Court stated that

> The employer, except as restricted by the collective agreement itself and except that it must engage in no unfair labor practice or discrimination, is free to select those he will employ or discharge. But the terms of the employment already have been traded out. There is little left to individual agreement except the act of hiring. This hiring may be by writing or by word of mouth or may be implied from conduct. In the sense of contracts of hiring, individual contracts between the employer and employee are not forbidden, but indeed are necessitated by the collective bargaining procedure.[22]

The Court believed that the individual hiring contract was "subsidiary" to the terms of the collective agreement and that workers could not waive its benefits. The Court reasoned that once the majority selected a union as exclusive bargaining representative, advantages or disadvantages provided in individual contracts would disrupt industrial peace and become a "fruitful way" of interfering with the organization of workers.[23]

If, however, a union is designated as majority representative in a professional sport with a tradition of individual contracts addressing salary and other compensation matters, the union might seek to negotiate a collective bargaining agreement ultimately limiting, but not necessarily eliminating, individual salary and compensation negotiations.

The unions and associations in sports have taken a variety of approaches to the relationship between the collective and individual agreement, especially as to compensation. Baseball, for instance, has two provisions in the agreement on this subject. In article 2, the clubs recognize the association as bargaining representative but provide "Special Covenants Contracts, which actually or potentially provide additional benefits to the Player."[24] The basketball agreement provides that individual contracts may not "provide for the waiver by a Player of any benefits or the sacrifice of any rights to which the Player is entitled by virtue of . . . this Agreement."[25] Basketball has attempted to preclude amendments to individual contracts.[26]

The soccer agreement is more ambitious and specific. The association may "disapprove" an individual contract for any of the following reasons: uncertainty or incompleteness in expression of its terms; "any conflict" between its terms and the collective agreement; the club or one of its officials has "made or agreed to make payment or convey anything of value to any firm or person for legal or representational services provided to a player in connection with the negotiation of a contract"; and finally, failure to disclose to the union the identity of an agent, attorney, or other representative.[27] The union is thus empowered to address abuses of agents, such as payments to agents by clubs when the clubs supposedly are representing the player's interests in an adversary context.

The collective agreement also states that "absent an express waiver by the Union, they [the League and clubs] could not negotiate or execute agreements with individual players."[28] The labor contract further states that when a club learns that a player or prospective player is to be represented by an agent, "it shall promptly notify the Union."[29] The union has an "absolute right" to attend all individual contract negotiations but no right to thwart or delay these negotiations. The subject matter that may be addressed in individual-club bargaining is specifically enumerated.[30] The standard player contract may not be amended.

The union's concerns in this area are threefold: (1) There are the problems with agents alluded to above; (2) conflicts or inconsistencies with the collective agreement may arise; (3) there may be an undermining of union goals through individual negotiations. An example of the first and the third problems is the increased use of deferred compensation, which may deflect player concern from pensions. Unless the union is able to control or influence such negotiations, it may be left with few subjects on which to bargain. Agents frequently do not defer *their* fees after negotiating such an agreement—a practice that seems particularly inequitable when the deferred compensation is not guaranteed.

It is quite probable that players' associations, particularly in soccer, will attempt to regulate the conduct of agents. The allegation that a "spurious" labor organization of agents has conspired to "undermine the NFL players' ability to improve their incomes" by a wage schedule that would adversely affect the agents' "profits"[31] has inspired antitrust litigation by the NFLPA against some of the agents. The theory of the litigation, ironically, is predicated on the view that the agents are entrepreneurs. If the associations are successful in regulating agents through licensing fees, limitations on agents' fees, and union member boycotts against agents who refuse to comply, the associations then must contend that agents are *not* a nonlabor group of businessmen to avoid antitrust liability.[36] This argument is highlighted by the Court's decisions in *American Federation of Musicians v. Carroll*[37] and *H.A. Artists & Associates v. Actor's Equity Association*,[38] where franchising arrangements and the boycotts of nonmembers were held to be within the labor exemption because unregulated agent fees would intensify wage competition among union members. It is contended that in this situation, "job hungry" athletes are prone to exploitation. Problems will continue while the agents play an active role in this process.

Indeed, this is why the 1982 agreement between the management council of the National Football League and the National Football League Players' Association has provided that reporting bonuses, additional salary payments, incentive bonuses, and other provisions that may be negotiated with the club are to be negotiated with the players' association and *its agent*. Pursuant to this authority the NFLPA has devised regulations that govern agents. In the first place, such regulations provide for the certification of agents and establish the guidelines for the granting or denial of certification by the players' association.

The regulations also provide for maximum fees that are a particular percentage of the compensation received in excess of the minimum salary provided for the player.

The regulations also obligate agents to avoid conflicts of interest, disclose relevant information, comply with law—in short, to provide the best representation possible.

Disputes about the procedures are to be resolved through arbitration, with the arbitrator being selected by the players' association. Provision is made for a hearing before the arbitrator. Again, this approach has really grown out of the tension between the players' association and the agents described above.

Another important issue is whether an employer may retain and honor individual employment contracts and enter into new contracts with athletes who are being recruited while such negotiations continue. The *North American Soccer League* litigation, which preceded the agreement referred to above, addressed this problem.[39] In that case, the board and the union took the position that adherence to or negotiation of such individual contracts was an unfair labor practice under the *J.I. Case* theory.[40] The board's position was that the employer could not act unilaterally as to wages, hours, and working conditions until the parties bargained to an impasse. This restriction would apply irrespective of the union's intent to contract collectively or individually. At the point of impasse, the employer could rely on individual contracts and relationships.[41]

In the context of temporary injunction proceedings[42] instituted by the board, the court in *North American Soccer League*[43] adopted the above position. The injunction prevented future negotiation of individual contracts, and the court also ordered additional relief.[44] The Second Circuit affirmed.[45]

In *North American Soccer League*, the clubs litigated the appropriate unit issue through unfair labor practice proceedings,[46] entered into individual contracts with players, and committed several unfair labor practices[47] subsequent to a secret ballot election in which the union obtained a majority vote and the board certified the union as exclusive bargaining agent. The unit issue eventually was resolved against the clubs. Meanwhile, 96.8 percent of the individual player contracts were negotiated and entered into subsequent to the union certification. The board sought a remedy that would render the individual contracts voidable at the union's option. Judge Motley stated that

> Respondents' claim that such power in the hands of the Union . . . would result in chaos in the industry and subject Respondents to severe economic loss and hardship since these individual contracts are the only real property of Respondents.
>
> It should be noted . . . that the relief requested by Petitioner is not a request to have all individual contracts declared null and void. It should be emphasized that Petitioner is not requesting that the "exclusive rights" pro-

vision of the individual contracts, which bind the players to their respective teams for a certain time, be rendered voidable.[48]

Judge Motley further ordered that contracts entered into before the certification be rendered voidable. The purpose of this remedy was to allow the collective bargaining process to function effectively. It is important to note that the remedy was limited to the portion of the agreement that did not affect the team's exclusive right to a player and thus the reserve system.

The situation in *North American Soccer League* differs from *J.I. Case* in that the employer in the former case did not consider the individual contract as a bar to collective bargaining over the subject matter that was previously negotiated. The crux of the employer's argument was that individual contracts may be entered into during continuous negotiations. The board's contention was that the Supreme Court authority precludes an employer from making unilateral changes in conditions of employment until an impasse or deadlock develops.[49] To permit the employer to negotiate with the individual would undermine the union's status as exclusive bargaining representative and erode its support among the players in the unit. The subtle message to the players is that the association is largely irrelevant and more likely a hindrance to their interests.

Since there is no legal demarcation between the subject matter covered by the individual agreement as opposed to the collective agreement, a major concern is whether all the subjects discussed at the bargaining table would be superseded by the individual contract. The employer, in its dealings with some players, might negotiate some terms that would constitute an incursion into that area that might be within the domain of the exclusive bargaining agent in its collective bargaining.

If individual negotiations with players are an unfair labor practice, notwithstanding its customary usage in the sports industry, the remedy raises troublesome problems. The remedy, even with the exclusive rights limitations, means that the union is in a position to utilize the most effective economic pressure to coerce the employer to accept its position. It raises problems somewhat analogous to other labor law issues that have been resolved, perhaps erroneously, against the unions.

For the past forty-eight years, the Court has taken the position that an employer may not only hire strikebreakers in the course of the strike but also may replace strikers permanently with these individuals.[50] The rationale is that the employer may show a business justification in keeping production optimal. This justification, under certain circumstances, outweighs the statutory policies supporting workers' rights to engage in strikes and other forms of economic pressure to further their self-interest. The employer, therefore, may enter into individual contracts, notwithstanding exclusivity considerations. If the employers' interest in production outweighs the right to strike, then there can be significant difficulties in reaching an accord with the union because the union can bring the industry to a grinding halt until impasse by voiding and refusing to enter into contracts involving both incumbents and applicants, until the dispute is resolved. The union has an interest in protecting itself as an institution from infringement through contracts embracing the same subject matter as the collective bargaining agreements. It is difficult, however, to view this interest as more significant than the strike weapon itself, which was made subordinate by the Court in *NLRB v. Mackay Radio & Telegraph Co.*[47]

GRIEVANCE ARBITRATION DECISIONS: TENSIONS BETWEEN THE COLLECTIVE AND INDIVIDUAL INTERESTS

The unions and associations in sports have taken a variety of approaches to the relationship between the collective and individual agreement, especially as to compensation. Baseball, for instance, has two provisions in the agreement on this subject. In article 2, the clubs recognize the association as bargaining representative but provide that "Special Covenants . . . [may] . . . be included in individual Uniform Player's Contracts, which actually or potentially provide additional benefits to the Player."[48]

The *Moore*[49] decision arose out of a special covenent between Alvin Moore and the Atlanta Braves. The National League president disapproved of this arrangement on the ground that the covenant was "inconsistent" with the basic agreement.[50] The covenant stated that Moore could not be traded without his consent and could become a free agent at the end of the 1977 championship season "if he so desires."[51] The players' association challenged the disapproval of the contract in a grievance.

The players' association argued that the individual contract could not be regarded as "inconsistent" with the collective bargaining agreement because it accorded benefits not available under the basic agreement. The clubs contended that the covenant struck "at the very heart" of the negotiated reserve system. The argument was that the Braves, by providing free agency for Moore without reference to the contractual scheme contained in the collective bargaining agreement, ignored other clubs' interest in maintaining a competitive balance—the very objective of the negotiated reserve system.[52]

At the time the grievance was filed, Moore did not have six years' service in the major leagues—a prerequisite to free agency under the labor contract between the parties. The covenant, moreover, made no reference to the quota and compensations of the basic agreement. In response, the association noted that the agreement contemplated free agency through methods other than the reentry draft. By way of rejoinder, the clubs maintained that these other avenues were designed for players whose careers were ending, younger players, players of marginal skills, or a default by the club.[53] With regard to the former category, the clubs contended that "[i]t was never contemplated that promises of outright release or termination would or could be used by individual Clubs and Players as a negotiating device or bargaining chip in order to evade the reentry procedure and other aspects of the reserve system."[54]

The arbitration panel held there was no reason that Moore could not negotiate conditional rights either to be traded or to become a free agent. The opinion stated:

> There is clear merit in the Association's argument that the words "additional benefits to the Player" should be liberally construed to support a wide variety of benefits to a player over and above the benefits accorded to him by the Basic Agreement. Though covenants containing such benefits may be "inconsistent" with a particular provision of the Agreement dealing with the same subject matter, there is logic in the Association's argument that they are not, in fact, "inconsistent" because Article II authorizes such inconsistencies where they provide benefit to the Player. The evidence . . . suggests the League Presidents have approved a number of special covenants in this light, where the "additional benefits to the Player" were within the Club's power to bestow.[55]

Inasmuch as the Braves were not terminating Moore for lack of playing skill, the arbitrator decided that Moore could not escape the reentry draft provided for in the collective bargaining agreement. The procedure and "its related quota provisions protect the interests of all 26 Clubs and cannot be waived by the Atlanta Club in the circumstances of this case."[56] Nevertheless, the modification of the length of service provisions negotiated between Atlanta and Moore, and circumvention of the reentry draft procedures, may affect the competitive balance in the league so as to promote the interests of some other clubs. If, for example, certain superstars became available earlier than provided for in the collective agreement, the resulting bidding wars would benefit wealthier teams such as the Yankees, Angels, and Braves. If, in contrast, the number of talented free agents available depressed the market, the impact could be immediate and substantial. In some instances, the players rather than the owners would be adversely affected. It is thus difficult to establish a clearly logical demarcation between length of service and other aspects of the reentry draft because one element protects the clubs in the league and the other does not. The *Moore* decision is probably the correct one. The additional benefits secured by individual players must be reconciled with the overriding procedures established by the collective agreement's reentry draft.

The second important case involved Mike Marshall, the 1974 Cy Young Award winner and erstwhile relief pitcher for the Minnesota Twins.[57] Marshall negotiated a special covenant with the Twins that permitted him to become a free agent after the 1978 season but "without regard to the compensation provisions therein."[58] The arbitrator, following *Moore*, concluded that the compensation provisions were designed for the benefit of all clubs and not merely the individual club that lost the player to free agency. While the arbitrator conceded that the club losing the player might waive its right to compensation, it would not waive the "detriment" or "cost" that the signing club would incur in the normal reentry draft procedure.[59]

The recent Dave Winfield free-agency episode created another problem. The Yankees, fearful that they would not be one of the thirteen teams able to draft Winfield, reportedly negotiated with the Padres to provide for an agreement between the Yankees and Winfield and a trade between the Padres and the Yankees based on that deal.[60] This alleged agreement circumvented the reentry draft procedure and compensation and, in theory, imposed a cost on the signing club. The players' association, however, accepted this procedure as compatible with the agreement because Winfield was able to use the prospect of free agency, limited only by the amateur draft compensation, as a vehicle to bargain for acceptable contract terms.

The final group of baseball-related cases involves option clauses and right of refusal clauses in special covenants. In 1976 Carlton Fisk, Rick Burleson, and Gary Maddox negotiated provisions giving their respective clubs the right of first refusal at the end of their contracts. Their theory was that a player could reap the financial benefits of a bidding war while remaining with the club in cities like Boston and New York where there are many fringe benefits to being a famous ballplayer. The association objected to these covenants on the theory that they inevitably depress the bidding between clubs.

An arbitrator took the position, in a dispute involving pitcher Dick Tidrow, that a right of first refusal "could not possibly create anything better than free agency."[61] This position seems flawed given the advantages that players might reap from such a provision. To take an extreme example, players cannot waive their right to be part of the free-agent draft after six years, although they may do so indirectly by entering into a long-term contract. The grievance thus was settled in favor of the association:[62] a further step toward collectivizing the relationship.

Another important variation on this theme of individual/collective tension involves negotiated option clauses. The *Carlton Fisk* award[63] decided that substantial performance by the Red Sox was not adequate to meet the option tender date of December 20 established under the collective agreement.[64] The arbitrator rejected the club's reliance on extreme forfeiture as an excuse of the condition because the Red Sox already had received Fisk's performance for salary paid between 1976 and 1980. This rationale is questionable in light of Fisk's inability to play during most of 1979—although Fisk played in 1980 under adverse circumstances. The arbitrator's comment that free-agency status for Fisk was an "unfortunate consequence for the Club in comparison to the minor inconvenience to him flowing from the related contract tender"[65] understates the matter.

Another option clause case, the *Tidrow* arbitration,[66] was of more precedential value. Tidrow, prior to joining the Chicago Cubs, signed a contract with the Yankees for 1977 to 1979 and then in 1978 negotiated an extension for 1980. The contract provided for compensation, some of it deferred, and stated that the club reserved the right to exercise an option on Tidrow's services at a salary of $200,000 for 1981 by notifying Tidrow before December 20, 1980.[67] The renewal option was exercised by a letter dated August 28, 1980. The players' association objected to the renewal that purportedly blocked Tidrow's access to reentry draft on the ground that the special covenent containing the option did not constitute an actual or potential benefit to the player.[68] The club contended that Tidrow had executed a contract for the succeeding season that was a contractual limitation on free-agent rights.

The arbitrator, however, held that the individual contract's special covenants referred to the 1980 season.[69] Tidrow thus could not be deemed to have executed a contract for 1981. The arbitrator also concluded that the agreement extracted from Tidrow all irrevocable offers to enter into a future contract. Moreover, since the players' association successfully resisted incorporation of an option year in the collective bargaining agreement as a prerequisite to free agency—except for players like Fisk who contracted prior to August 9, 1976[70]— the arbitrator found the bargaining history to be "strong evidence" of an intent not to eliminate free agency through an option clause.[71]

Since *Moore* held that a contract could be inconsistent and yet acceptable if it provided an actual or potential benefit, further arbitral inquiry was requested. The arbitrator discussed the contention that Tidrow had benefitted through the economic "package" that he received with a guaranteed contract rather than the standard contract. Any detriment, reasoned the arbitrator, could be offset by a potential benefit. The option clause, however, must provide its own benefit. Tidrow, experienced in negotiations and aware of free agency's benefits, could have perceived an option clause as being more advantageous.

In making his determination, the arbitrator found the following to be conclusive: "By remaining silent until the latter part of 1979 and retaining $100,000 in bonuses for signing the contract he now seeks to overturn, Tidrow led the Cubs—who acquired his contract in apparent good faith—to act in reliance on his evident acceptance of all its terms."[72] Tidrow accordingly was estopped because of his tardy disavowal, his actual or constructive knowledge that he was losing free agency, and detrimental reliance by the Cubs. While the arbitrator stated that clubs might attempt to circumvent the collective bargaining agreement through such covenants as making optional renewal clauses a condition precedent to all contracts, such was not the case in *Tidrow. Tidrow* is thus a "narrow holding" that again emphasizes the tension between collective and individual interests.

A series of cases arising out of the 1981 strike highlights the tension between individual and collective interests. In the first of this series, Panel Decision No. 42,[73] the arbitrator concluded that players on strike while disabled were not entitled to salary by virtue of their disability alone. The arbitrator concluded that the payment of medical and hospital expenses during the strike to such players was not inconsistent with the failure to provide compensation inasmuch as in the former case "the fact of disability itself . . . gives rise to the expenses . . . [and thus] no current right to reimbursement could possibly exist until the disability. In this context, therefore, disability is the *sole entitling factor*—not one that threatens loss of compensation otherwise payable."[74] The arbitrator distinguished this from benefits which were in the nature of an accrued right and related to past service. Disability payments, said the arbitrator, are "in no way related to past service. The fact is they are nothing more than a *substitute for* salary for current services and therefore are not due during the period of a strike where no salary could be payable had the Player not been disabled."[75]

The *Frank Tanana* case, arising out of a contract entered into between the former Red Sox pitcher under a contract assumed by that club from the California Angels, posed the tension between individual and collective interests more dramatically. Here the arbitrator concluded that no salary was to be paid to players during the strike where the individual contract was silent on the matter. The Messersmith contract had explicitly provided for salary payments in the event of a strike. On the other hand, a number of individual contracts provided for no payment in the event of a strike. As noted above, the Tanana agreement was silent on this subject—as were a substantial number of other player contracts.

At the outset the arbitrator noted that under federal labor law an employer is generally not obligated to compensate employees while they are on strike. Indeed, as the arbitrator noted, the National Labor Relations Board has held that the NLRA does not oblige an employer to finance an economic strike against itself by remunerating strikers for work not performed.[76] The arbitrator stated that the general payment provision in Tanana's contract that "all compensation and benefits payable to the Player hereunder shall be paid in any event" was "inherently vague" and noted that such imprecise wording could not be utilized to create "such an unusually open-ended salary obligation that it would be applicable when Tanana was withholding his services during a strike."[77]

The players' association contended that a player's failure to perform during a strike did not preclude pay in the absence of explicit language in the contract to the contrary because it was not "an arbitrary refusal" within the meaning of the individual agreement. The association argued that the refusal during the strike was not "a capricious exercise of personal choice, without valid or rational reason." However, the arbitrator rejected this view and noted that Webster's Dictionary does not make capriciousness an indispensable factor in determining whether conduct is arbitrary and that conduct may be arbitrary when engaged in because of "personal preference" or because of a selection "at random" or a "convenient selection or choice" rather than because it is based on "reason or nature." Nevertheless, this aspect of the arbitrator's reasoning is the most troublesome. As he noted:

> In the specialized context of an Addendum to a Uniform Players contract, of course, dictionary definitions of the word "arbitrary" have limited usefulness. Nonetheless, the proviso is worded broadly enough to *allow it to be read*

as precluding the extraordinary requirement of compensation to an employee who has *willfully* withholding services because of participation in a strike.[78]

Perhaps the most persuasive portion of the opinion relates to the arbitrator's reference to the primary purpose of the salary payment provision: that is, payment because of lack of playing ability, disability, or death. But another difficulty with the arbitral conclusion here relates to the fact that many clubs had entered into contracts specifically precluding pay in the event of a strike. Thus, went the Players' Association argument, the clubs were on notice and knew that failure to make an exception meant that an obligation existed. But, said the arbitrator, the specific exception for strikes might have been simply to eliminate any question relating to the accepted situation. Here, as elsewhere in the guaranteed contract cases, the arbitrator noted that those dealing on behalf of the clubs were generally not lawyers. Said Arbitrator Goetz:

> [T]he practice by the Angels and other Clubs of obtaining express exceptions to salary guarantees fall[s] far short of establishing clear recognition by the Clubs that salary payments had to be made unless there was an express exception covering that contingency. The probative value of such circumstantial evidence of intention depends on the reasonableness of the inference sought to be drawn. Other inferences as to the purposes of such conduct [clarification] seem equally reasonable. Consequently, the Association's evidence of other contracts is inadequate to carry the burden of persuasion as to intent with respect to the asserted narrower interpretation of the "arbitrarily refuse" proviso, which is fundamental to its case.[79]

Under other circumstances, however, Tommy John, as of this writing with the California Angels, was successfully able to claim pay during the strike from the New York Yankees. In Panel Decision No. 50c and d[80] owner George Steinbrenner of the New York Yankees was found to have been insisting uniformly on contracts that precluded payments in the event of a strike. Here John, who was disabled during a portion of the strike, was held to be entitled to pay because of the initial insistence on an express exclusion for strikes by the Yankees and a final "grudging deletion" of this exclusion by the club in order to gain other concessions. Generally, pay during a strike has been precluded where the contract is silent or where players are disabled—in the absence of some peculiar legislative history such as that reflected in the *John* arbitration.

NOTES TO CHAPTER 8

1. 29 C.F.R. §101.18a (1975).
2. NLRA §9(b)(2), 29 U.S.C. §159(b)(2)(1976).
3. In Mallinckrodt Chemical Works, 162 N.L.R.B. 387, 397 (1966), the board lists maintenance of separate identity as one of six criteria to be considered in determining the propriety of allowing craft unit severance.

4. Ed Garvey, executive director of the NFLPA, testified before a congressional special subcommittee that the sixteen-club NFL had been the only employer signatory to the first collective bargaining agreement in 1968. In 1970, however, the owners refused to negotiate unless the NFLPA agreed to amend its certification petition by deleting the league as a joint employer. This refusal eventually resulted in the creation of the National Football League Management Council. See Proposed Amendments to the National Labor Relations Act: Hearings on H.R. 7152, Subcom. of Education and Labor, 92d Cong., 2d Session, 13-15 (1972).

5. As to approval of the standard player contract, see, for example, NBA Uniform Player Contract, para. 14:

> This contract shall be valid and binding upon the Club and the Player immediately.
> ... If, pursuant to the Constitution and By-Laws of the Association, the Commissioner disapproves this contract within ten (10) days after the filing thereof in his office, this contract shall thereupon terminate and be of no further force or effect

Id., reprinted in Practicing Law Institute, Representing the Professional Athlete 1978, at 52-53. The requirements of the player contract have similar effect. NFL Player Contract, *id.* at 27. This approach seems to ignore two cases where players were not held to contracts entered into by them but repudiated before the commissioner's approval. *See* Detroit Football Club v. Robinson, 186 F. Supp. 933 (E.D. La.), *aff'd*, 283 F.2d 657 (5th Cir. 1960); Los Angeles Rams v. Cannon, 185 F. Supp. 717 (S.D. Cal. 1960).

The commissioner's disciplinary powers are accorded to him in the constitution and bylaws of all leagues, though recent collective bargaining agreements have modified these powers. Certain disciplinary powers often are alluded to in the player contract itself or attached as addenda. *See, e.g.,* NBA Uniform Player Contract, Excerpt from Constitution of the Association, para. 35, *reprinted in* Representing the Professional Athlete 1978, at 56-58.

6. 236 N.L.R.B. 1317 (1978), *aff'd*, 501 F. Supp. 633 (S.D.N.Y.) *aff'd*, 632 F.2d 217 (2d Cir. 1980).

7. *Id.* at 1318.

8. *Id.* at 1318-19.

9. *Id.* at 1320.

10. National Labor Relations Board Region 2, Case Nos. 2-RC-19518 and 2-RC-19522, May 18, 1983.

11. *Id.* at 4.

12. *Id.* at 8.

13. 246 N.L.R.B. 743 (1979).

14. *Id.* at 11.

15. *See, e.g.,* Hines v. Anchor Motor Freight, 424 U.S. 554 (1976); Vaca v. Sipes, 386 U.S. 171 (1967); Ford Motor Co. v. Huffman, 345 U.S. 330 (1953); Steele v. Louisville & Nashville R.R., 323 U.S. 192 (1944).

16. *See, e.g.,* Rusicka v. General Motors Corp., 523 F.2d 306 (6th Cir. 1975).

17. "A wide range of reasonableness must be allowed a statutory bargaining representative in serving the unit it represents, subject always to complete

good faith and honesty of purpose in the exercise of its discretion." Ford Motor Co. v. Huffman, 345 U.S. at 338.

18.   *See* Players Want Easier Route to Gain Free-Agent Status, N.Y. Times, Dec. 8, 1979, at 17, col. 2.

19.   Oates, Is NFL Ready for Equal Pay for All?, L.A. Times, July 22, 1979, pt. III at 1, col. 2.

20.   321 U.S. 332 (1944).

21.   *Id.*

22.   *Id.* at 335–36.

23.   *Id.* at 336, 338.

24.   1976 Baseball Basic Agreement, art. 2.

25.   NBA Agreement, 1980, art. 23, §8.

26.   *See id.* §1 (b).

27.   NASL Agreement, 1980, art. 23, §8.

28.   *Id.* §1.

29.   *Id.* §2.

30.   *Id.* §4.

31.   Upshaw v. Trope, Civil Action No. 80–03680 (C.D. Cal., Aug. 20, 1980.)

32.   United States v. Hutcheson, 312 U.S. 219 (1941).

33.   391 U.S. 99 (1968).

34.   449 U.S. 991 (1981).

35.   *See* note 6 *supra.*

36.   *See* note 20 *supra.*

37.   *Id.*

38.   Section 10 (j) of the NRLA provides that

> The Board shall have power, upon issuance of a complaint as provided in subsection (b) of this section charging that any person has engaged in or is engaging in an unfair labor practice, to petition any United States district court, within any district wherein the unfair labor practice in question is alleged to have occurred or wherein such person resides or transacts business, for appropriate temporary relief or restraining order. Upon the filing of any such petition the court shall cause notice thereof to be served upon such person, and thereupon shall have jurisdiction to grant to the Board such temporary relief or restraining order as it deems just and proper.

29 U.S.C. §160 (j) (1976).

39.   501 F. Supp. 633 (S.D.N.Y. 1979), *aff'd*, 632 F.2d 217 (2d Cir. 1980).

40.   Judge Motley also enjoined the league "[f]rom giving effect to these individual contracts of employment or any modification, continuation, extension or renewal thereof 'to forestall collective bargaining'" which were entered into prior to September 1, 1978. *Id.* at 640.

41.   632 F.2d 217 (2d Cir. 1980).

42.   Morio v. NASL, 501 F. Supp. at 635. Certification of unions as exclusive bargaining agents may be reviewed by virtue of an employer's refusal to bargain. American Fed'n of Labor v. NLRB, 308 U.S. 401 (1940).

43.   Judge Motley sets forth the unfair labor practices the North American Soccer League had engaged in:

> Respondents conceded that they have unilaterally changed the conditions of employment by requiring employees to obtain permission from their respective clubs before wearing a particular brand of footwear other than that selected by each

Respondent Club; that they have changed the conditions of employment by initiating plans for a new winter indoor soccer season which began in November, 1979 and ended in March, 1980; that they unilaterally changed conditions of employment by requiring employees to play or otherwise participate in the winter indoor soccer season; that they unilaterally changed conditions of employment by initiating plans to increase the 1980 summer outdoor soccer season by two games and two weeks over the 1979 format, which is presently in operation; and that they unilaterally changed employment conditions by initiating plans to reduce the maximum roster of all the Respondent Clubs during the regular summer outdoor season from 30 players to 26 players beginning on or about October 16, 1979, and continuing to the present.

501 F. Supp. at 637–38.

44. *Id.* at 693.
45. In NRLB v. Katz, 369 U.S. 736 (1962), the Supreme Court held that unilateral action by an employer without prior discussion with the union may constitute an unfair labor practice in violation of §8(a)(5) of the NLRA.
46. NLRB v. Mackay Radio & Tel. Co., 304 U.S. 333 (1938).
47. *Id.*
48. 1976 Baseball Basic Agreement, art. 3.
49. Major League of Professional Baseball Clubs v. Major League Baseball Players Ass'n (Moore), No. 77–18 (Sept. 7, 1977).
50. *Id.* at 2.
51. *Id.*
52. *Id.* at 8.
53. *Id.* at 11–12.
54. *Id.* at 12.
55. *Id.* at 14–15.
56. *Id.* at 17.
57. Major Leagues of Professional Baseball Clubs v. Major League Players' Ass'n (Marshall v. Minnesota Twins), No. 78–15 (Oct. 25, 1978).
58. *Id.* at 2.
59. *Id.* at 13–14.
60. *See* Yanks Seek to Land Winfield Before He Is a Free Agent, N.Y. Times, Oct. 23, 1981, §4, at 19, col. 4.
61. Decision of the Arbitration Panel, Major League Baseball Players Ass'n v. Chicago Cubs (Tidrow), No. 80–18 (Nov. 4, 1980) [hereinafter cited as Tidrow].
62. "The league presidents who originally approved the contracts [Lynn, Burleson, Fisk and Maddox] since have stricken those clauses." Chass, Miller Sees a Ripoff in Agents' Acts, N.Y. Times, Jan. 27, 1977, §C, at 25, col. 1.
63. Major League Baseball Players Ass'n (Fisk), No. 80–35, (Feb. 12, 1981) [hereinafter cited as *Fisk*].
64. *Id.* at 16.
65. *Id.* at 20.
66. *See* Tidrow, *supra* note 61 and accompanying text.
67. Clubs' Memorandum, Major League Baseball Players Ass'n v. Chicago Cubs 3 (Tidrow), No. 80–18 (Nov. 4, 1980).
68. *Id.* at 14–15.

69. *See* Tidrow, *supra* note 61 and accompanying text.

70. *Id.* at 19.

71. *Id.* at 16.

72. *Id.*

73. Major League Baseball Players Association & Major League Baseball Players Committee (June 29, 1983).

74. *Id.* at 25.

75. *Id.* at 36.

76. General Electric Co., 80 N.L.R.B. 510 (1948). *See also* Die Tool & Engineering Co., 3 Lab. Arb. 156, 158 (1946).

77. Panel Decision No. 50a & b at 25.

78. *Id.*

79. *Id.* at 33.

80. Major League Baseball Player Relations Committee & Major League Baseball Players' Ass'n (Dec. 19, 1983).

9 THE FUTURE

"History teaches no lesson but change," said H.A.L. Fisher.[1] Assuredly, the professional sports industry has experienced a great deal of change during the past few years. Memories of a straw-hatted owner sitting contentedly in his first base box behind the dugout and the players "aw shuckin' " it between chaws are fast fading. George Steinbrenner has replaced Cornelius McGillicuddy; and Steve Garvey is no Dizzy Dean. The boys of summer—and of fall, winter, and spring—may come to play, but they come to be paid as well. They bring with them agents and union reps to back their demands. Professional sports was always commerce, Justice Holmes notwithstanding, but commerce has now transformed into industry. In these industries, labor relations are a focus, and the changes wrought by collective bargaining are deep and decisive.

The metamorphosis is not complete. New rumblings make themselves felt. The 1970s brought the greatest upheavals yet in professional sports history, with multiple antitrust suits, sweeping collective bargaining provisions, decisive arbitration on a host of issues, and substantial tax reforms affecting team depreciation of players contracts. For many, it was the worst of times; for others, the best. In the 1980s there have been two major strikes by ballplayers, unprecedented in the industries as to duration and devisiveness. The NBA referees also walked,[2] as did the major league baseball umpires for a brief time at the start of the 1984 playoffs.[3]

THE SHIFTING NATURE OF SPORTS LEAGUES

The challenges met by one league predictably will eventually affect all. Whether affected by litigation, further concessions through collective bargaining, governmental intervention, changing technologies, or fluctuations in the national economy, sports leagues are not static. The next ten years will witness change, but how will these events occur and what will be their net effects?

We noted several chapters earlier that in the past few years the labor movement has been the central catalyst for change in the sports industry. Having now examined sport by sport the intricate relationships that have developed among these sports, we feel that assertion is confirmed. The intriguing question is whether the labor movement will dominate the industry for the next few years. The alternative is that the leagues will undergo such significant redirection that the revised league structures will force limitations and restraints on the collective bargaining process. Will the efforts by labor become more reactive than proactive? There are several possible scenarios, none necessarily exclusive of the others.

New Technologies

The developing technologies of cable, satellite transmissions, videodiscs, and videocassettes may alter the basic economics of existing leagues and encourage the growth of rival leagues and new sports. Leagues may form their own broadcast networks, just as other companies invade the cable market and as single stations become superstations beaming their product to much of the country. As the new commissioner of baseball assumed his post in 1984, among his earliest targets were the superstations. He charged that these stations were diluting baseball's product, causing decreased attendance in both major and minor league cities. While the figures did not immediately confirm his assertions, the point was made.[4] The traditional exclusivity that a club has to its home territory was being challenged, as was the ultimate control that the league has in deciding what should be shown and where. A response was demanded. Battle lines were drawn.

It is only a small step from condemnation of what others are doing to an adoption of the philosophy, "if we can't beat 'em, then join 'em." Several professional sports clubs already have combined with other interests to form mini-networks.[5] These early efforts have seen mixed results, from failure to tentative success. Clearly, though, the promise is there. The possible financial rewards undoubtedly vary from league to league, but all leagues and clubs will move as technology increases their choices.

For example, the NFL already televises all its games over national network feeds. While only a small percentage of the telecasts reach the entire nation on a given Sunday, all games are televised, at least regionally. Suppose, then, that the NFL enters the telecasting business and develops facilities to broadcast all its games. It will be possible to televise the games, beam them to a satellite, and let the viewer choose which game from among the dozen or so telecast he or she would like to receive. With new television sets having a capacity of sixty or seventy channels, reserving a few frequencies on Sunday for the NFL would not be difficult.

Of course, the NFL would still want to protect the home gate by imposing regional blackouts and perhaps restricting the number of signals that could be received at the precise time the home team was playing. But these are minor problems. The technological problems are solvable. The remaining question is "Why not?" Why not cut out a middleman, such as the networks? The only possible argument against such a course would be insufficient financial gain, and this seems to be unrealistic. The NFL can potentially sell its product at both ends—to sponsors and consumers—in a manner that far surpasses its current lucrative contracts with the networks.

A scenario similar to this is set forth in Peter Gent's novel, *The Franchise:* [6]

> The FCC is falling in line, the private companies are launching their DBS satellites, the technology is all in place and shortly professional football will go to pay-television: subscription, cable, direct broadcast. I'll bet *the League launches its own satellite.* You're talking about billions to each team. Each franchise. The Super Bowl reaches between fifty and seventy-five million households now. [Each team] will eventually reach a million households, at twenty bucks a game, twenty million per *game.* . . . Twenty games a season is four hundred million a season. . . .

The $400 million per team of course compares with the $14.5 million currently realized by each NFL club from the three network contracts. Even allowing for exaggeration on a large scale, the spread is impressive. The fantasizing over the possibilities is not restricted to novels; others have speculated on similar potentials. While the NFL is the most obvious possibility for its own network, clubs in other sports are actively pursuing less grandiose schemes—and other leagues may not be far behind. While not yet at the level of launching their own satellites, clubs are getting into the business of participating in the ownership of the televised product. The reverse is also true. Communications interests are becoming the masters of sports franchises. [7]

New Sports Leagues and New Sports

As technologies develop, opportunities for new sports leagues and even the popularity of new sports are enhanced. The American Football League's survival in the 1960s was owed largely to its contract with NBC. Other leagues have faltered because of an inability to attract a network contract. The WFL is a prime example; and the USFL may at length falter if it cannot increase, let alone maintain, its network agreement. The stakes were made clear in late 1984 when the USFL filed its 1.3 billion dollar lawsuit against the NFL, charging among other things that the NFL had "persuaded" the networks not to deal with the USFL over a possible contract when the new league switched to a fall schedule in 1986.[8]

The flip side of past failures, however, is the opportunity to succeed where success was not previously possible. This may occur as technologies improve and resulting expansion implodes, then saturates. The expanded media will need product, and sports is a prime and desirable source of that product. New leagues may be encouraged to form simply to fill air time. Even absent direct involvement by the media, those who form new leagues may find willing media purchasers. This will not be true for all leagues, as the USFL has discovered, but at least some sports newcomers may benefit.

New sports may appear, or perhaps conglomerates of existing ones will emerge. We tend to think of the sports we play as established in antiquity. In fact, the development of sports as consuming passions is of recent vintage, and the rules of the games are constantly changing. As the histories of the development of individual sports in the earlier chapters suggest, today's baseball and football, for example, were at earlier times quite different games. Other sports may evolve (such as indoor soccer), and existing ones (outdoor soccer?) may at length capture the public fancy. Developing technologies will aid this process, opening opportunities for exposure unknown a few years ago.

As product is needed, the media reach out and embrace new ideas. If large audiences are not demanded immediately, if narrow-casting is used to massage relatively small numbers of viewers, then new sports may be allowed time to mature. One difficulty with the USFL was that it tried to move too quickly and did not stick with the cautious approach announced at its creation. If the USFL had stuck to a spring schedule, on a limited budget, content to be minor league for a time, the league's early history might have been far different. Other sports may appear that do not repeat this mistake. If so, their long-run prognosis should be improved, and competition with the established sports eventually will be more a reality. This in turn would induce further change in the existing sports leagues.

Future of Leagues as Cartels

Sports leagues have proceeded as cartels, controlling the player and consumer market, dividing territories, protecting all within the cartel. Outside challenges to the cartel have met with limited success. While some restrictions on player mobility were struck down in the 1970s in suits engendered in part by rival leagues,[9] and a few other restraints removed, such as the NFL rule prohibiting its owners from having ownership interests in clubs in other leagues,[10] most league rules that protect the members of the cartel have remained intact, impervious to legal attack from the outside.[11] Even the player mobility rules are still largely in place, aided by the protections afforded by the labor exemption to the antitrust laws.[12]

Then attack was launched from within. The Oakland Raiders wanted to move, and they combined with the Los Angeles Memorial Coliseum Commission to unleash a broadside against the NFL. At the least, this action may force the leagues to reassess how they do business and control their members and to modify some of the more stringent requirements on franchise movement and other attributes of franchise ownership. The worst case, from the league perspective, would be to obliterate the cartel, force clubs to be all-out competitors, allow teams to move when and where they desire,[13] abolish revenue sharing, and leave an open field to clubs to market their product on television and cable however and wherever they wish.

The worst case is unlikely to happen. First, the courts lean strongly to "rule of reason" analysis, and courts have suggested that sports leagues are unique and that a club should not have to compete too vigorously with others in its league. These judicial predispositions indicate that leagues can continue as cartels, up to certain limits. Those limits must be discovered without too much cost or damage. Leagues will have to bend further than they have been willing to in the past, draw realistic bottom-lines that can be tolerated, and not attempt to control members beyond what is truly necessary. Whether leagues will accept this kind of curtailment of their power is problematical. The NBA changed its rules to allow franchise movement on a simple majority vote of its members. When the San Diego Clippers announced it was moving to Los Angeles without seeking or receiving this approval, it was the league that filed suit.[14] On the other hand, the NFL has refused to amend its rules pending the final outcome of the Raiders suit, and in the meantime the Colts forsook Baltimore by night to move to the pleasures of Indianapolis, and other teams talk about moving without consulting the league.[15] The NFL approach must be modified: A league can keep its basic structure intact only if it relinquishes some of its traditional control.

One possible alternative available to the leagues—one already pressed but unsuccessfully—is to obtain congressional relief from the antitrust burdens imposed by decisions such as *Los Angeles Coliseum*. Under the primary impetus of the NFL, sports leagues have convinced members of Congress to introduce bills that would grant sports leagues antitrust immunity as to much of their internal activities, including revenue sharing and decisions on franchise ownership and movement.[16] Not only have these bills aroused intense opposition from other affected interests, they have provoked a backlash. Bills have been introduced that would require arbitration outside a league's auspices to determine if a franchise move is justified under objective criteria established under the proposed law.[17] This proposal has incurred leagues' opposition.[18]

The most likely outcome of this proposed legislation is that Congress will at length do nothing and leave the disposition of the antitrust problems to the courts under existing law. The political forces have been too strongly called forth on all sides for Congress quietly to enter this arena. Gone are the 1960s where the NFL could go to Congress and within a few weeks, over the objections of only a few, obtain legislation that would allow the NFL to deal as a league with television networks and would allow its merger with the AFL.[19] The halcyon days for professional sports leagues, where congressional relief was only a few well-placed phone calls away, are over. Congress might act; but it could well be not to the leagues' liking. Today, other interests—notably labor, consumers, and municipalities with stadia and arenas—exert influence as well.

As these many variables are tested, change is assured. Different approaches will be tried; and predictably the patterns will not be identical from one league to another. Each league may increasingly go its own way, spurred by special concerns for its economic base and the power balances, largely between management and labor, within its own confines.

Sports as an Entertainment Industry

Whatever else, professional sports leagues are entertainment; they seek those illusive dollars that people are willing to spend to fill their leisure time. Clubs within a league seem to agree on this and do not see themselves ultimately as competitors with themselves, notwithstanding the sentiments expressed by the majority in *Los Angeles Memorial Coliseum Commission v. NFL*. Sports leagues vie primarily interleague and with other forms of entertainment—motion pictures, the theater, music, videogames, book publishing, even their constant companion, television. On the one hand, the sports league's fortunes are tied to the overall health of the entertainment industry as a whole. At the same time, a sports league has to be concerned that its present popularity compared with other entertainment forms does not shrink. Competition is a key.

Sports leagues have ridden waves of publicity, popularity, and general profitability for the past twenty years. In many respects, professional athletes have replaced movie stars as folk heroes to an increasingly large share of the consumer market. That market may still be developing. For example, the growth of women's participation in sports should benefit the professional leagues, though it may be years before the leagues benefit from this phenomenon. Whether female participation in sports greatly increases female interest in spectator sports is debatable. In general, however, the assessment of interest in sports is still auspicious.

This should not lull sports leagues into being overly sanguine about their prospects. The entertainment business as an industry is still adolescent. The motion picture industry has witnessed dizzying highs and abysmal lows, and is still feeling its way. Television has encountered the sobering realities of cable. Live theatre reels from spiraling costs on the one hand and enticements for its fans to sample other, newer attractions on the other. The sports industry existed for a long time as leagues operating as fairly small enterprises; its track record is too short to support much speculation.

All entertainment is a gamble. More motion pictures lose money than make it. Perhaps one in five record albums shows a profit. Sports leagues, and thus their clubs, are basically the same. A *Star Wars*, or a Michael Jackson "Thriller," or a National Football League is not the norm. And as with the NFL, nothing is assured. Next year may see reversals.

Sports leagues are show biz. So long as the glamour persists, potential buyers hover. But sports leagues may have to adapt as tastes in entertainment change, as technologies improve, as legal pressures make old practices prohibitive to maintain. If the leagues can accommodate these changes, the ball then passes to labor.

PROSPECTS FOR THE UNION MOVEMENT IN SPORTS

As sports leagues undergo transformations, so do the players' associations. Their progress during the past twenty years has been significant, and they are determined that this progress should continue. They must capitalize on their strengths, address issues that they have not been able fully to resolve, and be watchful of what happens to the leagues, not only currently but in five or ten years in the future. These are not simple tasks.

Strengths: Using Weapons to Gain Leverage

Several elements interact to determine a union's power base: strong leadership, cohesion and resolve among the members, and realism in setting and seeking goals. Added to those should be an "edge," a means of exploitation that at some critical point can tip the scales in one's favor. Put another way, a union needs leverage; the leverage may be economic, political or legal.

Some leverage goes with the territory—whatever the circumstances allow at the time. Most advantages, though, are earned. There are five weapons at the disposal of the unions: collective bargaining, strikes (actual or threatened), litigation, arbitration, and political lobbying. Some of these have been used more often by certain unions than others—strikes, for example—but all are potentially vital.

For twenty years, sports unions have devised and deployed the right strategies. The results certainly have not been completely one-sided, but given the unions' position in the early 1960s, the labor movement in sports has progressed dramatically. Often, the results have been a consequence of sage leadership, surprising cohesiveness among a disparate membership, and a game plan that was not overreaching. Sports unions have also often been able to spring that added ingredient—some type of leverage. The unions have forced owners to concede more than they were willing. On the other hand, where leverage was missing, or where the union designs were too grand, the results were much more disappointing from the union perspective.

The most significant example of leverage was that obtained from the Messersmith and McNally arbitration[20] in baseball. With that award knelling the virtual demise of the reserve system, the owners were faced with the prospects of all players becoming free agents. The results of the award, upheld in the courts,[21] brought the owners to the bargaining table in a manner uncontemplated before that time. The leverage gained through legal maneuvers rapidly translated into a potential economic squeeze that sent owners reeling.

Similar were legal advantages gained by the players' associations in both the NBA and NFL in the mid-1970s. The *Robertson* case[22] altered the power balance in the NBA and resulted in a settlement and collective bargaining agreement predictably far different than would have been the case without such leverage. While the NFLPA has been criticized for not capitalizing fully on the *Mackey* and *Alexander* cases,[23] the economics of the league and the history of the union to that point suggest that matters were more complex than the criticisms recognize. It is possible, in fact, to use the NFL and NFLPA situations to illustrate some of the problems that may face all sports unions these next few years.

The NFLPA in doing battle with its league has not fared particularly well in collective bargaining. The scorecard reflects mixed results, with several key issues definitely weighing in favor of management. Free agency is practically nonexistent in the NFL. Although salaries have been on the rise since 1983, this is more an influence of the competitor USFL than the efforts of the NFLPA. If the USFL had formed in 1981, before the prior collective bargaining agreement in the NFL expired, the history of the 1982 negotiations and strike might have been far different. By the time the next NFL agreement expires, the USFL may have disbanded, and the NFLPA will have lost the economic leverage induced by a competitor league that it so badly needs. The NFLPA could not control the timing of this move. Where one's strengths can be manipulated, however, timing is often crucial.

Despite this bleak picture, the union movement in the NFL has been far from ineffectual. In the areas of benefits, minimum salary scales extending over multiple years, severance pay, and control over player agents, the NFLPA has accomplished notable gains.

Each sports union—its successes and failures—was analyzed in the earlier chapters. Given the shifting nature of sports leagues, it is likely that sports unions will face mixed results in the future. The old approaches may have to be altered. A union will still work from its strengths, but this must be done in the context of what is happening not only to its league, but also to the sports industries as a whole and to the entertainment industries in general. These are no simple, short-range tasks.

Unresolved Issues for Sports Unions

Players' associations must continue to grapple with the unresolved issues that emanate from their internal structures. Most industry problems are peculiar to professional sports, but to a limited extent analogies can be drawn to the other entertainment industries. These are constant issues that affect how sports unions proceed and how well they fare. Three problems, largely discussed in Chapter 8, are (1) defining the unit, (2) exclusivity in representing the player, and (3) individual versus collective interests among the players. The three are interrelated and underscore the uniqueness of sports unions. The problems facing the union leadership are not simple ones: The membership changes constantly, and a union has almost a 50 percent turnover in its membership every two years. Active membership support and participation is essential, but the fluctuating composition of the membership creates exceptional obstacles. Add to that a bifurcated process where individual attorneys and agents supplant the union in several of its vital functions, normally assumed by a union in the traditional model, and the challenges multiply. Finally, economics and the representational process can remove the interests of many of the individual members far from the norm for the union membership, raising issues of fair representation by the union and conflicts between general member interests and provisions in individual contracts. Those conflicts are numerous and intrinsic. If allowed to expand, they can enervate a union's strength and influence.

The players' associations have made several responses to these problems. The NFLPA has sought greater control over agents through the collective bargaining process and resulting regulations imposed on all who represent players in individual contract negotiations. Other unions have contested individual contracts on the grounds that players were induced to forfeit benefits guaranteed by the collective agreement. Arbitration awards have upheld the players' associations in several instances and rejected their contentions in others. Problems of the unit have gone before the NLRB and regional boards in connection with certification elections. Because of the persistent nature of these problems, they will undoubtedly trigger future contests. Individually, the problems are addressed and resolved. The long-term nature of the issues suggests, however, that other approaches may be required that may change the structure of unions as the nature of leagues shift.

More unions may seek the way of the Federation of Professional Athletes[24] and join an organization that cuts across several sports. Whether the collective strength would be enough to overcome the possible divisiveness is an open question. But if sports leagues are either forced or choose to change because of economic incentives or pressures, sports unions will find it necessary to adapt as well.

At some point in the near future, all sports unions will have to deal directly with the union/agent dichotomy. An uneasy truce has existed, flaring openly on occasion. It is an ongoing conflict between two groups seeking the same base, the players. While there may be no sweeping changes, at least certain steps will be taken. These may be direct moves at control, such as the NFLPA regulations concerning agents; or the moves may be toward mutual accommodation. Matters are volatile, and substantial abuses surface from time to time: Pressure on the unions to respond will grow. Asbent this, more states will follow the lead in California and move toward licensing of sports agents.[25] Whether the magnitude of the problem justifies this approach is beside the point. It takes only a few abuses and the resulting publicity for political pressures to mount. Sports unions should seize the initiative rather than see the political processes take control.

Finally, it is more than arguable that the procedure of collective bargaining developed by sports unions is relevant, if not a model, for other unions that are attempting to cope with the siege laid down against the entire American labor movement. The Report of the AFL–CIO Committee on the Evolution of Work, issued in February 1985, has noted that " . . . in some bargaining units workers may not desire to establish a comprehensive set of hard and fast terms and conditions of employment, but may nonetheless desire a representative to negotiate minimum guarantees that will serve as a floor for individual bargaining . . . " While the sports unions are becoming more deeply enmeshed in aspects of individual bargaining, such as regulation of agents, deferred compensation agreements with clubs which may not be economically viable and the major arbitration issues, their relationship with individuals and clubs will be instructive for unions that seek to attract professional and white collar employees who are reticent about unions because of their perceived rigidities. If the labor movement is to recapture the considerable amount of ground given up in recent years, it must focus its attention ever more carefully on such groups. Sports unions will have a role to play in all of this.

Future Areas of Negotiation

Future areas of negotiation in collective bargaining will be determined by the economic realities and prospects for a league. While there also will be issues that are largely noneconomic, they will not dominate either the time or efforts devoted to negotiations, nor will they generate the controversy that surrounds the economically based proposals. The money has grown so large—and the pie sits there so temptingly to be split—that economics have to prevail. On the one hand, player salaries have escalated; on the other, potentially great caches of revenues await exploitation, then division. Whether salaries outstrip revenues or vice versa are central questions that may vary by league. One league may argue division of spoils, while another may concentrate on holding down salaries under some sort of cap. It will be apparent, though, that whatever the individual league situation at a given time, economics will be the chief determinant for framing the issues.

The NBA went to the salary cap in 1983, and the verdict is not in on what it has wrought. Other leagues are studying the NBA's cap closely. The potential effect on player mobility, to the extent this can be ascertained given the multiple variables affecting mobility, is subject to persisting scrutiny. Finally, with future prospects for profiting from new technologies dangling tantalizingly before all eyes, sharing in those future riches is of overriding concern.

For both labor and management, the problems are immediate, but it is difficult for either side to know just how to proceed. Dealing with what is known, one can assess that prospects for all leagues are positive, but several conditions could materialize to alter the prognosis. Thus, in approaching collective bargaining, one must be mindful of both the known and the possible. While the sides in framing their collective bargaining agreements have always had to gamble on the net effects of the agreements, the risks taken have been cautious ones. The greatest risk taken to date has probably been the NBA clubs and players agreeing to a salary cap—a short-term one for the clubs with possible long-term consequences and a decidedly long-term gamble for the union. Other than that gamble, sports leagues, through collective bargaining, have not been particularly adventuresome.

Even the NBA, which instituted the cap, has failed to resolve the question of who controls rights in the area of cable, pay TV, videocassettes, and other technological advances. During the last two negotiations, the NBA owners and players have gone to the bargaining table over these issues. So far, they have agreed only that they disagree.[26] The matter may not be avoided much longer. In fact, it should be on the top of the agenda for every league—except, of course, that the owners basically like matters as they now stand. If collective bargaining negotiations falter, however, the next predictable step will be litigation. This should not comfort the owners. The eventual outcome in the courts may or may not favor their position.

Other collective bargaining issues will be added to the agendas. Player drug abuse is one problem that will not disappear. Just as leagues and unions address this potential blot on the integrity of sports, new cases appear.[27] In general, the image of a league must be maintained, and the aberrations of owners or players that potentially besmirch the image must be countered. The unions must become concerned about their players. This is two-edged, since involvement may mean discipline and potential conflict within the union. The players' associations, particularly the MLBPA, were at first understandably reluctant to be directly responsible for drug use.[28] That phase has passed, and the problem must be recognized as a top priority union concern.

Safety issues, rules of the game, schedules, lengths of the season, and the quality of officiating are, in a technical sense, separate issues, but they are interrelated. The players' concerns in these issues may increasingly be brought to the bargaining table. Potential items, such as the quality of officiating, could bring the players' associations in conflict with other sports unions, notably those of umpires or referees. Even so, increased player concerns over these may well occur.

The remaining future bargaining issues are matters traditionally identified as management prerogatives, such as the movement of franchises, qualifications for ownership of a franchise, expansion of leagues, and league mergers. Some in management pale at hearing of possible union intervention in these issues, but given the events in recent years, intervention is inevitable. The NBA players through the *Robertson* case intervened in the efforts of the NBA and the ABA to merge. In the future these issues could be brought to the bargaining table. Indeed, in early negotiations in baseball as the collective bargaining agreement wound down in late 1984, the players discussed with the owners such potential problems as league expansions, interleague play, or three-division alignments in each of the major leagues.[29] While owners may resist discussing league and club structures in the collective bargaining context, the hidden value for the league might be that certain of its rules could thereby be immunized through the labor exemption. It would be a calculated gamble, given the realities of collective bargaining and the uncertainties surrounding the labor exemption, but it might be worth the risk from both league and union perspectives.

THE 1985 BASEBALL NEGOTIATIONS

The prior pages were written before the 1985 negotiations in major league baseball were fully underway. Tracing the subsequent events that occurred through early August 1985 confirms that many of the future concerns are already with us, were tackled by the baseball negotiators, and were at best resolved only by temporizing measures.

Baseball's old agreement, born through the trials of the 1980 negotiations and tribulations of the 1981 protracted strike, expired in December 1984. Ostensibly, negotiations over a new pact got underway before the expiration date; in fact, little was negotiated for several months. Both sides waited to determine the other side's real focus. The owners were particularly recalcitrant, memories of 1981 burning deeply in their collective consciousness.[30]

The real sparring began with the teams already in spring training. The owners released economic data purporting to show that many baseball franchises were in serious economic difficulty.[31] The owners stopped short of claiming an inability to pay and thus did not immediately obligate themselves to open their books for inspection. However, their pleas were such that, if credence was to be accorded them, the eventual opening of the books in some fashion was inevitable.

The owners' initial economic report, released March 12, 1985, cited 1983 losses totaling $66.6 million, 1984 losses in excess of at least $40 million (not all clubs had reported 1984 data), and projected losses in 1985 of $58 million.[32] Predictably, the union leaders challenged the owners' claims. Donald Fehr, the acting executive director of the players' union, noted that club expenses, according to the report, totaled $558 million in 1983. He claimed that players' salaries totaled just over $200 million for that year and, adding the owners' contribution to the player pension plan, the total player expenses in 1983 still came to only $220 million. Fehr questioned how other expenses could possibly amount to $338 million.[33]

The debate over the true state of baseball's economic health continued for several months. The players demanded access to the books. Contrary to past experiences, the owners acceded.[34] After examining the books, the players charged that the claims of millions in losses were false and that the owners had collectively made a profit of $9 million in 1984, not a loss in excess of $40 million.[35] The owners later revised downward their claims of 1984 losses to $28.5 million but nevertheless continued to forecast heavy losses in the future, as much as $86 million by 1986.[36]

From these and other exchanges, the economics of baseball dominated the 1985 negotiations, even to the final areas of dispute over the amount of television revenues that would go to the players' pension fund and the number of years service required before players were eligible for salary arbitration.

In 1983 the NBA players were largely concerned with retaining what they already had, and the owners were trying to chip away, claiming that the system in place had created substantial financial problems. The scenario repeated itself in baseball in 1985. Similar proposals to those weighed in the NBA negotiations surfaced in the 1985 baseball talks. In late May, for example, the owners proposed a salary cap that would establish maximums for all clubs based on their 1985 payroll but would not affect existing individual contracts. The players immediately rejected the proposal.[37]

The owners also suggested limiting a free agent player's ability to negotiate with other clubs to only those clubs that were below the average team salary for the leagues in the prior two years. The union protested that this would essentially eliminate free agency, since a player would be deprived of negotiating with the very clubs most able and likely to make the player an attractive offer.[38]

To what extent the owners' proposed salary cap and restrictions on free agent dealing were offered with any realistic expectation that either would be adopted is unclear. Despite the owners decrying the state of baseball's finances, baseball franchises were in better financial condition than many NBA clubs in 1983. The likely explanation is that the salary cap and significant restrictions on free agency were bargaining chips to be discarded by the owners as actual bottom-line concessions were gained.

The progress in the negotiations was slow. Few significant accords were reached. In April, the owners and players did agree to expand the two leagues' championship playoffs to a 4-of-7 game format, which would yield an additional $9 million in television revenue. The two sides agreed that the split of the $9 million ultimately would be resolved when the overall division of television revenues was settled. In the interim, a third of the money was to be put in escrow.[39]

With progress only on peripheral issues, the players' executive board requested a strike authorization by the players. Through a club-by-club vote, the players overwhelmingly approved. The board then set an August 6 strike date if no settlement was reached. Even with this impetus, little agreement was reported during June and July over the most controversial issues. Parties from each side disagreed among themselves whether there would be a strike. Several suggested that Peter Ueberroth, the new commissioner of baseball, should intervene.[40] Some recalled the black humor about ex-commissioner Bowie Kuhn's lack of action in 1981. Said the wags, "the '81 strike would never have happened had Bowie been alive."

In truth, a commissioner's role in collective bargaining in league sports is shadowy. As discussed in earlier chapters, the leagues and clubs have in several instances created special organizations to remove the commissioner from direct involvement in labor relations. This is the case in baseball. The Players Relations Committee is in place to deal collectively with the players. Raymond Grebey headed the PRC in 1980 and 1981; that position, in 1985, was now occupied by Lee MacPhail, a long-time baseball man and former president of the American League. Commissioner Ueberroth was free to cajole, but he had no official status in the negotiations. Even, so, since Ueberroth had been instrumental in getting the umpires back to work for the 1984 World Series and had somehow forced the terms of agreement in that instance, several parties urged his intervention again.[41]

Ueberroth was quoted almost daily as the August 6 strike date loomed. He seemed perplexed over his proper role. First he said he would not allow a strike to occur;[42] then he said he had no real power and could not really act.[43] He said he would announce some compromise plans that should be considered seriously by the two sides as starting points to steer the talks toward a successful conclusion.[44] When he announced his proposals, however, both sides quickly shrugged them off.[45] Finally, when the actual settlement was reached, Ueberroth was on the scene, but the accounts place him as arriving at MacPhail's apartment after the terms were actually concluded. At an ensuing press conference, Ueberroth stated he played no role in the final negotiations.[46] Some owners, though, said the commissioner kept the negotiations going; others disagreed.[47] In sum, the commissioner's contributions were difficult to assess, and observers disagree whether his actions helped or hindered the final stages.[48]

The last few days before the strike deadline were bittersweet. Everyone, it seemed, hoped a strike would be averted. Some owners expressed optimism that a settlement would be reached. Others, along with the commissioner, were more pessimistic.[49] Ueberroth in fact went so far as to say that a strike appeared inevitable so why not start it immediately and get it over with.[50] The players' spokesmen were guarded, asserting that the owners were not forthcoming with good-faith proposals; there was a discernable underlying tension among the players. Some players might have strongly favored a strike, but many quite obviously hoped it could be avoided.[51] The players' resolve in general seemed weak as compared with that of 1981. A prolonged strike might bode ill for union steadfastness.

Fans also entered the act as ad hoc groups formed to protest a strike. Activists burned tickets outside a few stadia.[52] Others suggested a later boycott for each day a strike would run.[53] Although most fans seemed indifferent to the actual issues dividing labor and management,[54] in principle, the public favored the owners and viewed the players as wanting, once again, too large a piece of the pie.[55] This reaction of strongly favoring management was in contrast to 1981, when the public support for players or owners split almost evenly.[56]

While attention focused on the pending strike, the game itself enjoyed glory days. The final Sunday before the strike saw two milestones. Tom Seaver, a pitcher now with the Chicago White Sox, won his 300th game, and Rod Carew of the California Angels collected his 3,000th hit. In major league history, fewer than twenty players in either category had reached those plateaus. In the meantime, Pete Rose was closing in on Ty Cobb's all-time 4,191 hit record, a mark that baseball experts long believed unbeatable. Some division races were red hot. The New York Mets overtook the St. Louis Cardinals in the National League East to enter the projected strike period with a narrow one-half game lead. No sports fan wanted to see that race interrupted. The Mets had their sensational sophomore pitcher, Dwight Gooden, and the Cards countered with rookie outfielder Vince Coleman, who by the end of July already had stolen more bases than any other rookie ever had in an entire season. Even so, on the final weekend, the talks made little progress,[57] and the media focused on the impacts of a strike on club and player finances and on the various economic interests of cities, stadium owners, and others swept into a labor stoppage.[58]

No last-minute solution materialized. On August 6, as threatened, the players struck. A popular prediction was that the strike would likely be a long one. The season itself was threatened. Of course, this did not happen. The strike lasted only one day. Both sides were obviously closer to agreement than was publicly announced. Thus, in a meeting removed from media glare, the negotiators for management and labor pulled back from previously asserted positions to reach compromises on all major issues. A significant movement by the owners' negotiators removed demands for a salary cap. That hurdle aside, the players responded by also granting concessions and in effect surrendered certain gains realized in earlier collective bargaining agreements.[59]

The two major compromise areas concerned television revenues to be paid by owners to the players pension plan and eligibility for salary arbitration. As to television revenues, the players had demanded that one-third of national television revenues go to the players pension plan, a figure that had been allocated in prior collective bargaining agreements by the dollars actually stipulated. Since the latest national television package with two networks greatly increased the total dollars involved, and with players' salaries continuing to escalate rapidly, the owners argued that one-third was too much as this would entail an increase from $15.5 million to $60 million per year. The owners instead had offered a yearly increase to $25 million. The compromise under the 1985 agreement has the owners contributing on average over the term of the new agreement some $32.6 million per year.[60] Although it was not specified in precise language, there was also an understanding that the difference between the $32.6 million granted and the $60 million requested should be used, if necessary, to aid clubs suffering financial difficulties.[61] On this important economic issue, the players succeeded in more than doubling the yearly contribution previously made by the owners, but the owners were able to modify a precedent that one-third of television revenues should go to the players fund. In fact, the figure under the new contract was now closer to one-sixth.

For salary arbitration, the owners tried to extend eligibility from two years to three and to place a limit on how much a player could seek through salary arbitration, specifically that a player could not seek more than a 100 percent increase over his prior year's salary. In most commercial settings, a 100 percent increase is ludicrous. In professional sports, however, it is not. During the three years prior to the new agreement, twenty-three players requested and received, through salary arbitration, increases over 100 percent. For example, in 1983, Fernando Valenzuela went from $350,000 to $1,000,000 (186%), Tim Lollar from $50,000 to $300,000 (500%), Damasco Garcia from $130,000 to $400,000 (208%); in 1984, George Frazier jumped from $125,000 to $425,000 (240%); and in 1985, Dave Schmidt rose from $115,000 to $344,000 (199%).[62] Both the actual dollar and percentage increases for these and others, both over and just under the 100 percent increase level, have been startling.

The owners nevertheless withdrew their demands for this cap on salary arbitration awards. But they received two important concessions in return. Beginning in 1987, a player must have three full years of major league service to qualify for salary arbitration.[63] The implementation of this provision was obviously timed to give everyone on a major league roster in 1985 a chance to complete two full years of service and not be affected by the new three-year rule.

The other concession is harder to assess. It stipulates that effective in 1987 an arbitrator shall "give particular attention, for comparative salary purposes, to contracts of players with Major League Service not exceeding one annual service group above the Player's annual service group."[64] The language goes on to clarify, however, that a player can argue special accomplishment and assert the relevance of other players' salaries without regard to length of service. Under this, "the arbitrator shall give whatever weight to such argument as he (or she) deems appropriate."[65] Thus, it is suggested to an arbitrator that the major criterion should be a comparison of the player in arbitration with other players similarly situated in terms of major league service, but it is only a suggestion.

The player can argue, and the arbitrator can consider, other circumstances. This makes it difficult to predict what depression in salary arbitration awards will be felt after 1987.

One veteran players attorney, Dick Moss, has also suggested that this might signal a return to spring training holdouts by players, particularly those with two years of service who will henceforth be ineligible for salary arbitration. He reasons that, by the end of two years, players are usually able to assess their value to a club. Since salary arbitration will no longer be available, a player who believes he is not being properly valued will have only the option of sitting out. A two-year veteran will be more likely to be assertive than a player just completing his rookie year.[66]

A substantial irony of the 1985 accord is that it returns free agent compensation in baseball to its pre-1981 posture. The single issue that sparked the 1981 strike was effectively eviscerated in the 1985 settlement. In 1980 and 1981, the owners fought hard, with limited success, for an implementation to free agent compensation that would cause certain free agent signings to result in a major league player being awarded to the old club as compensation. The selected player was to come from a pool created by all clubs and not necessarily from the new club that signed the free agent. In the 1981–1985 period, eight players were awarded as compensation. One of these was Tom Seaver, who in posting victory 300 did so for the club that claimed him as compensation. Overall, though, the resort to the player pool was sufficiently negligible that the owners were willing to abandon it. With the 1985 agreement, draft choices were reinstated as the sole means of free agent compensation.[67]

Most of the other provisions in the 1985 settlement had an economic base, including increased reimbursements,[68] an immediate increase in the Major League minimum salary from $40,000 to $60,000 (retroactive to the start of the 1985 season),[69] an increase in the players' World Series share,[70] and other financial benefits. One provision was not directly economic and received little media attention. Under this provision, the union was recognized as reserving the power to certify and thus regulate agents who negotiate individual contracts for the major-league players.[71] This provision tracks what the NFL Players Association had included in its 1982 agreement with the NFL owners. This union control device, discussed earlier in this chapter, is growing in professional sports and will be a source of increasing tension between unions and agents.

The 1985 baseball negotiations resolved little in terms of long-run prospects for either baseball or professional sports in general. The settlement was just one step in a process by which management and labor in the several leagues are feeling their way toward meeting the challenges facing unique industries with special economic problems. This is not to suggest an absence of notable events. The shaky finances of franchises once again were influential, as with the NBA in 1983. The owners' willingness, however begrudgingly, to allow the players access to their books signals more to come. But even as the talks dragged on, the baseball owners sent out conflicting messages. While the Pittsburgh Pirates indicated a possibility of filing for bankruptcy [72] and other owners claimed staggering losses, [73] there was talk of future expansion of the leagues. [74] Consequently, the true financial state remained an unknown. Offsetting current operating losses are always the possibilities of increased worth of the franchises.

The 1985 agreement did little to address the issue of greatly escalating salaries. In all probability, the new restrictions on salary arbitration are only bromides, not antidotes. An open market for players' services will likely continue. As the 1985 strike neared, attention focused on what players stood to lose for each day of a strike. The sums were substantial. Thirty-five major leaguers were earning $1 million a year or more. At the top of the scale, players such as Mike Schmidt and Jim Rice earned about $13,000 *per game*. [75] These players would lose substantial sums if a strike occurred; then again, they could well afford it. The real question is whether the 1985 agreement will slow the inexorable salary spiral in baseball. Will the current 35 million-per-year players double or triple during the several years of the new accord? That prospect seems likely, unless factors beyond the 1985 agreement cause the owners to stem their spending urges. [76]

In 1985 the role of a commissioner in labor relations continued to be something of an anomaly, but this phenomenon only attended the uncertain roles played by most owners and players. In fact, there are many parties interested in a sports labor dispute, but only a few on each side of the bargaining table who actually grapple with and reach agreement on the issues. While involvement on each side by the rank and file is important, certain functions must be handled by their delegates. Not everyone will be pleased by the ultimate results, as was evidenced by the grumblings from certain players and owners alike over the 1985 terms. [77]

As a continuing trend, the 1985 negotiations were conducted under substantial publicity and scrutiny. This attention has become inevitable in professional sports labor negotiations and creates unique problems. The media heighten public awareness, and thus response. Even Congress is heard rumbling in the background, passing resolutions urging the parties toward settlement. In professional sports, it seems, the players are everywhere, not just on the field.

NET EFFECTS: "HIT 'EM WHERE THEY AIN'T"

It is fitting to conclude our discussion with homage to William Henry Keeler, known in sports annals as Wee Willie Keeler. As with sports unions, Keeler early faced tough odds on his way to baseball immortality. At five feet four inches tall, he had to rely on skills other than those attributable to physical size. He was not strong; he parlayed speed, coordination, and brains. Wee Willie's start in professional ball as a left-handed third baseman was not auspicious, but he persevered and became one of baseball's all-time great rightfielders.

Wee Willie Keeler's axiom was "Hit 'em where they ain't." His words have been an inspiration for today's players as well—if not on the field, at least at the negotiating table, before the arbitrator, in court, or on the picket line. Where the owners have said, "They can't be serious about striking," the players have been. Where the owners have said, "A judge (or an arbitrator) would never decide it that way," the players have pressed the issues and have won more than they have lost. Where the owners have said, "We'll never agree to that term," the combined leverages of persistence, litigation, arbitration, and walkouts have forced agreement. The intriguing question is how long this leverage will persist.

Conceivably, the net legal effects may be a redefinition of both the league and union structures in sports. Either the leagues may become looser associations of teams, or they may adopt a partnership model. Unions will be forced to modify their own structures to respond to changing league models. In the process, there will be a redefining of the employer/employee relationship in sports. While retaining unions, players may move toward independent contractor status. At the very least, accountability for league activities should rest more fully on players and unions, as well as clubs and leagues.

Wee Willie Keeler would have been proud. His philosophy might now become a watchword for labor relations in general in professional sports. But can both labor and management successfully emulate his style? After all, Yogi Berra warned, "If you can't imitate him, don't copy him."

Whatever the outcome, there will always be another game—at least until the next strike.

NOTES TO CHAPTER 9

1. *See* Wyzanski, History and Law, 26 U. Chi. L. Rev. 237, 243 (1959).
2. For background on the NBA referees' strike, including the use of a federal mediator to help settle the dispute and the strike's aftermath, see the following accounts: Montville, Whistling for a Cause, Boston Globe, Nov. 13, 1983, at 45, col. 1; Goldaper, Referees' Union Seeks a Mediator in Dispute, N.Y. Times, Nov. 23, 1983, at B11, col. 1; Mediator Enters Referees' Dispute, N.Y. Times, Dec. 2, 1983, at B15, col. 1; Whiteside, NBA, Referees Settle, Boston Globe, Dec. 10, 1983, at 25, col. 5; Thomas, With Union Referees on Job Coaches Say Order Restored, USA Today, Dec. 19, 1983, at 9C, col. 4; and A Frosty Peace, Sports Illustrated, Dec. 19, 1983, at 9.
3. *See, e.g.*, Umpires Say They'll Strike, San Francisco Chron., Oct. 1, 1984, at 51, col. 4; Rhoden, Umpires' Strike a Threat Today, N.Y. Times, Oct. 2, 1984, at 50, col. 2; Dickey, Umps' Strike Is What Baseball Doesn't Need, San Francisco Chron., Oct. 5, 1984, at 87, col. 1; More Discussions in Umpires' Strike, San Francisco Chron., Oct. 6, 1984, at 47, col. 5. The baseball umpires almost staged a one-game boycott in 1983 to protest the dismissal of an umpire in the International League. The boycott was of

a special exhibition game, which the umpires were not obligated to work under their existing collective agreement with the major leagues.

4. *See* Craig, Baseball Facing a Super Problem, Boston Globe, Dec. 9, 1984, at 95, col. 1.

5. *See, e.g.*, Craig, Celtics, Whalers Hope Cable Will Pay, Boston Globe, May 30, 1981, at 28, col. 1; Craig, Celtics Cable TV Plan Has Huge Potential, Boston Globe, May 27, 1981, at 37, col. 1; Craig, Sonic Cable Idea Could Boom, Boston Globe, Feb. 28, 1981, at 28, col. 1; Eskenazi, Cable TV Begins to Make Big Changes in Professional Sports, N.Y. Times, April 19, 1981, §5, at 1, col. 1. That not all plans are warmly received, see Craig, Realty of Cable a Jolt to Chicago Fans, Boston Globe, Dec. 7, 1980, at 82, col. 1.

6. P. Gent, The Franchise 394 (1983).

7. For example, in baseball, the Atlanta Braves and the Chicago Cubs are owned by the television stations that cover their games. In turn, their games are beamed to satellites, since WTBS in Atlanta and WGN in Chicago are among the so-called superstations. *See* Craig, Baseball Facing a Super Problem, Boston Globe, Dec. 9, 1984, at 95, col. 1.

8. *See* USFL "Discussing" Huge Antitrust Suit vs. NFL, San Francisco Chron., Oct. 6, 1984, at 44, col. 2; USFL Hits NFL with $1.3 Billion Suit, San Francisco Chron., Oct. 18, 1984, at 67, col. 1.

9. *See, e.g.*, Nassau Sports v. Hampson, 355 F. Supp. 733 (1972); Nassau Sports v. Peters, 352 F. Supp. 870 (1972); Philadelphia World Hockey Club v. Philadelphia Hockey Club, 351 F. Supp. 462 (1972); and Boston Professional Hockey Assn v. Cheevers & Sanderson, 348 F. Supp. 261 (1972).

10. NASL v. NFL, 505 F. Supp. 659 (1980), *modifying* 465 F. Supp. 665 (1979).

11. The USFL's suit against the NFL, if successful, would be the first to establish general predatory practices by the established league against a newcomer. The two notable earlier attempts that resulted in legal victories for the older leagues are AFL v. NFL, 205 F. Supp. 60 (1962), *aff'd*, 323 F.2d 124 (1963); and ABAPA v. NBA, 404 F. Supp. 832 (1975).

12. The labor exemption under the antitrust laws is discussed primarily in Chapter 4.

13. The move of the Colts from Baltimore to Indianapolis, done without consultation with the NFL and accomplished by a move in the night, captured the headlines in 1984. It epitomized the position that the NFL felt it had been placed in because of the decisions to date in Los Angeles Memorial Coliseum Comm'n v. NFL F.2d (1984). For reflections on this move, see Attner, Naptown and the Colts, Sporting News, Sept. 10, 1984, at 2; and Chick, A Diehard Colts Can Can't Believe They're Gone, Sporting News, Sept. 10, 1984, at 59.

14. *See* Clippers Quit San Diego to Play in Los Angeles, May 16, 1984, at B11, col. 4. *See also* Boston Globe, June 16, 1984, at 27, col. 3.

15. The shift of the NFL Colts' franchise is cited in note 13 above. Other NFL franchises were seriously considering moves, apparently without league

approval, in late 1984. The Philadelphia Eagles were thought to be on their way to Phoenix; and the New Orleans Saints were for sale, with a future move a possibility. *See* NFL Set to Discuss Tose, Boston Globe, Dec. 13, 1984, at 57, col. 1; Philadelphia Still Talking with Eagles, Boston Globe, Dec. 13, 1984, at 57, col. 1.

16. Among bills introduced at behest of professional sports leagues, in particular the NFL, *see* S. 2784, 97th Cong., 2d Sess. (1982); and S. 2821, 97th Cong., 2d Sess. (1982).

17. S. 2505, 98th Cong. 2d Sess. (1984), and attending Hearings to Provide a Right of First Refusal for Metropolitan Areas before a Professional Sports Team Is Relocated, and for Other Purposes, Senate Comm. on Commerce, Science and Transportation, 98th Cong., 2d Sess., No. 98–87 (1984).

18. *See* N.Y. Times, June 14, 1984, at D24, col. 4; It's 1984 for NFL, L.A. Times, July 2, 1984, pt. 3 at 8, col. 1.

19. The statutory provisions authorizing leaguewide dealings on television contracts, as well as the authorization of the NFL/AFL merger, appear in 15 U.S.C. §§ 1291–95 (1976). The original action on the merger can be found in H.R. Rep. No. 2308, 89th Cong., 2d Sess. 4, *reprinted in* [1966] U.S. Code Cong. & Ad. News 4372, 4377–78.

20. Professional Baseball Clubs, 66 Lab. Arb. & Disp. Settl. 101 (1975) (Seitz, Arb.).

21. Kansas City Royals Baseball Corp. v. Major League Baseball Players' Ass'n, 409 F. Supp. 233, *aff'd*, 532 F. 2d 615 (1976).

22. Robertson v. NBA, 389 F. Supp. 867 (1975). See extensive discussion of *Robertson* in Chapter 6.

23. Mackey v. NFL, 407 F. Supp. 1000 (1975), *modified*, 543 F. 2d 606 (1976), *cert. dismissed*, 434 U.S. 801 (1977). Alexander v. NFL, U.S. Dist. Ct., Minn., 4–76 Civil 123. The *Alexander* case, initiated as a class action in light of the *Mackey* decision, was settled between the league and the class. Although a few player members of the class contested the settlement in Alexander, such efforts were not successful. *See* Reynolds v. NFL, 584 F. 2d 280 (1978).

24. The Federation of Professional Athletes is affiliated with the AFL–CIO. Current members of the FPA include the players' associations of the NFL, USFL, MISL (Major Indoor Soccer League), and NASL (North American Soccer League).

25. *See* California Labor Code §§ 1500 et seq. (1982).

26. *See* Collective Bargaining Agreement between NBA and NBPA art. 18 (Oct. 10, 1980); and Index to Memorandum of Understanding between the NBA and Players' Association, art. 4, 90 (June 6, 1983). These provisions are discussed in Chapter 6.

27. The NBA and the NBPA forged the first joint agreement on a drug program, reached by management and labor. The agreement, which took effect on January 1, 1984, provides that "any player who either is convicted of or pleads guilty to a crime involving the use or distribution of heroin or cocaine" or is found under newly instituted procedures "to have

illegally used these drugs, shall immediately be permanently dismissed" from the NBA. There is a minimum two-year wait for any appeal. *See* NBA, Players Association Unite to Drive out Drug Abusers, Boston Globe, Oct. 26, 1983, at 39, col. 1.

This of course did not stop all the problems. On the same day, in late 1984, it was announced that two players were suspended for drug use. One player, John Lucas, immediately announced his retirement, saying the lifestyle of players on the road was too conducive to a return to drugs. *See* Boston Globe Dec. 11, 1984, at 62, col. 6.

Other NBA players live under the threat of expulsion, one being Michael Ray Richardson of the New Jersey Nets. Richardson was first suspended, then filed a grievance. Before the decision on his grievance was announced, he reached settlement with his club. However, it is clear that another incident and his career is in great jeopardy. *See* Johnson, Richardson Fights to Get His Salary, N.Y. Times, Oct. 13, 1983, at B15, col. 5; Thomas, Richardson in Limbo until Ruling, USA Today, Dec. 20, 1983, at 4c, col. 4; and May, Richardson Must Stay Clear of Drugs, or He's Gone, Hartford Courant, Dec. 25, 1983, at D8, col. 1.

The NFL has had its problems: McDonough, A Tragic Story—Jordan Goes to Jail, May 4, 1976, at 37, col. 3; In Jail, Former Dolphins Are "Disappointed," N.Y. Times, Oct. 23, 1977, §E, at 9, col. 8; Tony Peters Indicted, N.Y. Times, Aug. 11, 1983, at B10, col. 3; Rozelle Admits Pro Football Has Drug Problem, St. Louis Globe-Democrat, June 19–20, 1982, at 5G, col. 1; Feds Allegedly Probing NFL Narcotics Ring, St. Louis Globe-Democrat, June 25, 1982, at 4C, col. 4; Are the Teams Doing Enough in N.F.L. Drug Cases?, N.Y. Times, July 31, 1983, §5, at 2, col. 1 (opposing views offered by ex-NFL players, Calvin Hill and Peter Gent); Forbes, NFL Leaning toward Local Drug Centers, USA Today, May 29, 1984, at 8C, col. 3.

28.   Drug problems in major league baseball have captured headlines the past three or four years. There have been suspensions of players, appeals of these suspensions through arbitration, and an agreement on the institution of a drug program, forged between the owners and the players' association.

As to suspensions, *see, e.g.*, Chass, Howe Punishment Criticized, N.Y. Times, July 1, 1983, at A13, col. 4; Durso, Kuhn Bans Four Players for a Year for Drug Use, Dec. 16, 1983, at B7, col. 1.

As to arbitration of grievances related to drugs, *see* In the Matter of Arbitration between Major League Baseball Players' Ass'n (Ferguson Jenkins) & Major League Player Relations Comm. (Commissioner Bowie Kuhn), Decision No. 41, Grievance No. 80-25 (1980); In the Matter of Arbitration between Bowie K. Kuhn, Commissioner of Baseball, & Major League Baseball Players' Ass'n (Willie Wilson, Jerry Martin), Decision No. 54, Gr. Nos. 84-1 & 84-2 (1984); In the Matter of Arbitration between Major League Baseball Players' Ass'n (Pascual Perez) & Bowie K. Kuhn, Commissioner of Baseball, Gr. No. 84-9 (1984).

As to the drug program, *see, e.g.*, Chass, Baseball Works Out Drug Program, N.Y. Times, May 4, 1984, at A23, col. 1; and Rogers, Baseball Players Vote Drug Plan, N.Y. Times, May 24, 1984, at D23, col. 5.

29. *See* Baseball Reps Meet Twice on Labor Contract, San Francisco Chron., Nov. 21, 1984, at 47, col. 1.

30. Chass, Baseball Owners Are Gathering Amid Gloomy Predictions, N.Y. Times, Dec. 2, 1984, at 23, col. 1.

31. Chass, Owners Request Help of Players, N.Y. Times, Feb. 28, 1985, at B9, col. 5; Chass, Baseball Talks Stay Uncertain, N.Y. Times, March 5, 1985, at B7, col. 5.

32. Chass, Baseball Clubs Disclose Losses, N.Y. Times, March 13, 1985, at B9, col. 5.

33. *Id.*

34. *See* Baseball Negotiations Chronology, Boston Globe, Aug. 6, 1985, at 58, col. 3.

35. *Id.*

36. *Id. See also* No Progress Reported at Baseball Talks, San Diego Union, July 19, 1985, at C6, col. 1.

37. Owners' Proposal Includes Salary Cap, Boston Globe, May 21, 1985, at 62, col. 2; Gammons, Owners Must Make Players Believers, Boston Globe, May 22, 1985, at 33, col. 1.

38. Jenkins, If Elected, These Embattled Stars May Not Serve, San Diego Union, July 3, 1985, at C3, col. 1.

39. *See* Baseball Negotiations Chronology, Boston Globe, Aug. 6, 1985, at 58, col. 3.

40. Holtzman, Ueberroth May Force a Settlement, San Diego Union, July 14, 1985, at H7, col. 1.

41. "Ueberroth could blackjack the owners into a settlement," one National League executive said. "He can make the owners do whatever he wants." *Id.*

42. Ueberroth Vows No Strike; Many Minor Issues Settled, San Diego Union, July 27, 1985, at C3, col. 1.

43. Kurkjian, Ueberroth May Lack Power to Avoid Strike, San Diego Union, July 28, 1985, at H13, col. 1; Ueberroth Not Optimistic on Settlement, San Diego Union, July 29, 1985, at C8, col. 1.

44. Ueberroth Suggests Solutions, San Diego Union, Aug. 2, 1985, at C1, col. 1.

45. MacPhail Rejects Proposals, Boston Globe, Aug. 3, 1985, at 29, col. 6; Reich, Neither Side Holds Much Hope for Ueberroth's Plan, L.A. Times, Aug. 3, 1985, Pt. III, at 1, col. 1.

46. Gammons, Baseball Strike Ends After 1 Day, Boston Globe, Aug. 8, 1985, at 1, col. 1.

47. *Id.*

48. *See e.g.*, Berkow, Polished Image For Ueberroth, N.Y. Times, Aug. 8, 1985, at B11, col. 1; Ostrow, Ueberroth Still Has That Golden Touch, USA Today, Aug. 8, 1985, at C1, col. 4; Vecsey, The Best of Times, N.Y. Times, Aug. 9, 1985, at A17, col. 1; Chass, Behind the New Baseball Pact,

Compromises, N.Y. Times, Aug. 9, 1985, at A1, col. 1; and Gammons, Empty Role for the Star, Boston Globe, Aug. 9, 1985, at 59, col. 5.

49. *See e.g.*, Owners, Union Now Ready to Tackle 'Major' Issues, San Diego Union, July 30, 1985, at D4, col. 6; Boswell, Stakes Are High In Strike Talks, Hartford Courant, Aug. 1, 1985, at C1, col. 1; Ueberroth Not Optimistic on Settlement, San Diego Union, July 20, 1985, at C8, col. 1.

50. Ueberroth Sees Strike, 'The Sooner the Better,' San Diego Union, July 15, 1985, at D5, col. 1.

51. Brady, Strike Three for Baseball Since 1972? USA Today, Aug. 6, 1985, at C1, col. 4.

52. *See e.g.*, Wayne Lockwood column, San Diego Union, July 27, 1985, at C1, col. 1.

53. *See* Boswell, Stakes Are High In Strike Talks, Hartford Courant, Aug. 1, 1985, at C4, col. 4.

54. *See* Fans Take Stand Against a Strike, Hartford Courant, Aug. 1, 1985, at C4, col. 5.

55. *Id. See also* Baseball Fans Sympathetic to the Owners, San Diego Union, July 28, 1985, at H4, col. 1.

56. *Id.*

57. Gammons, They're in Striking Range, Boston Globe, Aug. 5, 1985, at 25, col. 5; Chass, Baseball Talks Are at Standstill, N.Y. Times, Aug. 6, 1985, at A17, col. 5.

58. Ziegler, Some Cities Would Be Hit Worse Than Others, USA Today, Aug. 6, 1985, at 3C, col. 6; Czarniak, Ueberroth Gets Last-Pitch Talks Today, USA Today, Aug. 6, 1985, at A1, col. 3; Frongillo, Much to Lose in Fenway Area, Boston Herald, Aug. 6, 1985, at 64, col. 1; Blumenstock, Cities Fret About Loss of Revenue, USA Today, Aug. 6, 1985, at 3C, col. 4.

59. Chass, Behind the New Baseball Pact, Compromises, N.Y. Times, Aug. 9, 1985, at A1, col. 1.

60. The figure is $32.6 million per year, since $25 million is made retroactive to April 1, 1984. The prospective figures are $33 million for each of 1985–1988 and $39 million for 1989. Memorandum of Settlement between the Major League Clubs—Players Relations Committee and the Major League Baseball Players Association, Exhibit H, Aug. 7, 1985. (Hereafter, 1985 Baseball Memorandum.)

61. *See e.g.*, Gammons, Baseball Strike Ends After 1 Day, Boston Globe, Aug. 8, 1985, at 1, col. 1.

62. Chass, Players Score Major Victory in Defeat of Salary Cap, N.Y. Times, Aug. 11, 1985, §5, at 5, col. 1.

63. 1985 Baseball Memorandum, Exhibit E.

64. *Id.*

65. *Id.* One further provision relating to salary arbitration appears in 1985 Baseball Memorandum, Exhibit F, as follows: ". . . if a Player *wins* an award in excess of 50% of his prior years salary, the clubs may, if the Player appeals to arbitration again in the following year, submit a salary figure without regard to the maximum salary reduction provisions of the Basic Agreement." [Emphasis in original]

66. Chass, Behind the New Baseball Pact, Compromises, N.Y. Times, Aug. 9, 1985, at A18, col. 4.

67. 1985 Baseball Memorandum, Art. XVIII, Exhibit G.

68. *Id.*, Arts. VI, VII.

69. *Id.*, at 12.

70. *Id.*, Art. IX, at 6.

71. *Id.*, Exhibit A.

72. *See* Pirates May File for Bankruptcy, San Diego Union, June 26, 1985, at C6, col. 6.

73. *See* Brewers President Is Blaming 'Staggering' Losses on Salaries, San Diego Union, June 17, 1985, at D20, col. 1.

74. *See* Guidi, Baseball Seems Bent on Adding to Woes with Talk of Expansion, San Diego Union, June 27, 1985, at D17, col. 1.

75. *See* What Top Players Stand to Lose, USA Today, Aug. 6, 1985, at 3C, col. 3.

76. *See* Gammons, They Should Work on Control, Boston Globe, Aug. 11, 1985, at 50, col. 3.

77. *See e.g.*, Two Striking Reactions, Boston Globe, Aug. 9, 1985, at 66, col. 1.

INDEX